CHASING AFTER Aoi Koshiba 2

Created by
Hazuki Takeoka

Manga by
Fly

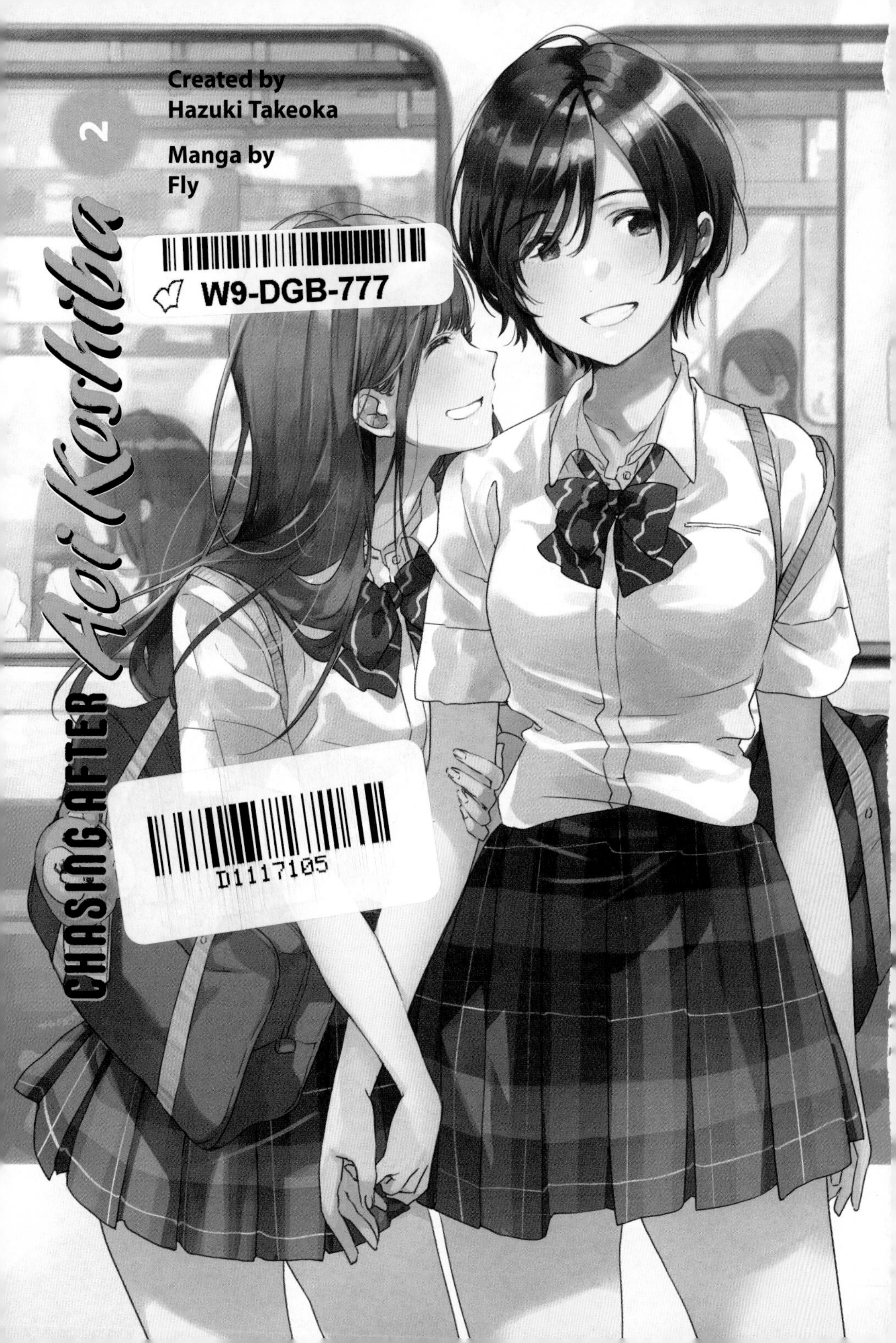

contents

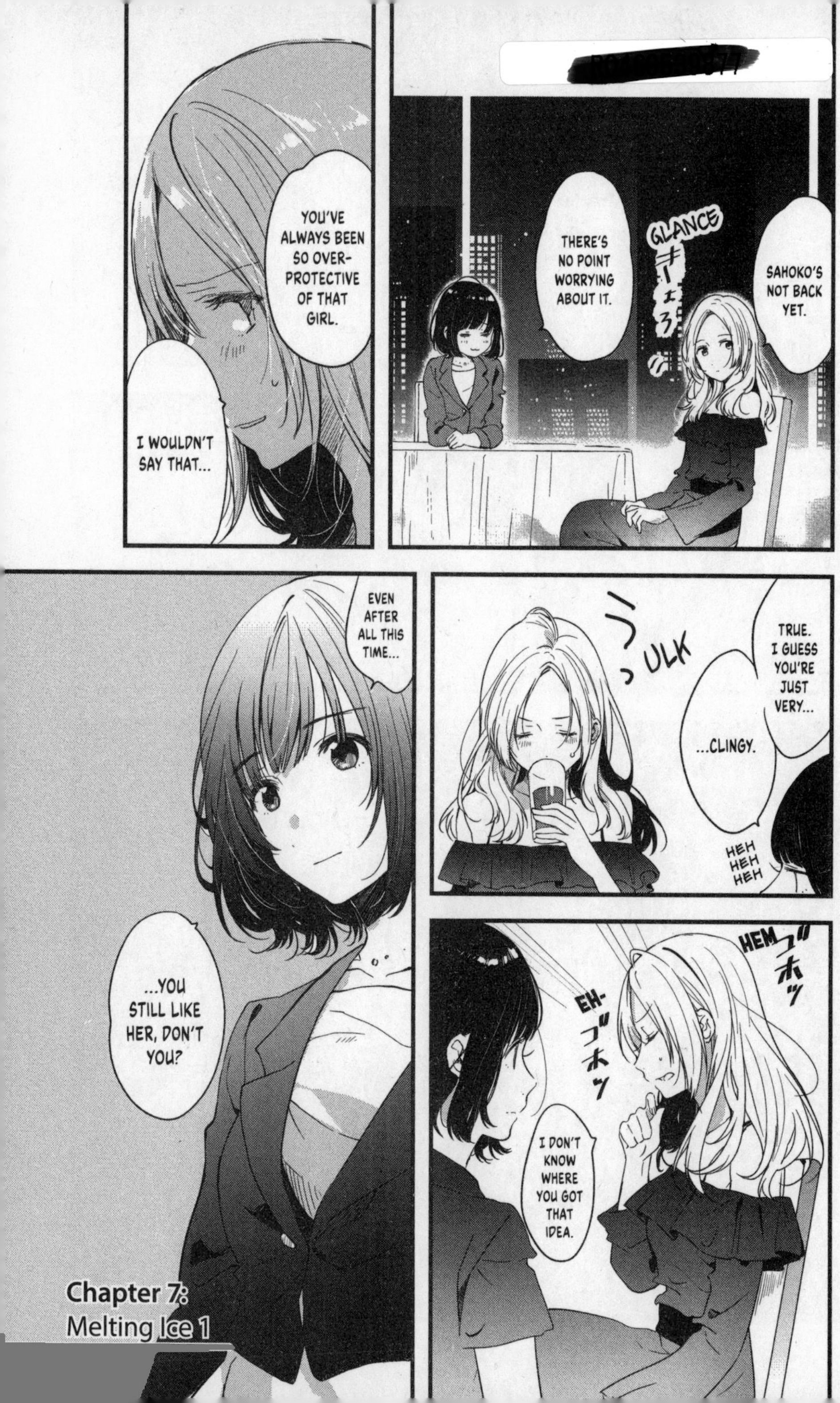
[redacted]
SAHOKO'S NOT BACK YET.
GLANCE
THERE'S NO POINT WORRYING ABOUT IT.
YOU'VE ALWAYS BEEN SO OVER-PROTECTIVE OF THAT GIRL.
I WOULDN'T SAY THAT...
TRUE. I GUESS YOU'RE JUST VERY...
...CLINGY.
ULK
HEH HEH HEH
HEM
EH-
I DON'T KNOW WHERE YOU GOT THAT IDEA.
EVEN AFTER ALL THIS TIME...
...YOU STILL LIKE HER, DON'T YOU?
Chapter 7: Melting Ice 1

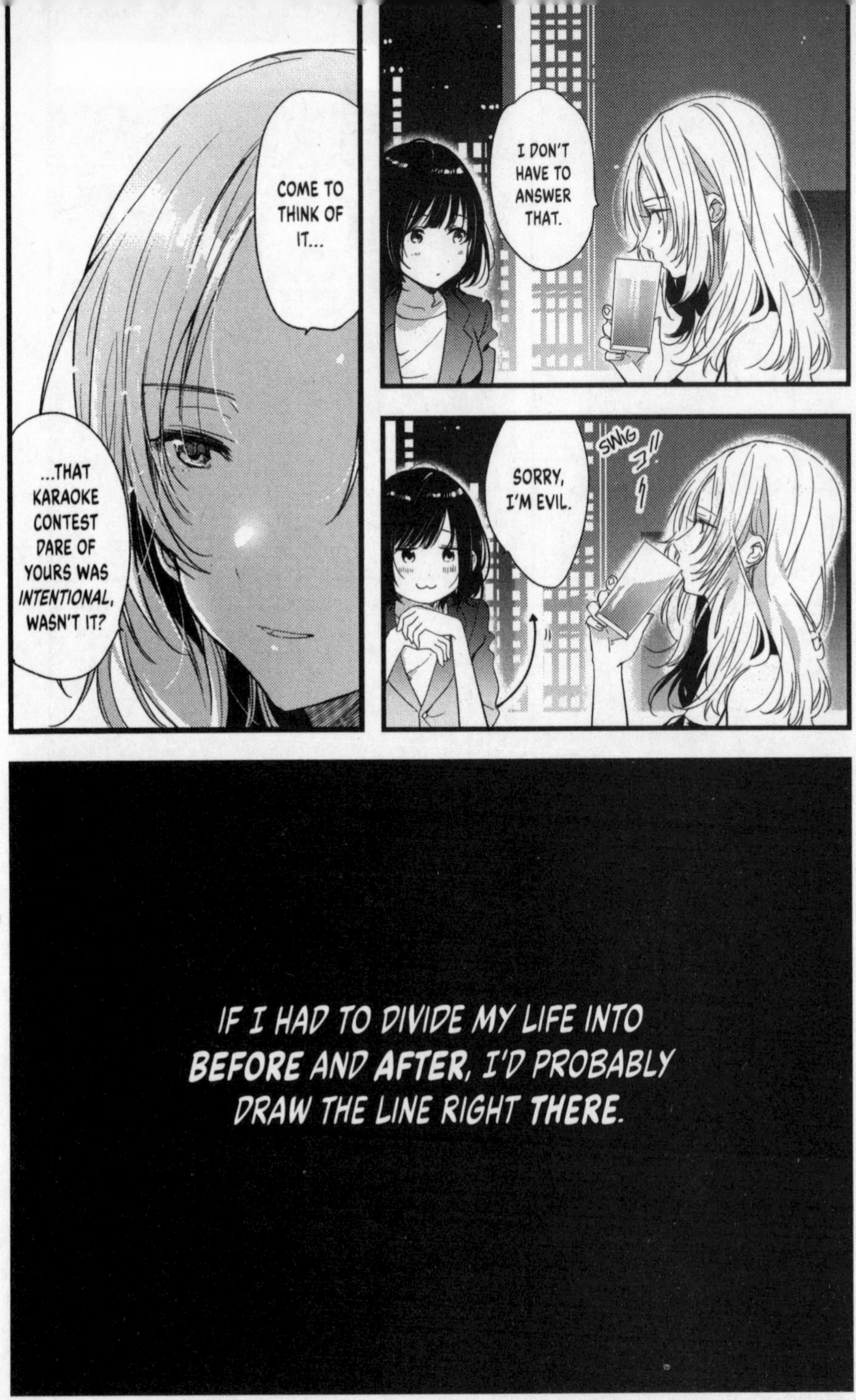
I DON'T HAVE TO ANSWER THAT.
SWIG
SORRY, I'M EVIL.
COME TO THINK OF IT...
...THAT KARAOKE CONTEST DARE OF YOURS WAS *INTENTIONAL*, WASN'T IT?
IF I HAD TO DIVIDE MY LIFE INTO **BEFORE** AND **AFTER**, I'D PROBABLY DRAW THE LINE RIGHT **THERE**.

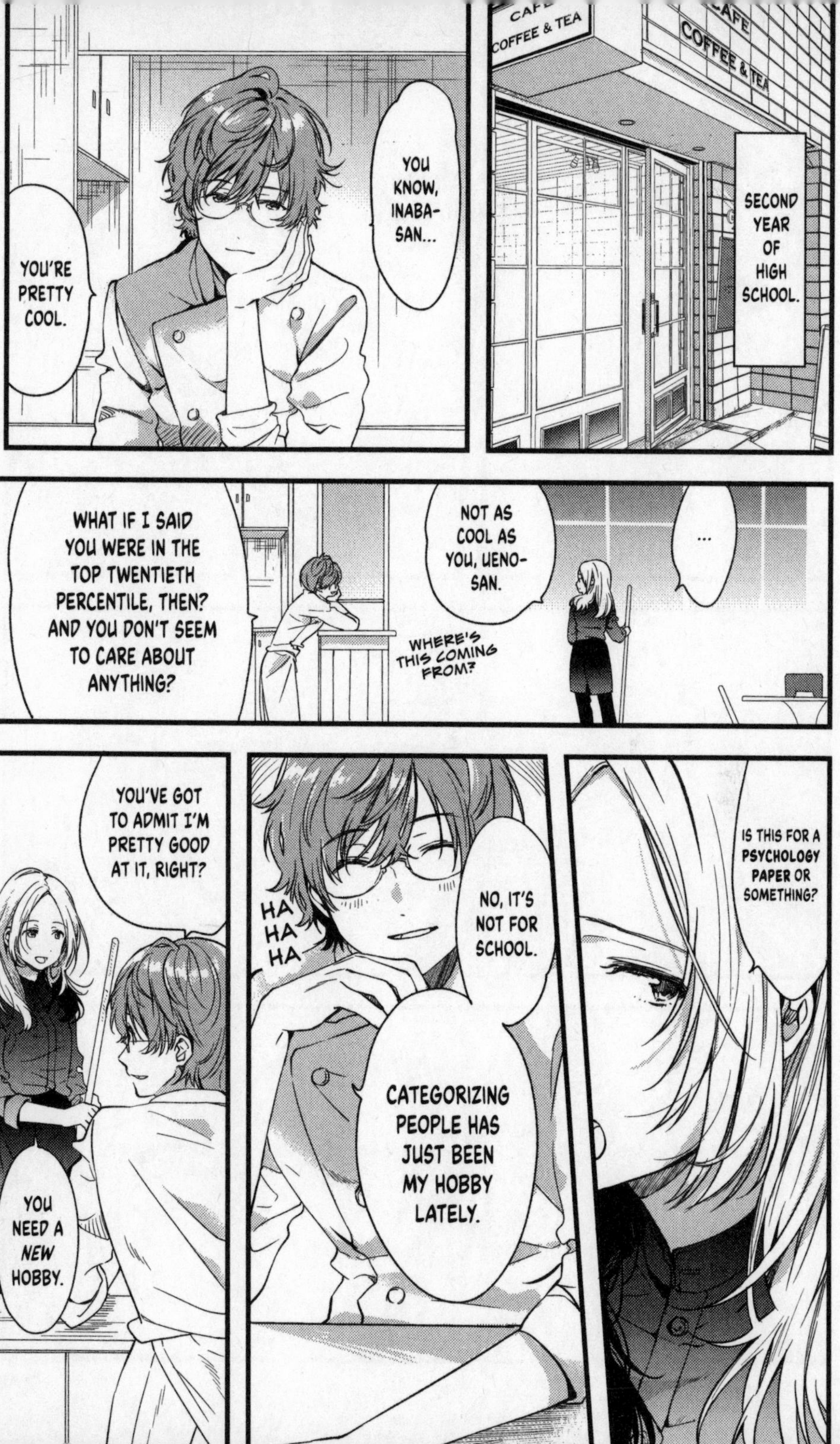
CAFE COFFEE & TEA
CAFE COFFEE & TEA
SECOND YEAR OF HIGH SCHOOL.
YOU KNOW, INABA-SAN...
YOU'RE PRETTY COOL.
...
NOT AS COOL AS YOU, UENO-SAN.
WHERE'S THIS COMING FROM?
WHAT IF I SAID YOU WERE IN THE TOP TWENTIETH PERCENTILE, THEN? AND YOU DON'T SEEM TO CARE ABOUT ANYTHING?
IS THIS FOR A PSYCHOLOGY PAPER OR SOMETHING?
NO, IT'S NOT FOR SCHOOL.
HA HA HA
CATEGORIZING PEOPLE HAS JUST BEEN MY HOBBY LATELY.
YOU'VE GOT TO ADMIT I'M PRETTY GOOD AT IT, RIGHT?
YOU NEED A *NEW* HOBBY.

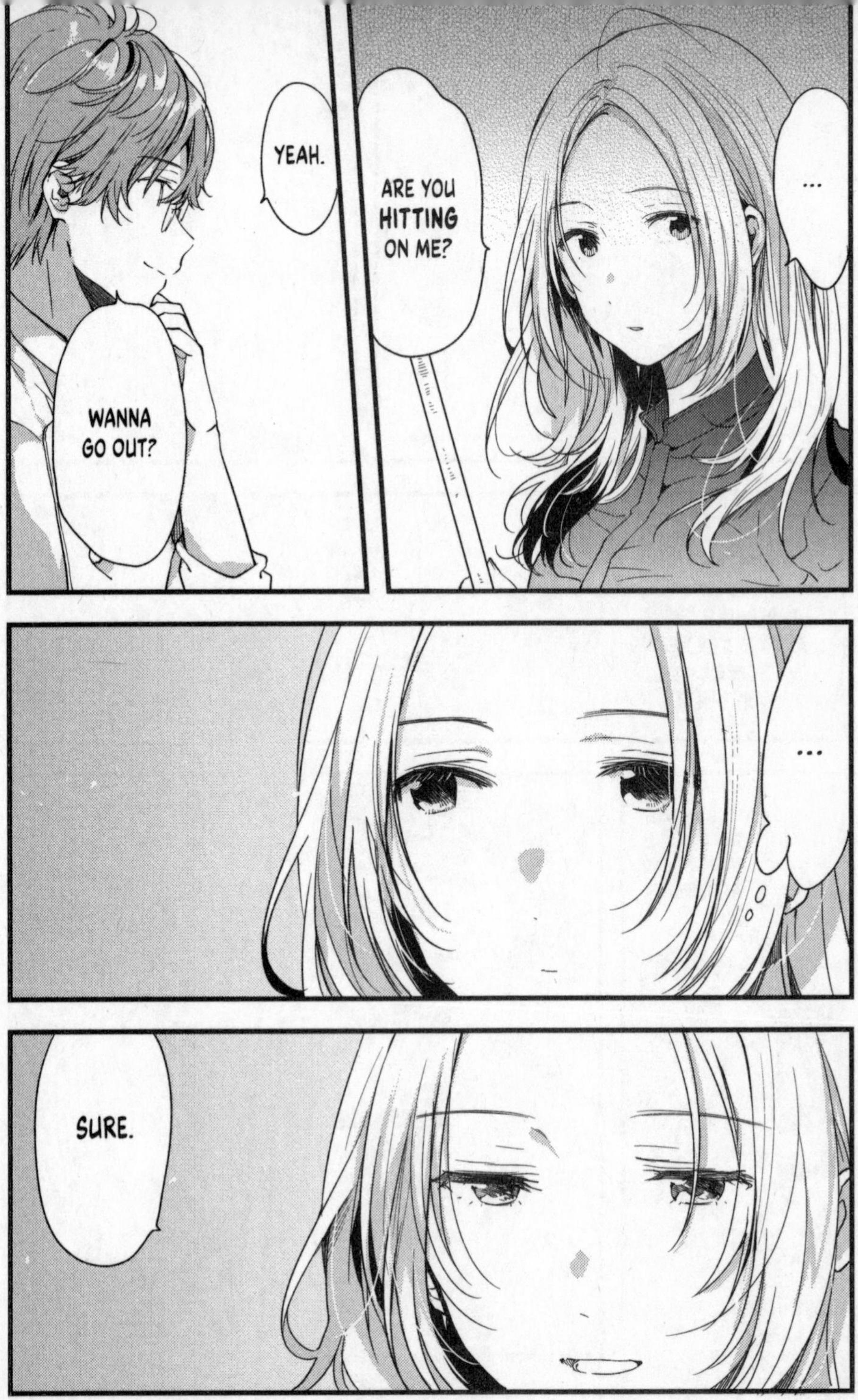
...
ARE YOU HITTING ON ME?
YEAH.
WANNA GO OUT?
...
SURE.

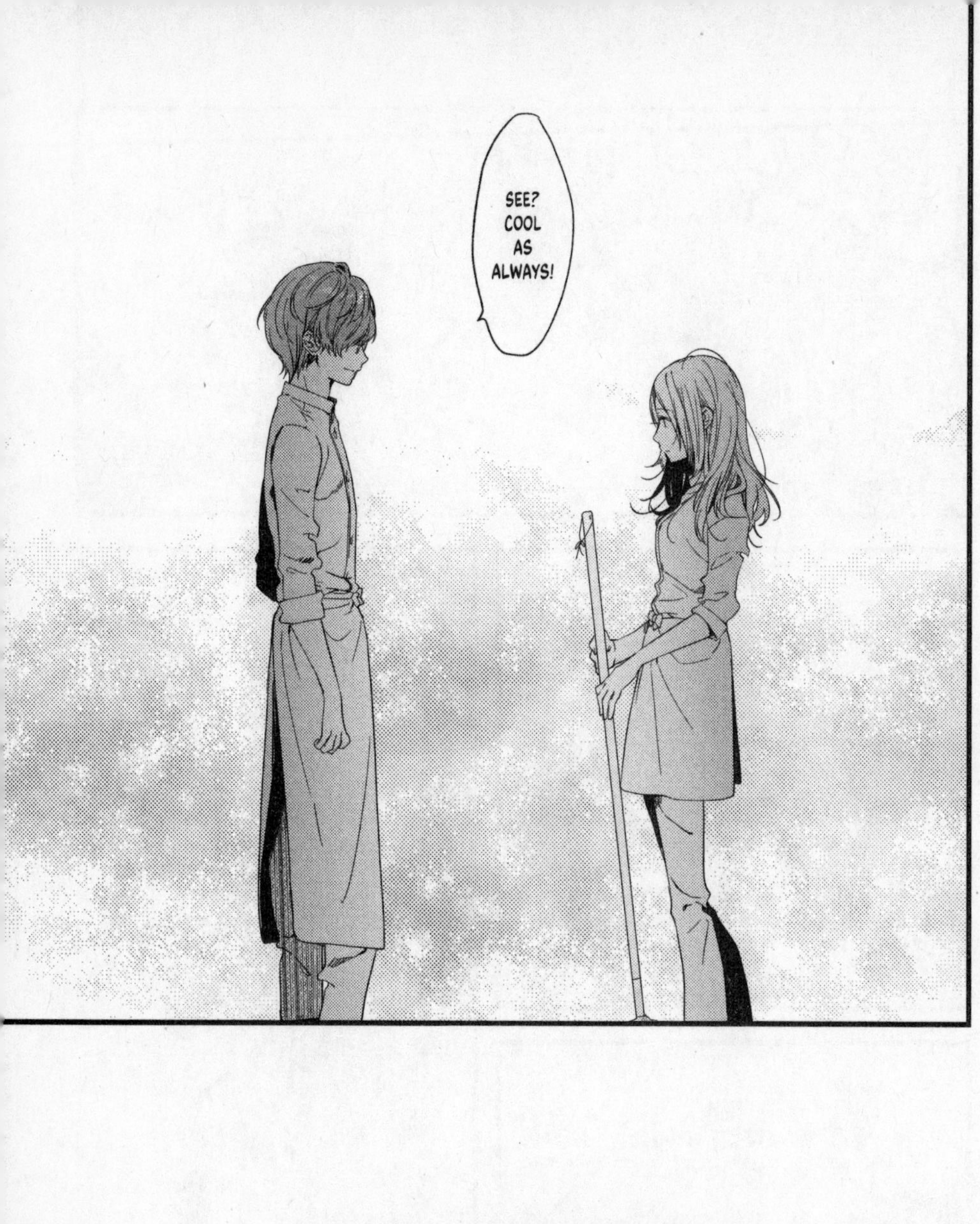
SEE? COOL AS ALWAYS!

AND THAT'S HOW I ENDED UP WITH A BOYFRIEND.

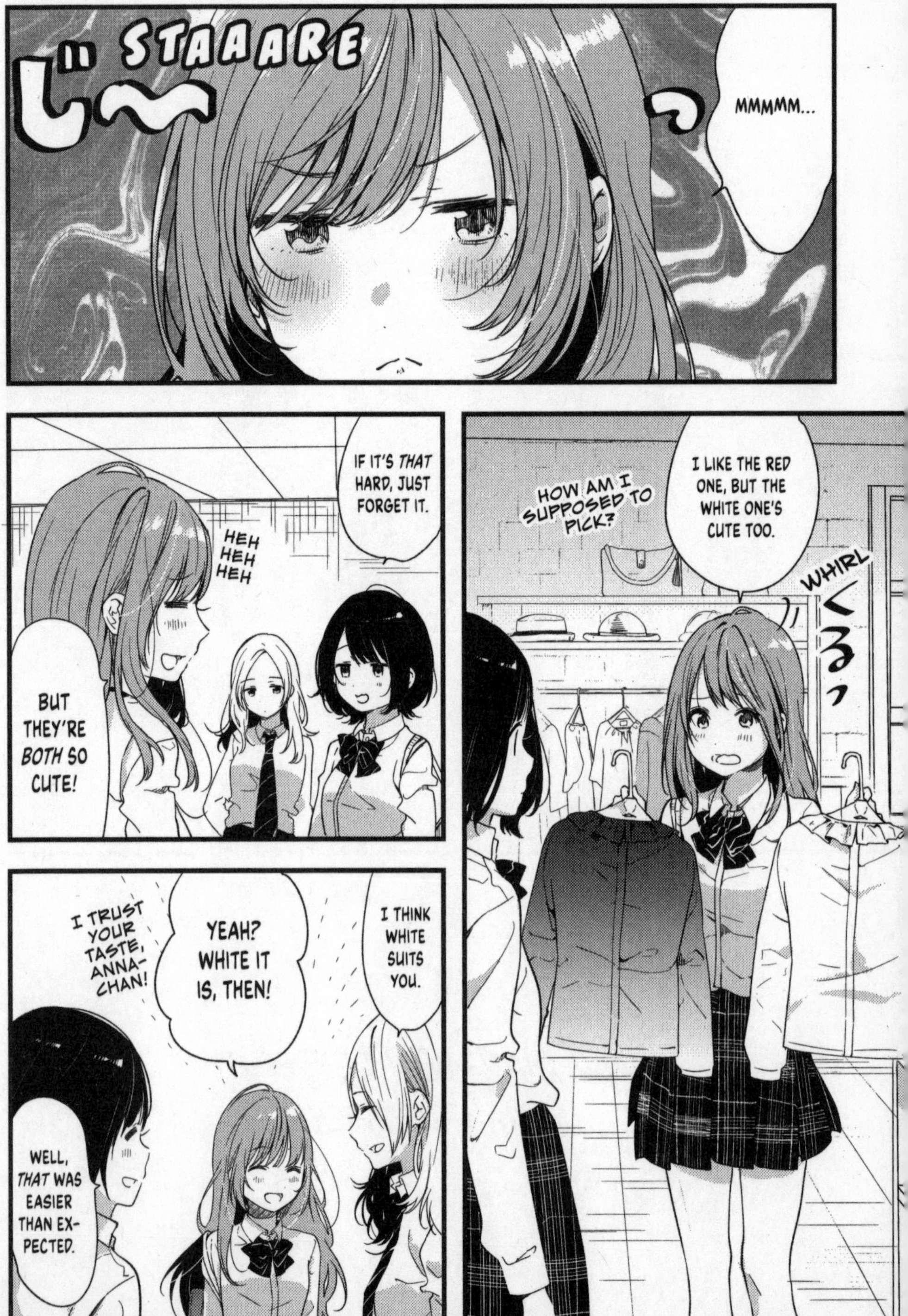
じ〜っ
STAAARE
MMMMM...
I LIKE THE RED ONE, BUT THE WHITE ONE'S CUTE TOO.
HOW AM I SUPPOSED TO PICK?
WHIRL
くるっ
IF IT'S *THAT* HARD, JUST FORGET IT.
HEH HEH HEH
BUT THEY'RE *BOTH* SO CUTE!
I THINK WHITE SUITS YOU.
YEAH? WHITE IT IS, THEN!
I TRUST YOUR TASTE, ANNA-CHAN!
WELL, *THAT* WAS EASIER THAN EX-PECTED.

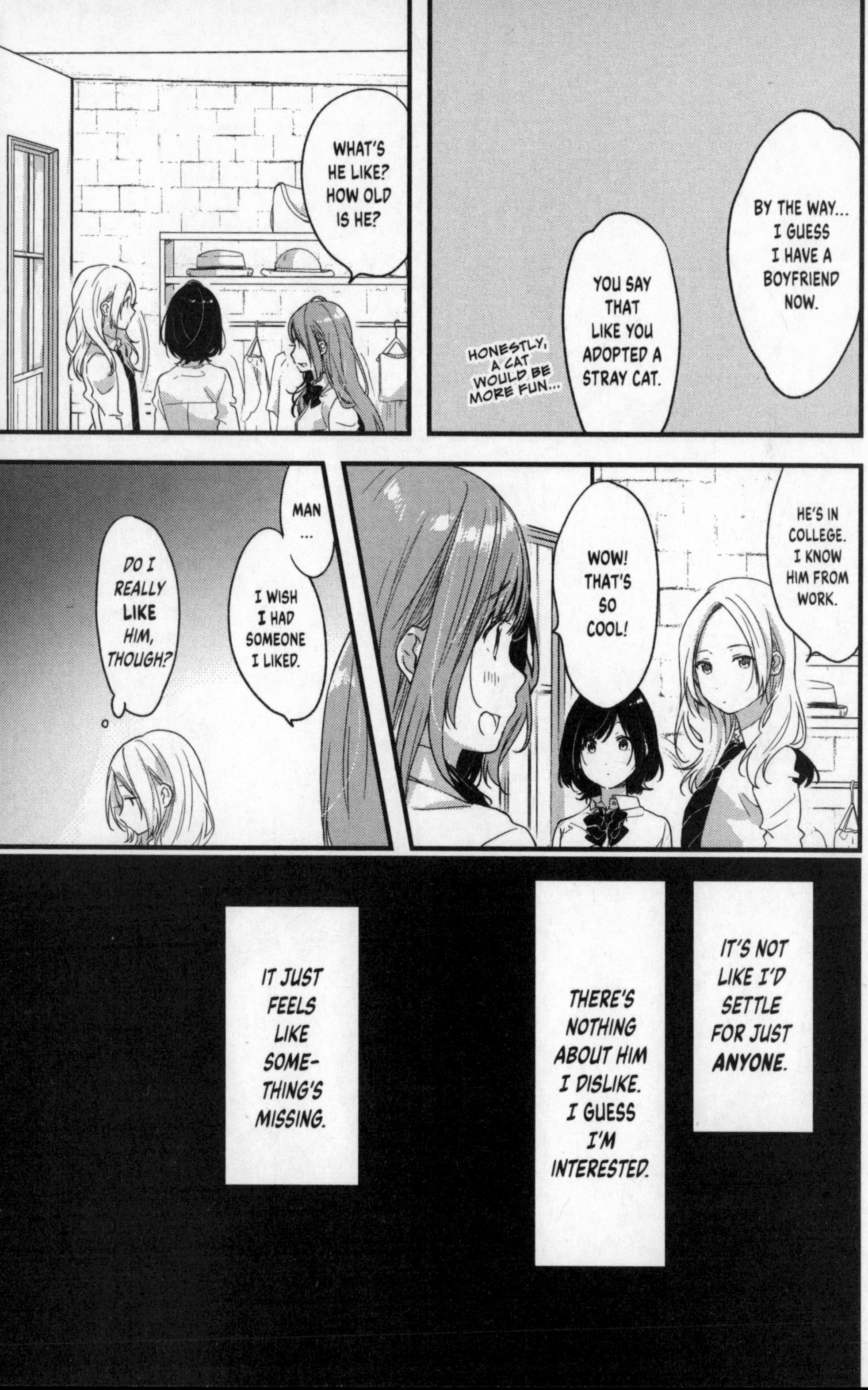
BY THE WAY... I GUESS I HAVE A BOYFRIEND NOW.
YOU SAY THAT LIKE YOU ADOPTED A STRAY CAT.
HONESTLY, A CAT WOULD BE MORE FUN...
WHAT'S HE LIKE? HOW OLD IS HE?
HE'S IN COLLEGE. I KNOW HIM FROM WORK.
WOW! THAT'S SO COOL!
MAN ...
I WISH I HAD SOMEONE I LIKED.
DO I REALLY LIKE HIM, THOUGH?
IT'S NOT LIKE I'D SETTLE FOR JUST ANYONE.
THERE'S NOTHING ABOUT HIM I DISLIKE. I GUESS I'M INTERESTED.
IT JUST FEELS LIKE SOME-THING'S MISSING.

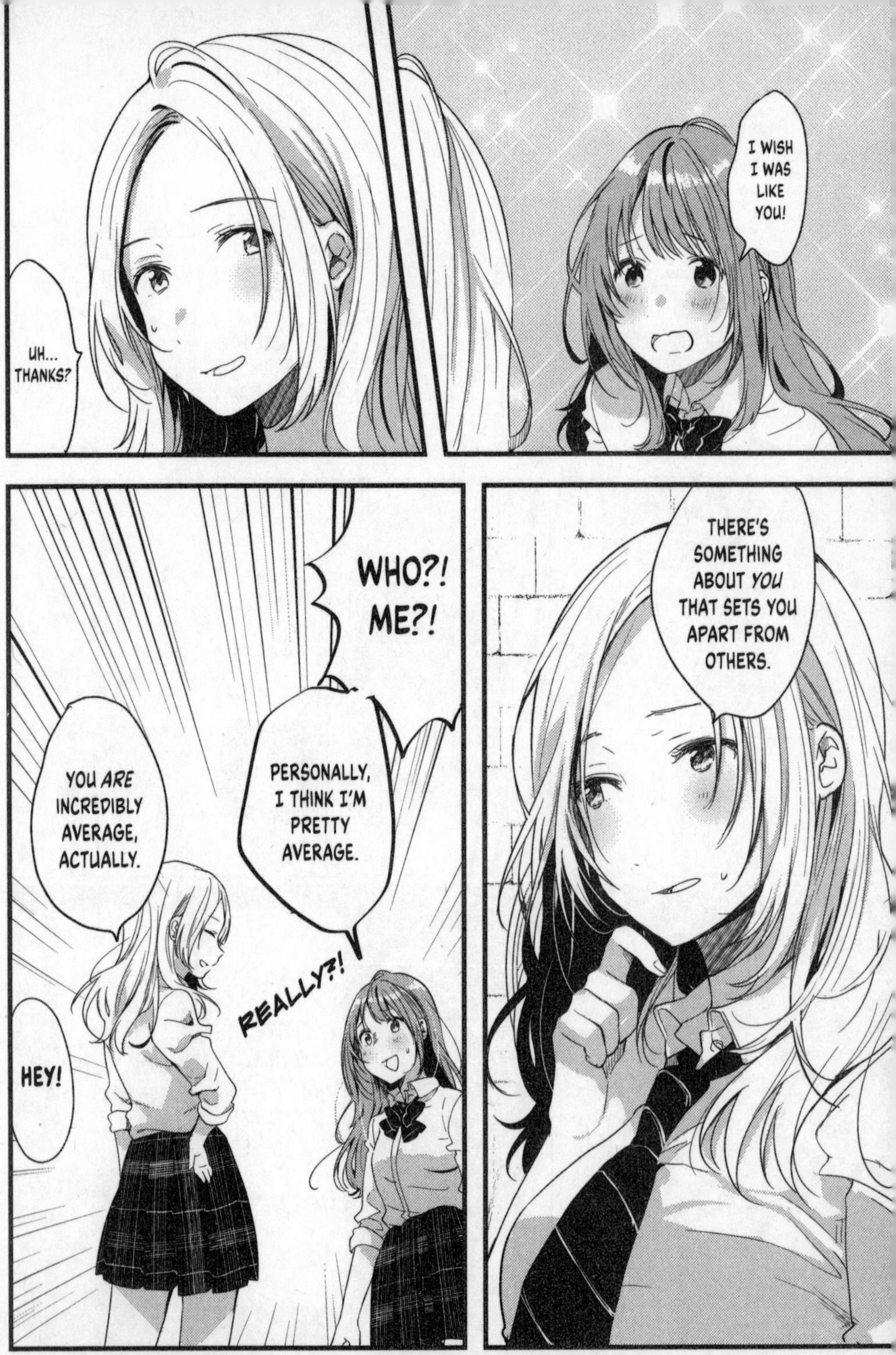
I WISH I WAS LIKE YOU!
UH... THANKS?
THERE'S SOMETHING ABOUT *YOU* THAT SETS YOU APART FROM OTHERS.
WHO?! ME?!
PERSONALLY, I THINK I'M PRETTY AVERAGE.
YOU *ARE* INCREDIBLY AVERAGE, ACTUALLY.
REALLY?!
HEY!

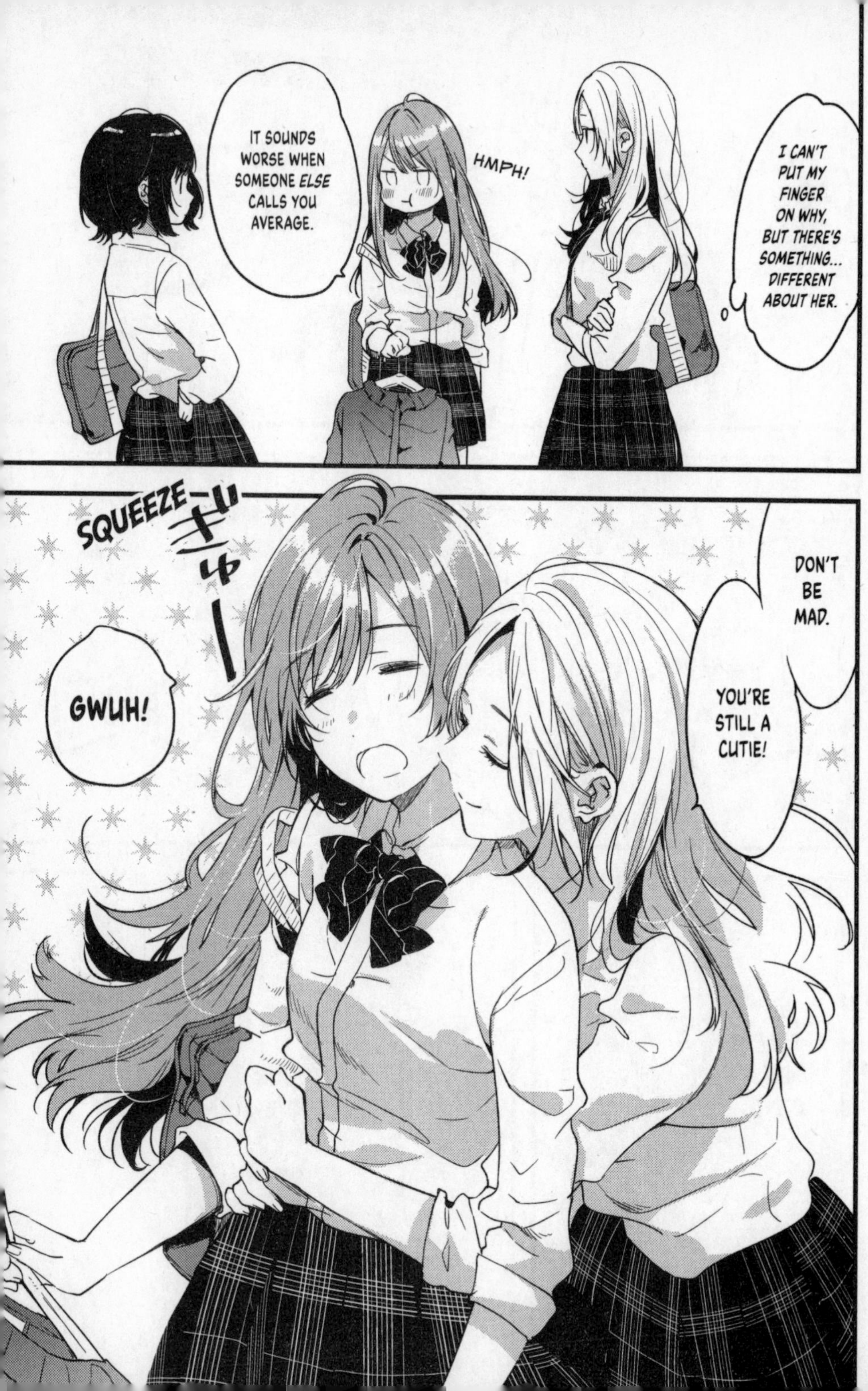
I CAN'T PUT MY FINGER ON WHY, BUT THERE'S SOMETHING... DIFFERENT ABOUT HER.
HMPH!
IT SOUNDS WORSE WHEN SOMEONE *ELSE* CALLS YOU AVERAGE.
DON'T BE MAD.
YOU'RE STILL A CUTIE!
SQUEEZE
ぎゅー
GWUH!

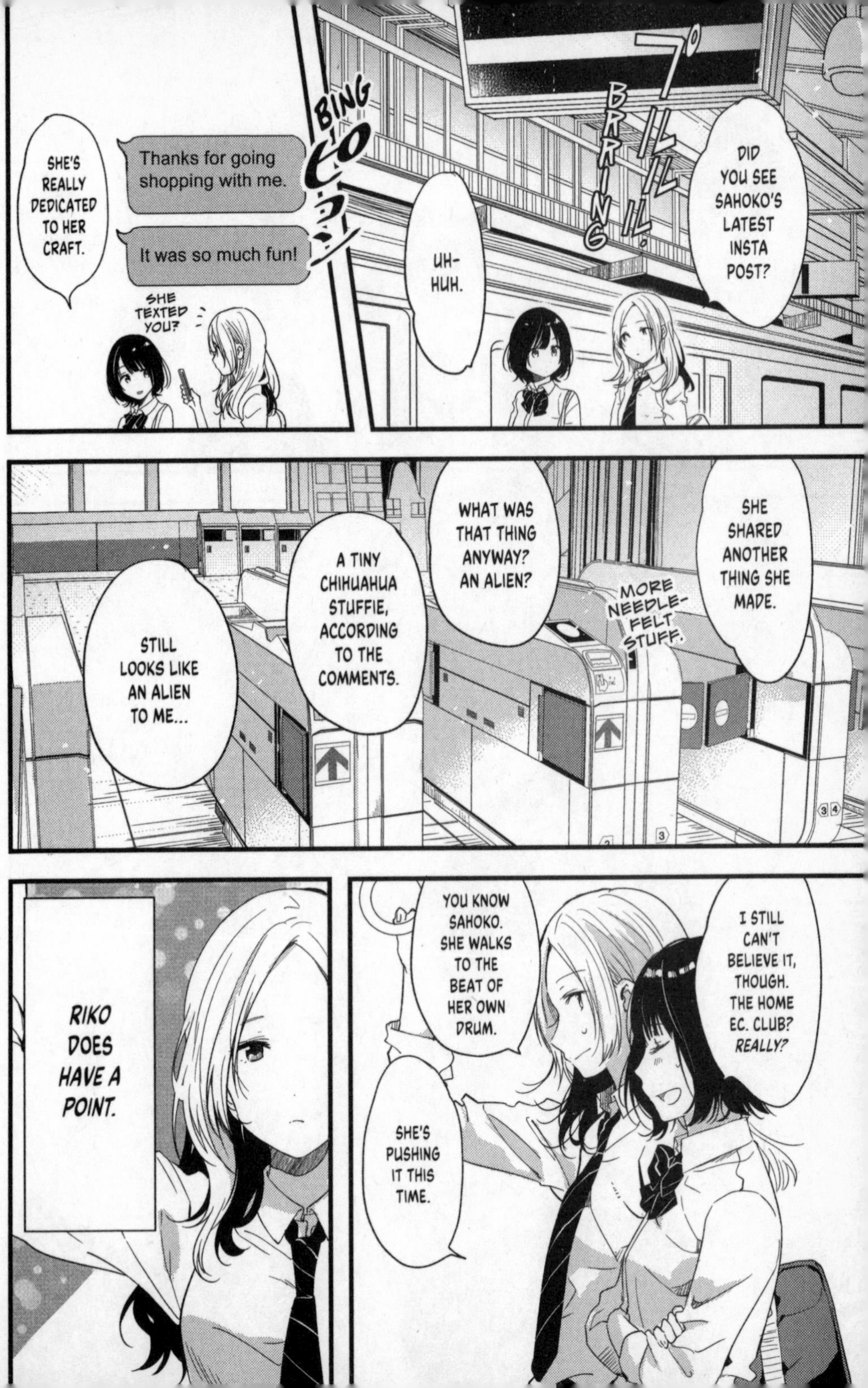
BRRING
DID YOU SEE SAHOKO'S LATEST INSTA POST?
UH-HUH.
BING
ピコン
Thanks for going shopping with me.
It was so much fun!
SHE'S REALLY DEDICATED TO HER CRAFT.
SHE TEXTED YOU?
SHE SHARED ANOTHER THING SHE MADE.
MORE NEEDLE-FELT STUFF.
WHAT WAS THAT THING ANYWAY? AN ALIEN?
A TINY CHIHUAHUA STUFFIE, ACCORDING TO THE COMMENTS.
STILL LOOKS LIKE AN ALIEN TO ME...
I STILL CAN'T BELIEVE IT, THOUGH. THE HOME EC. CLUB? *REALLY?*
YOU KNOW SAHOKO. SHE WALKS TO THE BEAT OF HER OWN DRUM.
SHE'S PUSHING IT THIS TIME.
RIKO DOES HAVE A POINT.

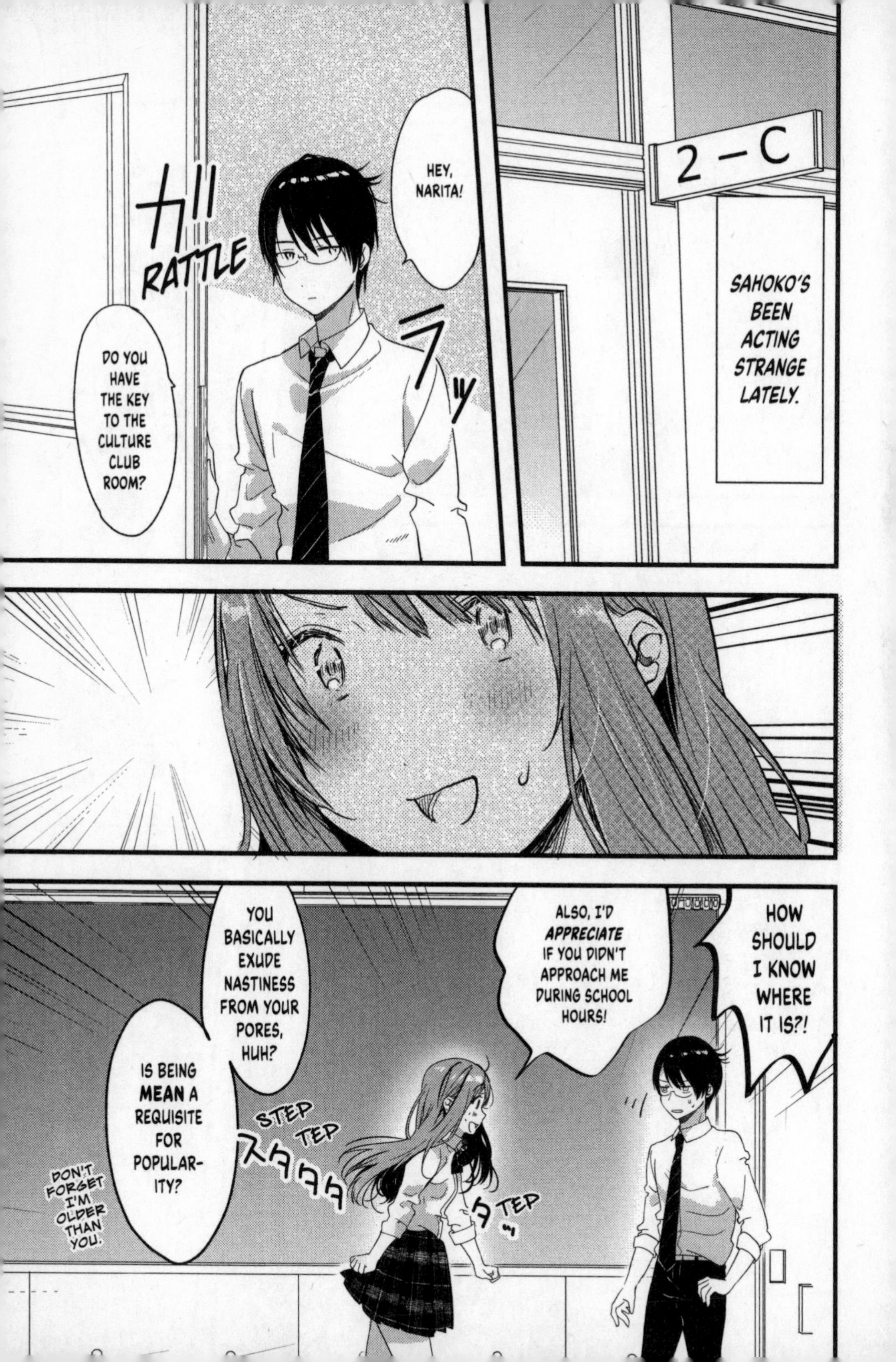
2 — C
SAHOKO'S BEEN ACTING STRANGE LATELY.
HEY, NARITA!
RATTLE
DO YOU HAVE THE KEY TO THE CULTURE CLUB ROOM?
HOW SHOULD I KNOW WHERE IT IS?!
ALSO, I'D *APPRECIATE* IF YOU DIDN'T APPROACH ME DURING SCHOOL HOURS!
YOU BASICALLY EXUDE NASTINESS FROM YOUR PORES, HUH?
IS BEING **MEAN** A REQUISITE FOR POPULAR-ITY?
STEP TEP
TEP
DON'T FORGET I'M OLDER THAN YOU.

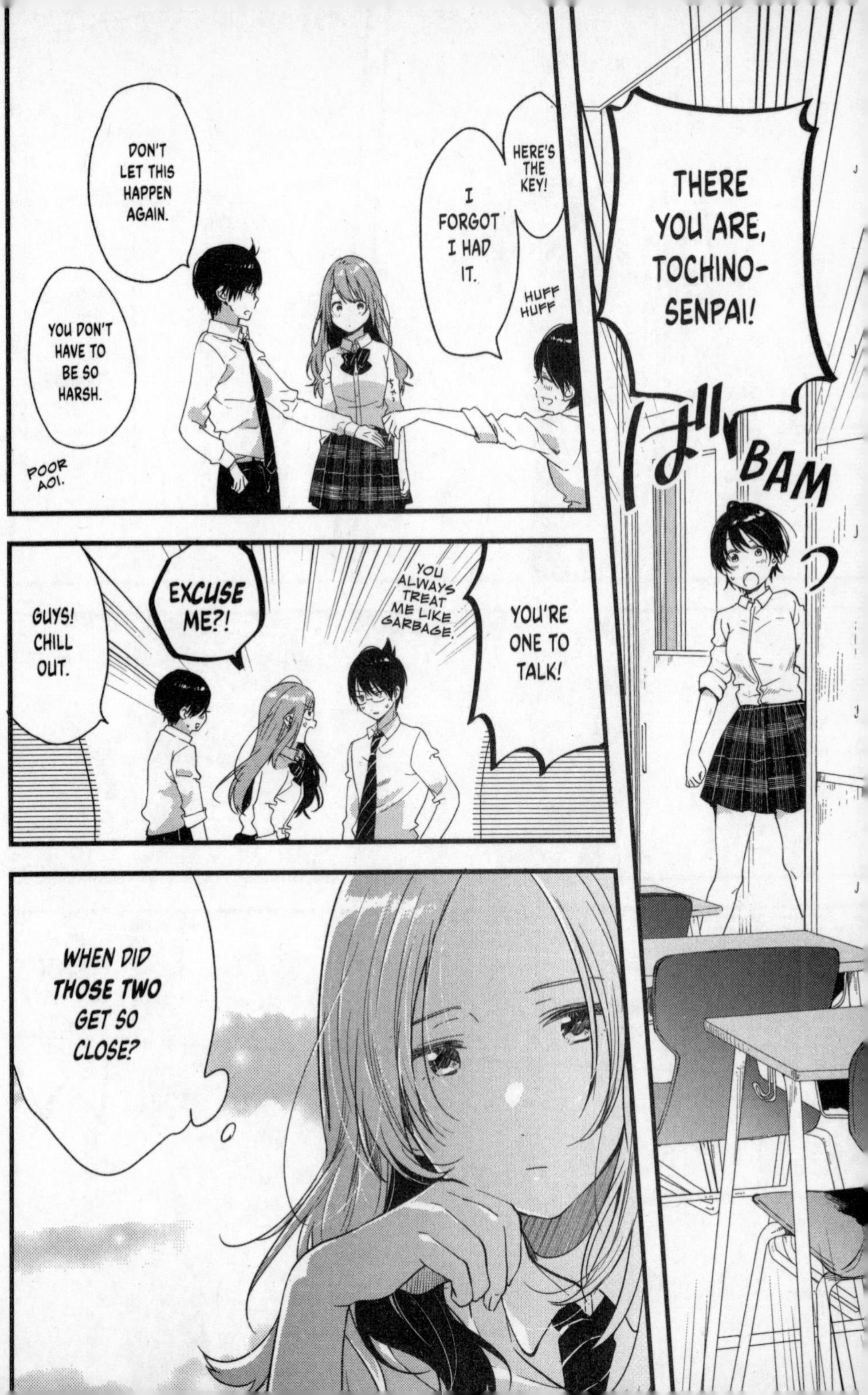
THERE YOU ARE, TOCHINO-SENPAI!
BAM
HERE'S THE KEY!
I FORGOT I HAD IT.
HUFF HUFF
DON'T LET THIS HAPPEN AGAIN.
YOU DON'T HAVE TO BE SO HARSH.
POOR AOI.
YOU'RE ONE TO TALK!
YOU ALWAYS TREAT ME LIKE GARBAGE.
EXCUSE ME?!
GUYS! CHILL OUT.
WHEN DID THOSE TWO GET SO CLOSE?

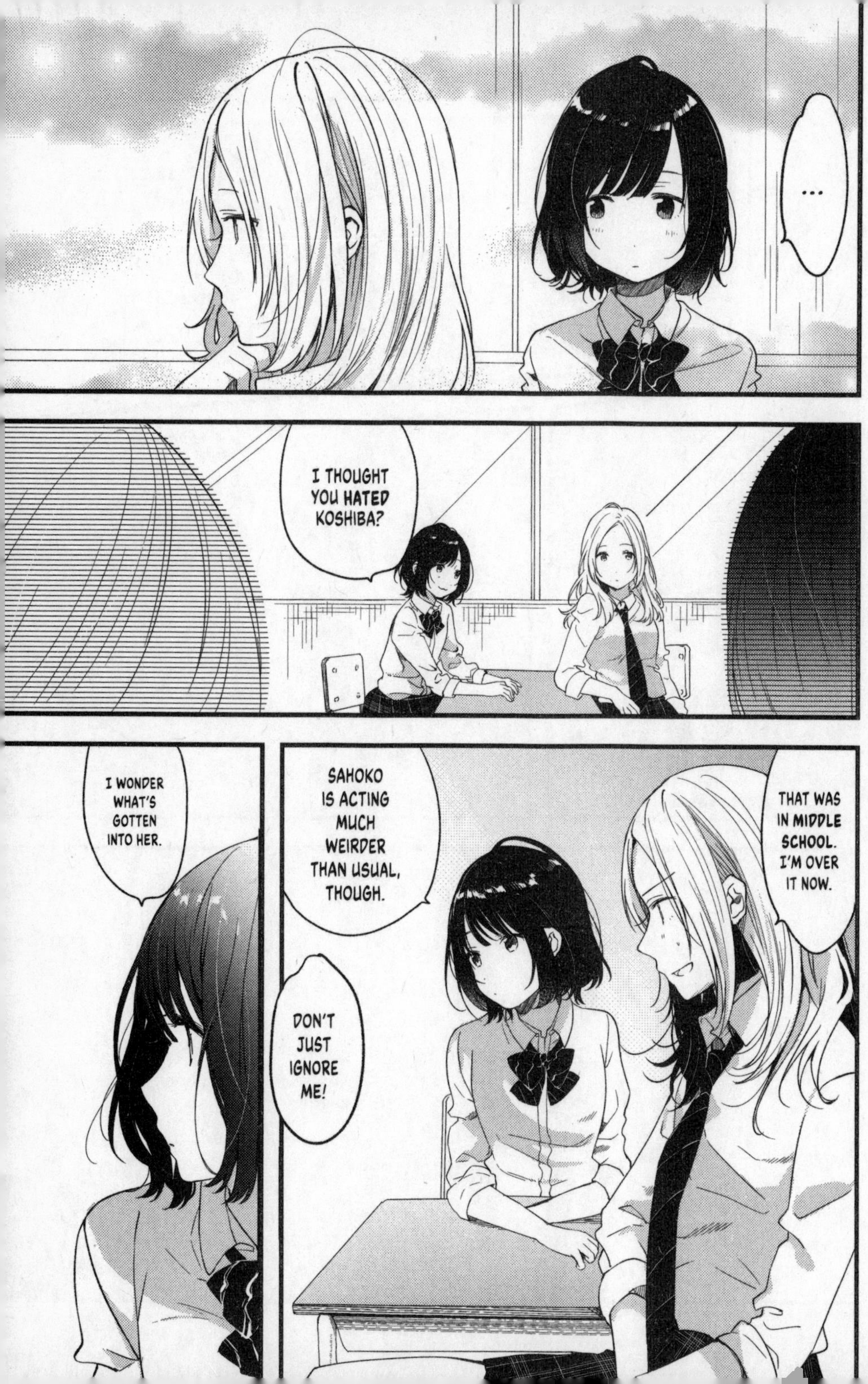
...
I THOUGHT YOU HATED KOSHIBA?
THAT WAS IN MIDDLE SCHOOL. I'M OVER IT NOW.
SAHOKO IS ACTING MUCH WEIRDER THAN USUAL, THOUGH.
DON'T JUST IGNORE ME!
I WONDER WHAT'S GOTTEN INTO HER.

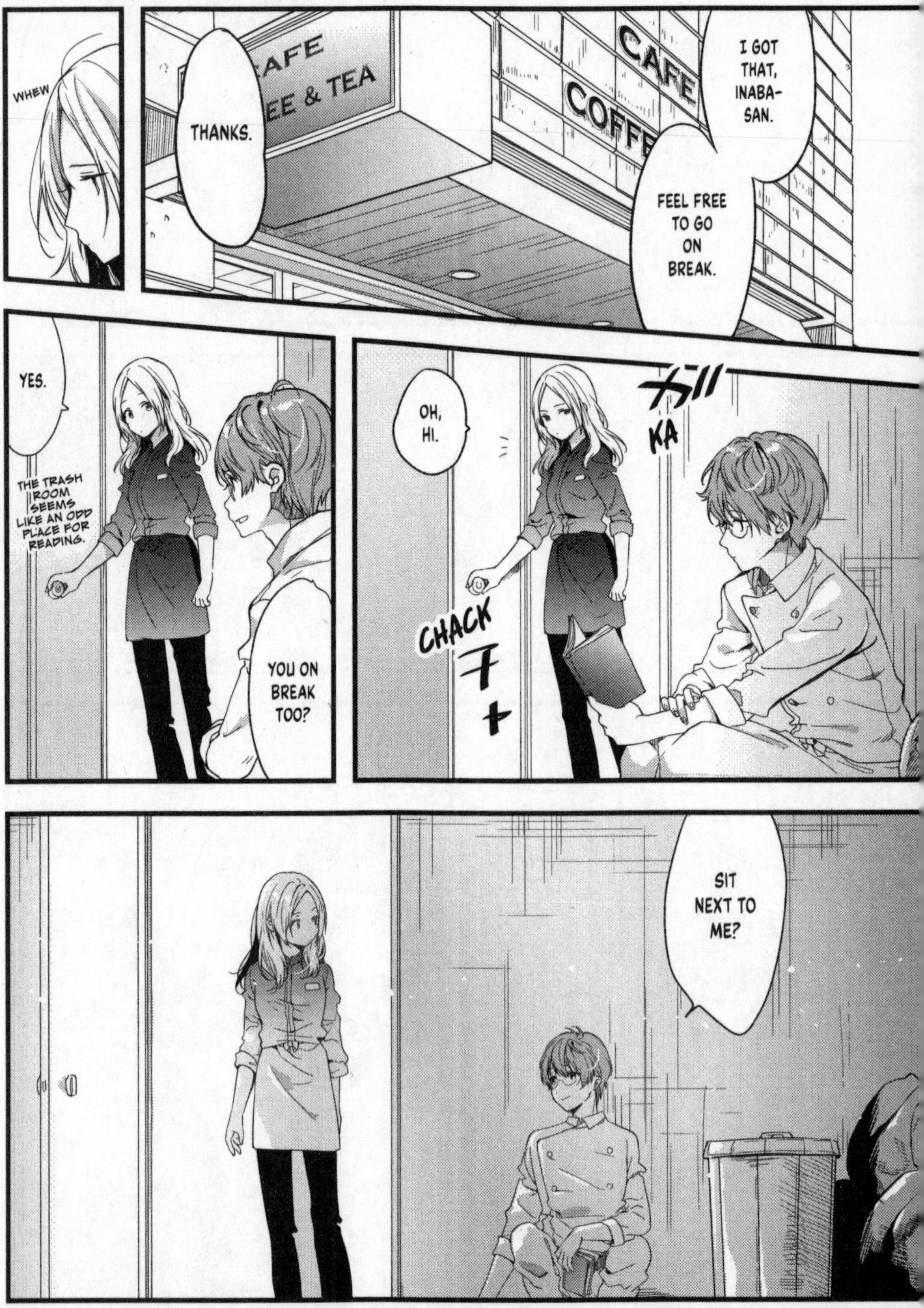
CAFE
I GOT THAT, INABA-SAN.
FEEL FREE TO GO ON BREAK.
THANKS.
WHEW
KA
OH, HI.
CHACK
YOU ON BREAK TOO?
YES.
THE TRASH ROOM SEEMS LIKE AN ODD PLACE FOR READING.
SIT NEXT TO ME?

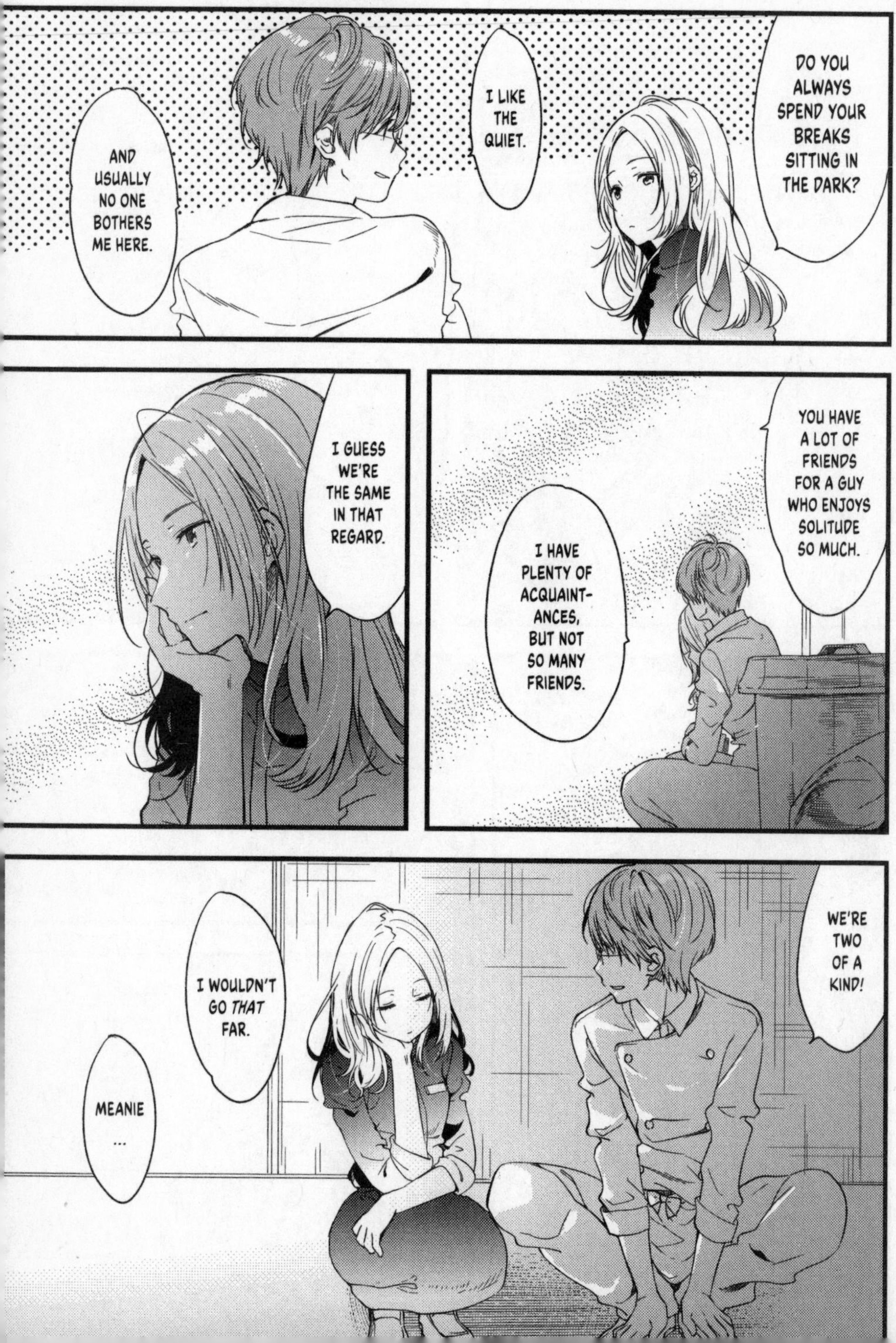
DO YOU ALWAYS SPEND YOUR BREAKS SITTING IN THE DARK?
I LIKE THE QUIET.
AND USUALLY NO ONE BOTHERS ME HERE.
YOU HAVE A LOT OF FRIENDS FOR A GUY WHO ENJOYS SOLITUDE SO MUCH.
I HAVE PLENTY OF ACQUAINT-ANCES, BUT NOT SO MANY FRIENDS.
I GUESS WE'RE THE SAME IN THAT REGARD.
WE'RE TWO OF A KIND!
I WOULDN'T GO *THAT* FAR.
MEANIE ...

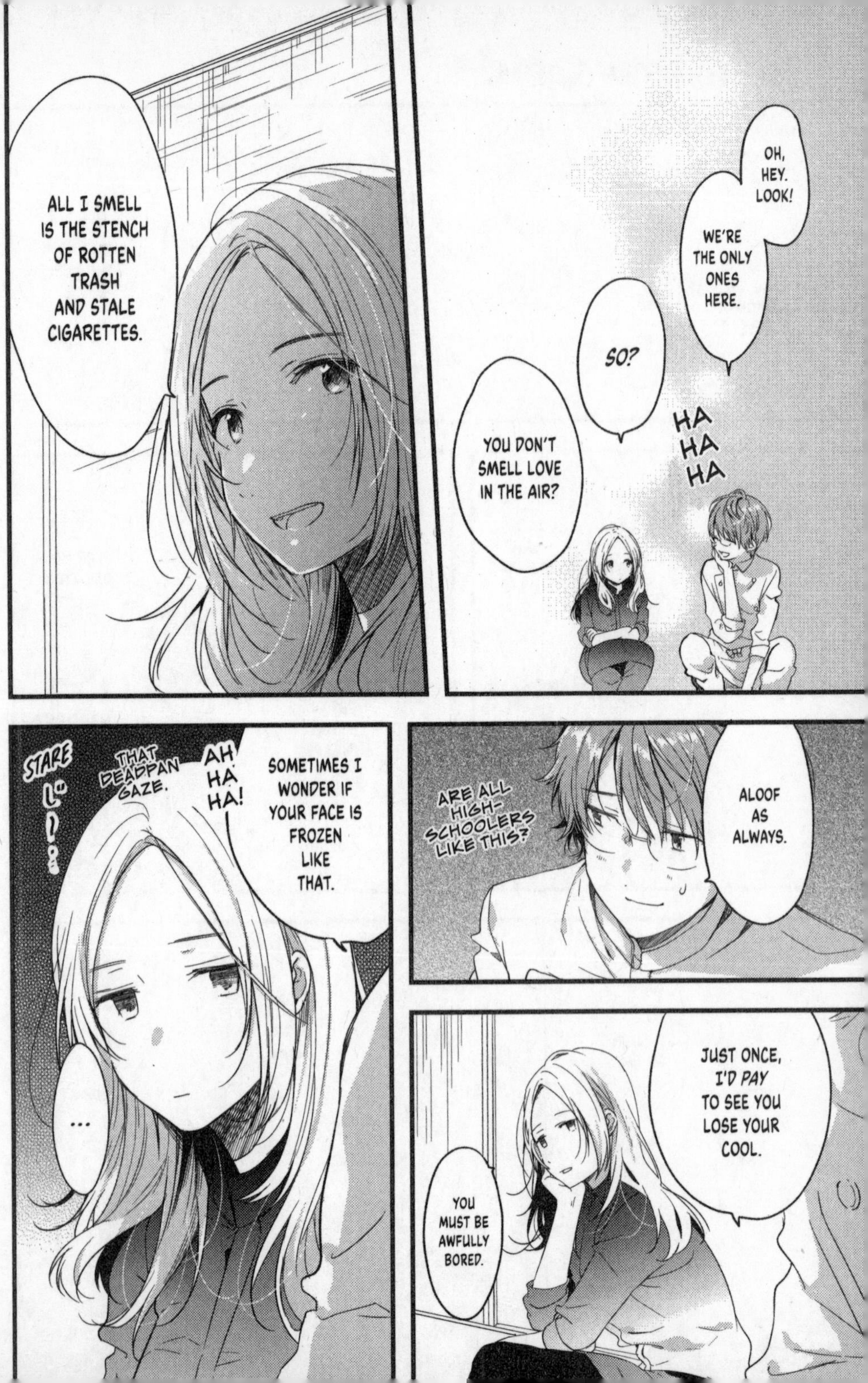
OH, HEY. LOOK!
WE'RE THE ONLY ONES HERE.
HA HA HA
SO?
YOU DON'T SMELL LOVE IN THE AIR?
ALL I SMELL IS THE STENCH OF ROTTEN TRASH AND STALE CIGARETTES.
ALOOF AS ALWAYS.
ARE ALL HIGH-SCHOOLERS LIKE THIS?
JUST ONCE, I'D *PAY* TO SEE YOU LOSE YOUR COOL.
YOU MUST BE AWFULLY BORED.
SOMETIMES I WONDER IF YOUR FACE IS FROZEN LIKE THAT.
AH HA HA!
THAT DEADPAN GAZE.
STARE
...

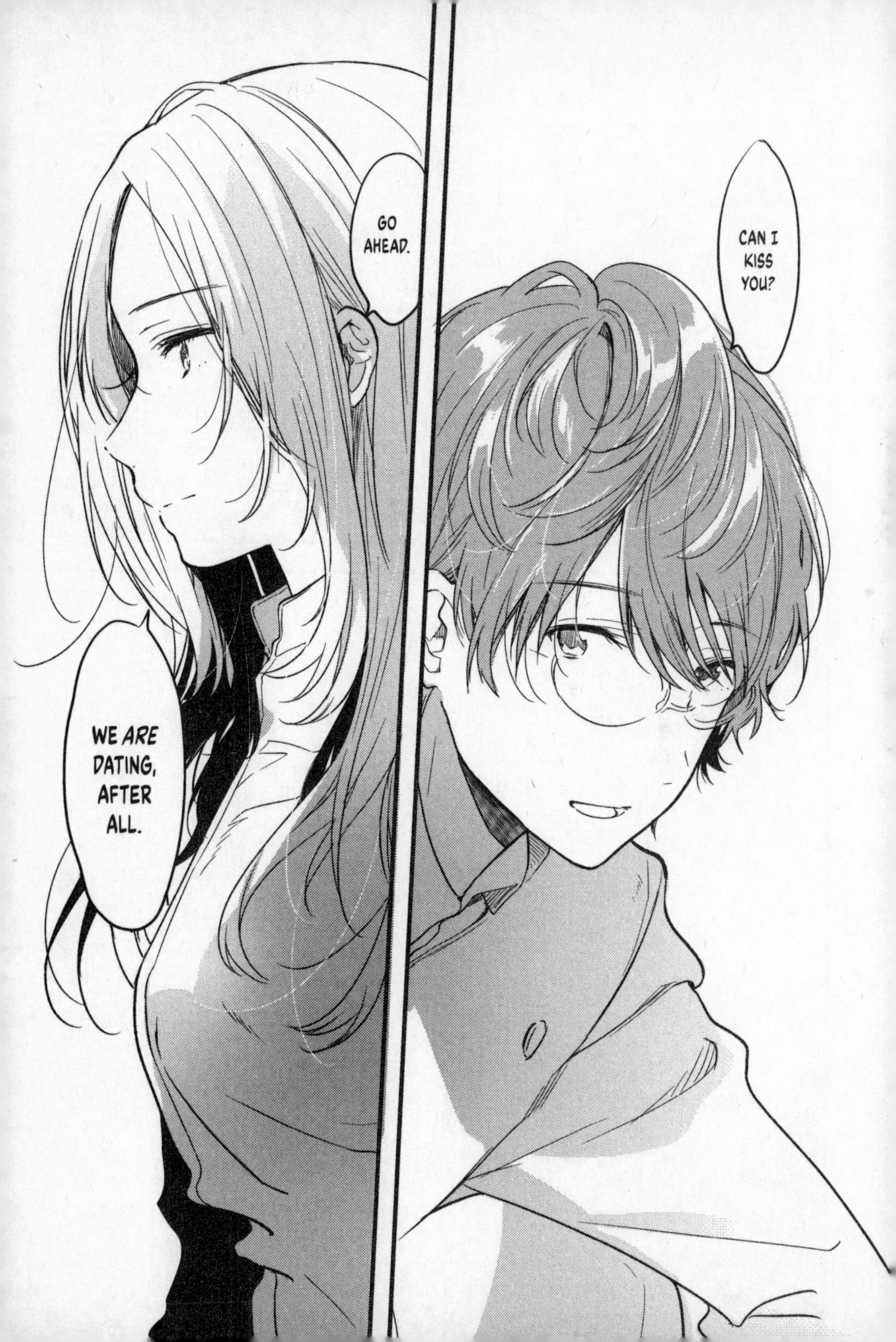
CAN I KISS YOU?
GO AHEAD.
WE *ARE* DATING, AFTER ALL.

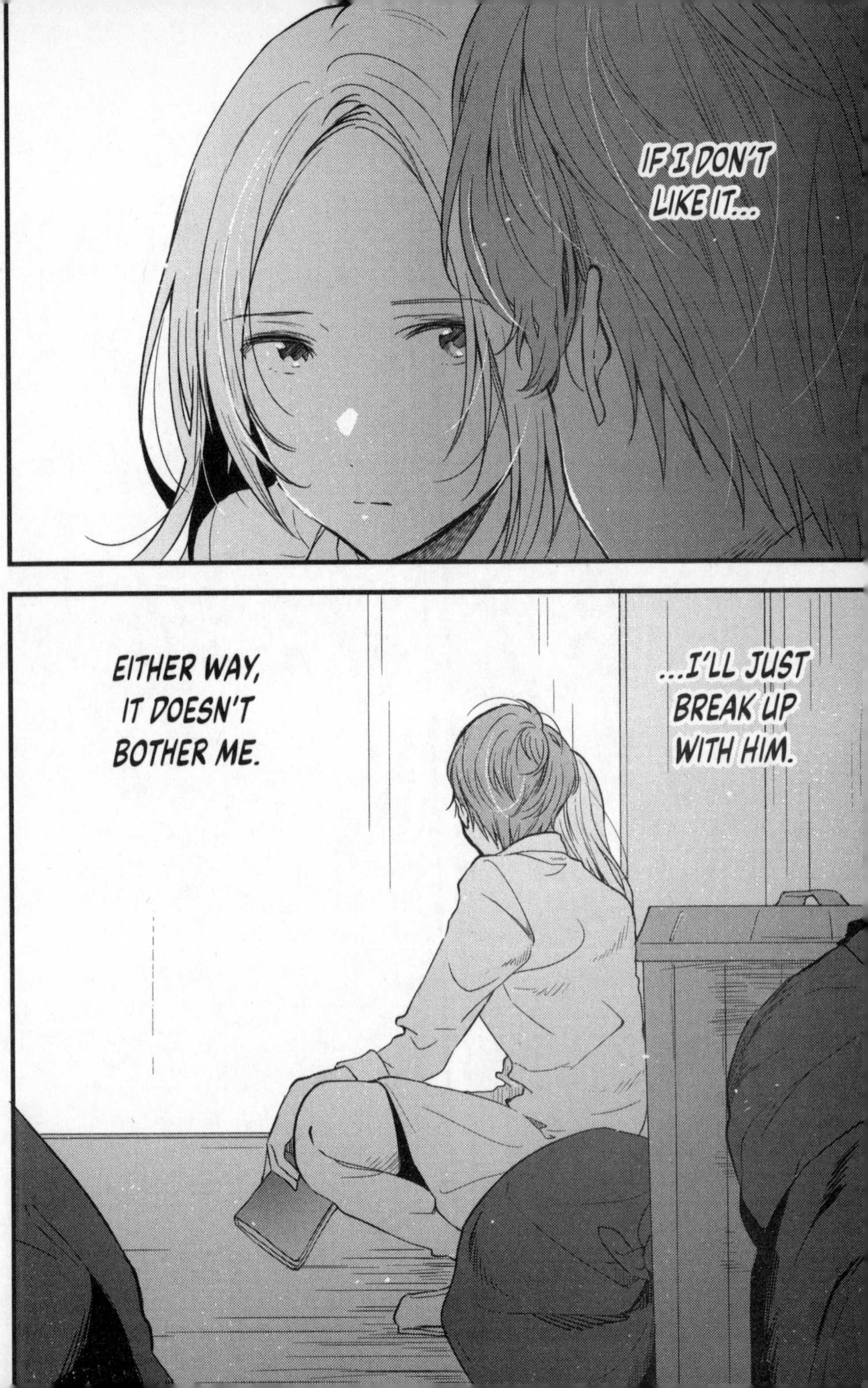
IF I DON'T
LIKE IT...
...I'LL JUST BREAK UP WITH HIM.
EITHER WAY, IT DOESN'T BOTHER ME.

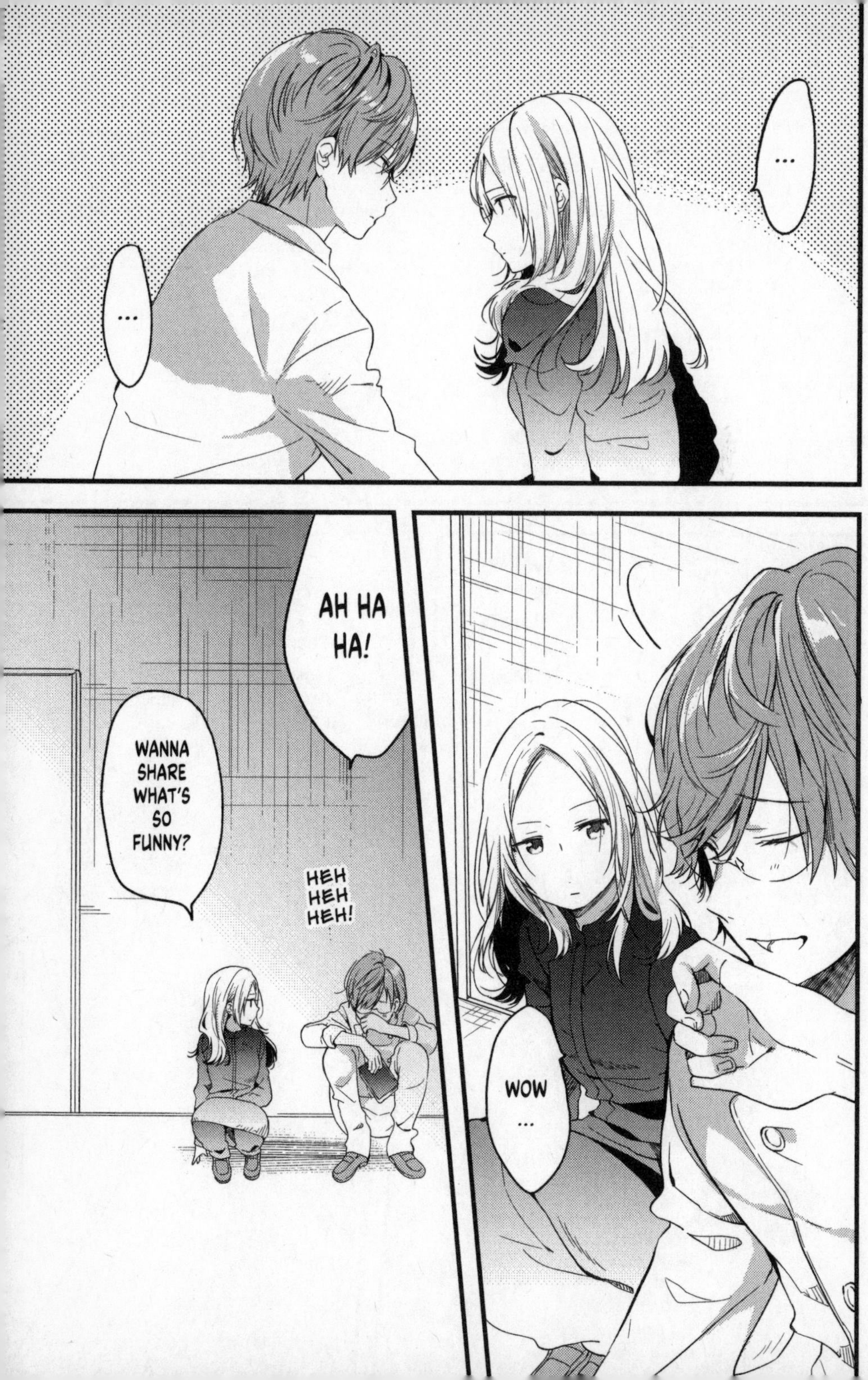
...
...
WOW ...
AH HA HA!
WANNA SHARE WHAT'S SO FUNNY?
HEH HEH HEH!

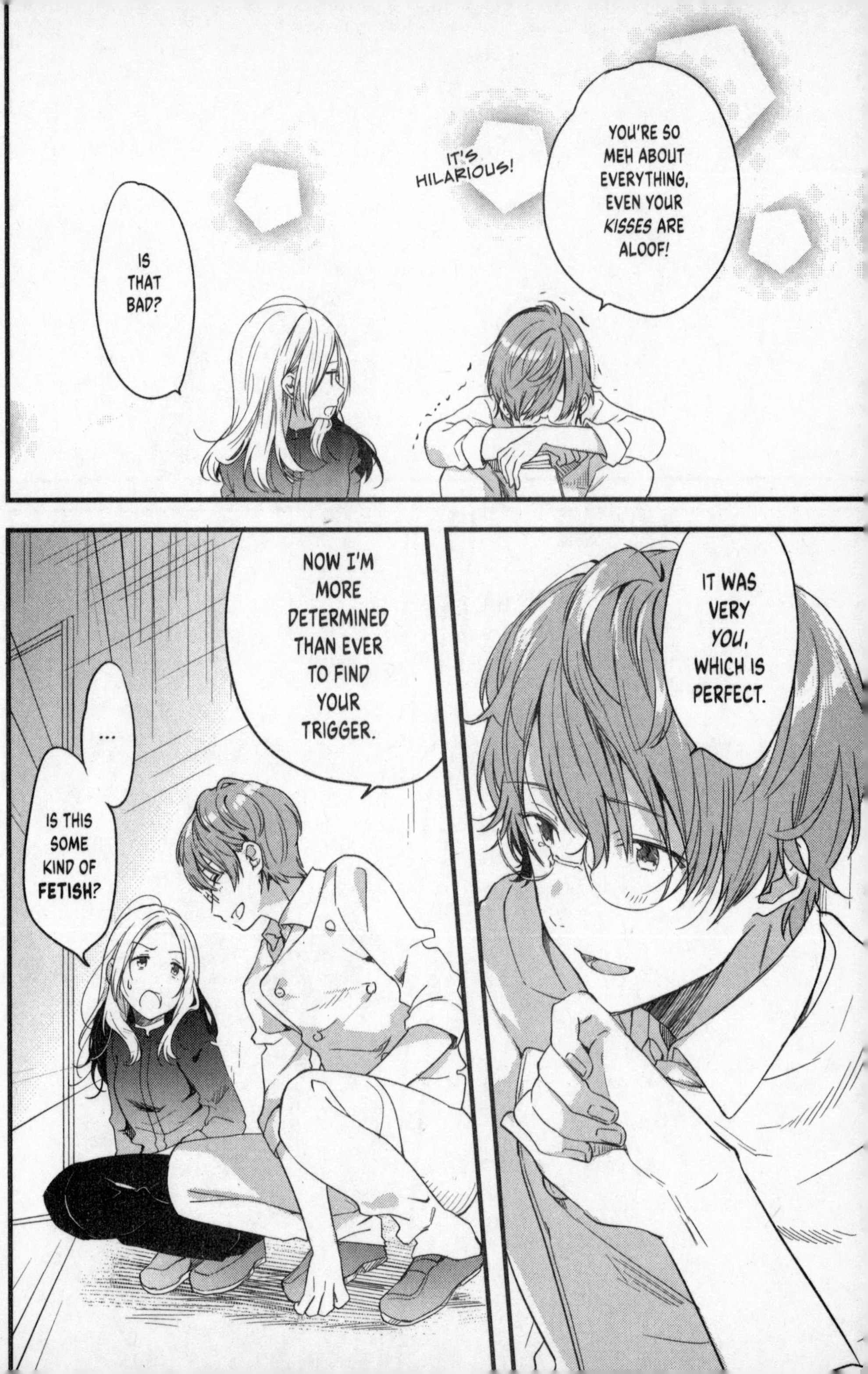
YOU'RE SO MEH ABOUT EVERYTHING, EVEN YOUR *KISSES* ARE ALOOF!
IT'S HILARIOUS!
IS THAT BAD?
IT WAS VERY *YOU*, WHICH IS PERFECT.
NOW I'M MORE DETERMINED THAN EVER TO FIND YOUR TRIGGER.
...
IS THIS SOME KIND OF **FETISH**?

Chapter 8:
Melting Ice 2

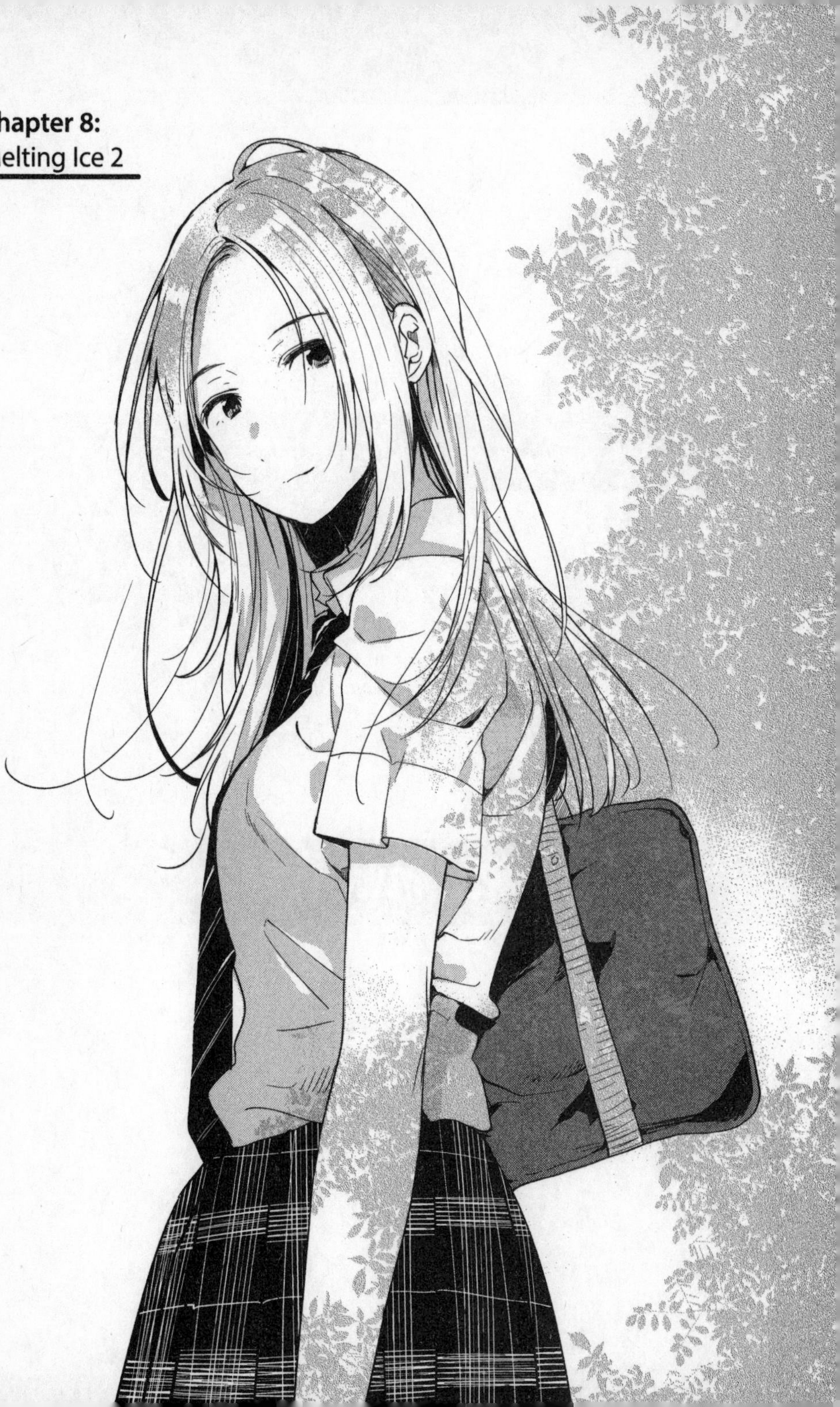

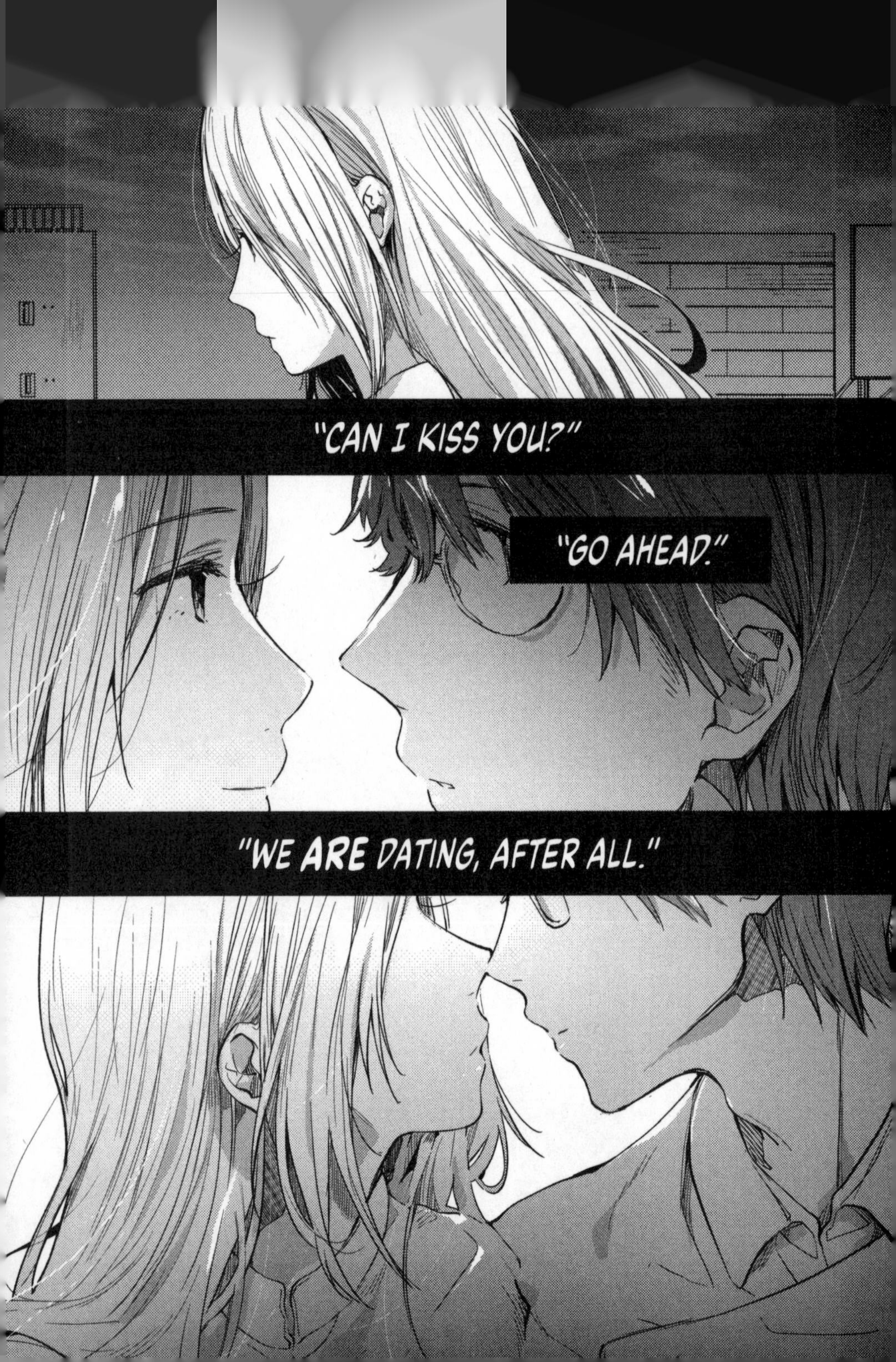
"CAN I KISS YOU?"
"GO AHEAD."
"WE ARE DATING, AFTER ALL."

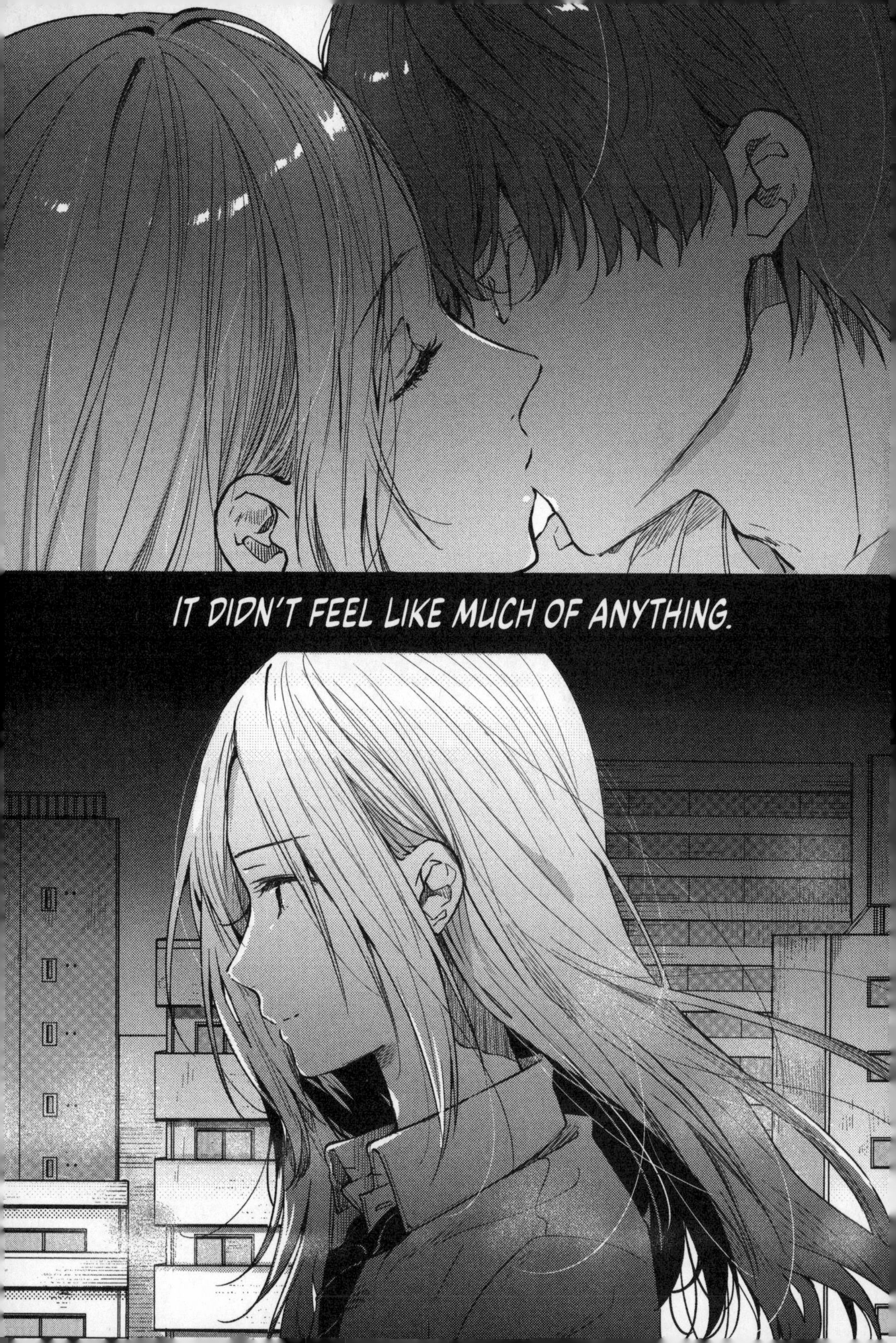
IT DIDN'T FEEL LIKE MUCH OF ANYTHING.

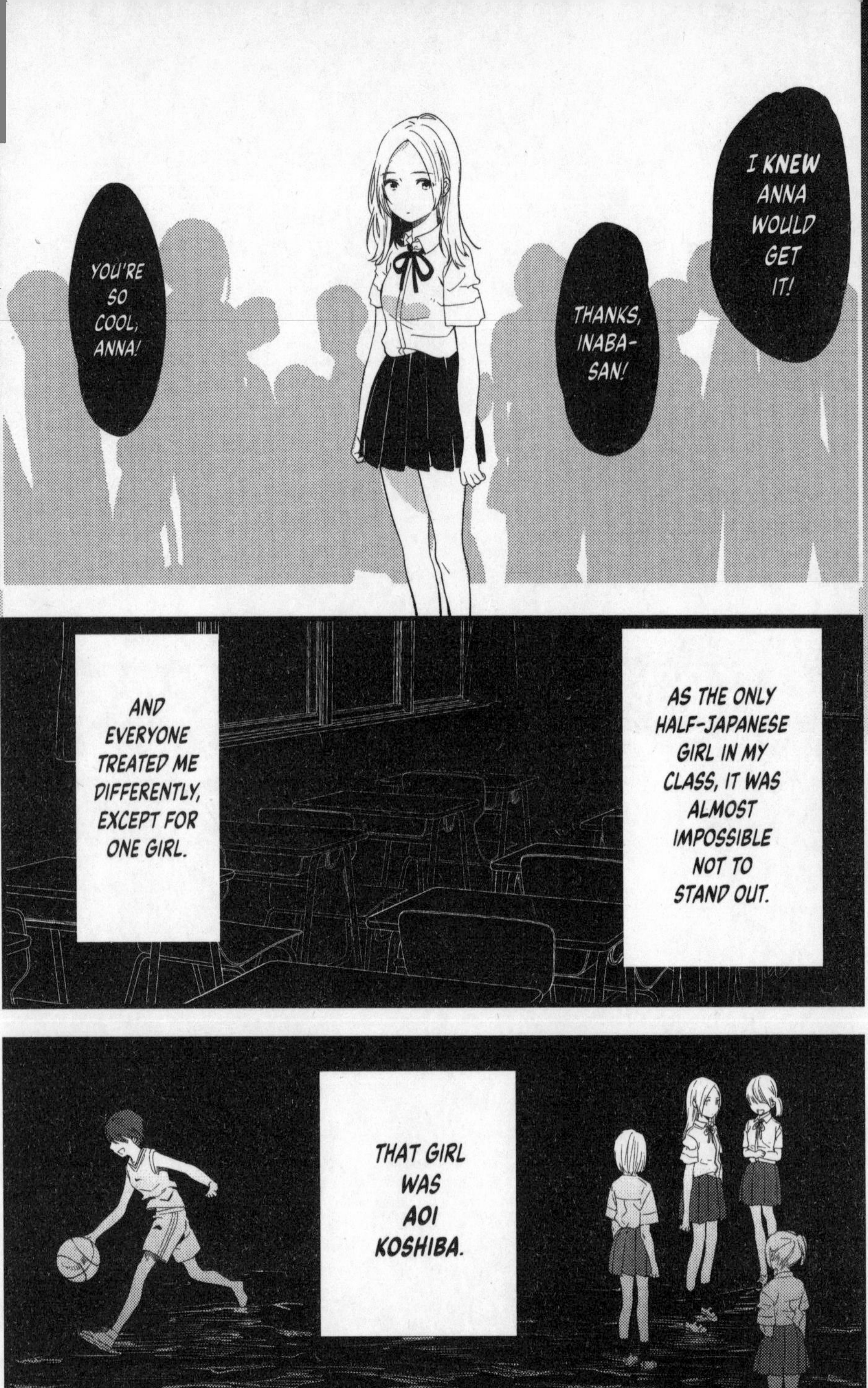

I KNEW ANNA WOULD GET IT!
THANKS, INABA-SAN!
YOU'RE SO COOL, ANNA!
AS THE ONLY HALF-JAPANESE GIRL IN MY CLASS, IT WAS ALMOST IMPOSSIBLE NOT TO STAND OUT.
AND EVERYONE TREATED ME DIFFERENTLY, EXCEPT FOR ONE GIRL.
THAT GIRL WAS AOI KOSHIBA.

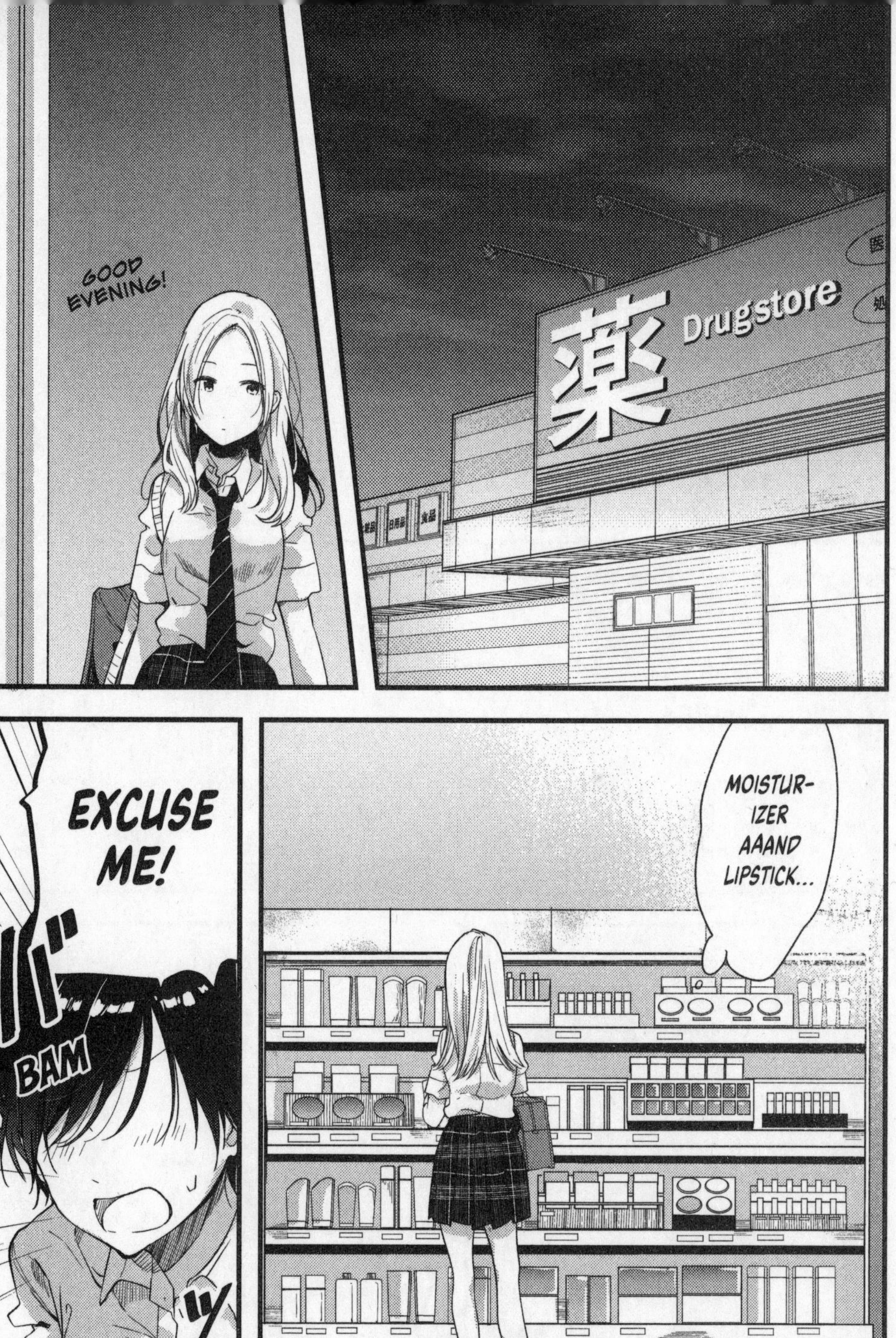
薬
Drugstore
GOOD EVENING!
MOISTUR-IZER AAAND LIPSTICK...
EXCUSE ME!
BAM

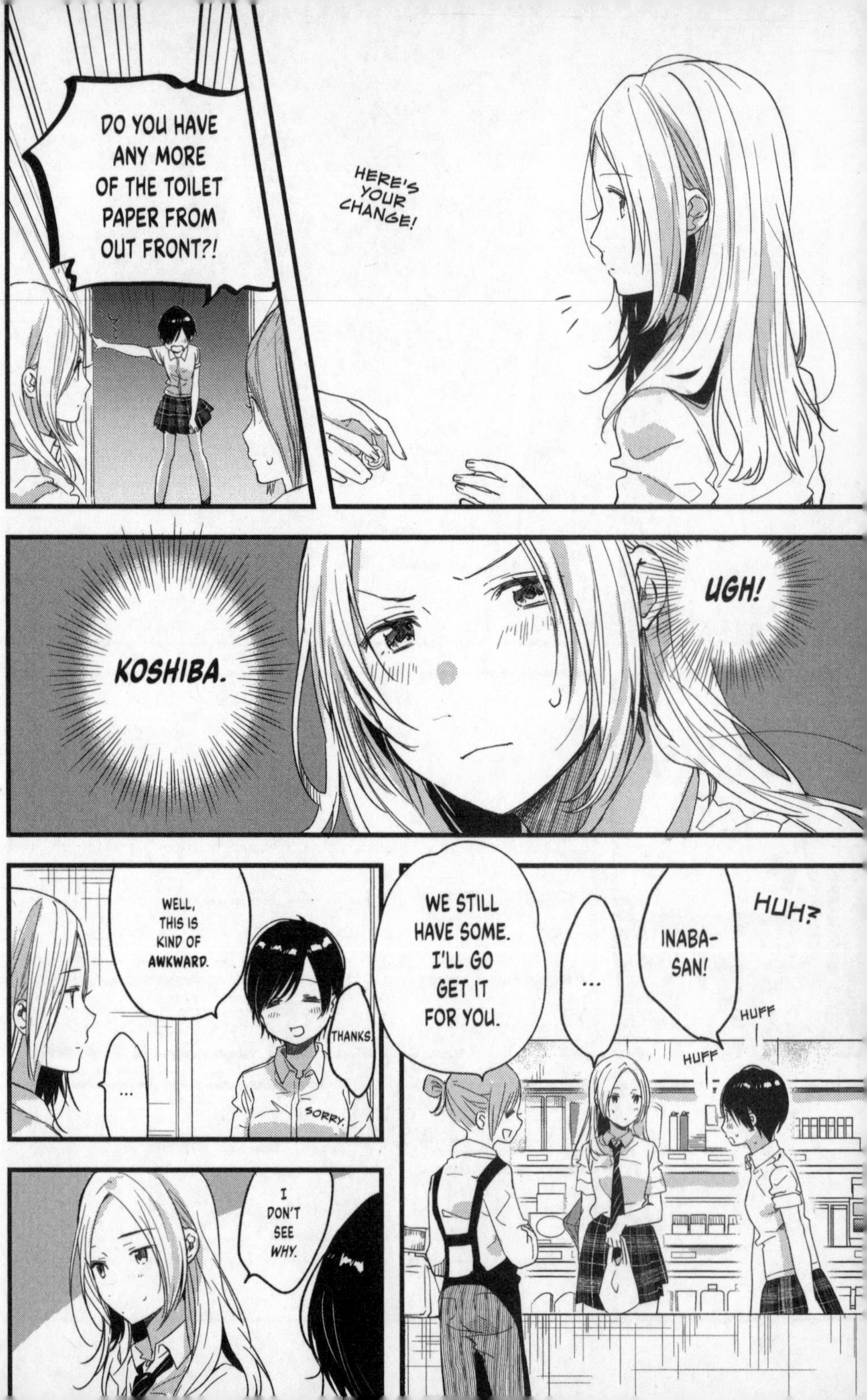

HERE'S YOUR CHANGE!
DO YOU HAVE ANY MORE OF THE TOILET PAPER FROM OUT FRONT?!
UGH!
KOSHIBA.
HUH?
INABA-SAN!
...
WE STILL HAVE SOME. I'LL GO GET IT FOR YOU.
HUFF
HUFF
WELL, THIS IS KIND OF AWKWARD.
THANKS.
...
SORRY.
I DON'T SEE WHY.

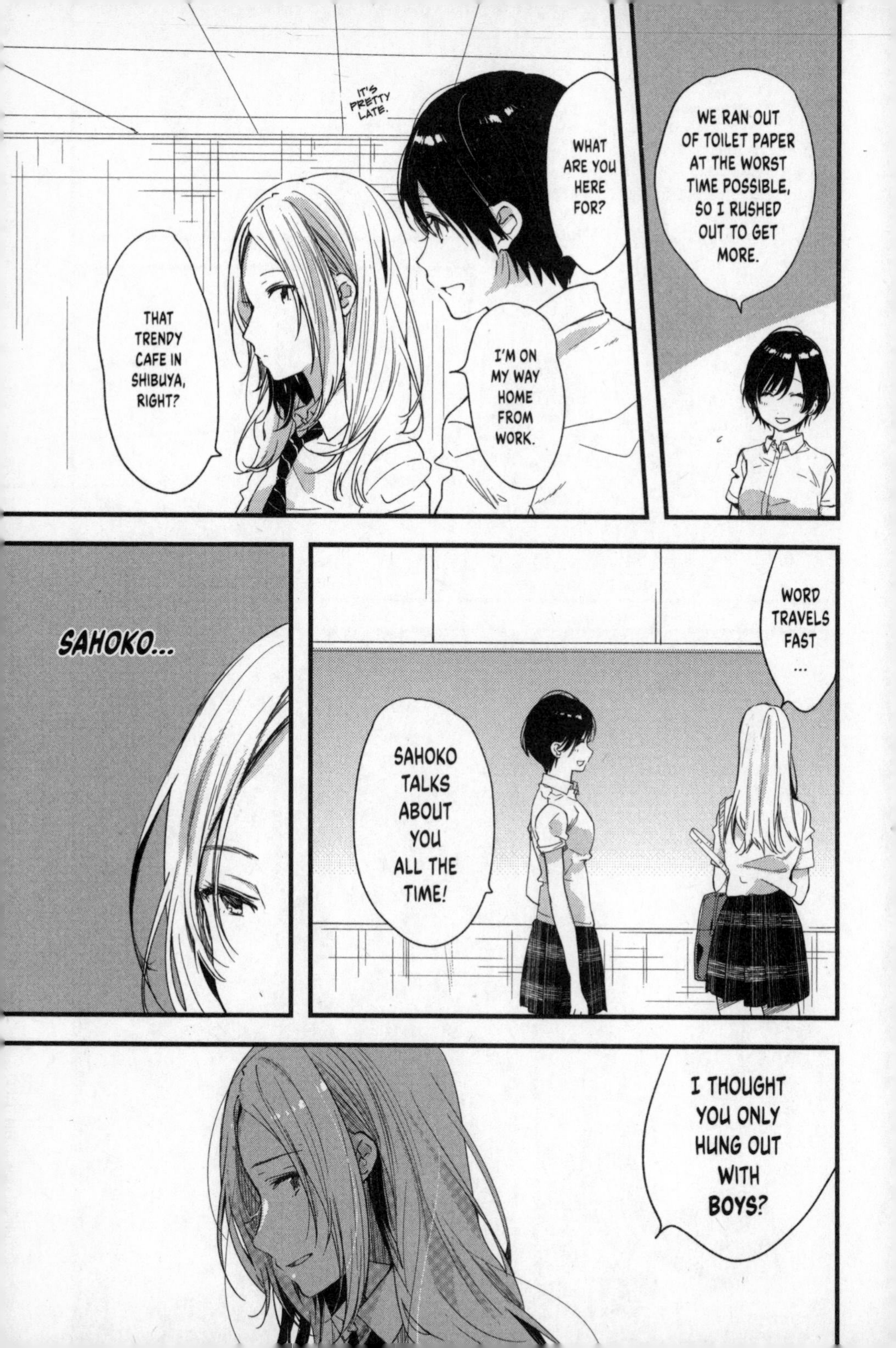
WE RAN OUT OF TOILET PAPER AT THE WORST TIME POSSIBLE, SO I RUSHED OUT TO GET MORE.
IT'S PRETTY LATE.
WHAT ARE YOU HERE FOR?
I'M ON MY WAY HOME FROM WORK.
THAT TRENDY CAFE IN SHIBUYA, RIGHT?
WORD TRAVELS FAST ...
SAHOKO TALKS ABOUT YOU ALL THE TIME!
SAHOKO...
I THOUGHT YOU ONLY HUNG OUT WITH BOYS?

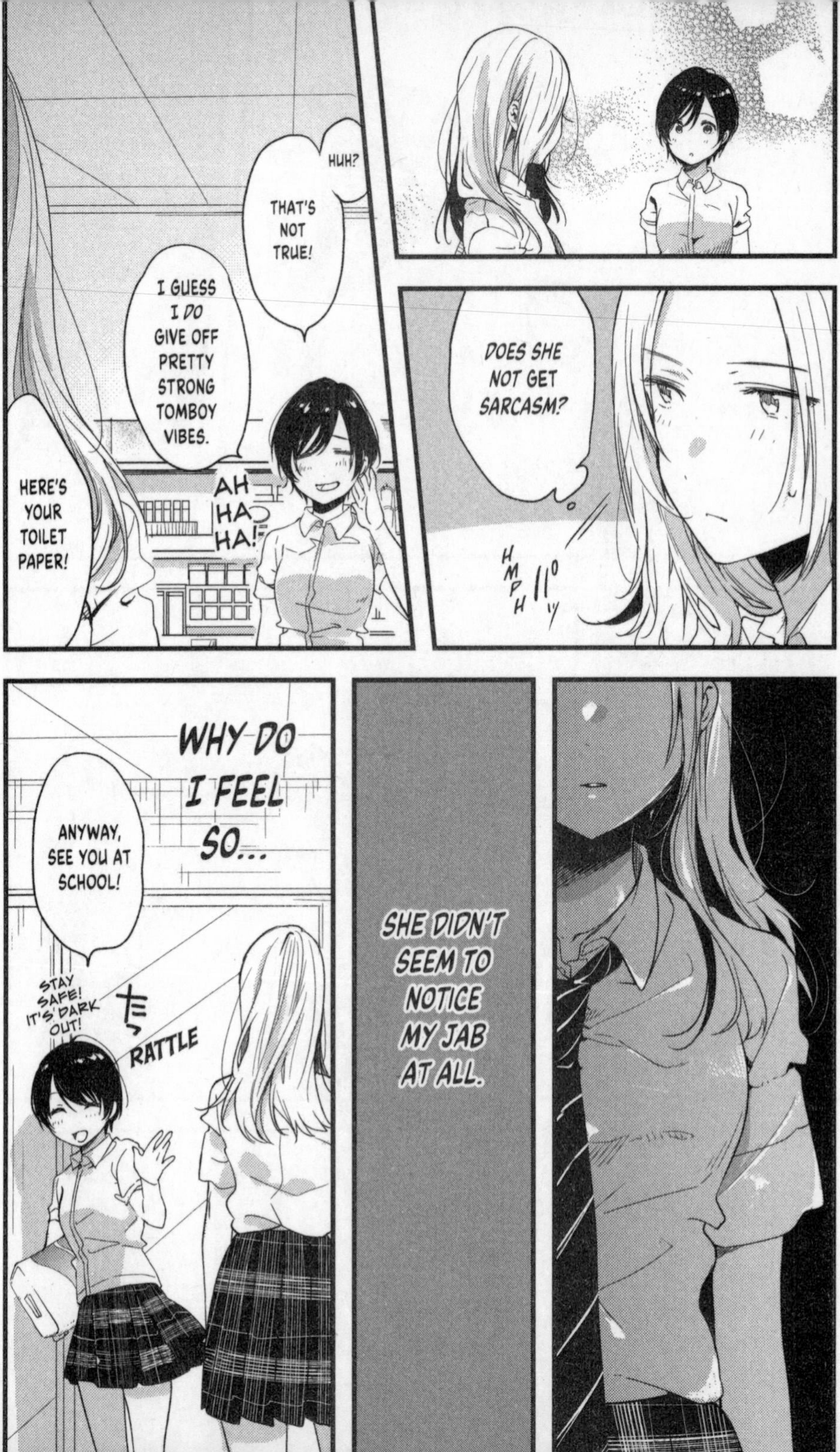
DOES SHE NOT GET SARCASM?
HMPH
HUH? THAT'S NOT TRUE!
I GUESS I DO GIVE OFF PRETTY STRONG TOMBOY VIBES.
AH HA HA!
HERE'S YOUR TOILET PAPER!
SHE DIDN'T SEEM TO NOTICE MY JAB AT ALL.
WHY DO I FEEL SO...
ANYWAY, SEE YOU AT SCHOOL!
STAY SAFE! IT'S DARK OUT!
RATTLE

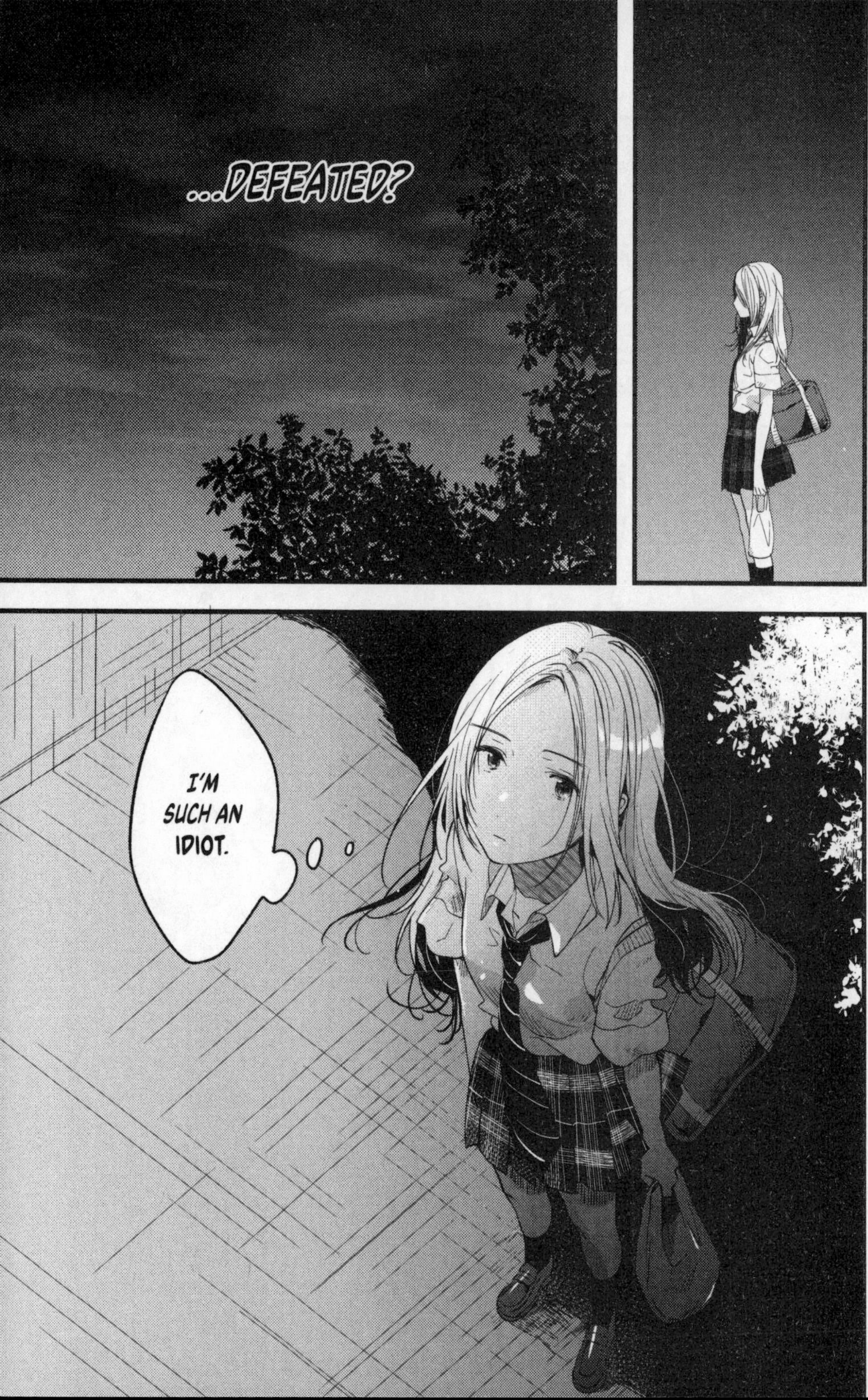
...DEFEATED?
I'M SUCH AN IDIOT.

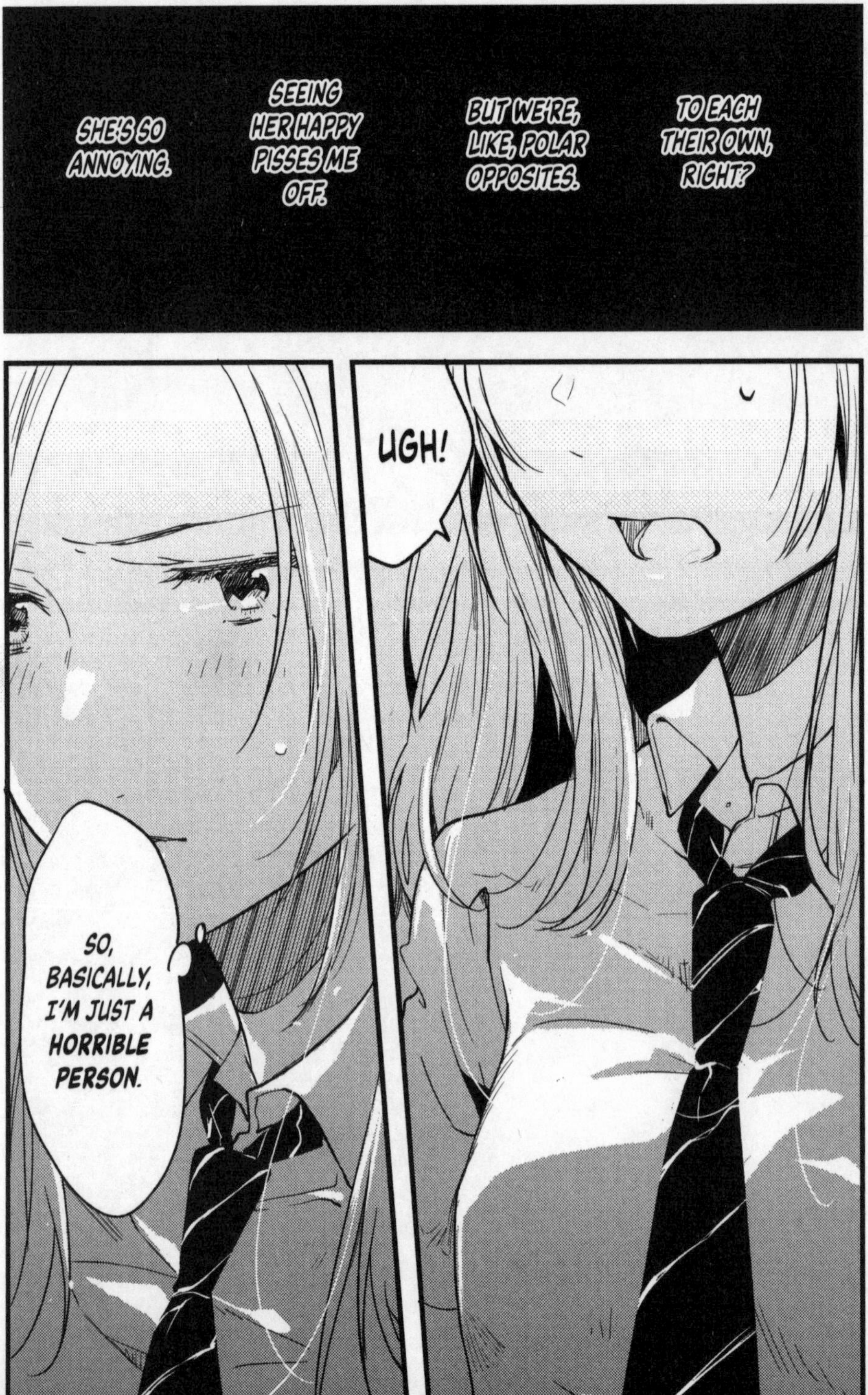
TO EACH THEIR OWN, RIGHT?
BUT WE'RE, LIKE, POLAR OPPOSITES.
SEEING HER HAPPY PISSES ME OFF.
SHE'S SO ANNOYING.
UGH!
SO, BASICALLY, I'M JUST A HORRIBLE PERSON.

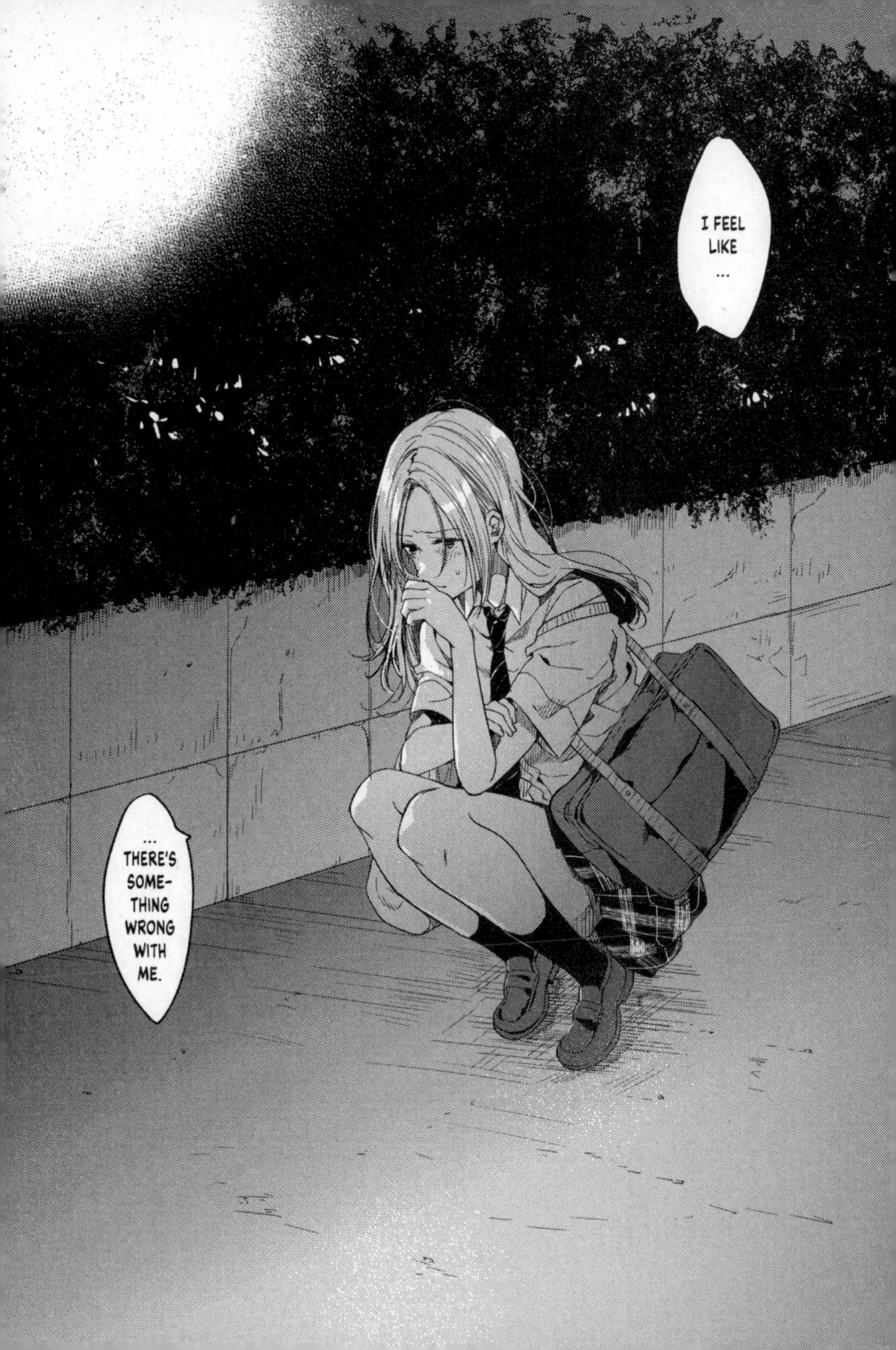
I FEEL LIKE ...
... THERE'S SOME-THING WRONG WITH ME.

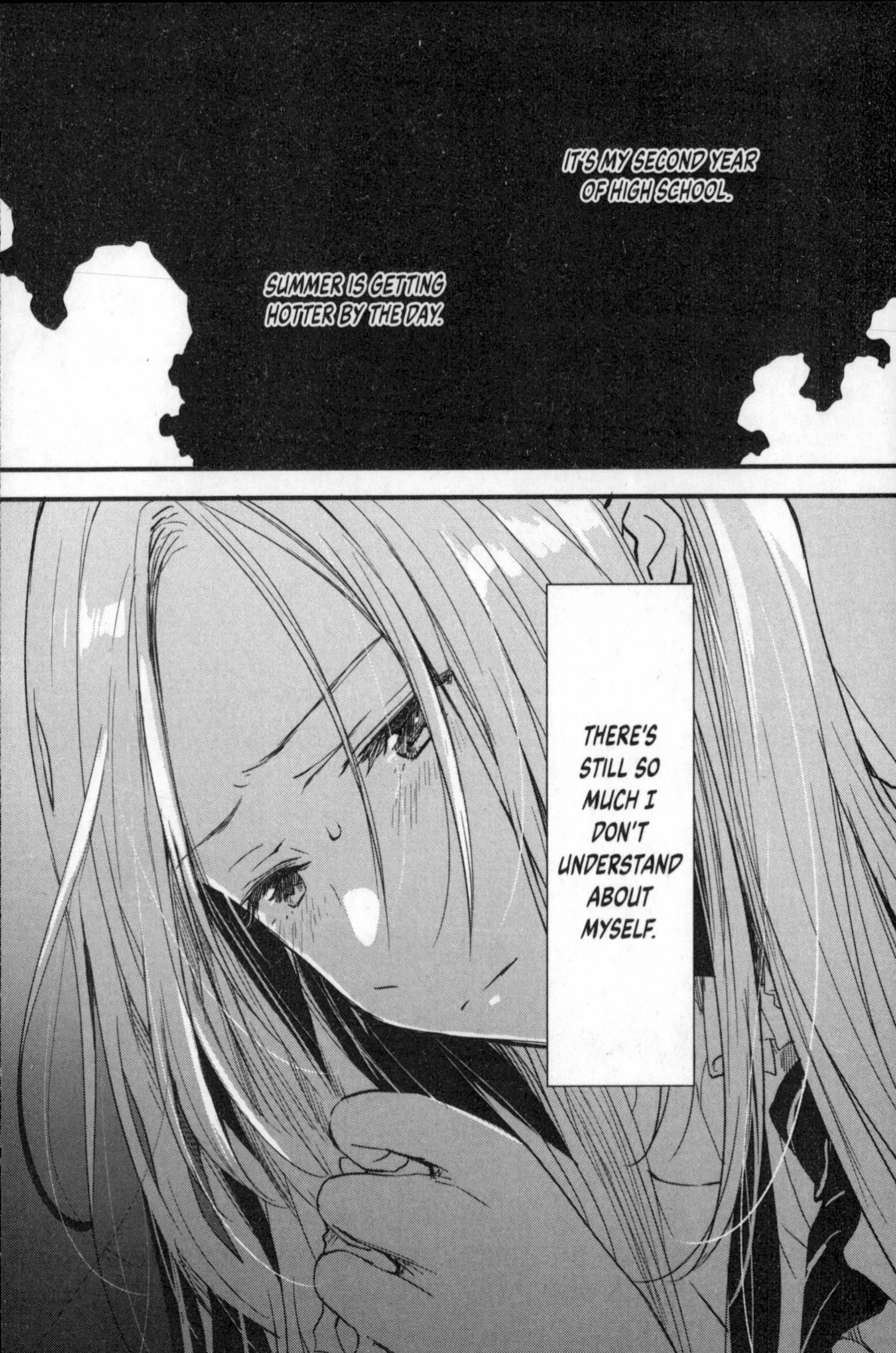
IT'S MY SECOND YEAR OF HIGH SCHOOL.
SUMMER IS GETTING HOTTER BY THE DAY.
THERE'S STILL SO MUCH I DON'T UNDERSTAND ABOUT MYSELF.

Chapter 9:
Melting Ice 3

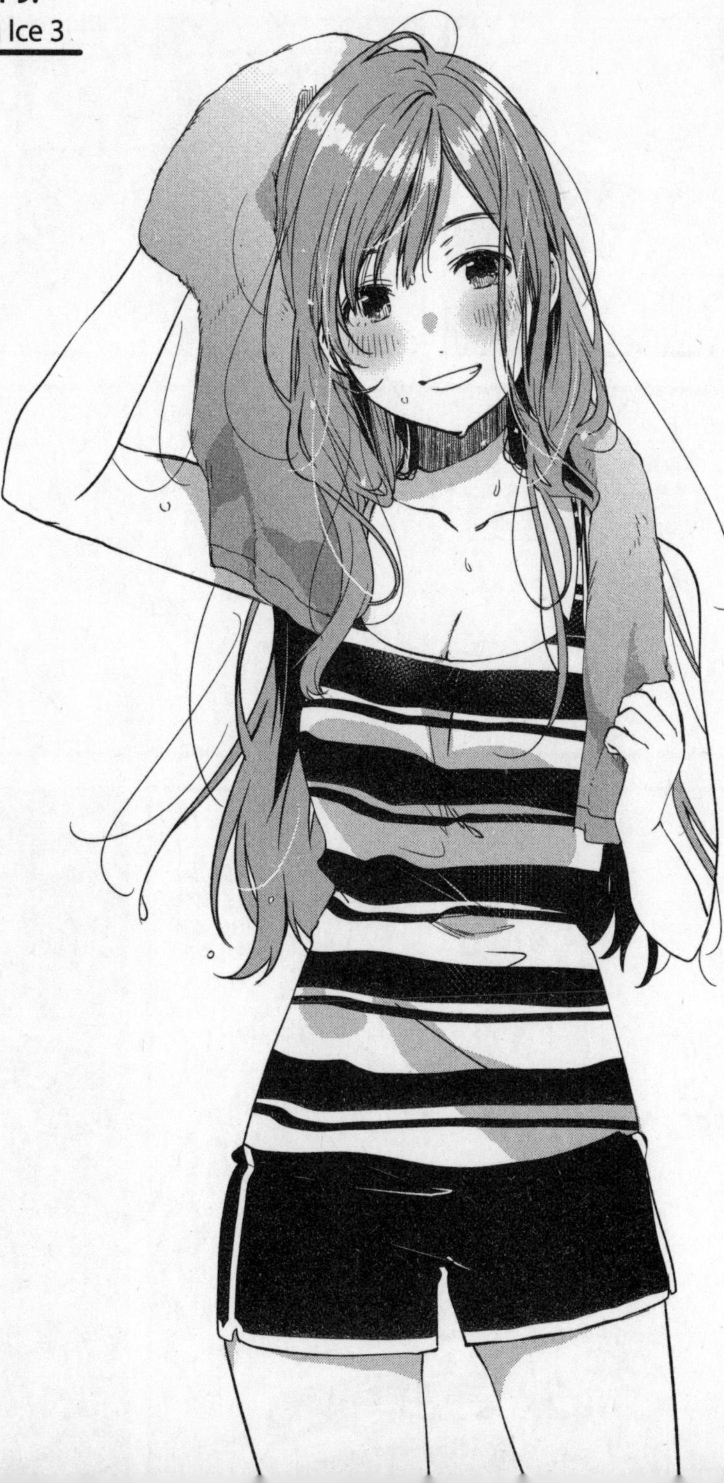

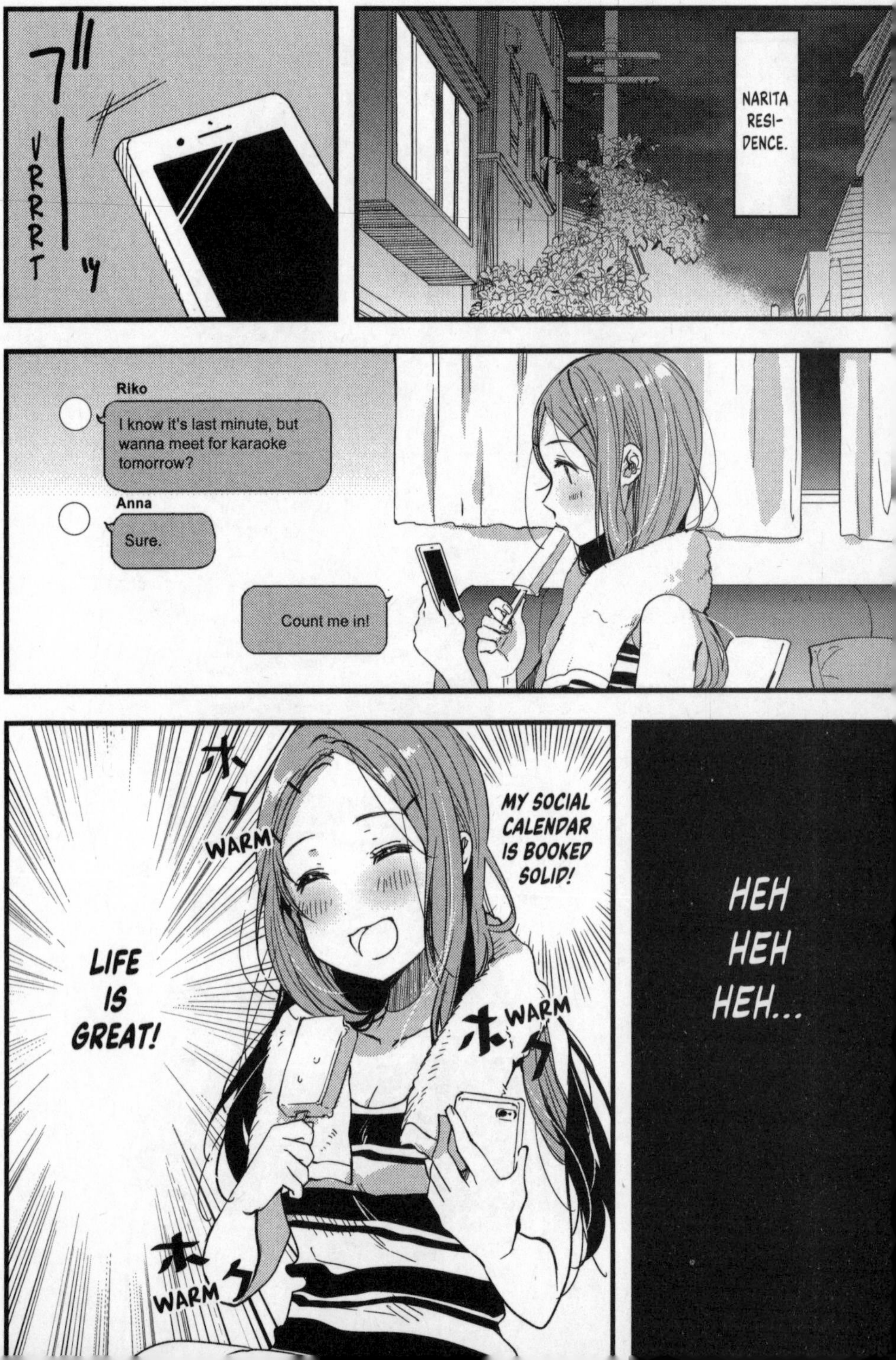
NARITA RESIDENCE.
VRRRT
Riko
I know it's last minute, but wanna meet for karaoke tomorrow?
Anna
Sure.
Count me in!
HEH HEH HEH...
MY SOCIAL CALENDAR IS BOOKED SOLID!
WARM
LIFE IS GREAT!
WARM
WARM

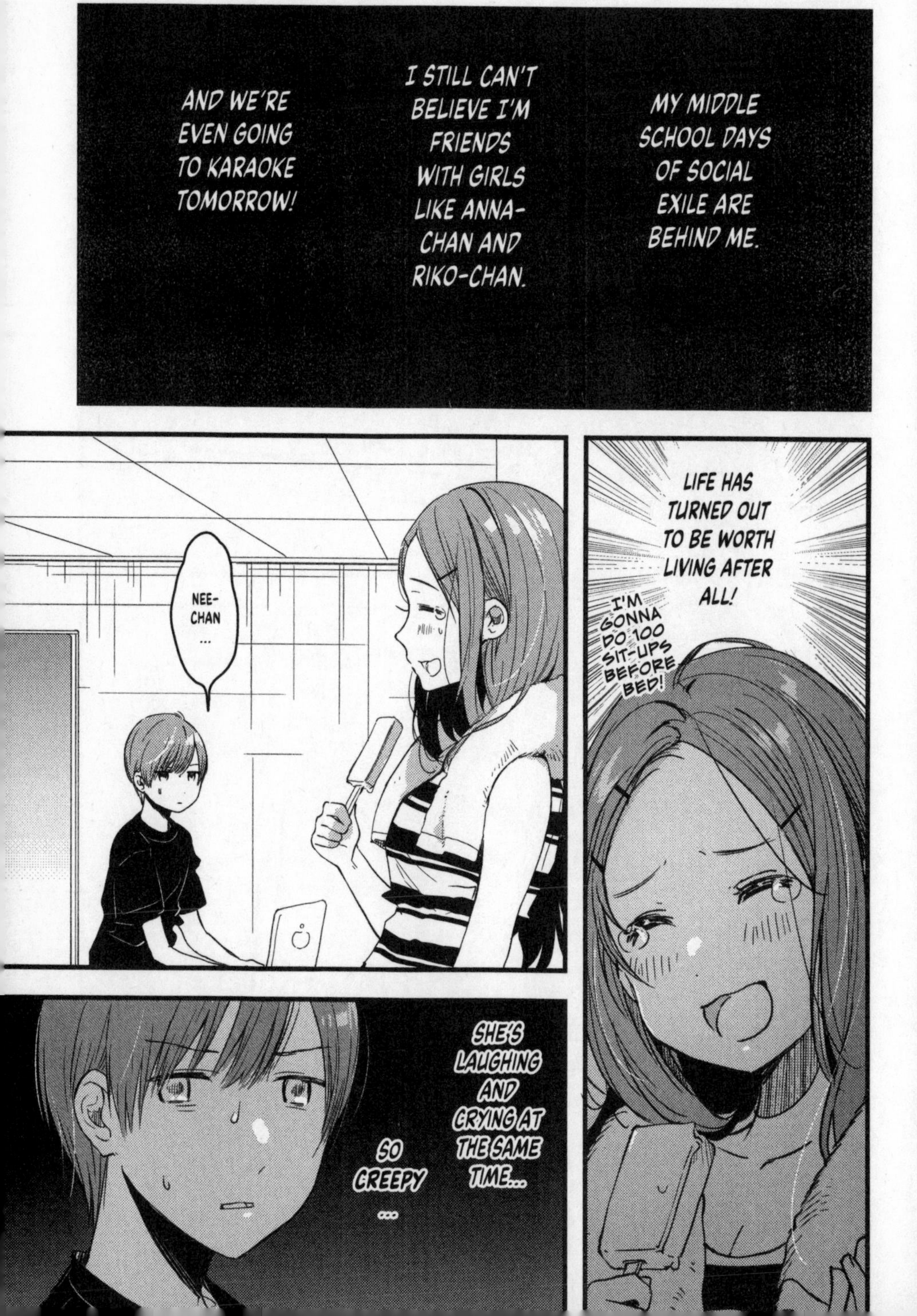
MY MIDDLE SCHOOL DAYS OF SOCIAL EXILE ARE BEHIND ME.
I STILL CAN'T BELIEVE I'M FRIENDS WITH GIRLS LIKE ANNA-CHAN AND RIKO-CHAN.
AND WE'RE EVEN GOING TO KARAOKE TOMORROW!
LIFE HAS TURNED OUT TO BE WORTH LIVING AFTER ALL!
I'M GONNA DO 100 SIT-UPS BEFORE BED!
NEE-CHAN ...
SHE'S LAUGHING AND CRYING AT THE SAME TIME...
SO CREEPY ...

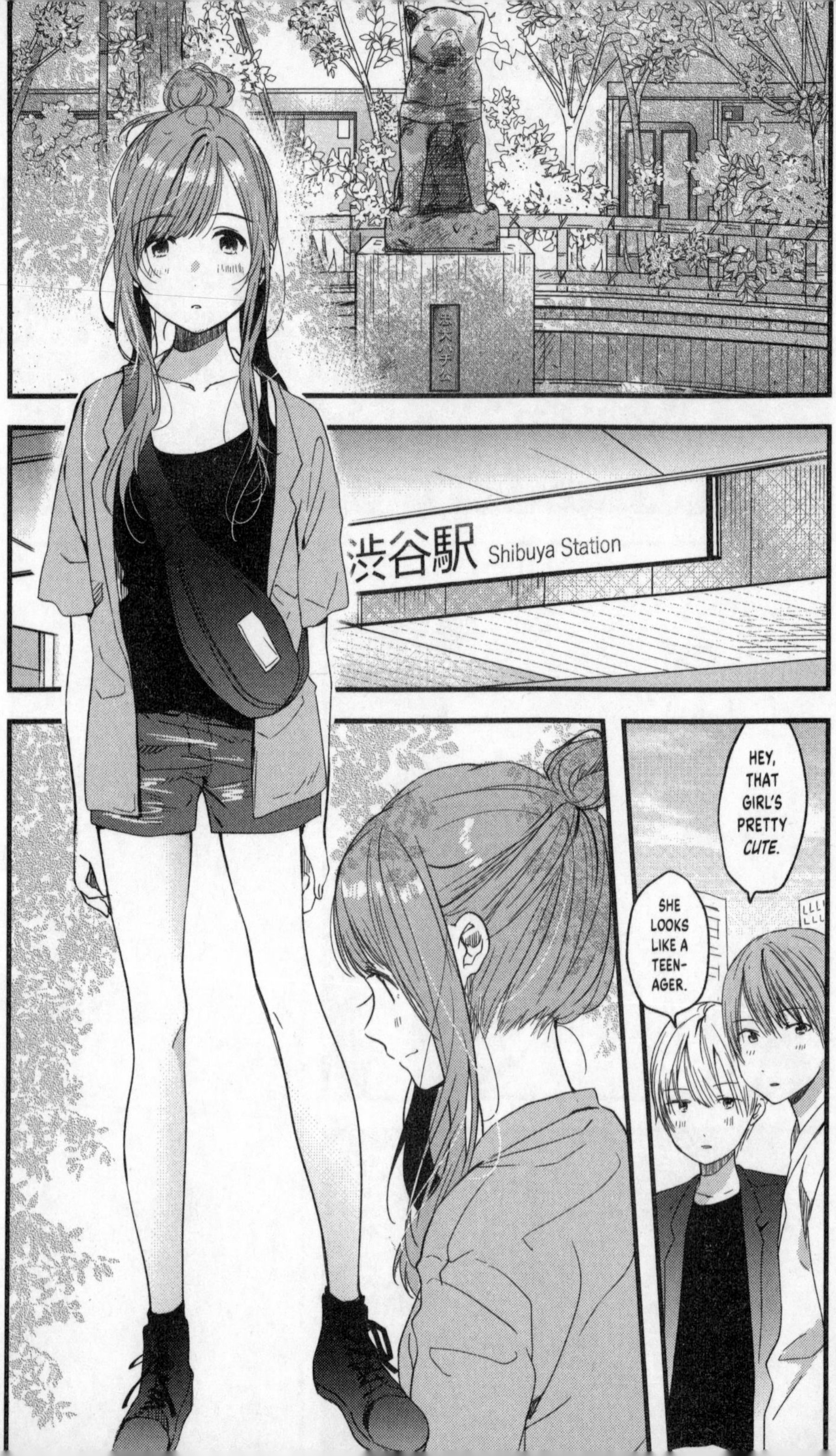
渋谷駅 Shibuya Station
HEY, THAT GIRL'S PRETTY *CUTE.*
SHE LOOKS LIKE A TEEN-AGER.

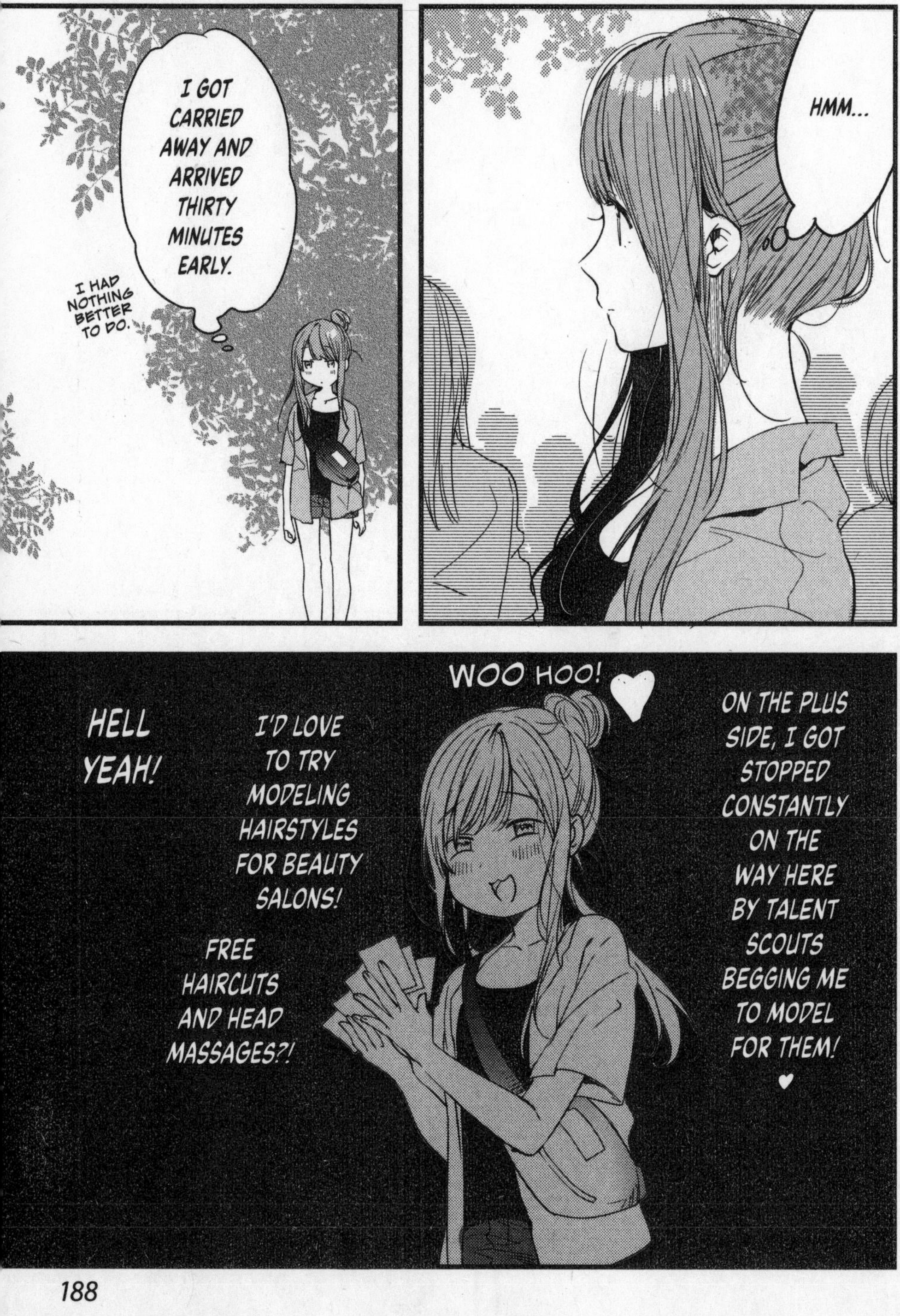
HMM...
I GOT CARRIED AWAY AND ARRIVED THIRTY MINUTES EARLY.
I HAD NOTHING BETTER TO DO.
ON THE PLUS SIDE, I GOT STOPPED CONSTANTLY ON THE WAY HERE BY TALENT SCOUTS BEGGING ME TO MODEL FOR THEM! ♥
WOO HOO! ♥
I'D LOVE TO TRY MODELING HAIRSTYLES FOR BEAUTY SALONS!
FREE HAIRCUTS AND HEAD MASSAGES?!
HELL YEAH!

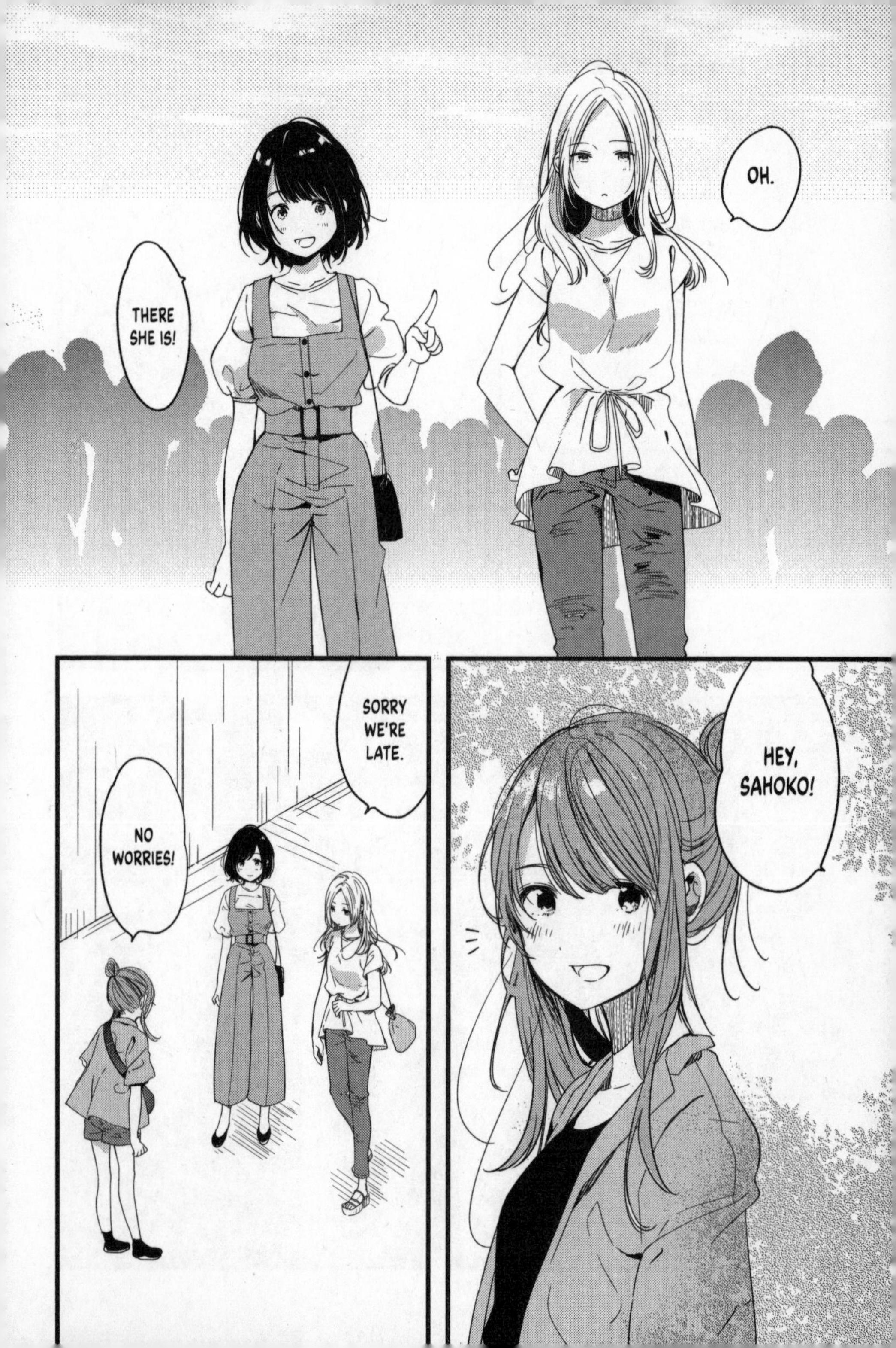
OH.
THERE SHE IS!
HEY, SAHOKO!
SORRY WE'RE LATE.
NO WORRIES!

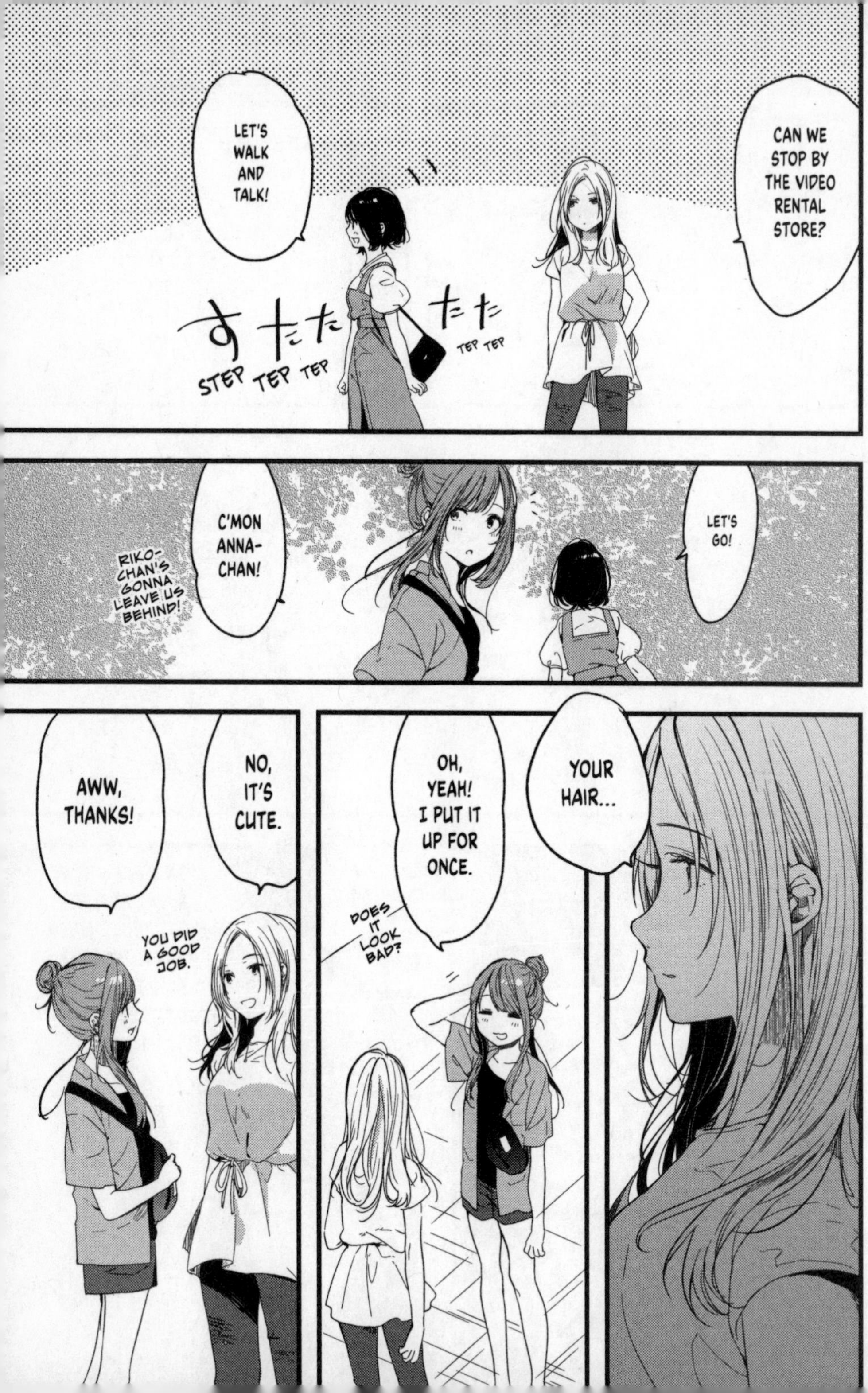
CAN WE STOP BY THE VIDEO RENTAL STORE?
LET'S WALK AND TALK!
すたた たた
STEP TEP TEP
TEP TEP
LET'S GO!
C'MON ANNA-CHAN!
RIKO-CHAN'S GONNA LEAVE US BEHIND!
YOUR HAIR...
OH, YEAH! I PUT IT UP FOR ONCE.
DOES IT LOOK BAD?
NO, IT'S CUTE.
AWW, THANKS!
YOU DID A GOOD JOB.

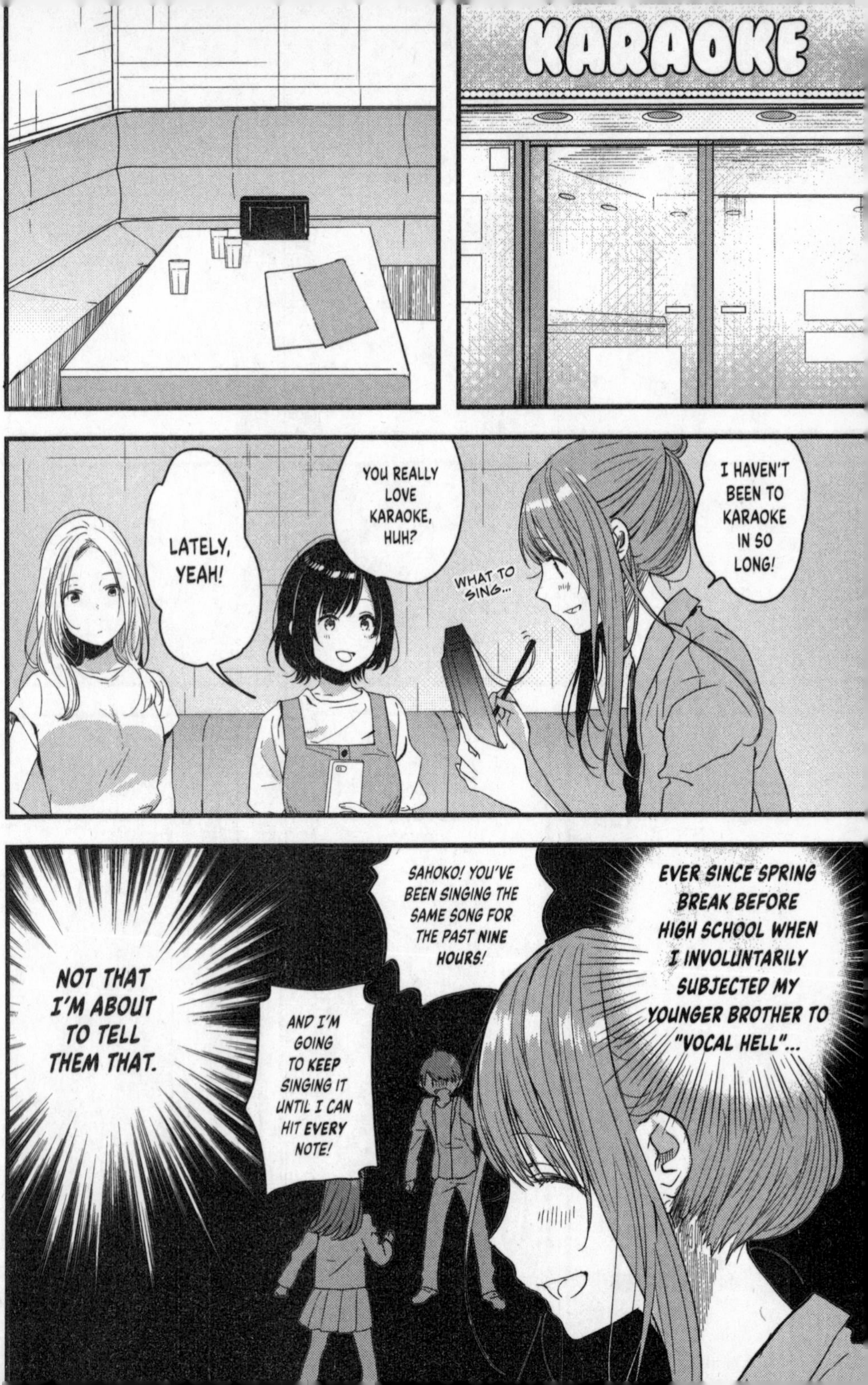
KARAOKE
I HAVEN'T BEEN TO KARAOKE IN SO LONG!
WHAT TO SING...
YOU REALLY LOVE KARAOKE, HUH?
LATELY, YEAH!
EVER SINCE SPRING BREAK BEFORE HIGH SCHOOL WHEN I INVOLUNTARILY SUBJECTED MY YOUNGER BROTHER TO "VOCAL HELL"...
SAHOKO! YOU'VE BEEN SINGING THE SAME SONG FOR THE PAST NINE HOURS!
AND I'M GOING TO KEEP SINGING IT UNTIL I CAN HIT EVERY NOTE!
NOT THAT I'M ABOUT TO TELL THEM THAT.

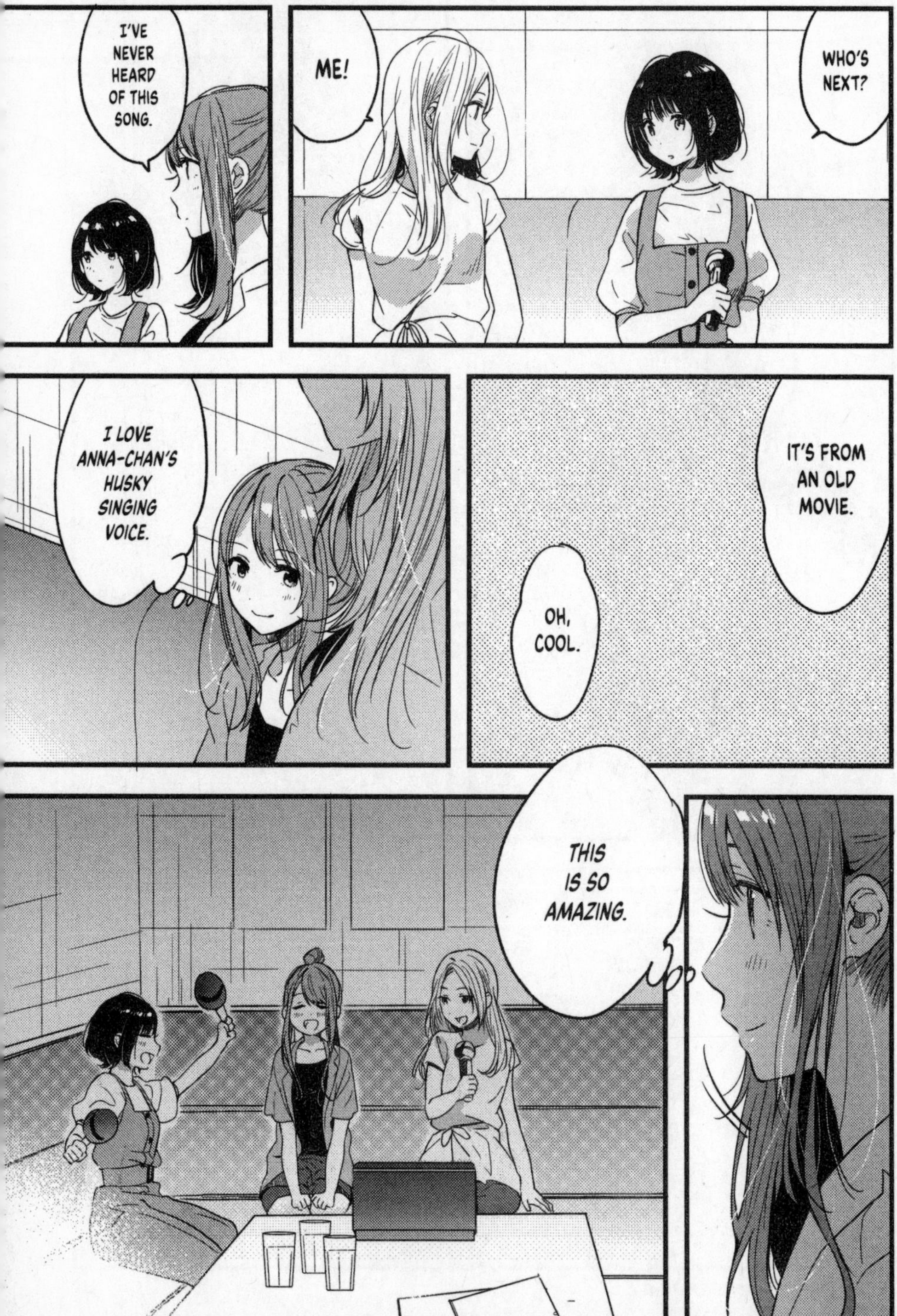
WHO'S NEXT?
ME!
I'VE NEVER HEARD OF THIS SONG.
IT'S FROM AN OLD MOVIE.
OH, COOL.
I LOVE ANNA-CHAN'S HUSKY SINGING VOICE.
THIS IS SO AMAZING.

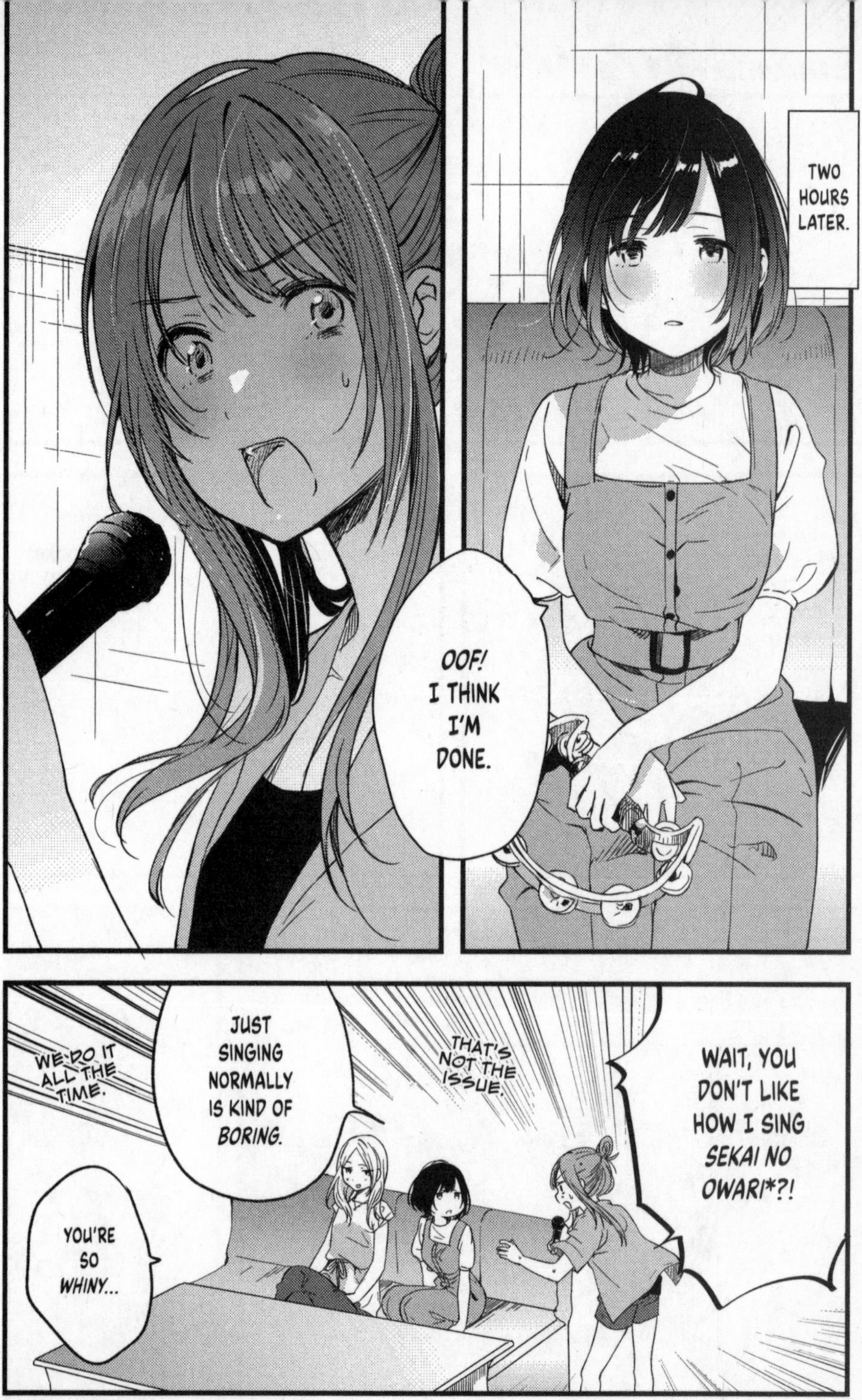
TWO HOURS LATER.
OOF! I THINK I'M DONE.
WAIT, YOU DON'T LIKE HOW I SING SEKAI NO OWARI*?!
THAT'S NOT THE ISSUE.
JUST SINGING NORMALLY IS KIND OF BORING.
WE DO IT ALL THE TIME.
YOU'RE SO WHINY...

*SEKAI NO OWARI IS A JAPANESE POP GROUP.

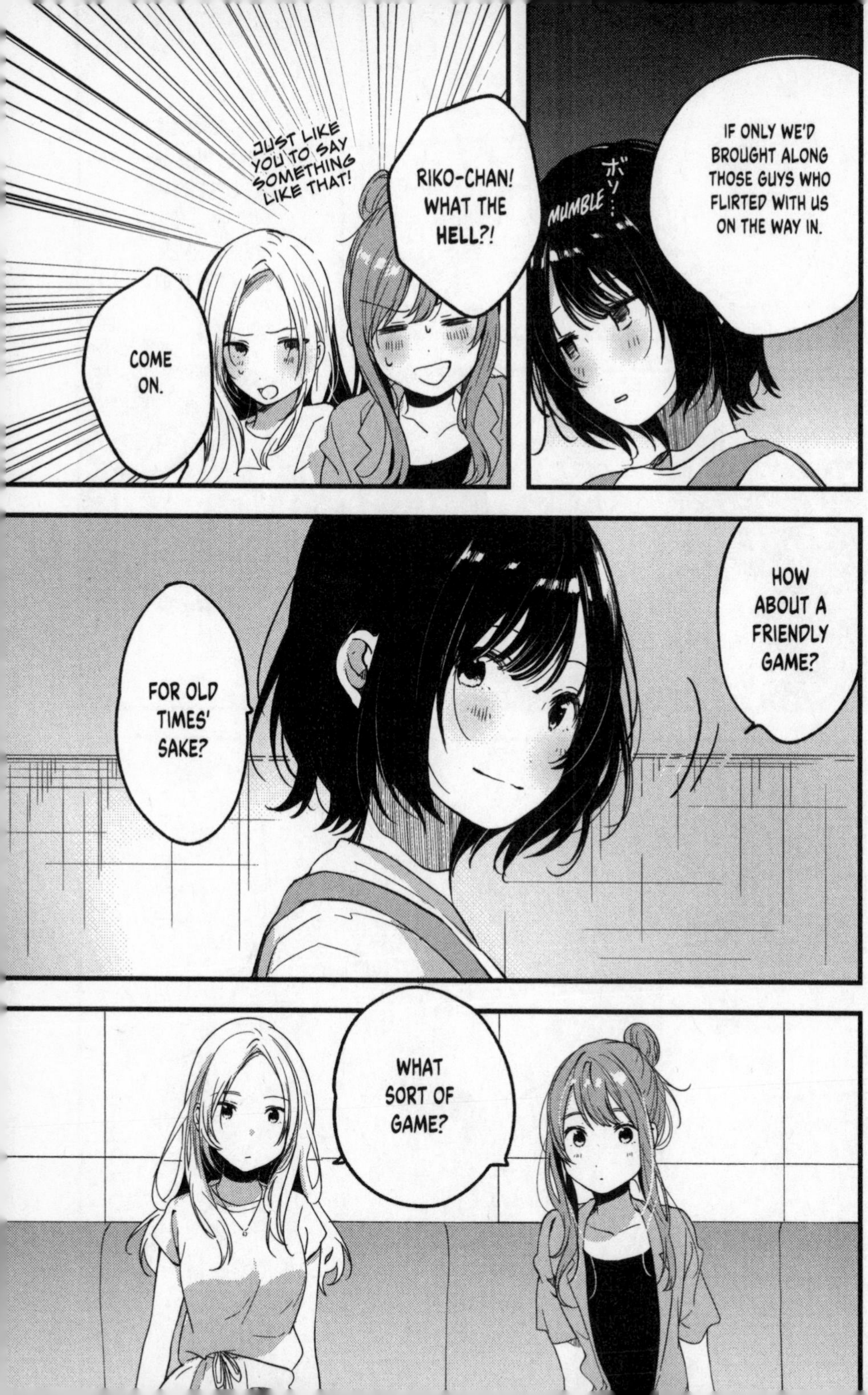
ボソッ…
MUMBLE
IF ONLY WE'D BROUGHT ALONG THOSE GUYS WHO FLIRTED WITH US ON THE WAY IN.
RIKO-CHAN! WHAT THE HELL?!
JUST LIKE YOU TO SAY SOMETHING LIKE THAT!
COME ON.
HOW ABOUT A FRIENDLY GAME?
FOR OLD TIMES' SAKE?
WHAT SORT OF GAME?

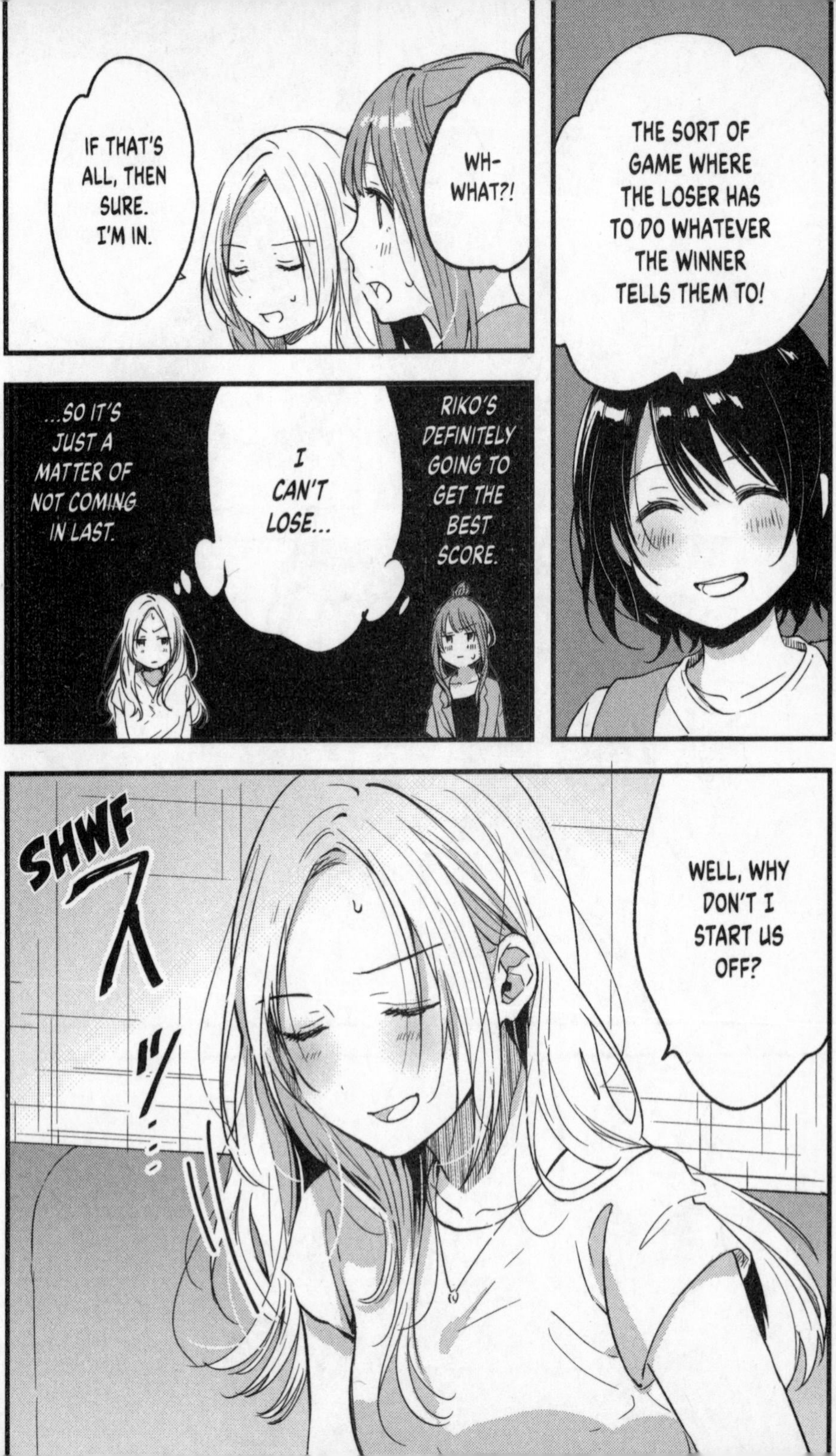
THE SORT OF GAME WHERE THE LOSER HAS TO DO WHATEVER THE WINNER TELLS THEM TO!
WH- WHAT?!
IF THAT'S ALL, THEN SURE. I'M IN.
RIKO'S DEFINITELY GOING TO GET THE BEST SCORE.
I CAN'T LOSE...
...SO IT'S JUST A MATTER OF NOT COMING IN LAST.
WELL, WHY DON'T I START US OFF?
SHWF

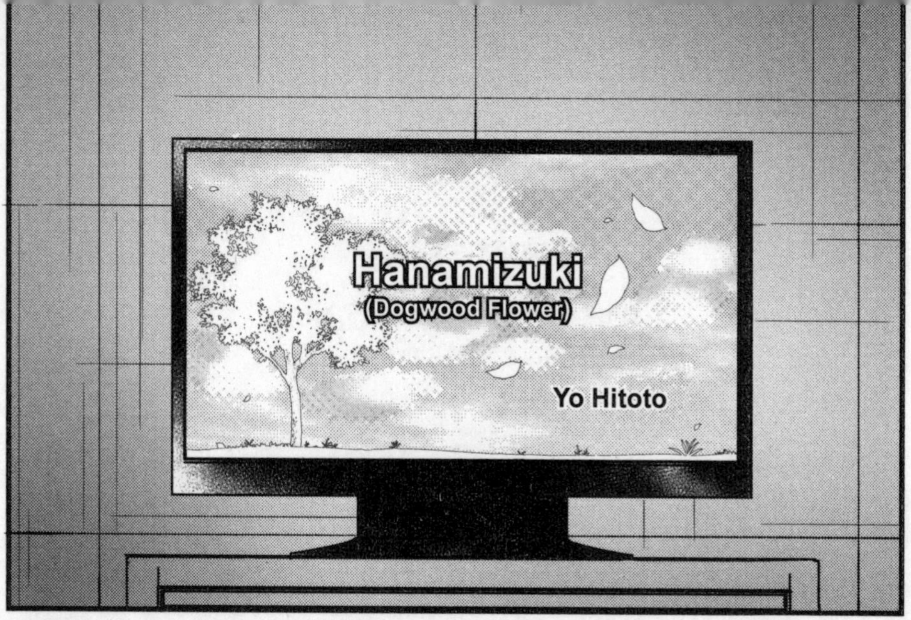
Hanamizuki
(Dogwood Flower)
Yo Hitoto

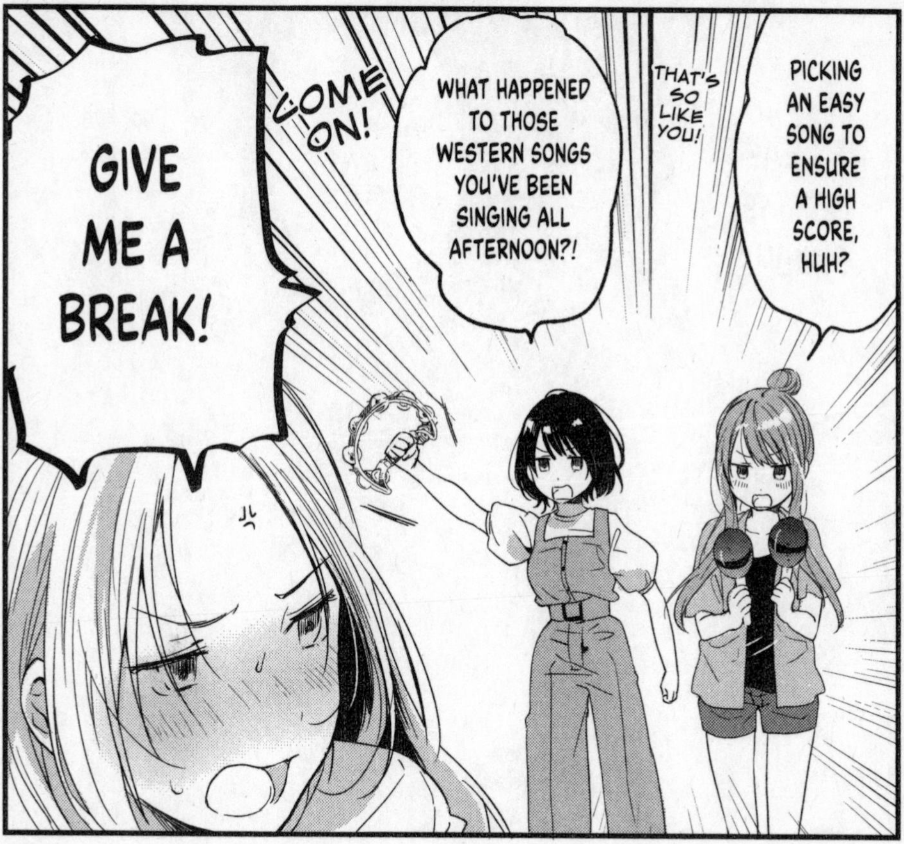
PICKING AN EASY SONG TO ENSURE A HIGH SCORE, HUH?
THAT'S SO LIKE YOU!
WHAT HAPPENED TO THOSE WESTERN SONGS YOU'VE BEEN SINGING ALL AFTERNOON?!
COME ON!
GIVE ME A BREAK!

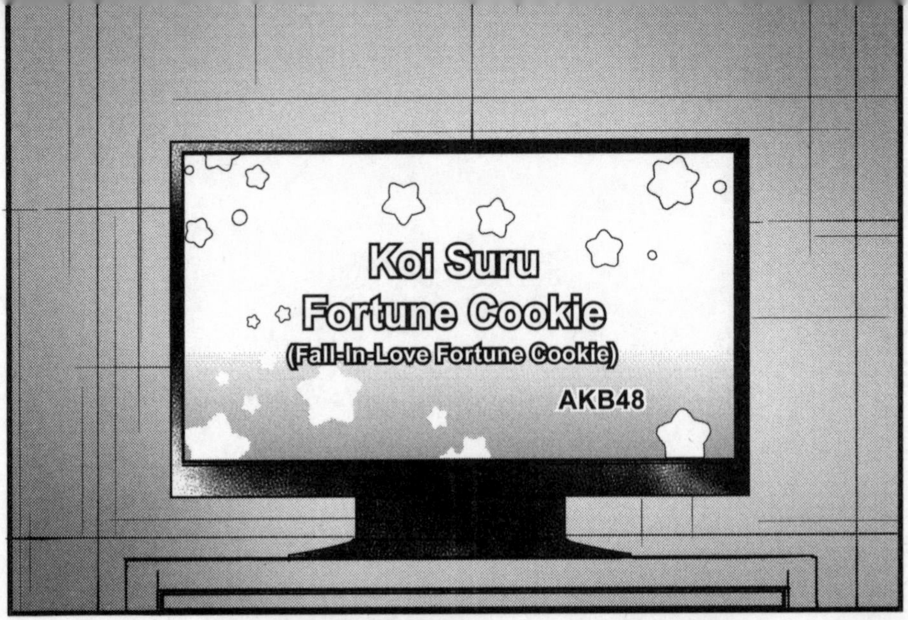
Koi Suru
Fortune Cookie
(Fall-In-Love Fortune Cookie)
AKB48

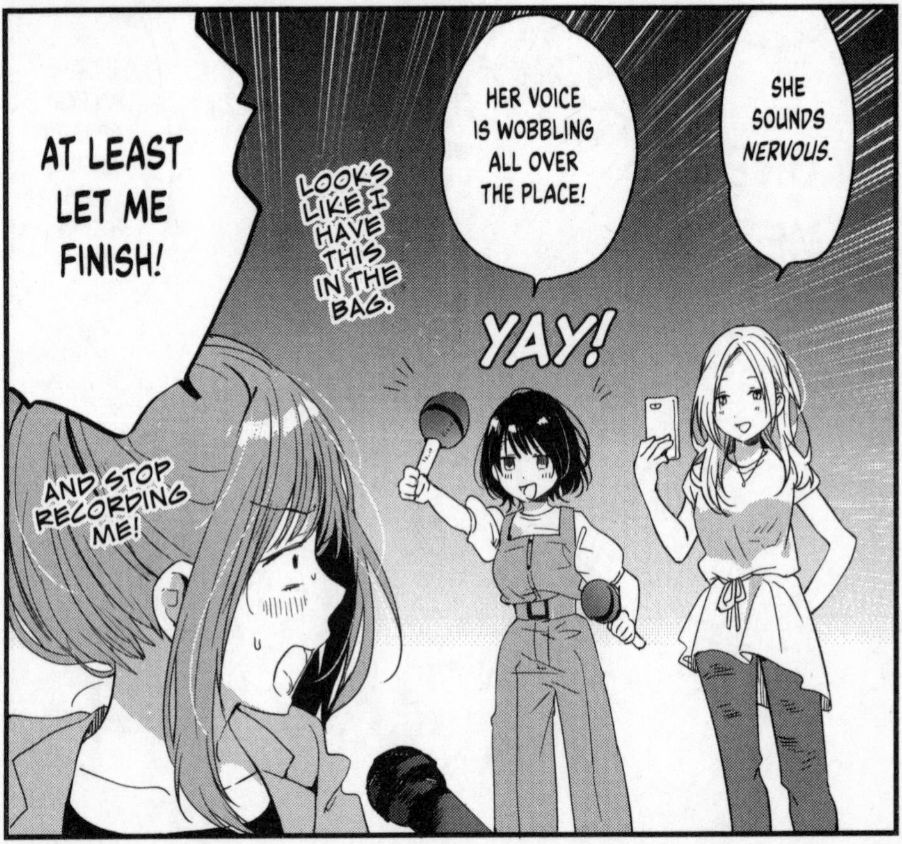
SHE SOUNDS NERVOUS.
HER VOICE IS WOBBLING ALL OVER THE PLACE!
YAY!
LOOKS LIKE I HAVE THIS IN THE BAG.
AT LEAST LET ME FINISH!
AND STOP RECORDING ME!

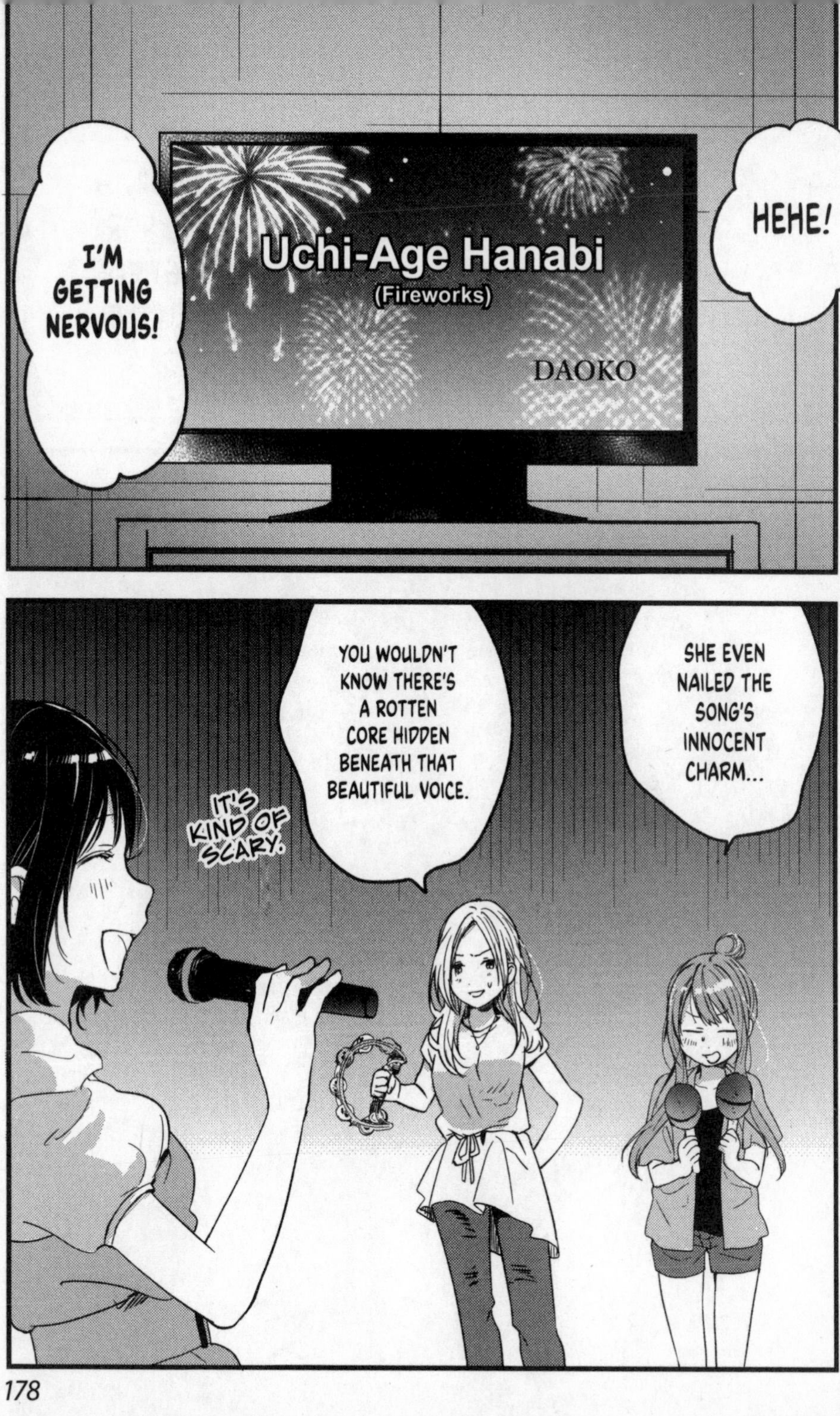
HEHE!
Uchi-Age Hanabi
(Fireworks)
DAOKO
I'M GETTING NERVOUS!
SHE EVEN NAILED THE SONG'S INNOCENT CHARM...
YOU WOULDN'T KNOW THERE'S A ROTTEN CORE HIDDEN BENEATH THAT BEAUTIFUL VOICE.
IT'S KIND OF SCARY.

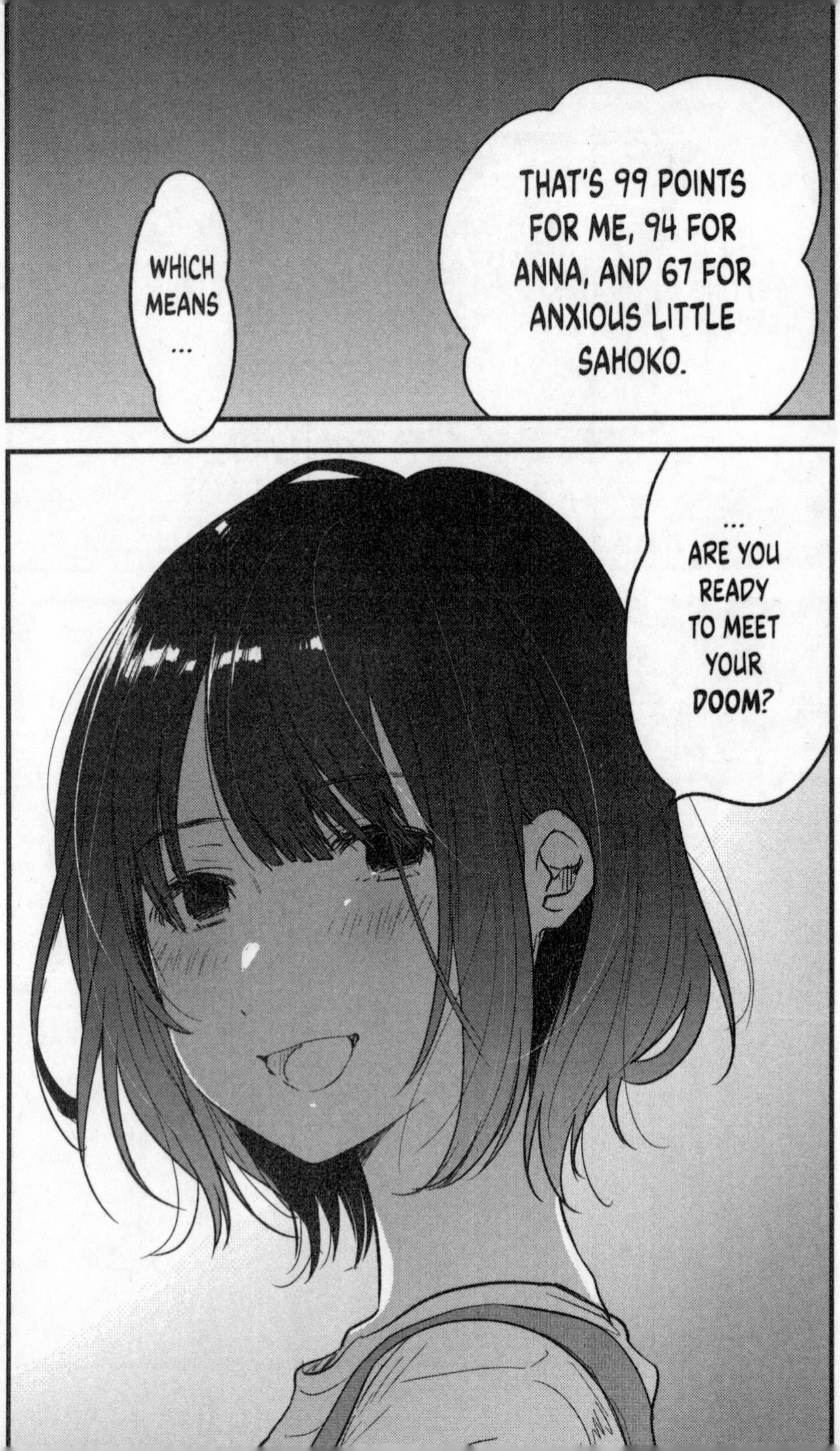
THAT'S 99 POINTS FOR ME, 94 FOR ANNA, AND 67 FOR ANXIOUS LITTLE SAHOKO.
WHICH MEANS ...
... ARE YOU READY TO MEET YOUR DOOM?

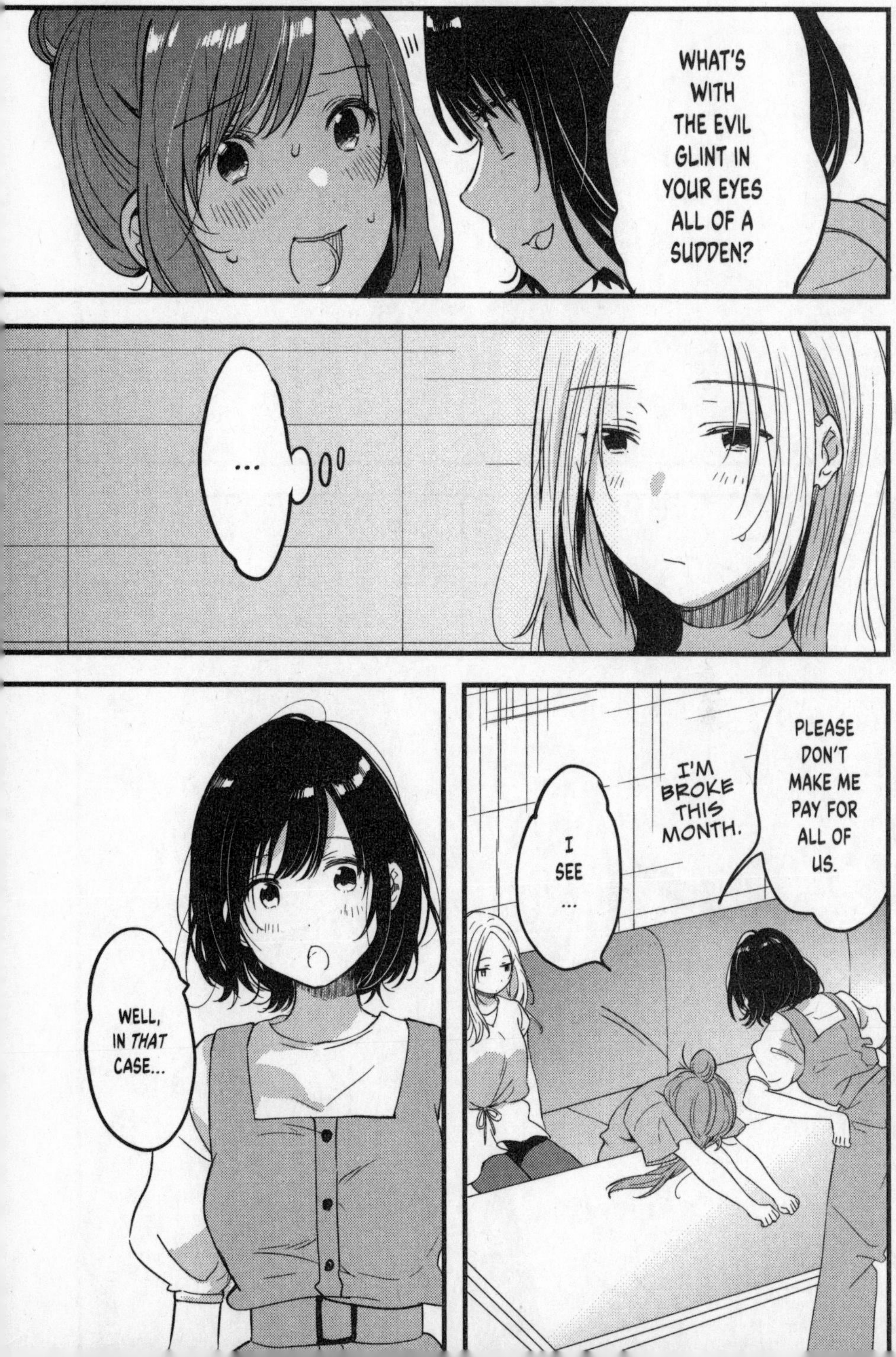
WHAT'S WITH THE EVIL GLINT IN YOUR EYES ALL OF A SUDDEN?
...
PLEASE DON'T MAKE ME PAY FOR ALL OF US.
I'M BROKE THIS MONTH.
I SEE ...
WELL, IN *THAT* CASE...

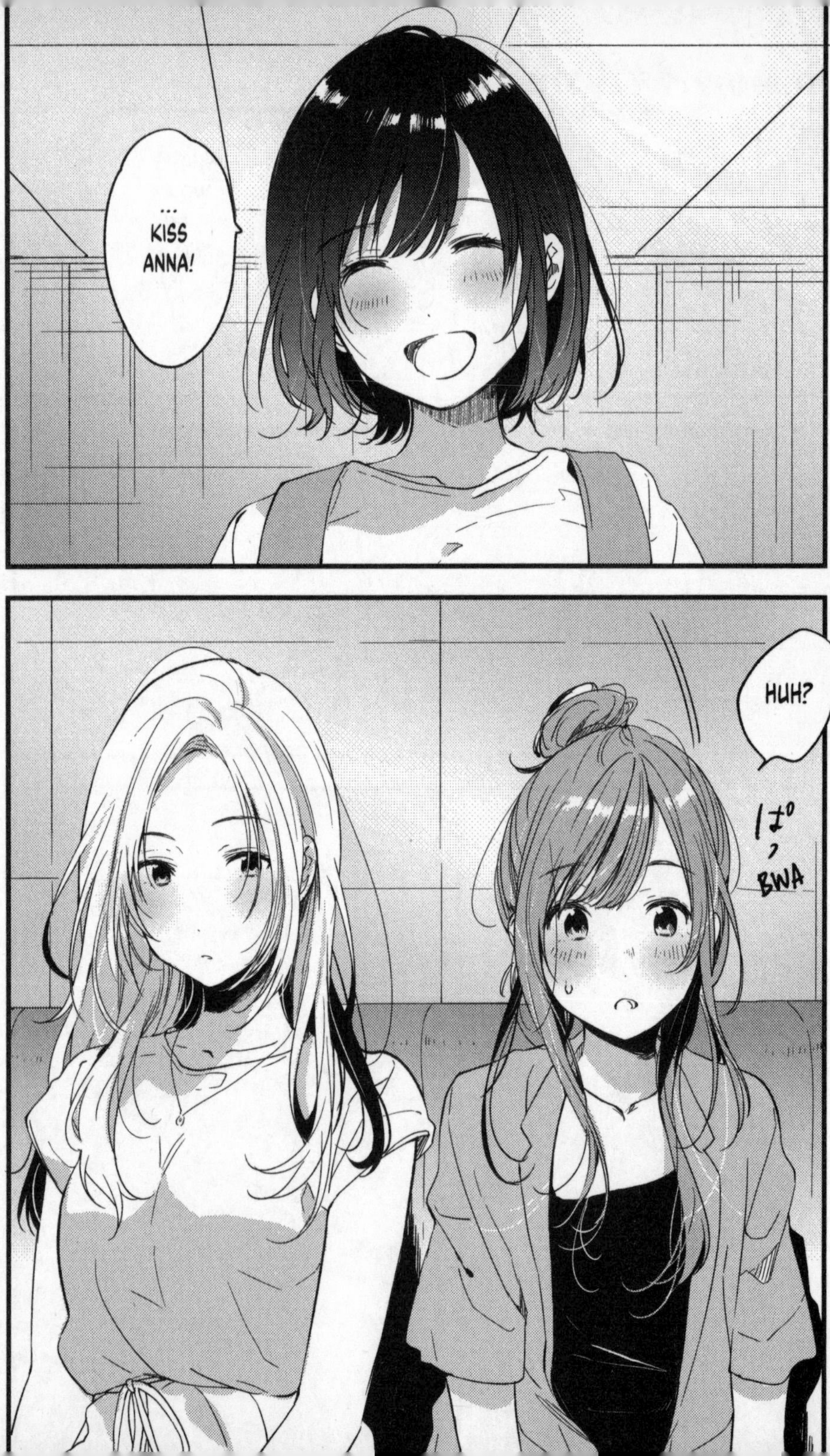

... KISS ANNA!
HUH?
ぱっ
BWA

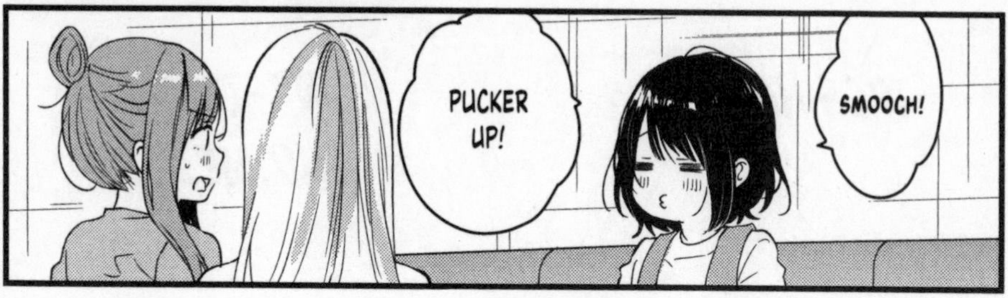
SMOOCH!
PUCKER UP!

IS THIS WHAT NORMAL FRIENDS REALLY DO TOGETHER?

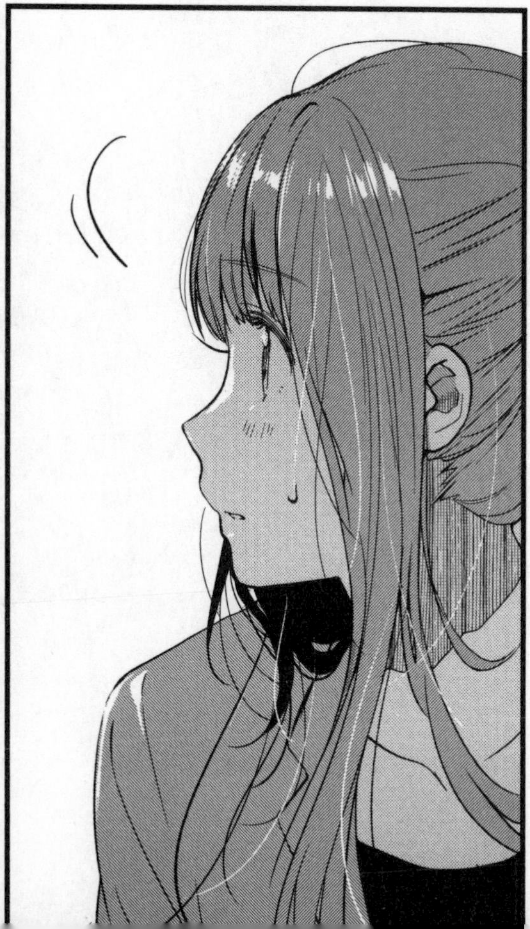

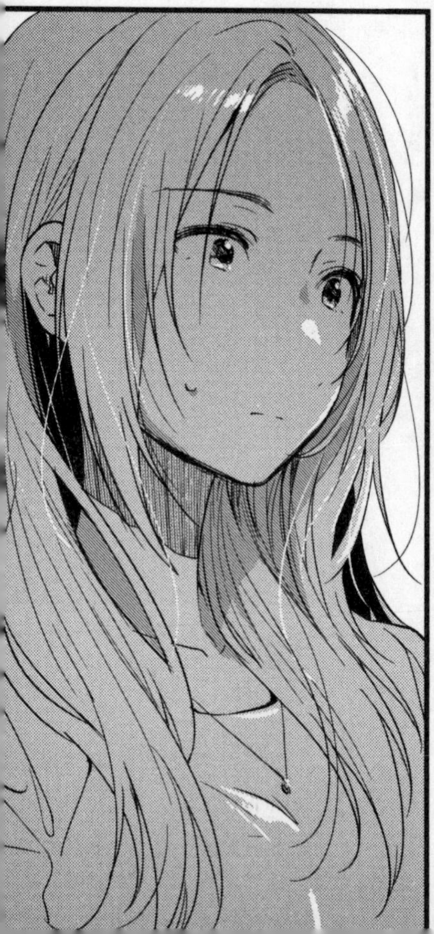

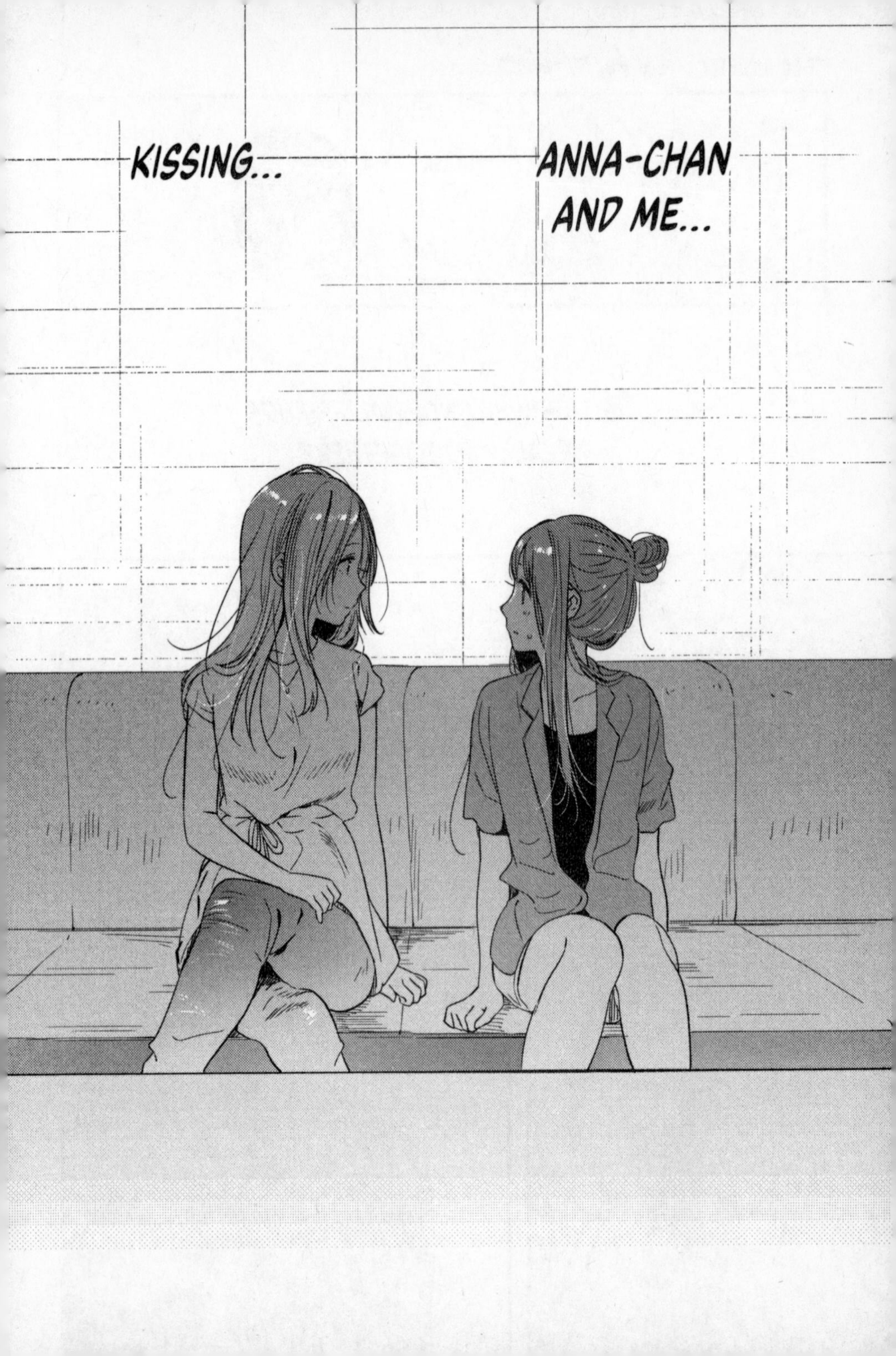
ANNA-CHAN AND ME...
KISSING...

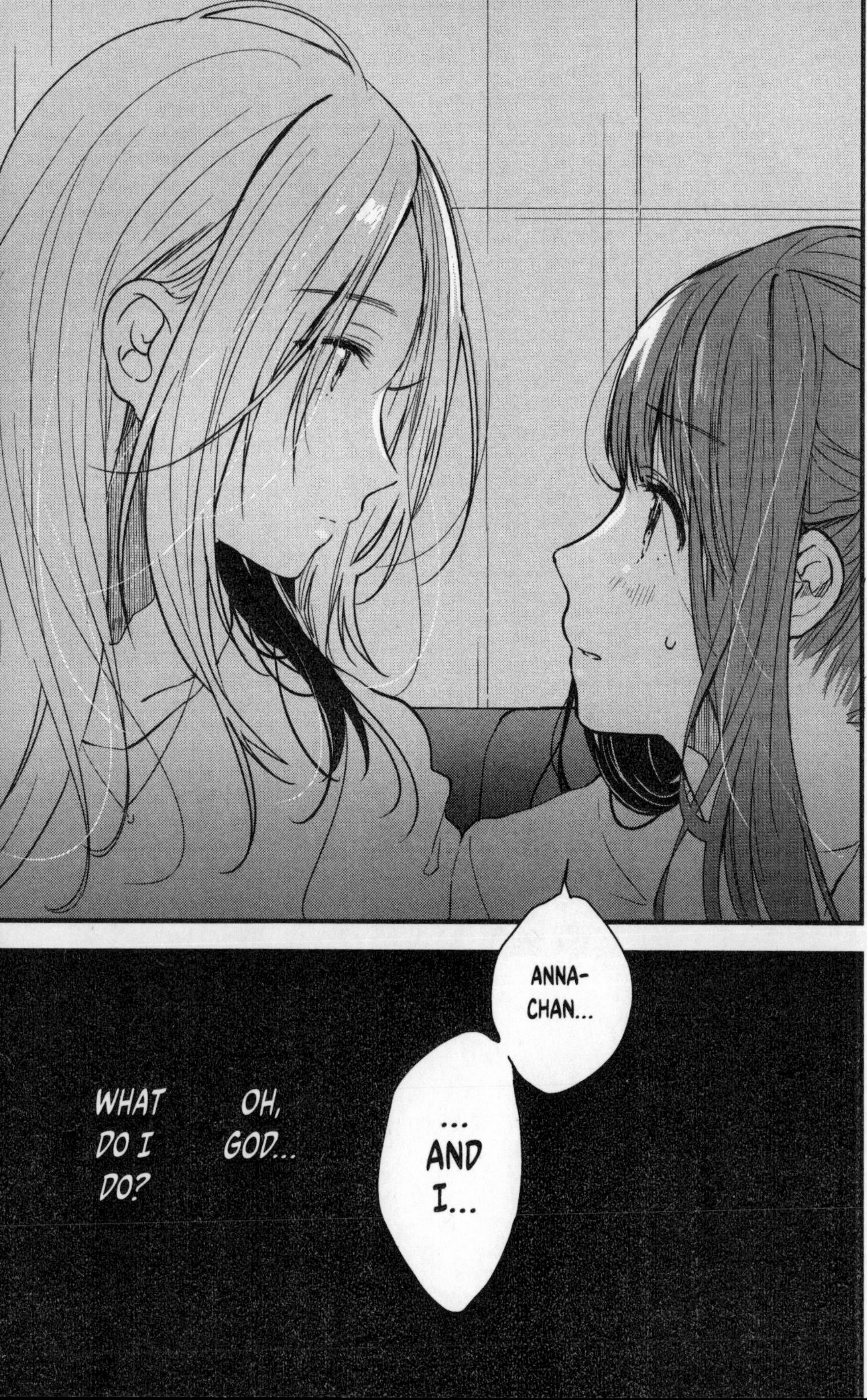
ANNA-CHAN...
... AND I...
OH, GOD...
WHAT DO I DO?

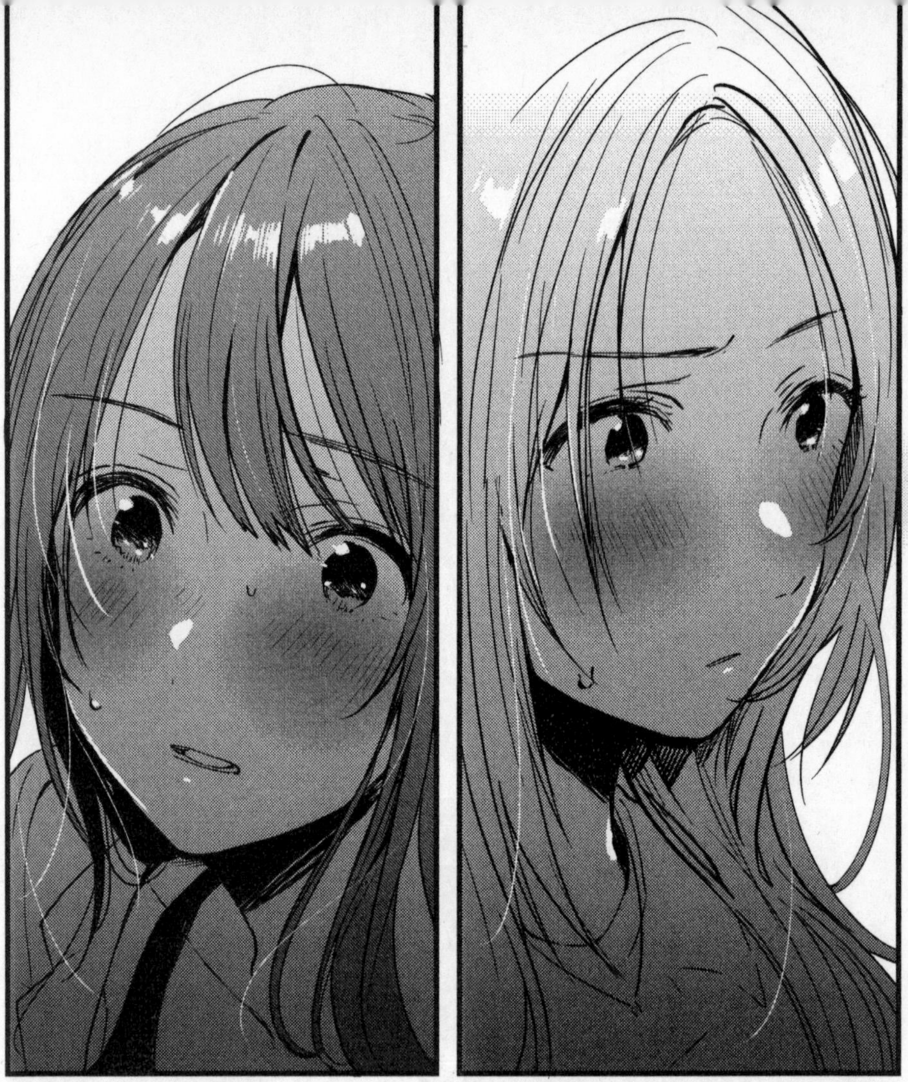
I NEVER IMAGINED I'D FIND MYSELF...
...IN A SITUATION QUITE LIKE THIS ONE.

Chapter 10:
Melting Ice 4

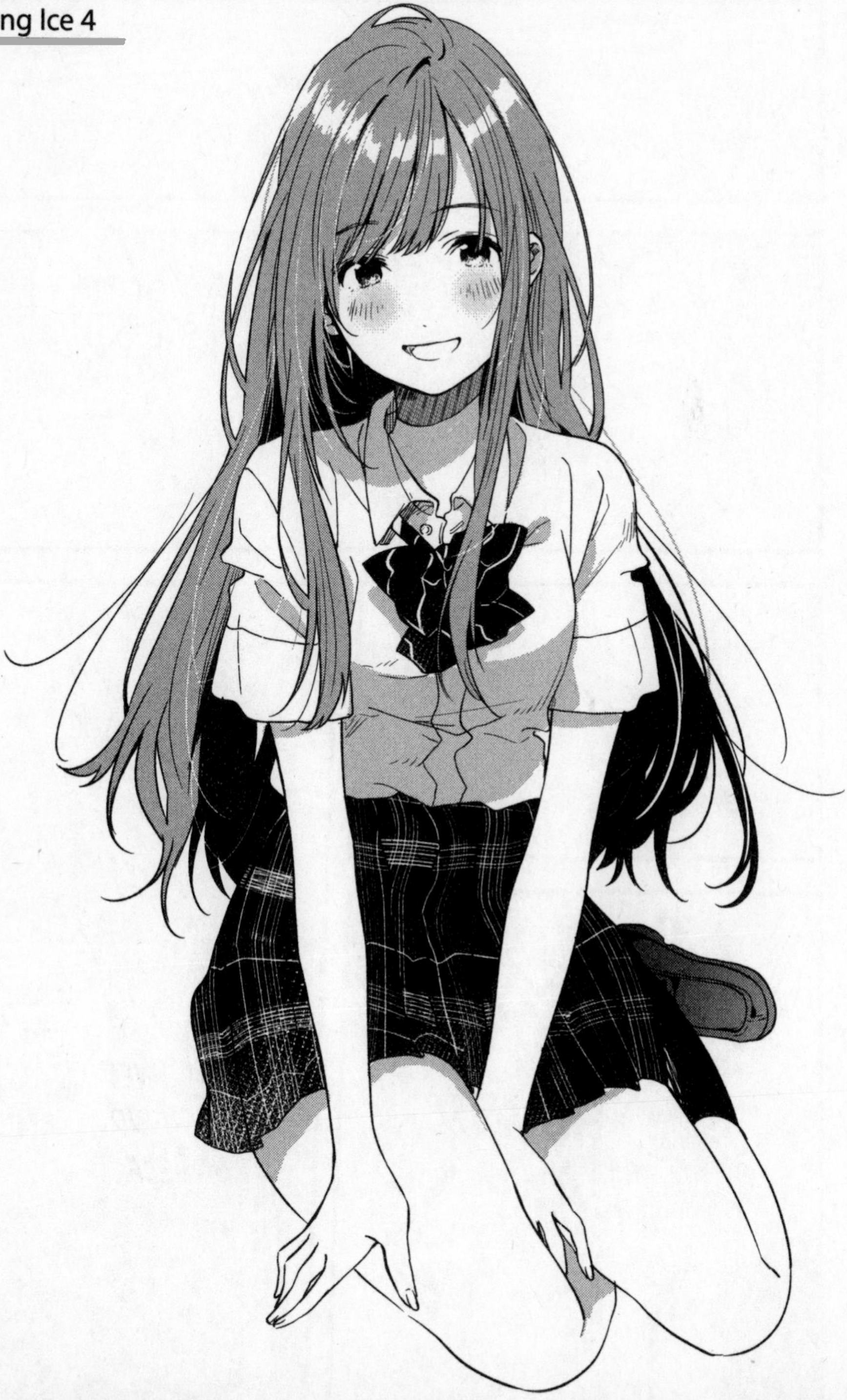

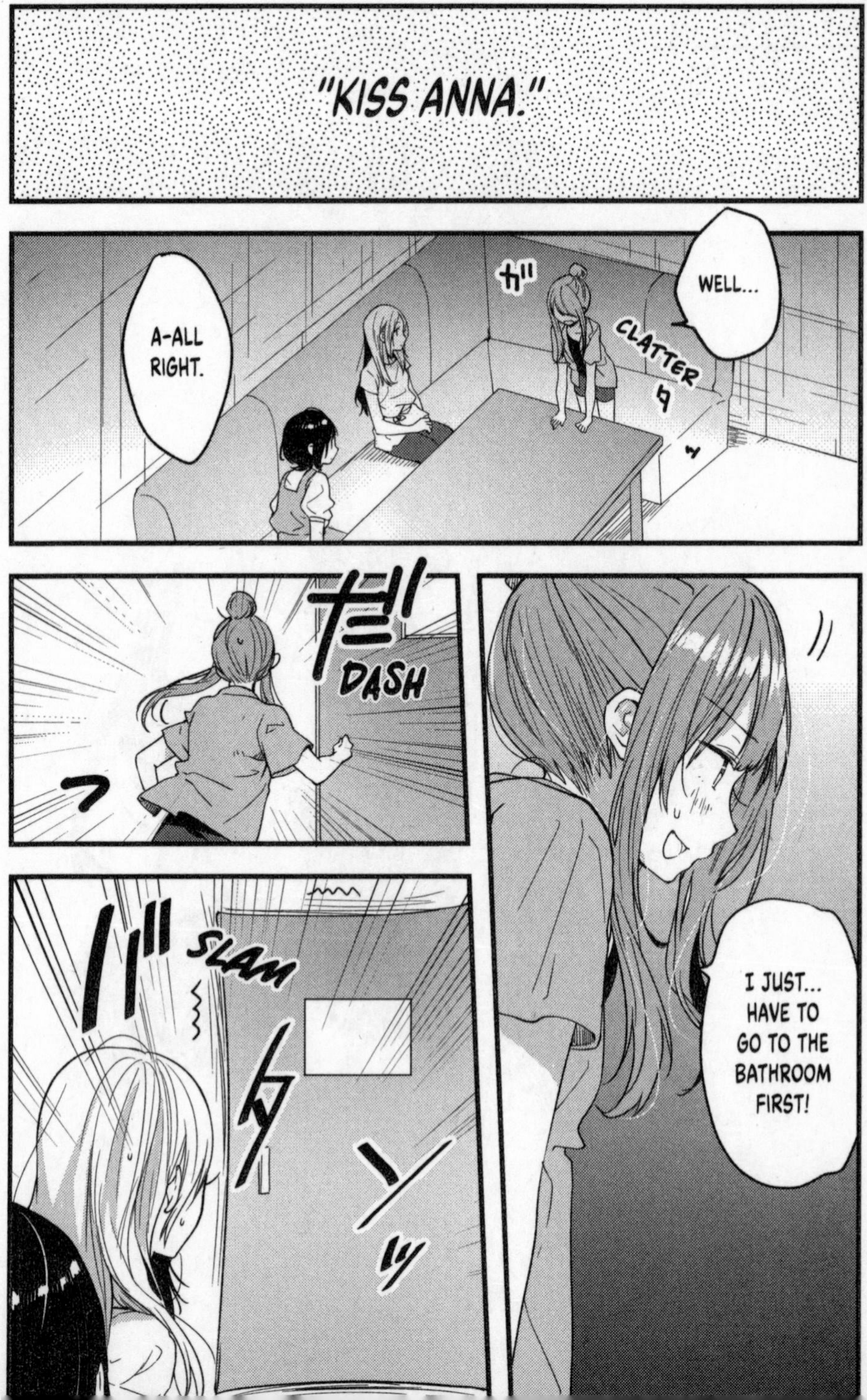
"KISS ANNA."
WELL...
CLATTER
A-ALL RIGHT.
I JUST... HAVE TO GO TO THE BATHROOM FIRST!
DASH
SLAM

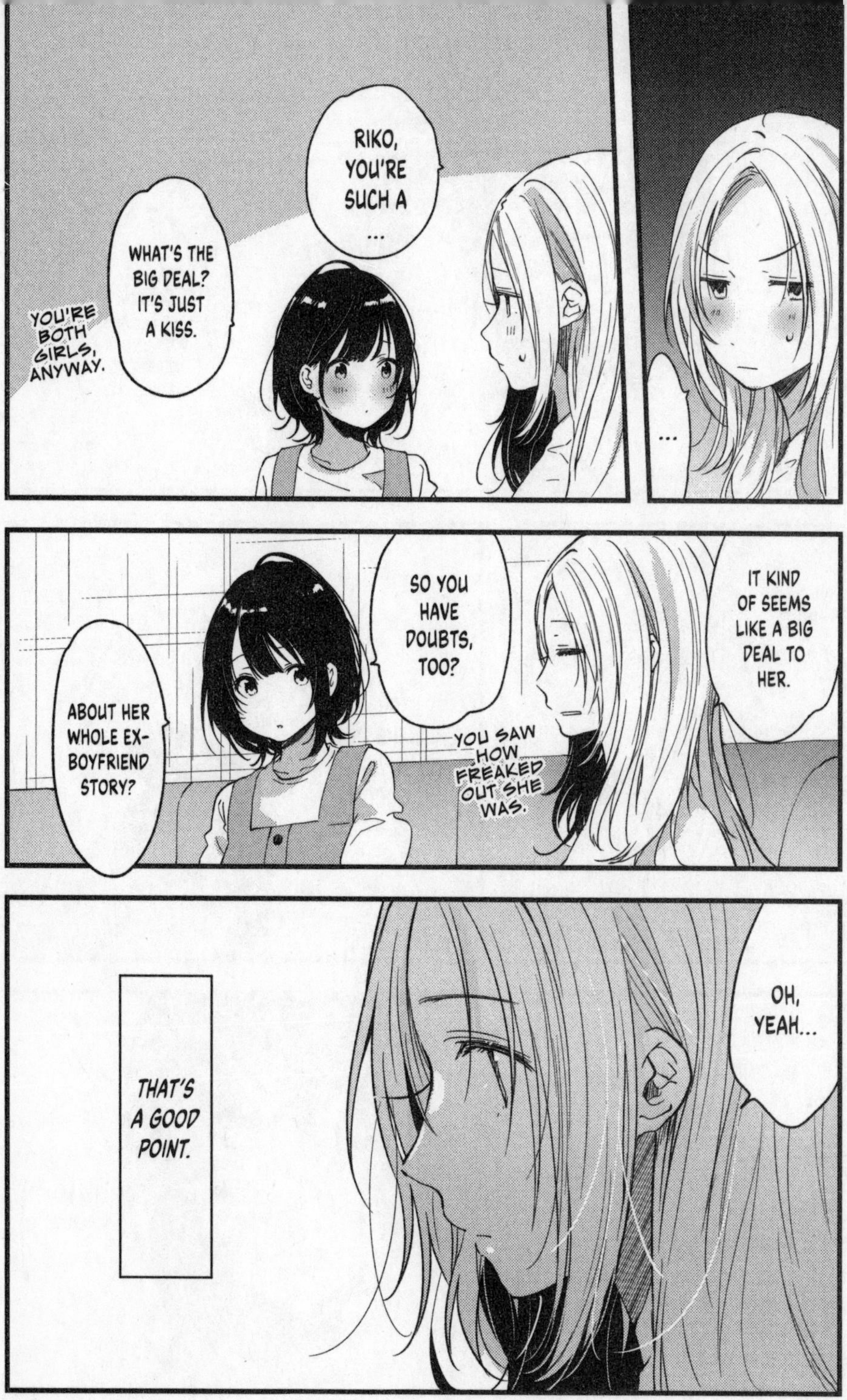
...
RIKO, YOU'RE SUCH A ...
WHAT'S THE BIG DEAL? IT'S JUST A KISS.
YOU'RE BOTH GIRLS, ANYWAY.
IT KIND OF SEEMS LIKE A BIG DEAL TO HER.
YOU SAW HOW FREAKED OUT SHE WAS.
SO YOU HAVE DOUBTS, TOO?
ABOUT HER WHOLE EX-BOYFRIEND STORY?
OH, YEAH...
THAT'S A GOOD POINT.

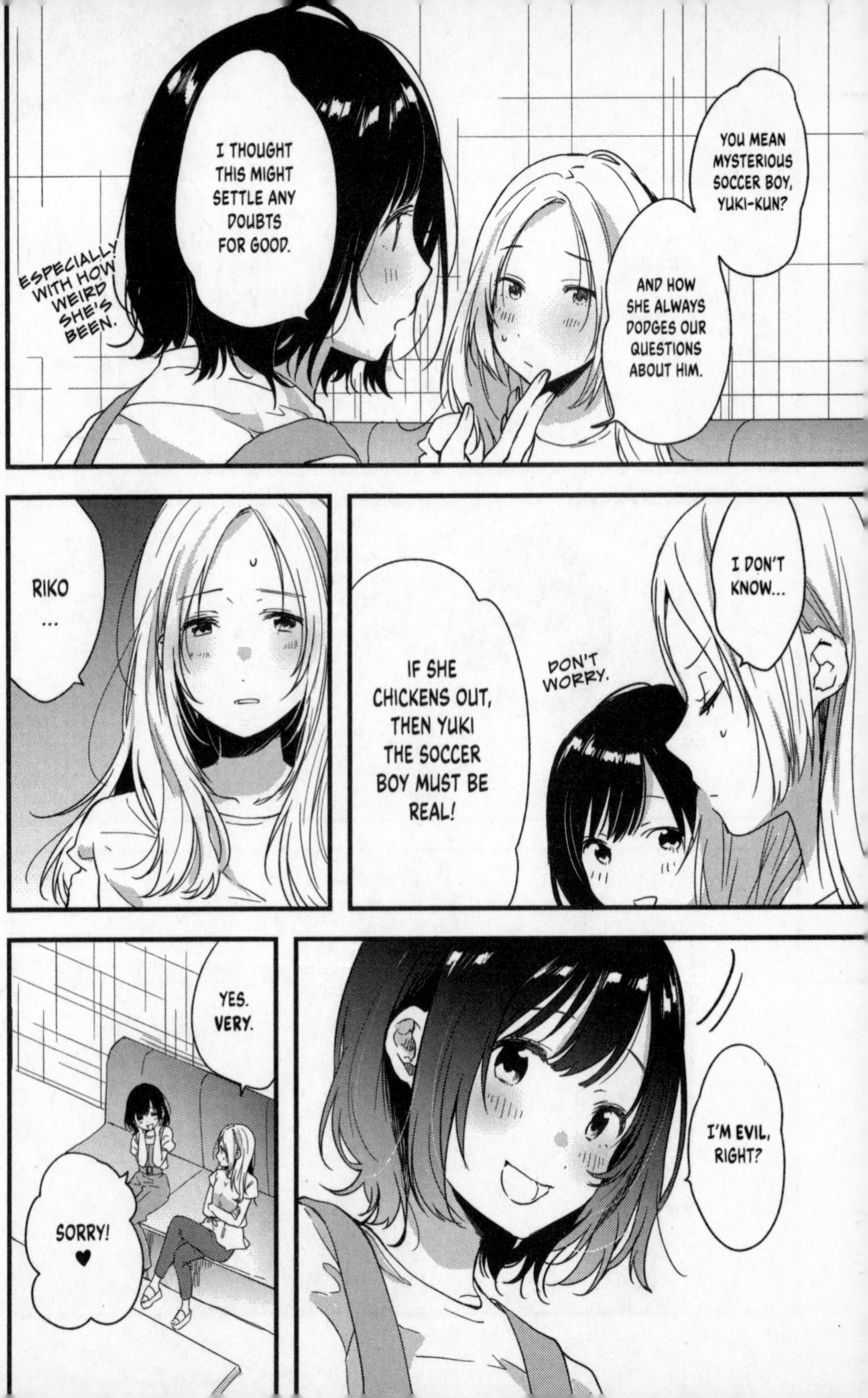
YOU MEAN MYSTERIOUS SOCCER BOY, YUKI-KUN?
AND HOW SHE ALWAYS DODGES OUR QUESTIONS ABOUT HIM.
I THOUGHT THIS MIGHT SETTLE ANY DOUBTS FOR GOOD.
ESPECIALLY WITH HOW WEIRD SHE'S BEEN.
I DON'T KNOW...
DON'T WORRY.
IF SHE CHICKENS OUT, THEN YUKI THE SOCCER BOY MUST BE REAL!
RIKO ...
I'M EVIL, RIGHT?
YES. VERY.
SORRY! ♥

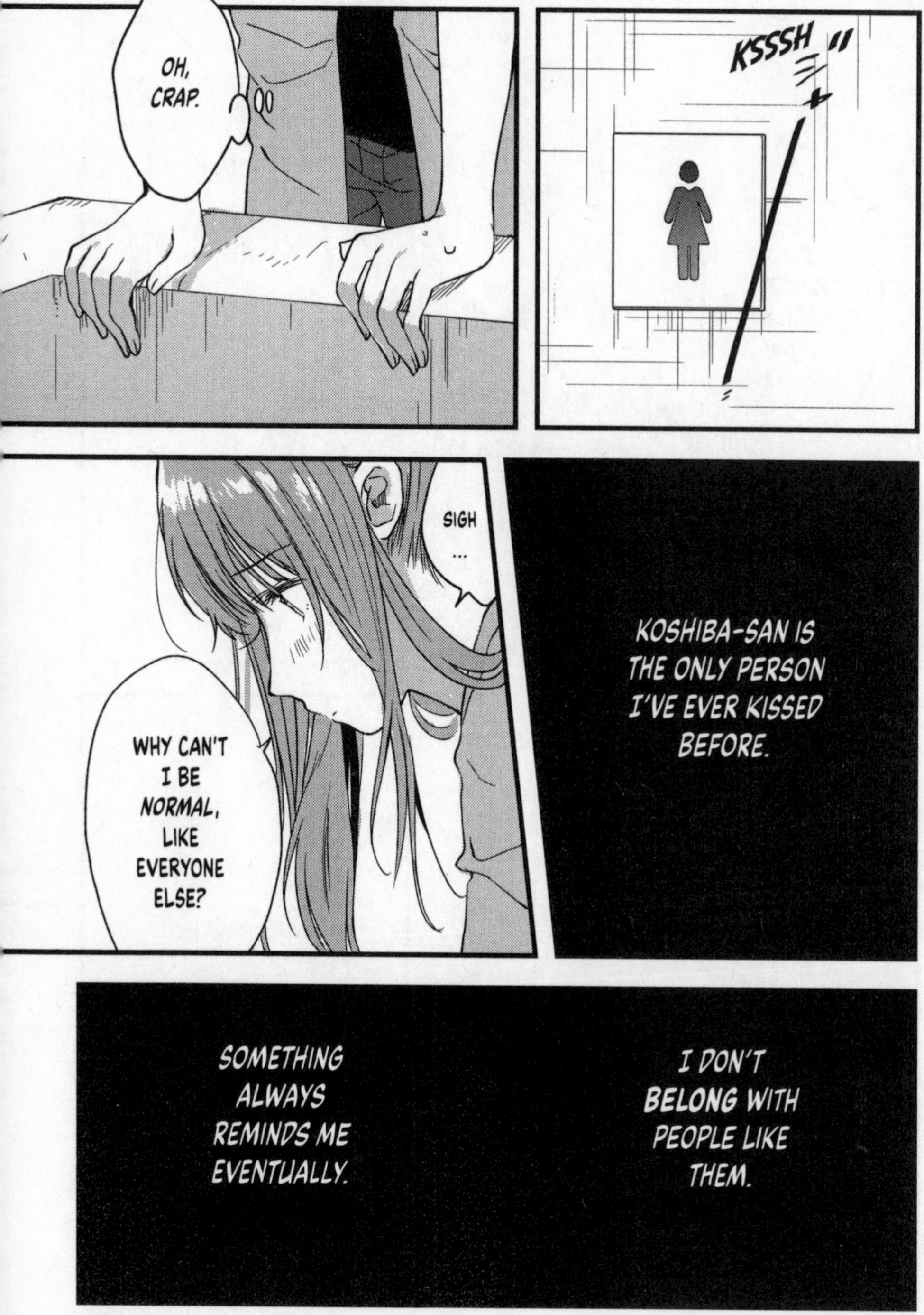
KSSSH
OH, CRAP.
KOSHIBA-SAN IS THE ONLY PERSON I'VE EVER KISSED BEFORE.
SIGH ...
WHY CAN'T I BE NORMAL, LIKE EVERYONE ELSE?
I DON'T BELONG WITH PEOPLE LIKE THEM.
SOMETHING ALWAYS REMINDS ME EVENTUALLY.

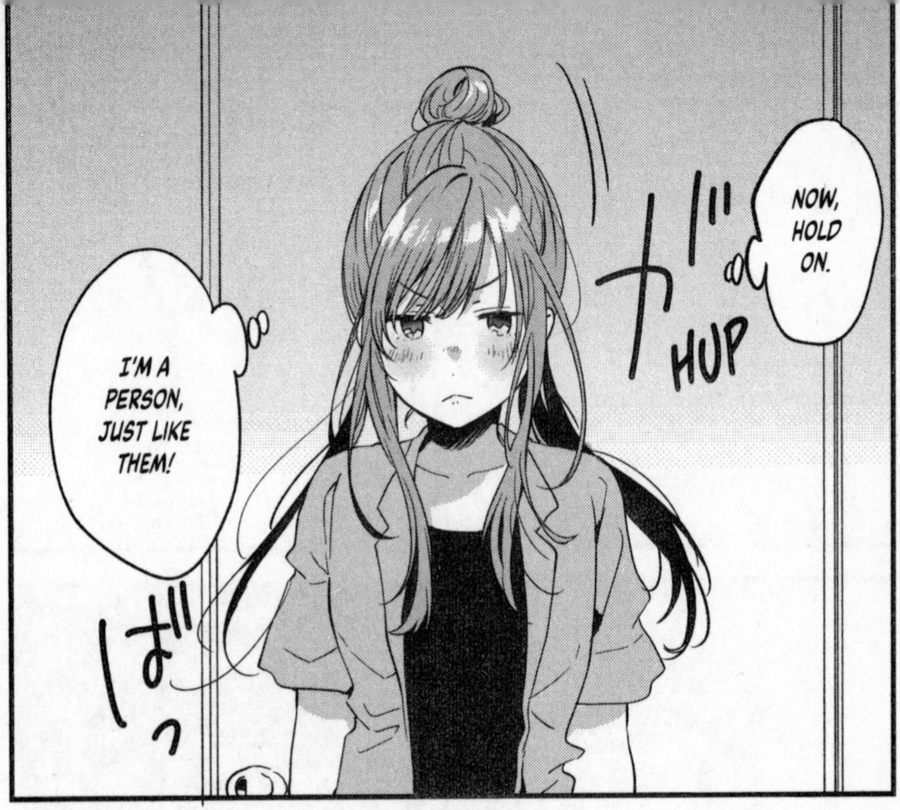
NOW, HOLD ON.
HUP
I'M A PERSON, JUST LIKE THEM!

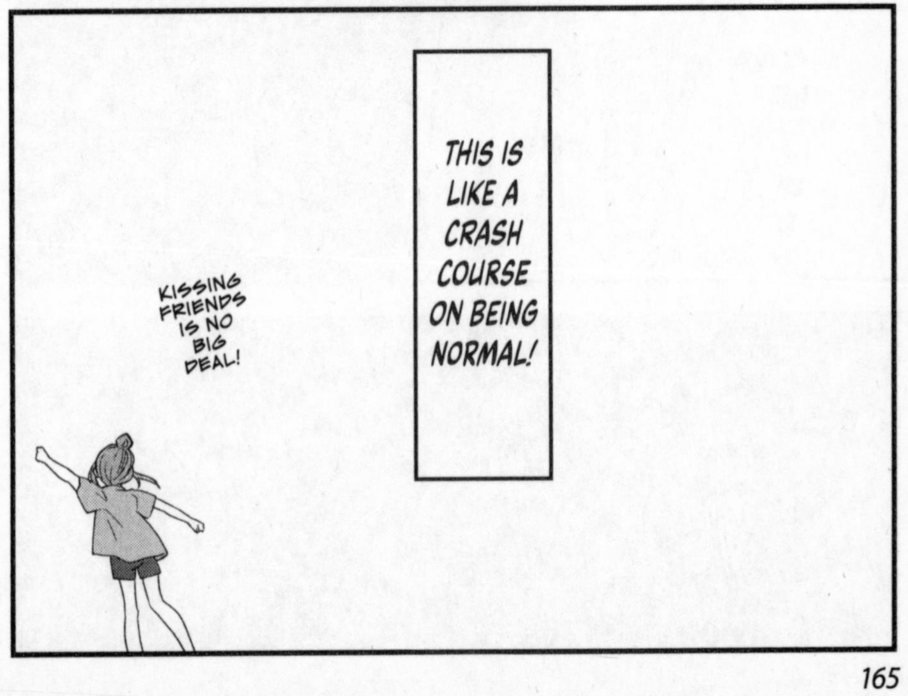
THIS IS LIKE A CRASH COURSE ON BEING NORMAL!
KISSING FRIENDS IS NO BIG DEAL!

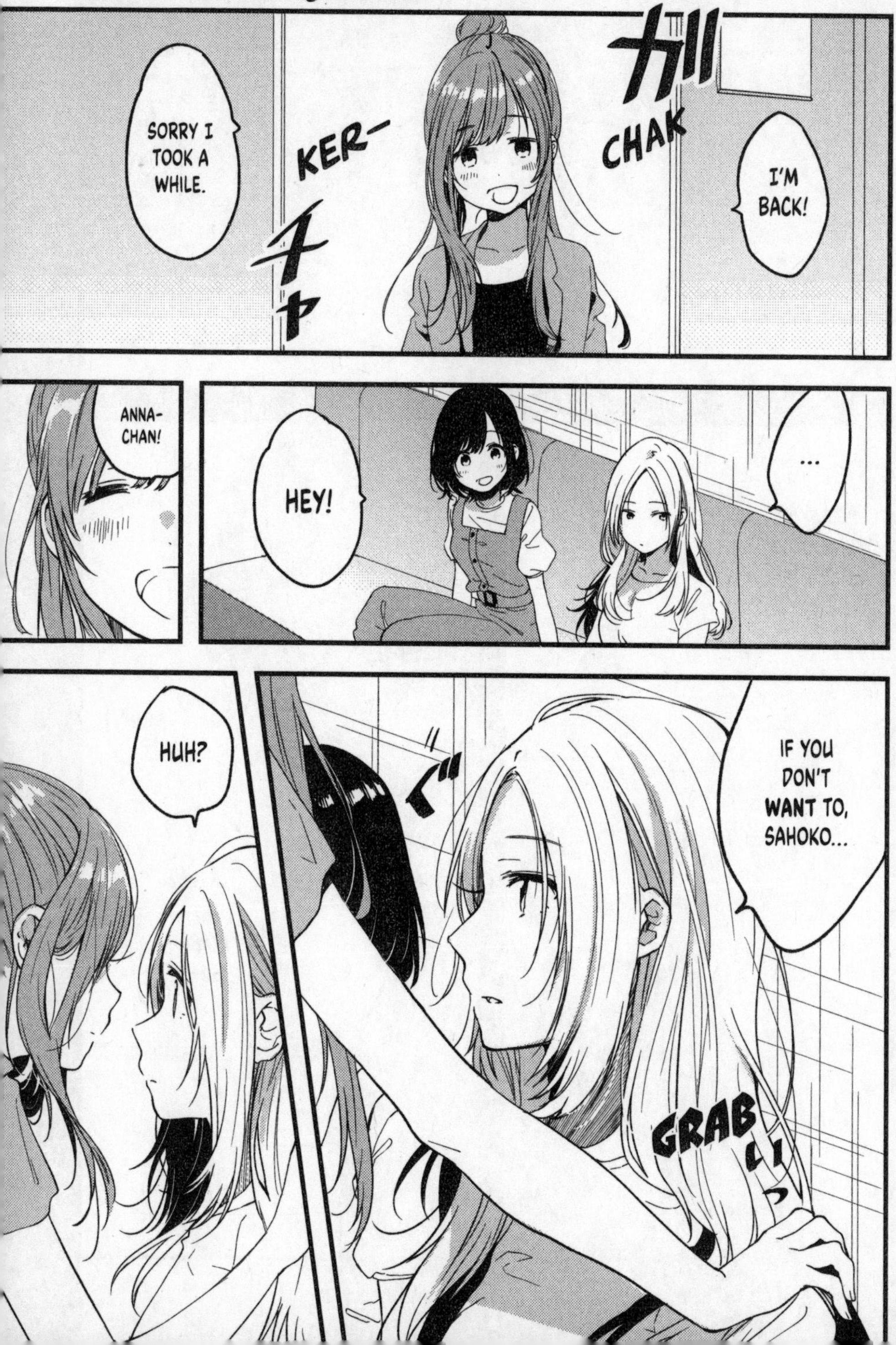
I'M BACK!
KER-
CHAK
SORRY I TOOK A WHILE.
...
HEY!
ANNA-CHAN!
IF YOU DON'T WANT TO, SAHOKO...
GRAB
HUH?

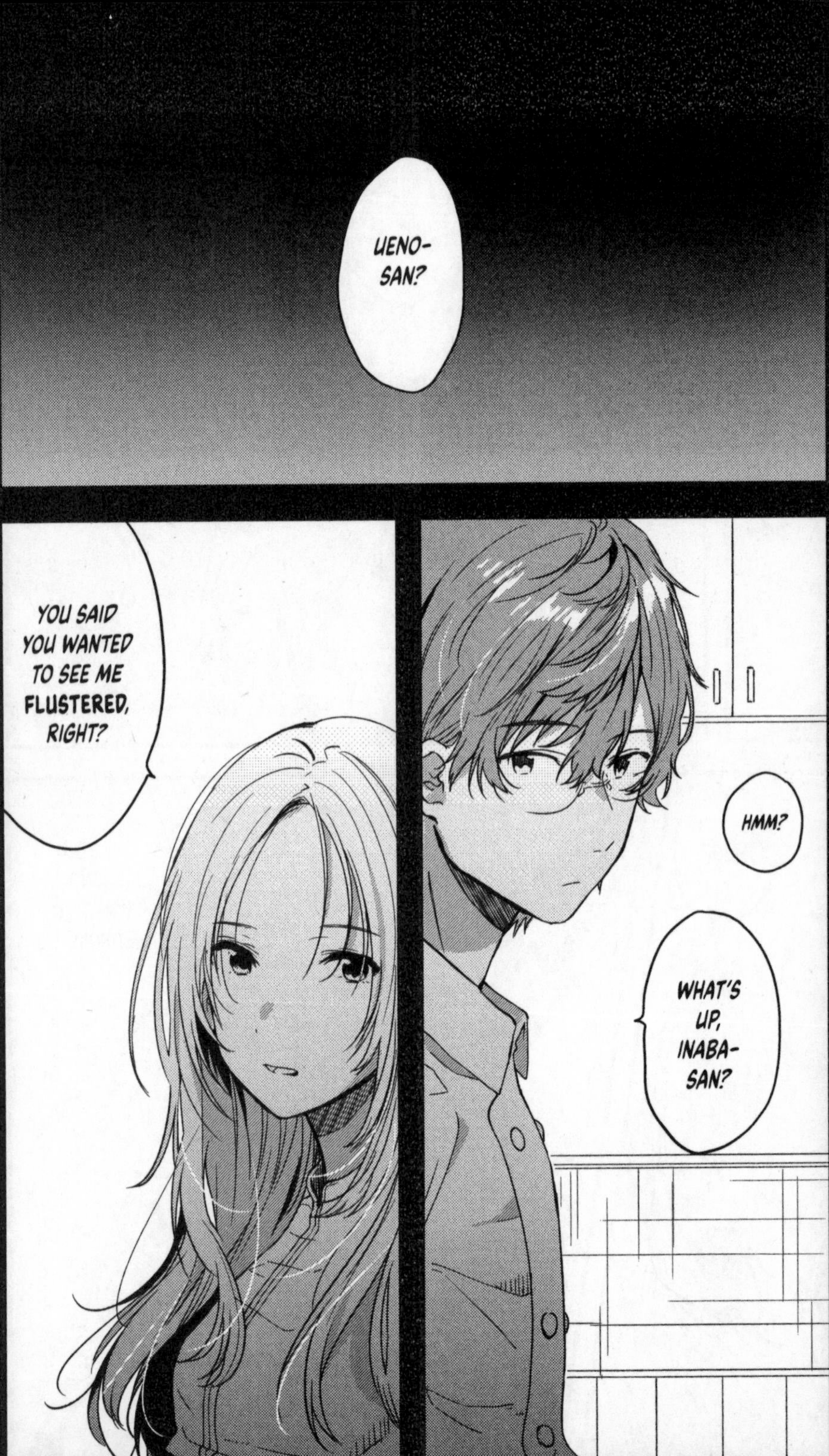
UENO-SAN?
HMM?
WHAT'S UP, INABA-SAN?
YOU SAID YOU WANTED TO SEE ME FLUSTERED, RIGHT?

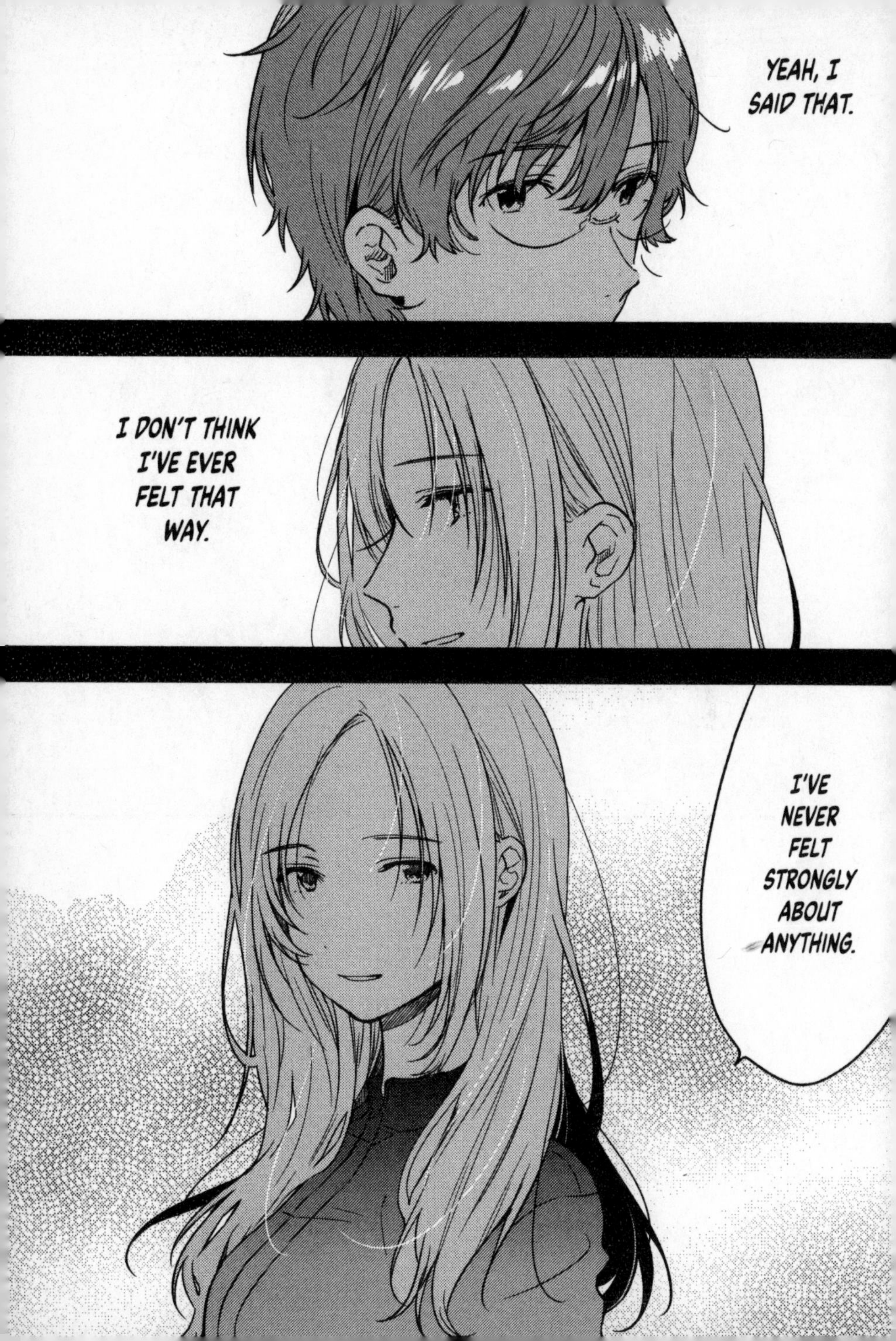
YEAH, I SAID THAT.
I DON'T THINK I'VE EVER FELT THAT WAY.
I'VE NEVER FELT STRONGLY ABOUT ANYTHING.

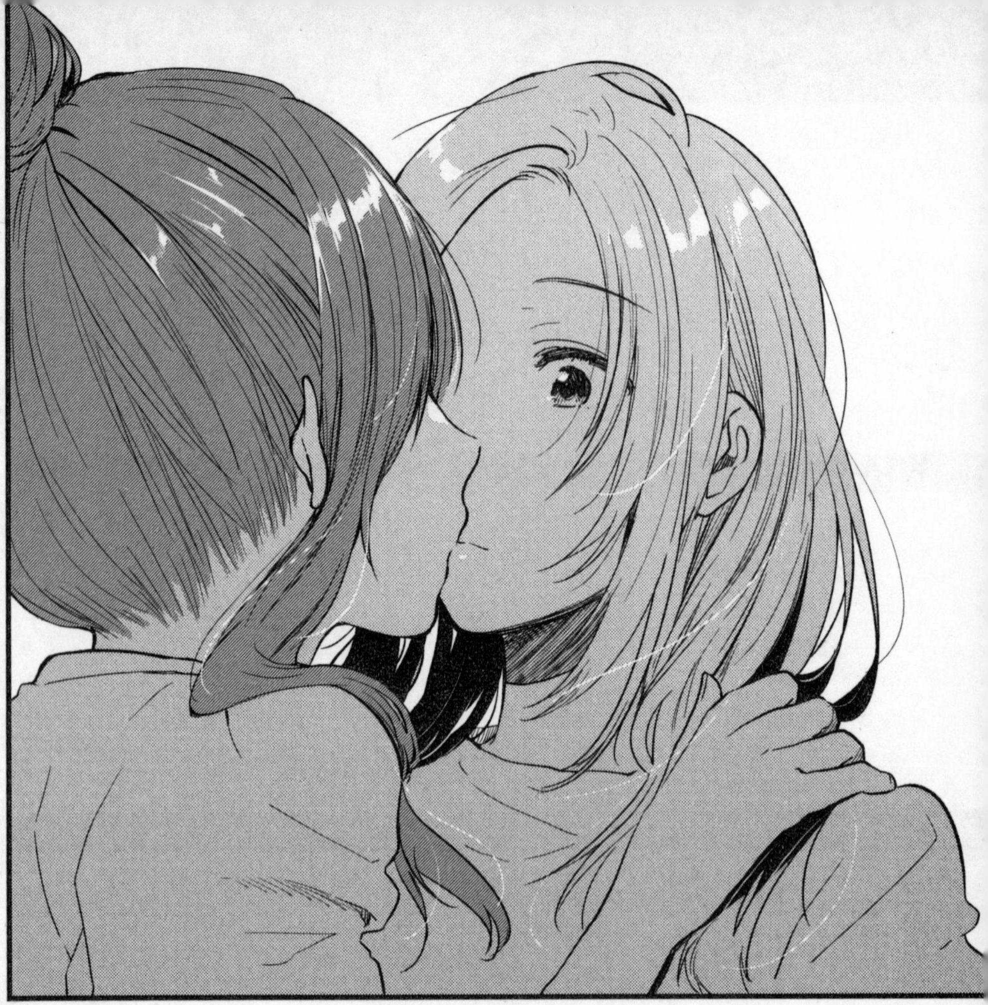

NOW I CAN
SAY FOR SURE...

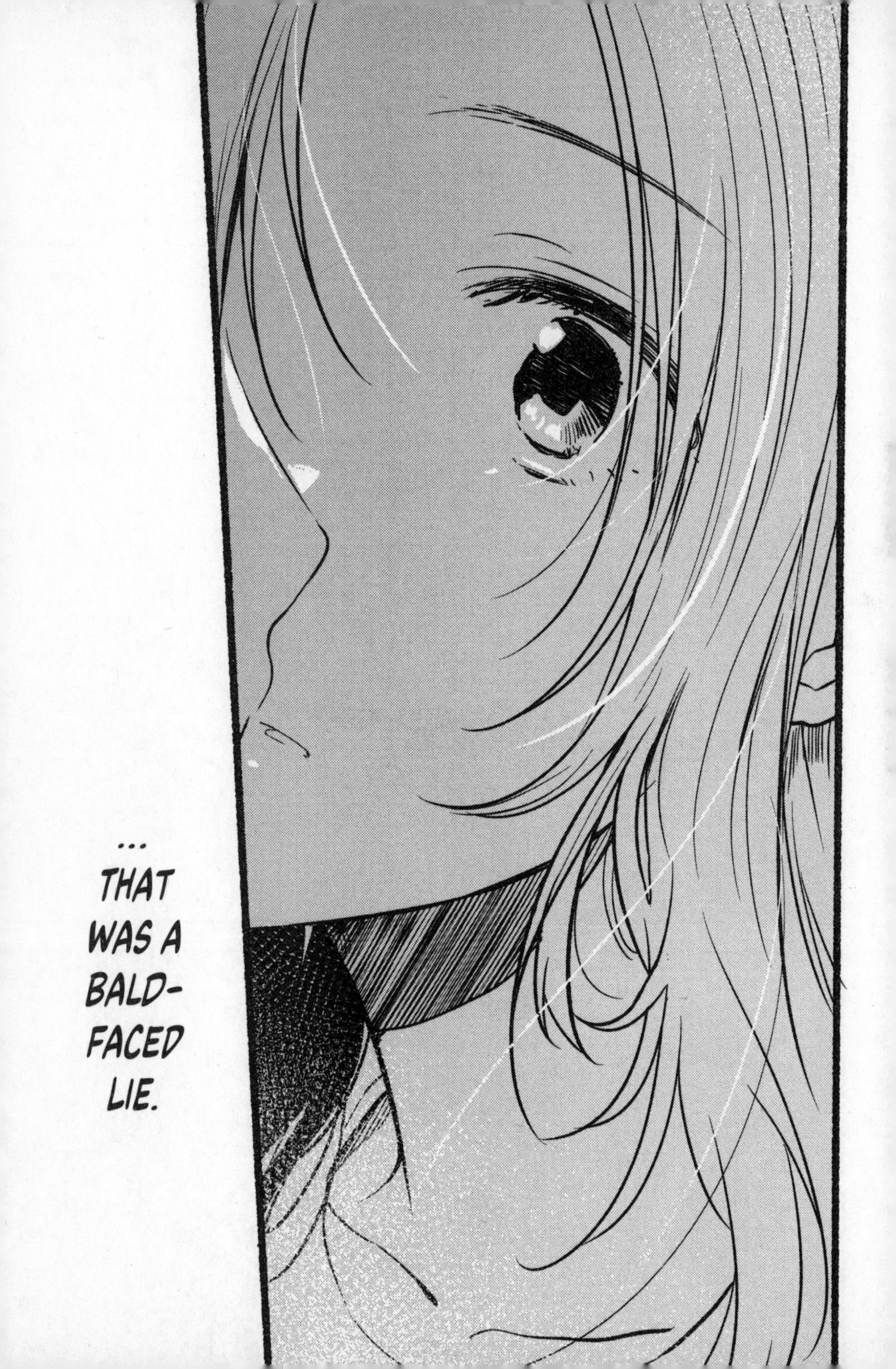
... THAT WAS A BALD-FACED LIE.

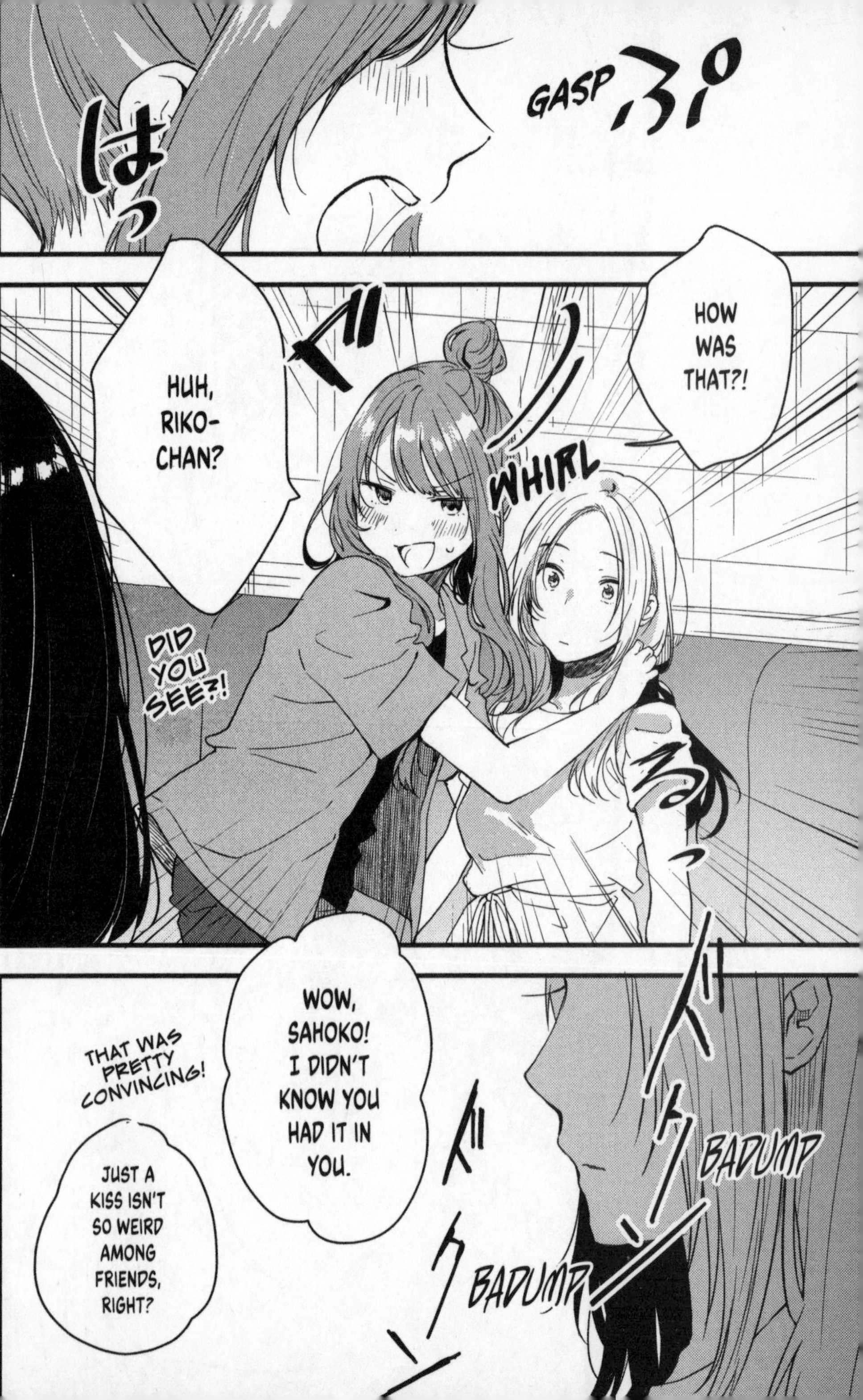
GASP ぷ
はっ
HOW WAS THAT?!
WHIRL
HUH, RIKO-CHAN?
DID YOU SEE?!
BADUMP
BADUMP
WOW, SAHOKO! I DIDN'T KNOW YOU HAD IT IN YOU.
THAT WAS PRETTY CONVINCING!
JUST A KISS ISN'T SO WEIRD AMONG FRIENDS, RIGHT?

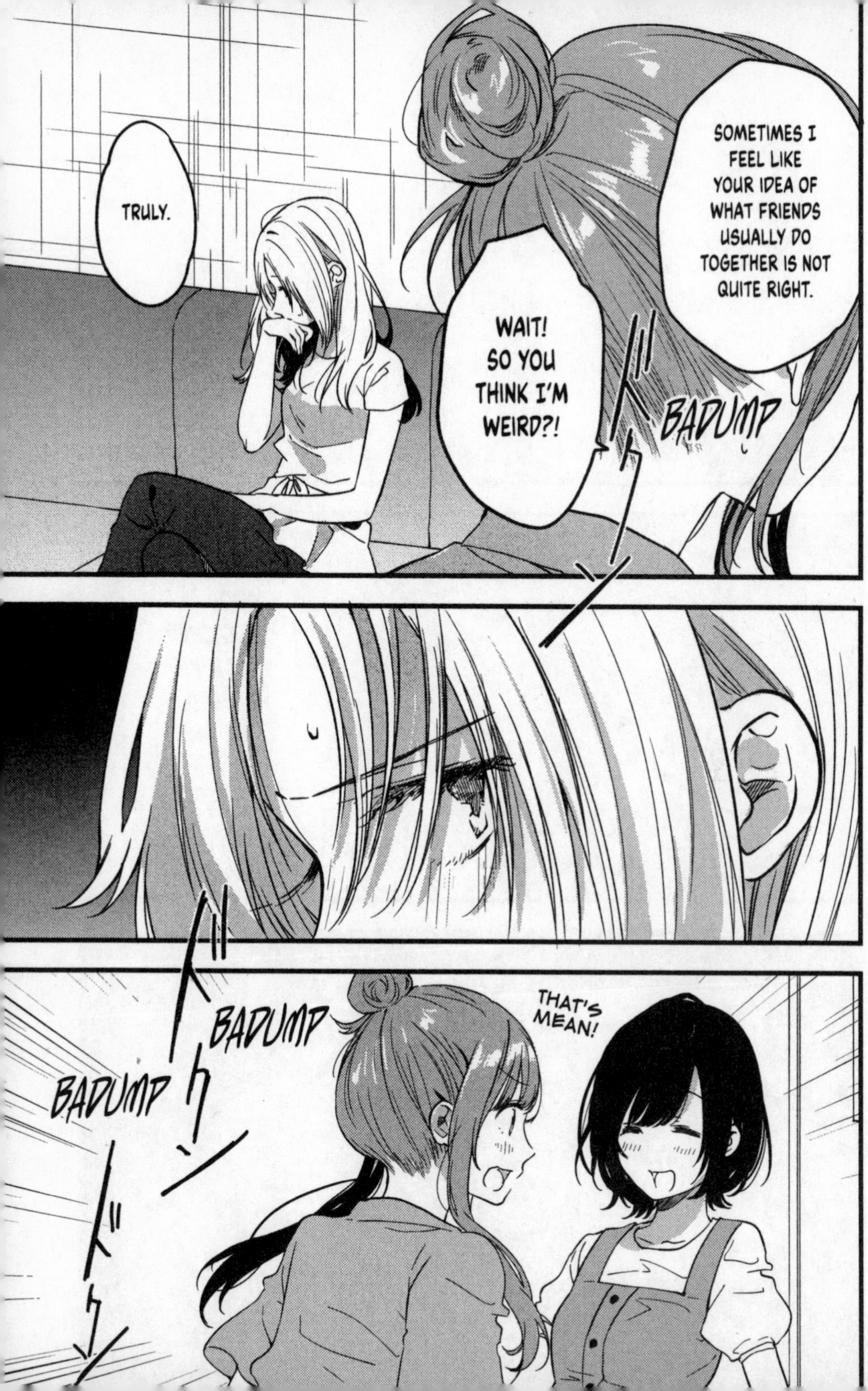
SOMETIMES I FEEL LIKE YOUR IDEA OF WHAT FRIENDS USUALLY DO TOGETHER IS NOT QUITE RIGHT.
WAIT! SO YOU THINK I'M WEIRD?!
BADUMP
TRULY.
THAT'S MEAN!
BADUMP
BADUMP

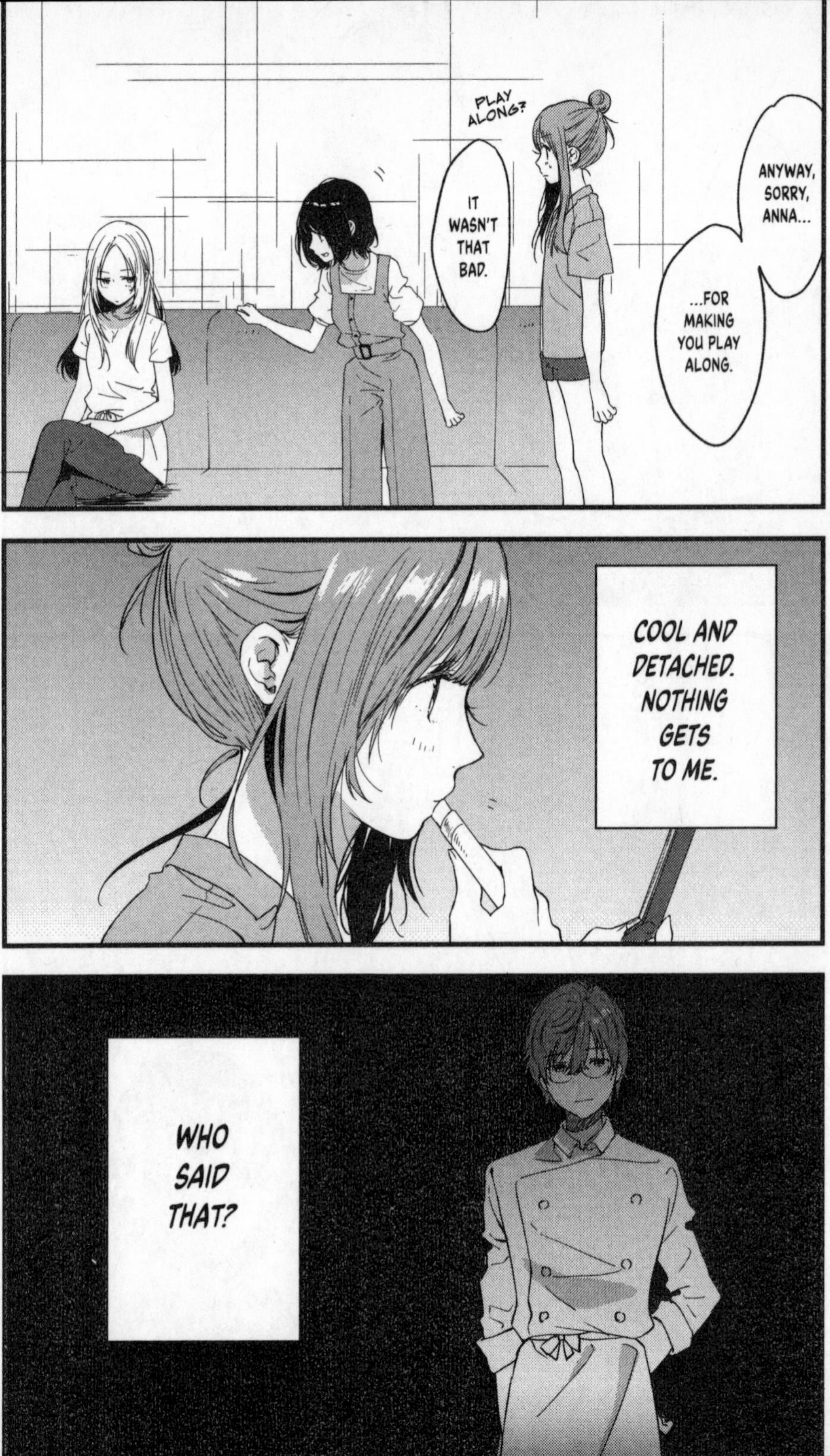
ANYWAY, SORRY, ANNA...
...FOR MAKING YOU PLAY ALONG.
PLAY ALONG?
IT WASN'T THAT BAD.
COOL AND DETACHED. NOTHING GETS TO ME.
WHO SAID THAT?

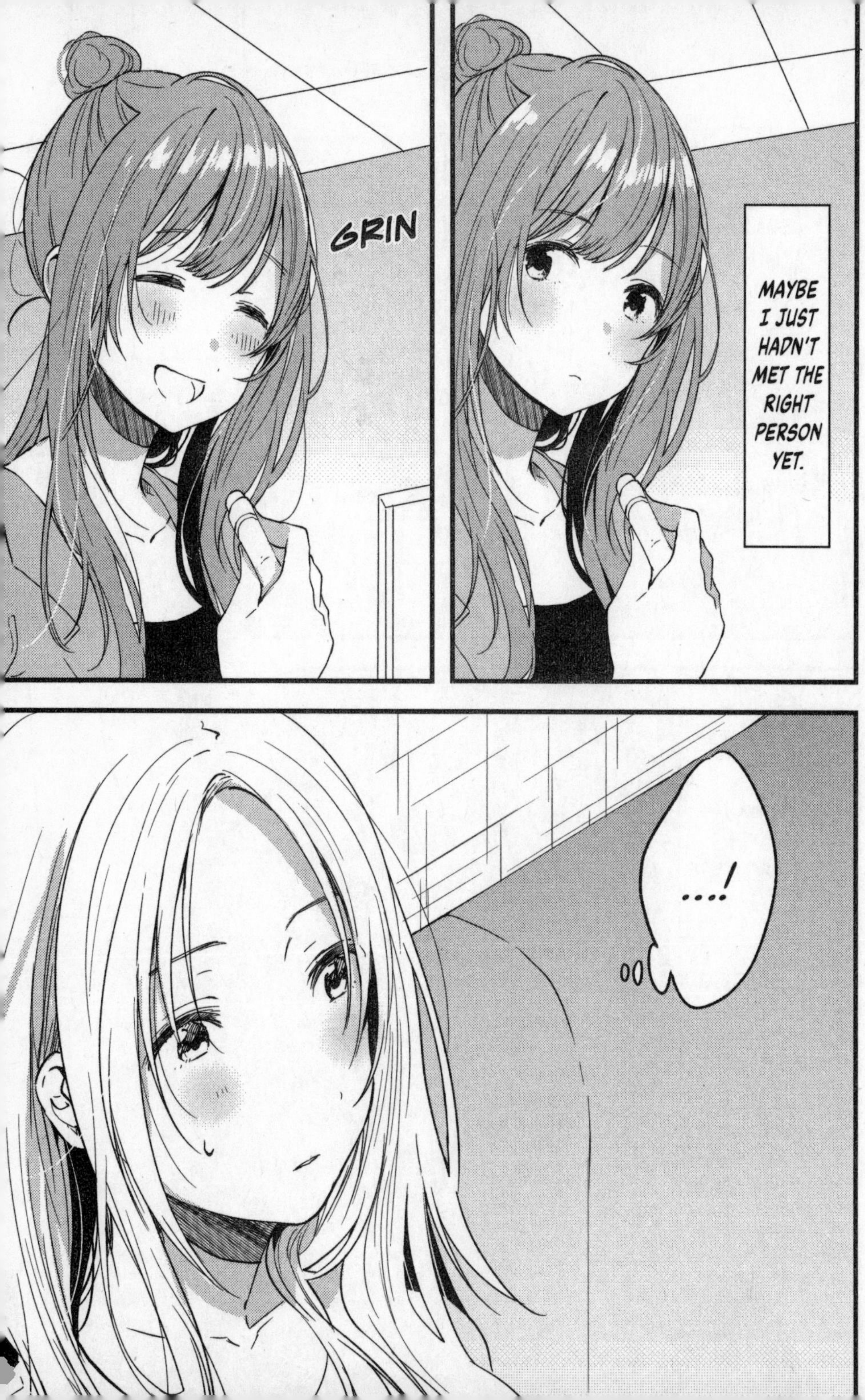
MAYBE I JUST HADN'T MET THE RIGHT PERSON YET.
GRIN
...!

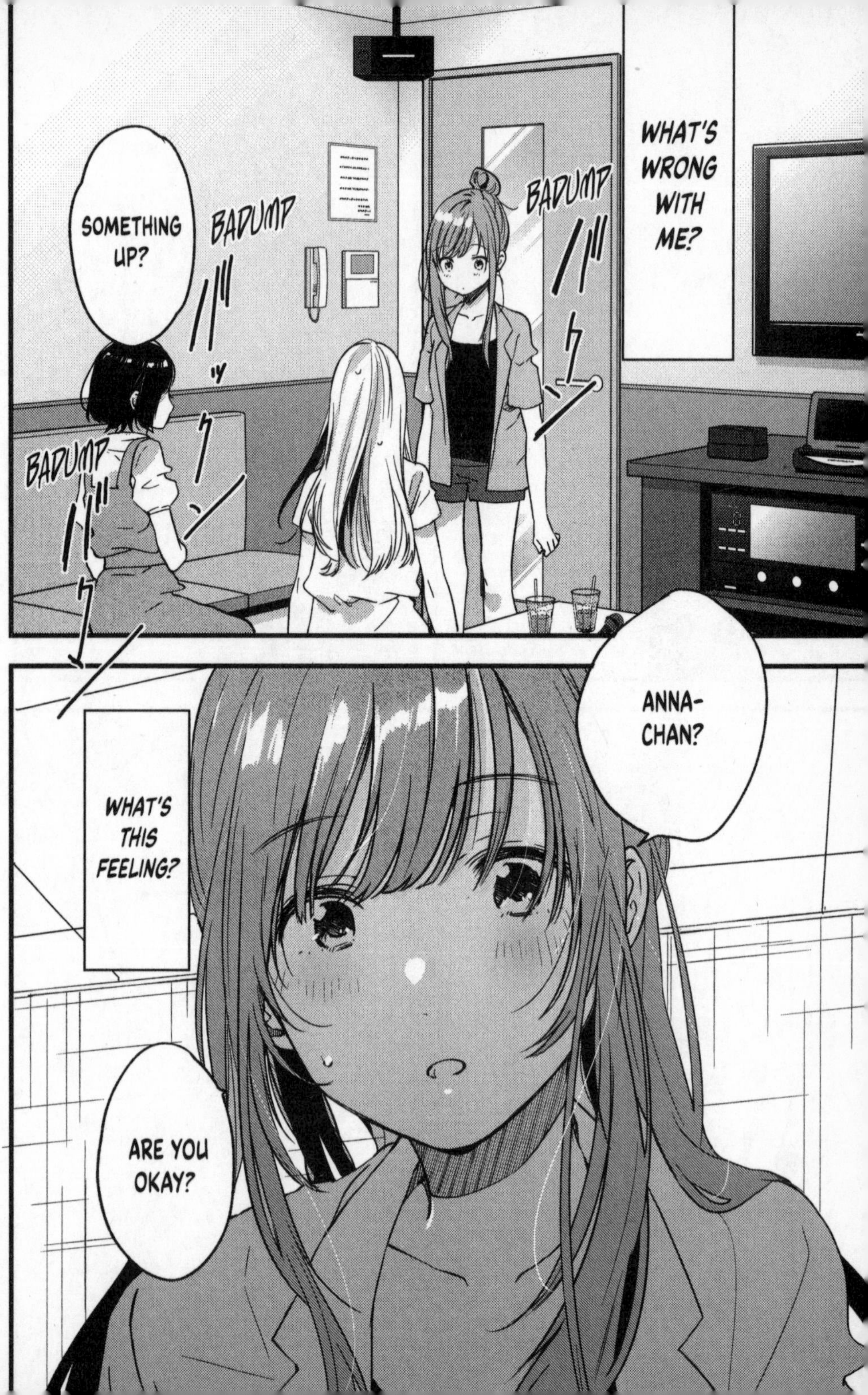
WHAT'S WRONG WITH ME?
BADUMP
BADUMP
SOMETHING UP?
BADUMP
ANNA-CHAN?
WHAT'S THIS FEELING?
ARE YOU OKAY?

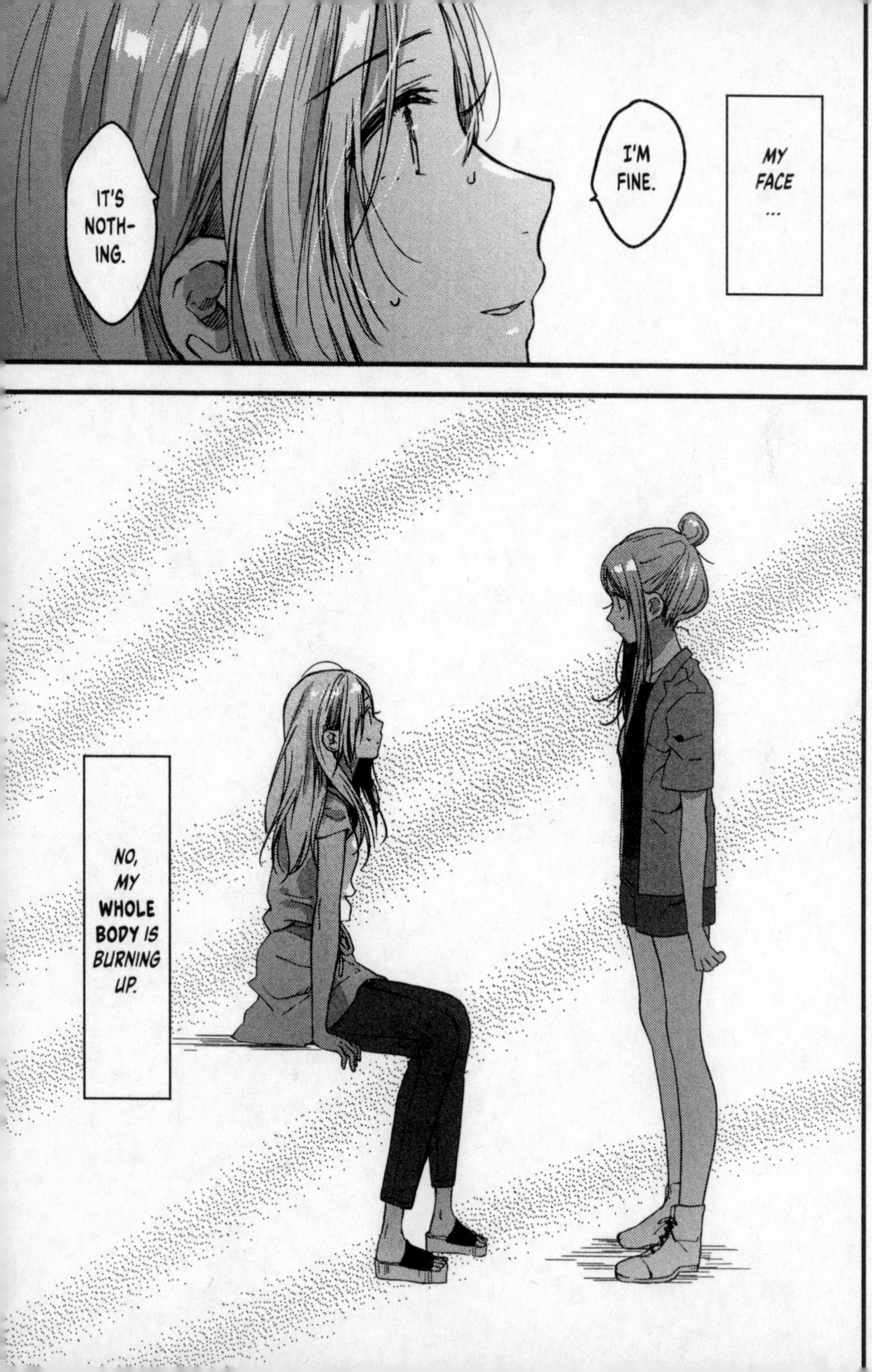
MY FACE ...
I'M FINE.
IT'S NOTHING.
NO, MY WHOLE BODY IS BURNING UP.

OH...
I GET
IT.

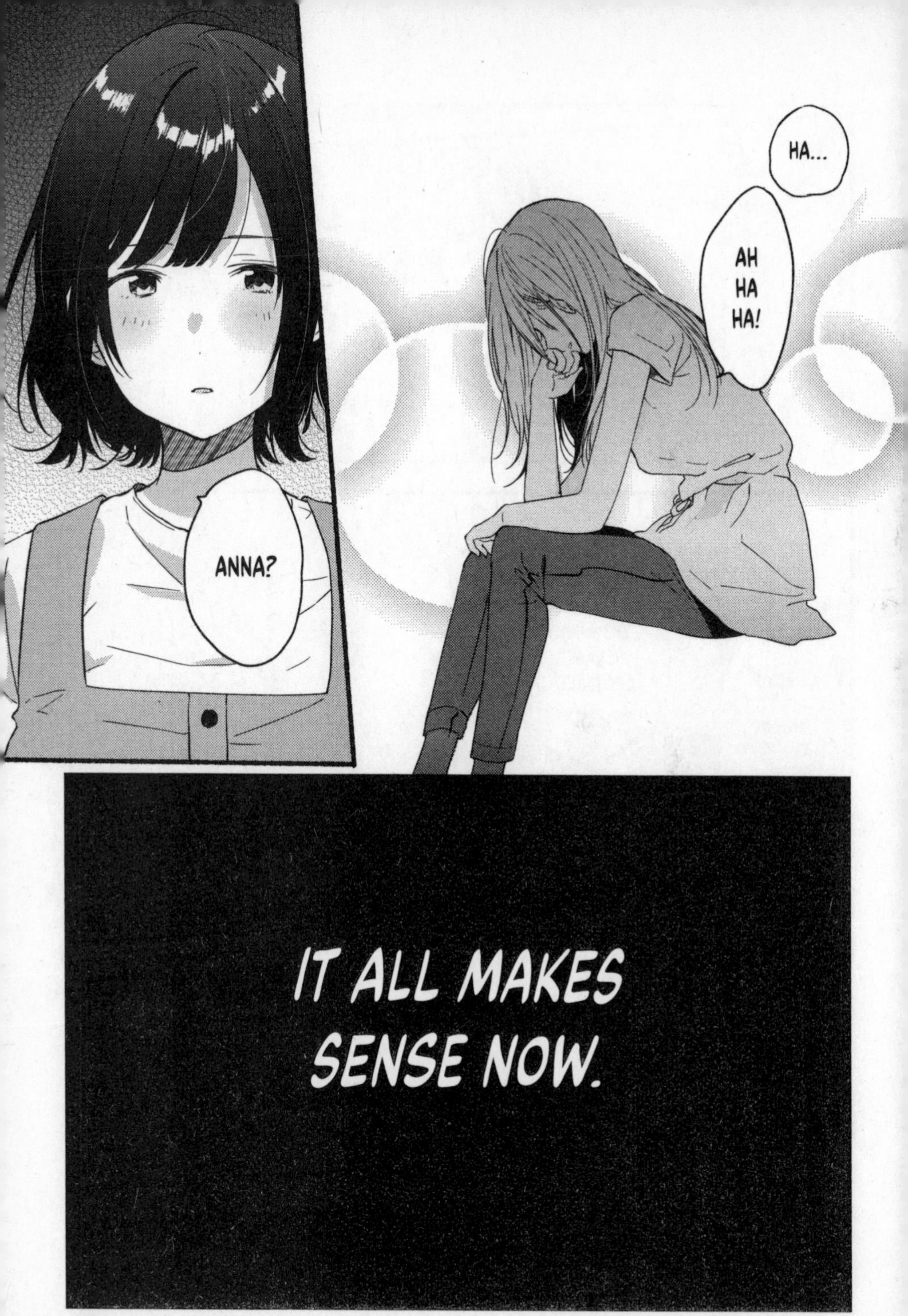
HA...
AH HA HA!
ANNA?
IT ALL MAKES SENSE NOW.

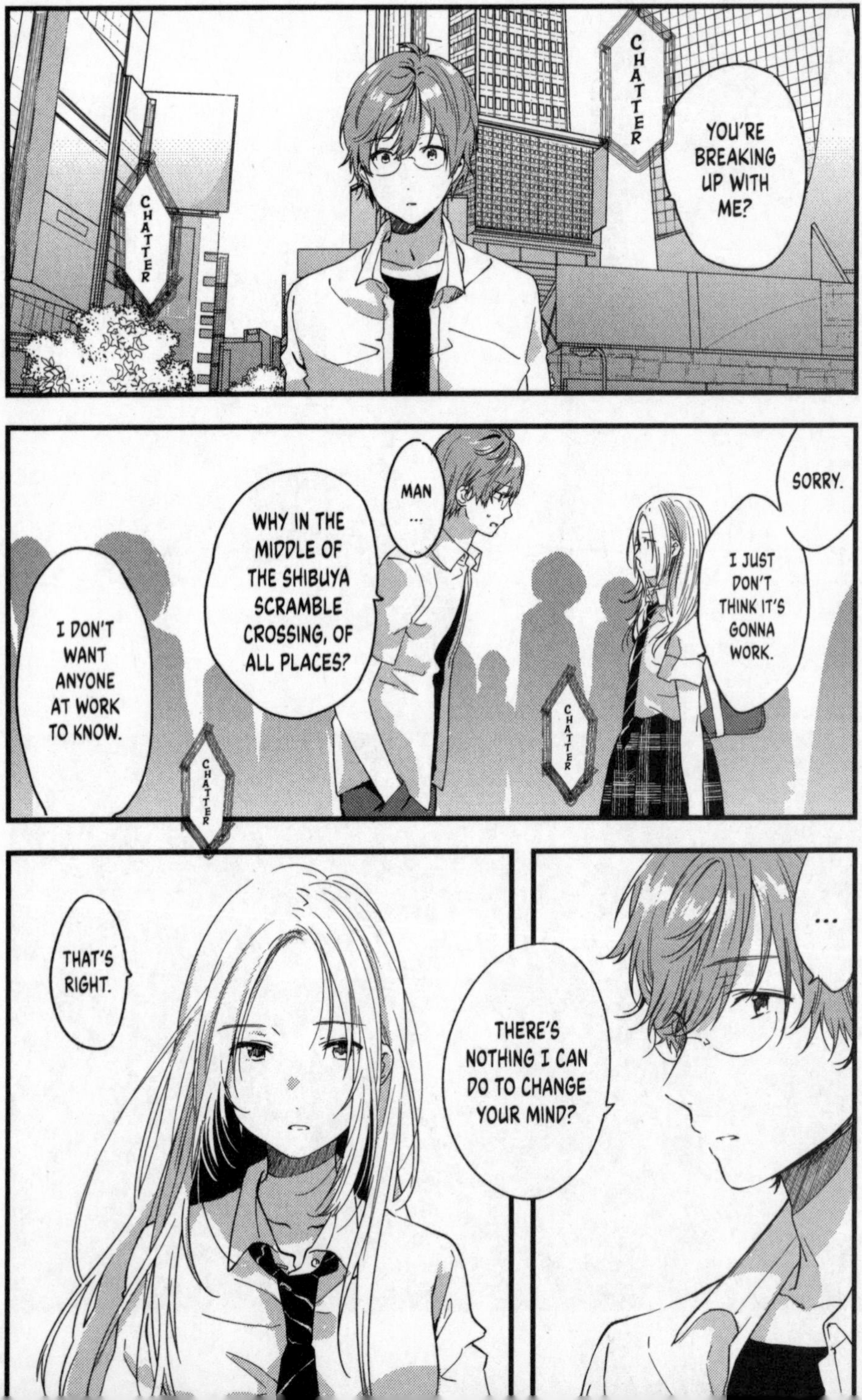
CHATTER
YOU'RE BREAKING UP WITH ME?
CHATTER
SORRY.
I JUST DON'T THINK IT'S GONNA WORK.
CHATTER
MAN...
WHY IN THE MIDDLE OF THE SHIBUYA SCRAMBLE CROSSING, OF ALL PLACES?
I DON'T WANT ANYONE AT WORK TO KNOW.
CHATTER
...
THERE'S NOTHING I CAN DO TO CHANGE YOUR MIND?
THAT'S RIGHT.

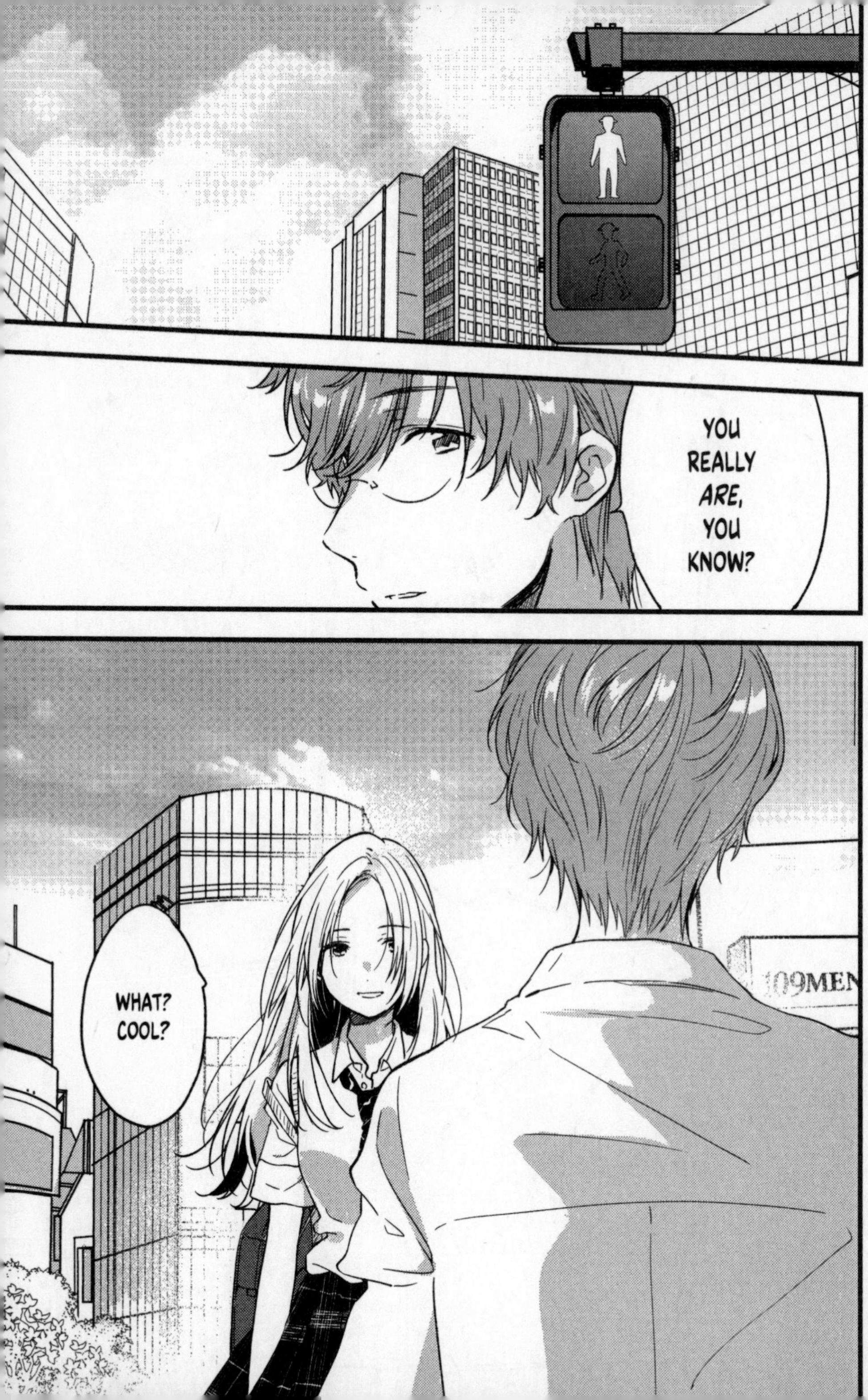
YOU REALLY ARE, YOU KNOW?
WHAT? COOL?

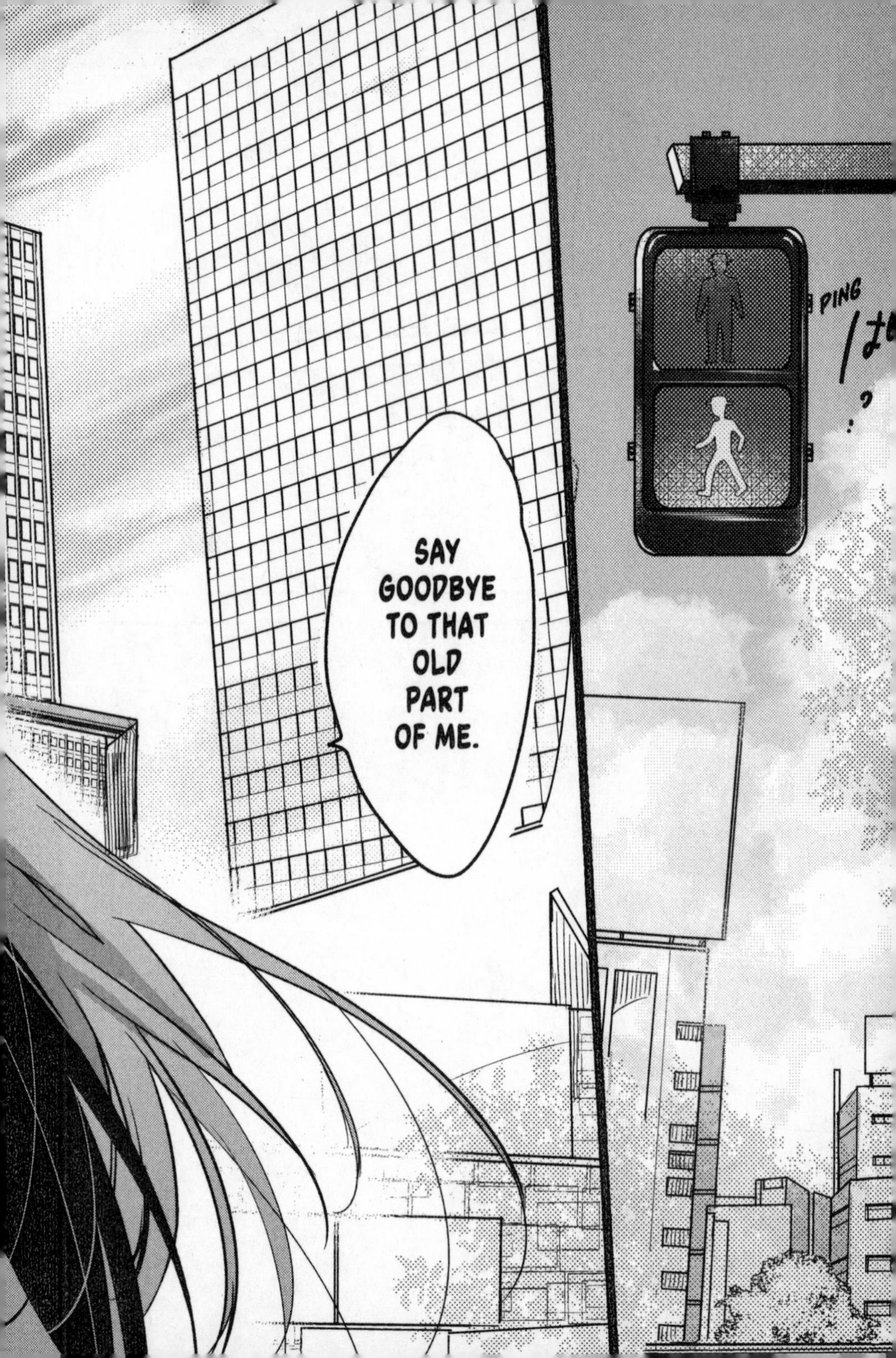
PING
SAY GOODBYE TO THAT OLD PART OF ME.

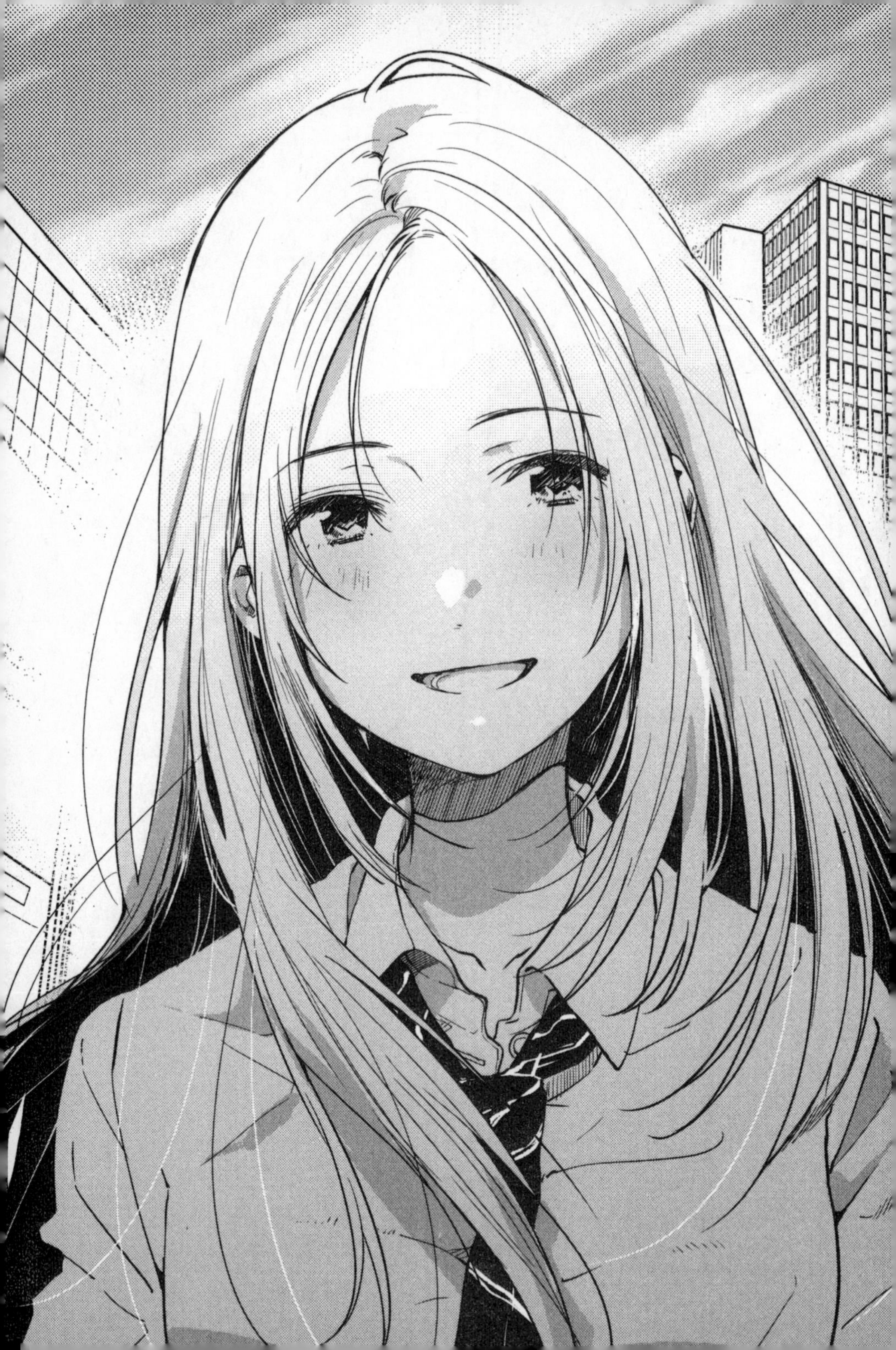

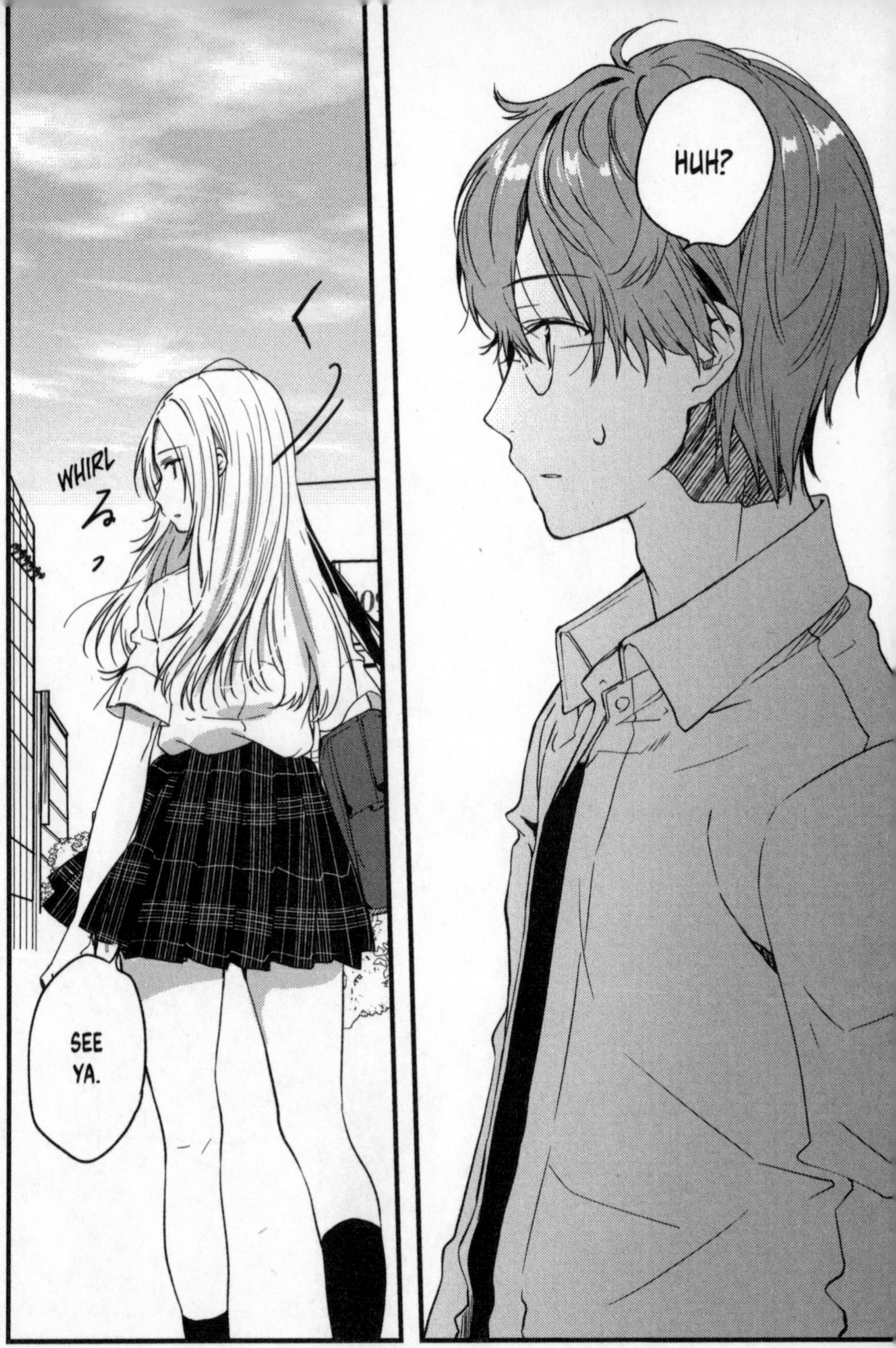
HUH?
WHIRL
SEE YA.

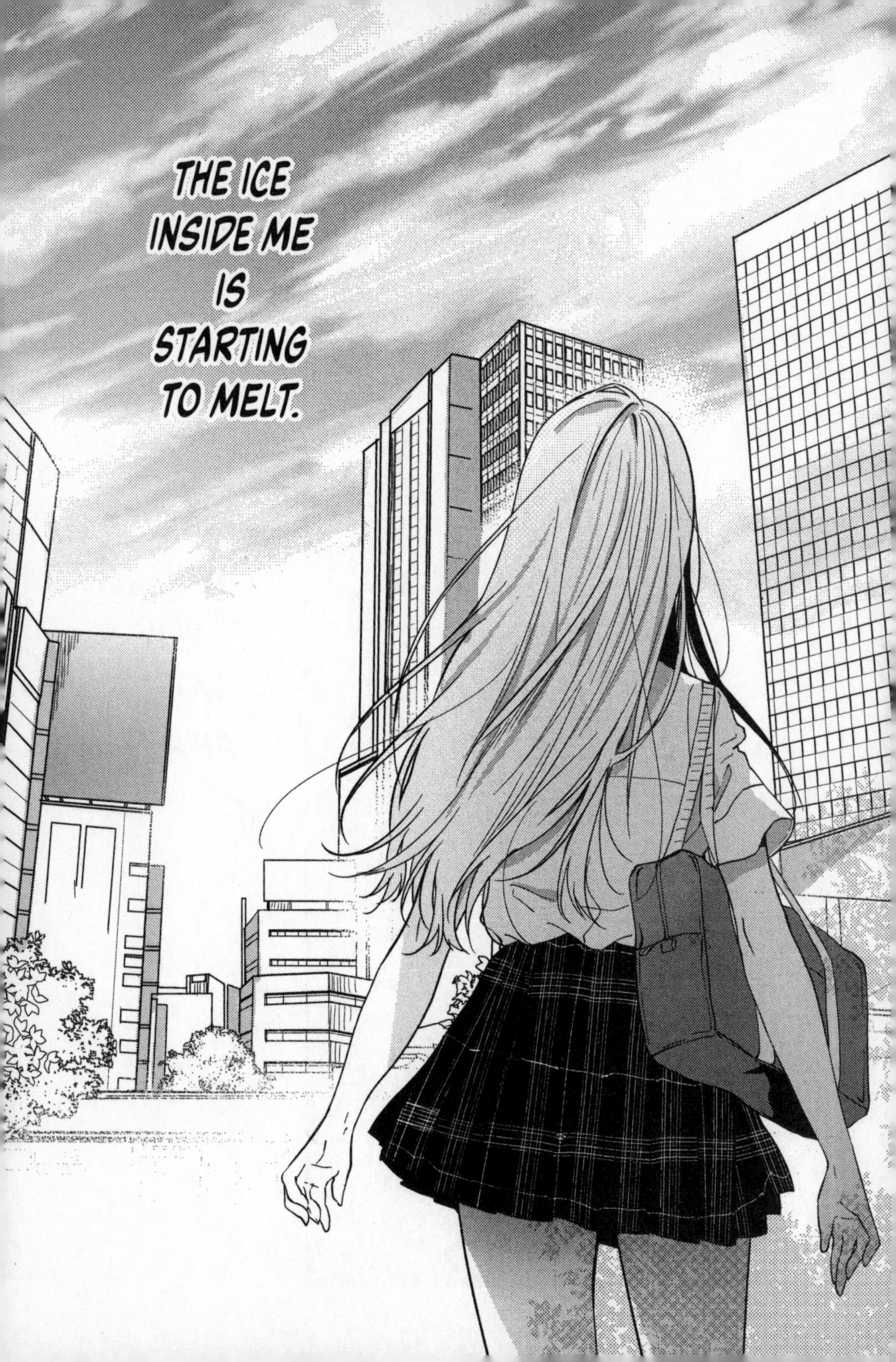
THE ICE INSIDE ME IS STARTING TO MELT.

AND A
WHOLE
NEW
WORLD
AWAITS.

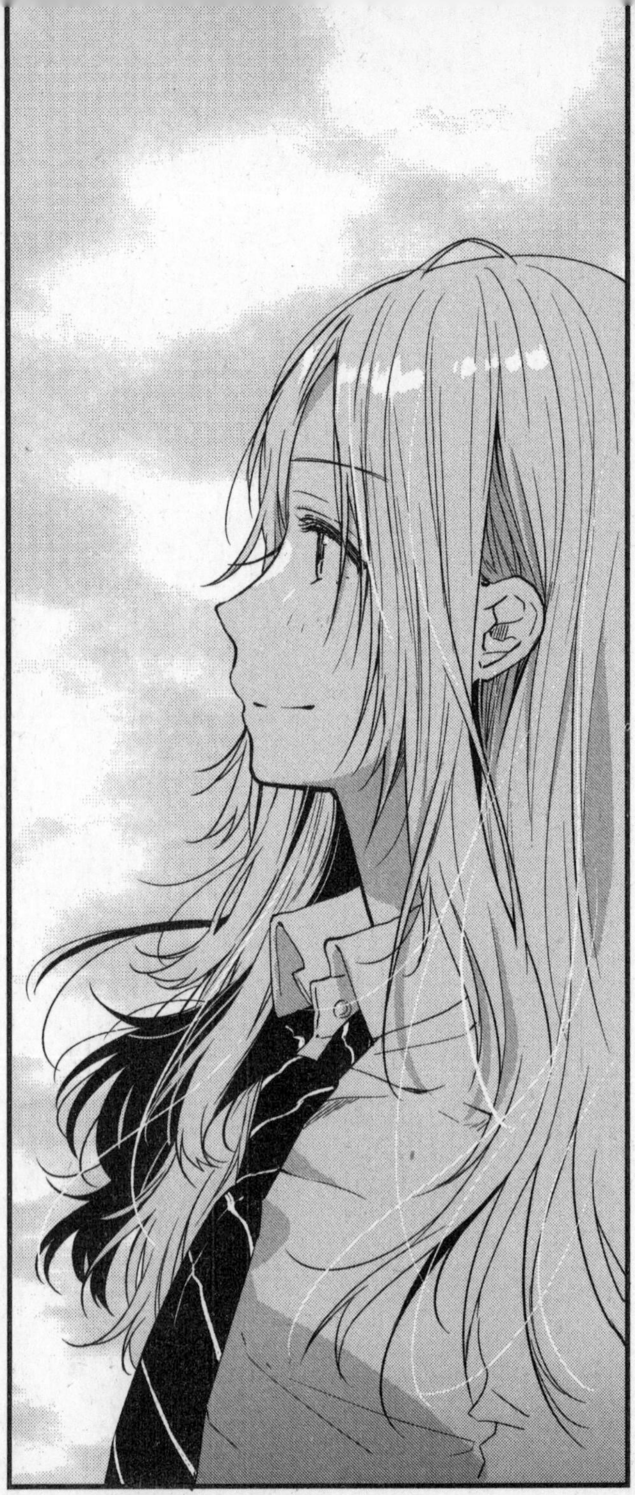

CHASING AFTER Aoi Koshiba

Summer | High School, Second Year

CHASING AFTER *Aoi Koshiba*

Summer | High School, Second Year

Chapter 11:
Oil and Vinegar 1

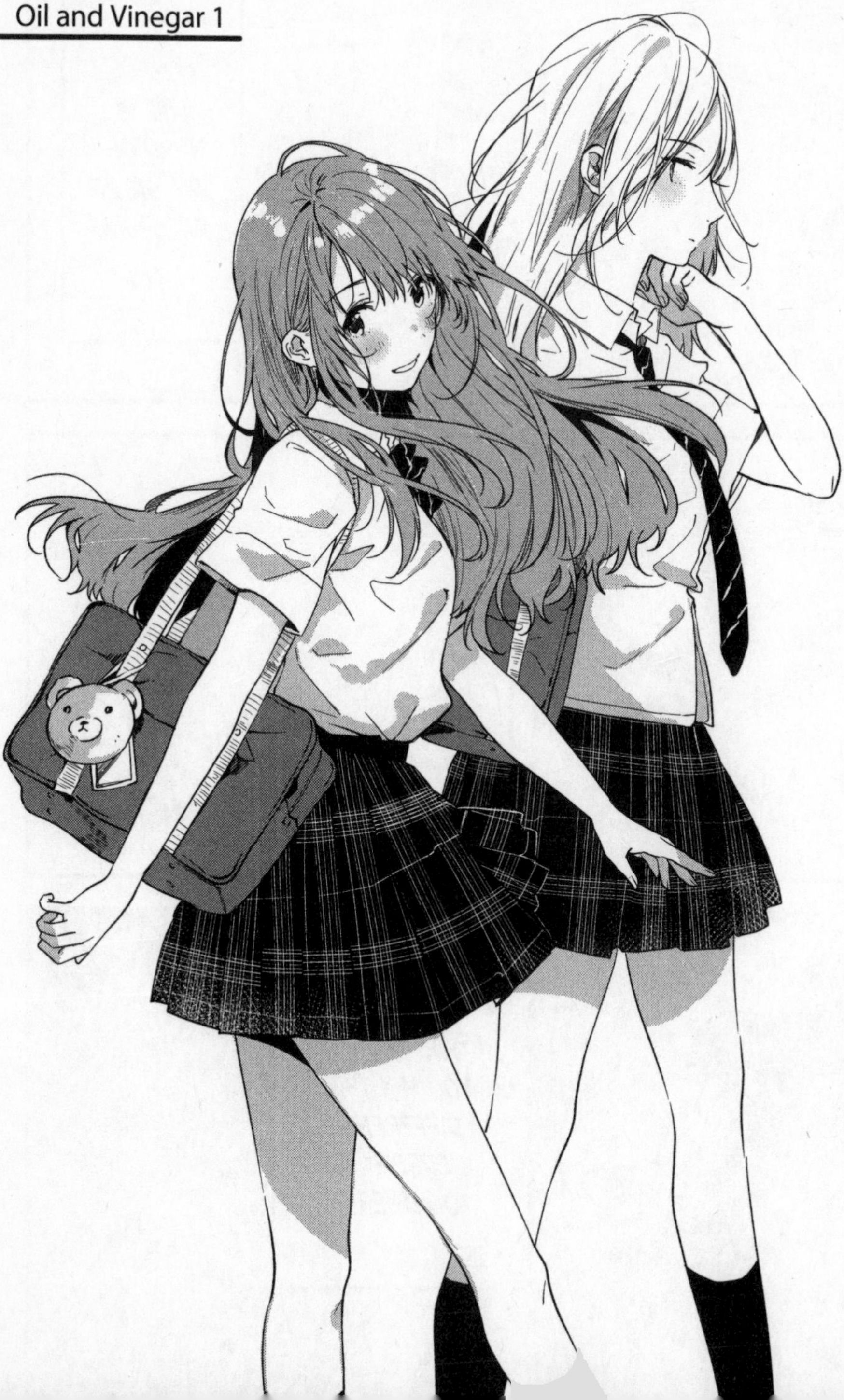

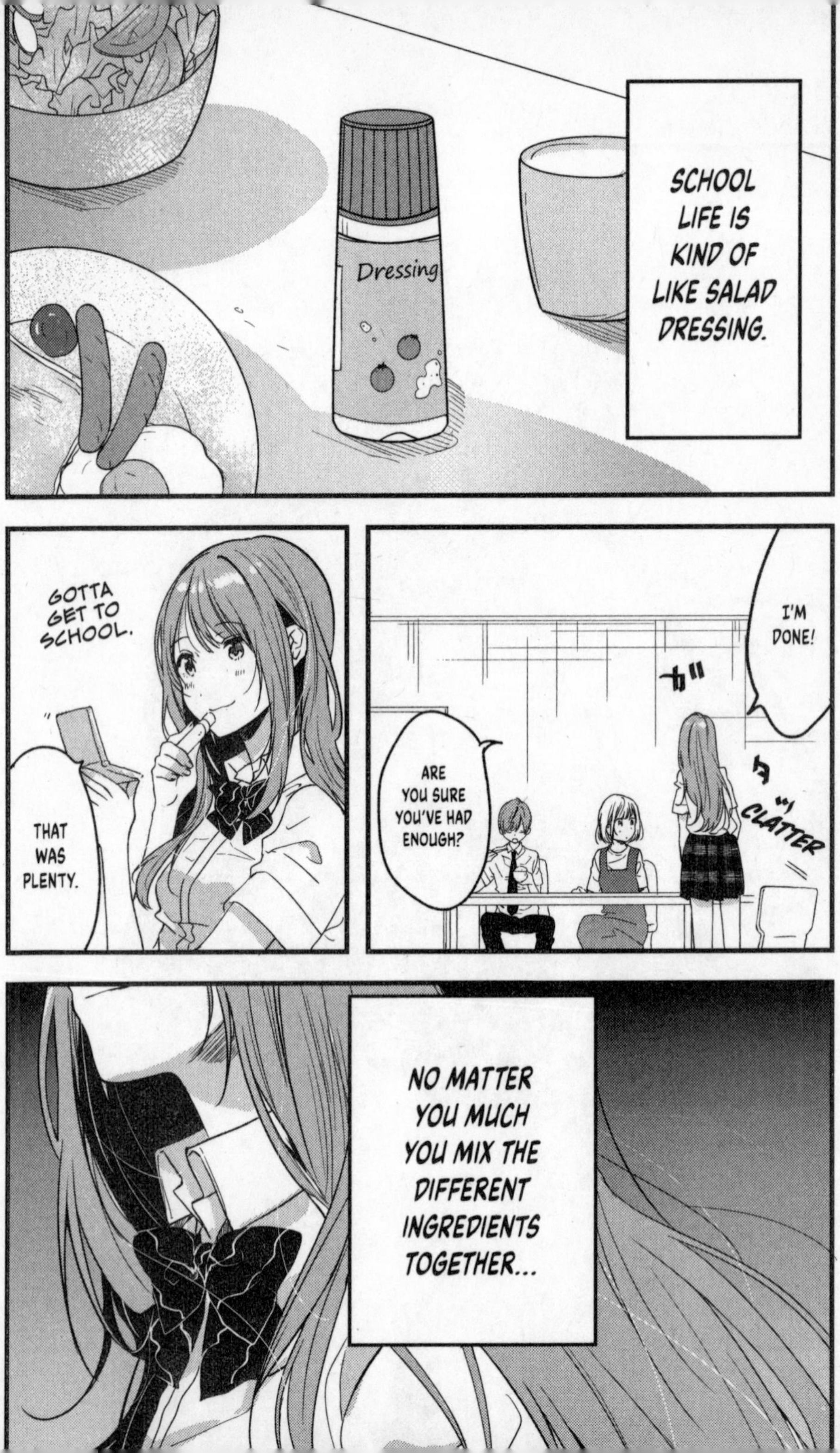
SCHOOL LIFE IS KIND OF LIKE SALAD DRESSING.
Dressing
I'M DONE!
ガ"
CLATTER
ARE YOU SURE YOU'VE HAD ENOUGH?
GOTTA GET TO SCHOOL.
THAT WAS PLENTY.
NO MATTER YOU MUCH YOU MIX THE DIFFERENT INGREDIENTS TOGETHER...

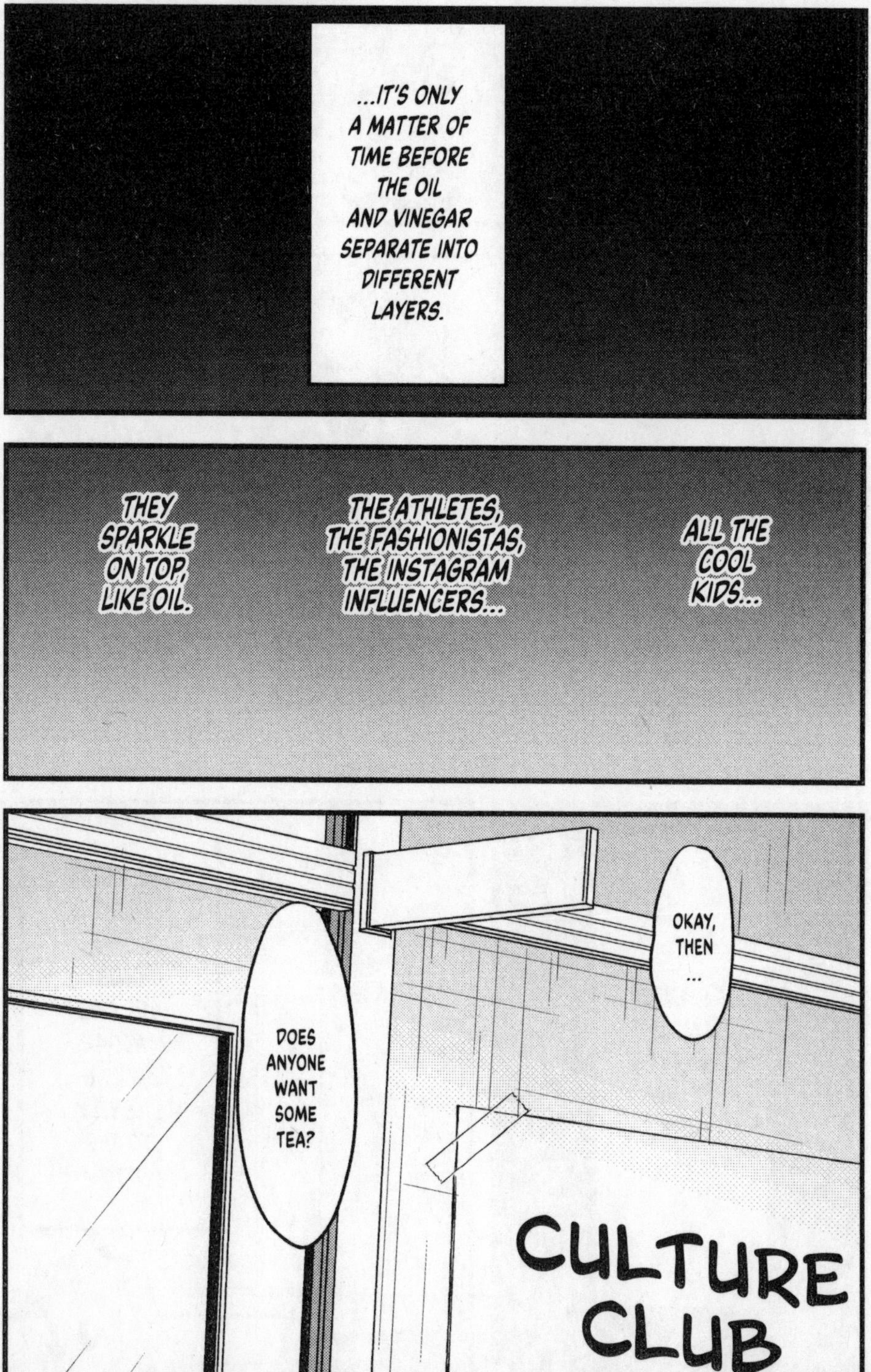
...IT'S ONLY A MATTER OF TIME BEFORE THE OIL AND VINEGAR SEPARATE INTO DIFFERENT LAYERS.
ALL THE COOL KIDS...
THE ATHLETES, THE FASHIONISTAS, THE INSTAGRAM INFLUENCERS...
THEY SPARKLE ON TOP, LIKE OIL.
OKAY, THEN ...
DOES ANYONE WANT SOME TEA?
CULTURE CLUB

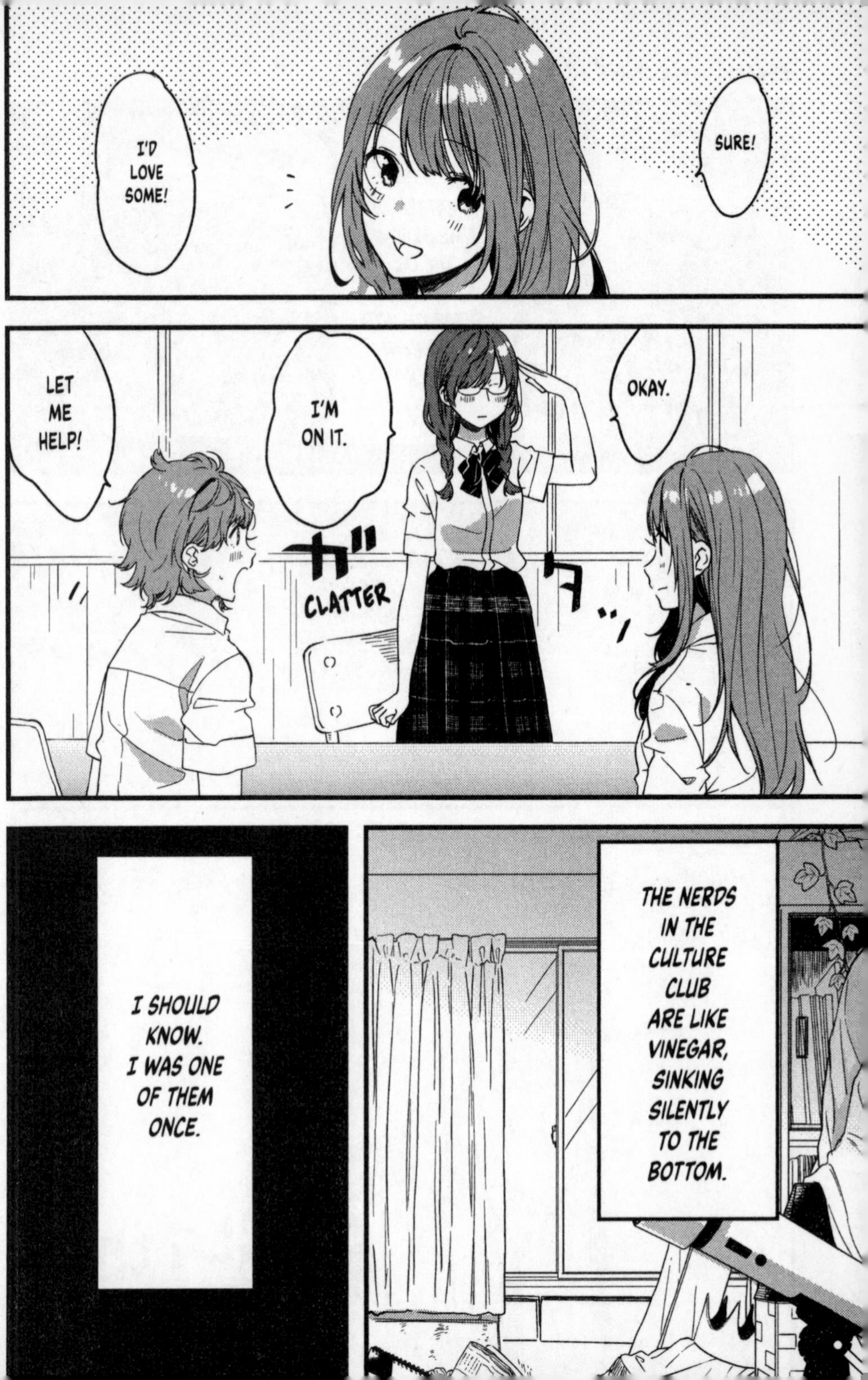
SURE!
I'D LOVE SOME!
OKAY.
I'M ON IT.
ガッ CLATTER
LET ME HELP!
THE NERDS IN THE CULTURE CLUB ARE LIKE VINEGAR, SINKING SILENTLY TO THE BOTTOM.
I SHOULD KNOW. I WAS ONE OF THEM ONCE.

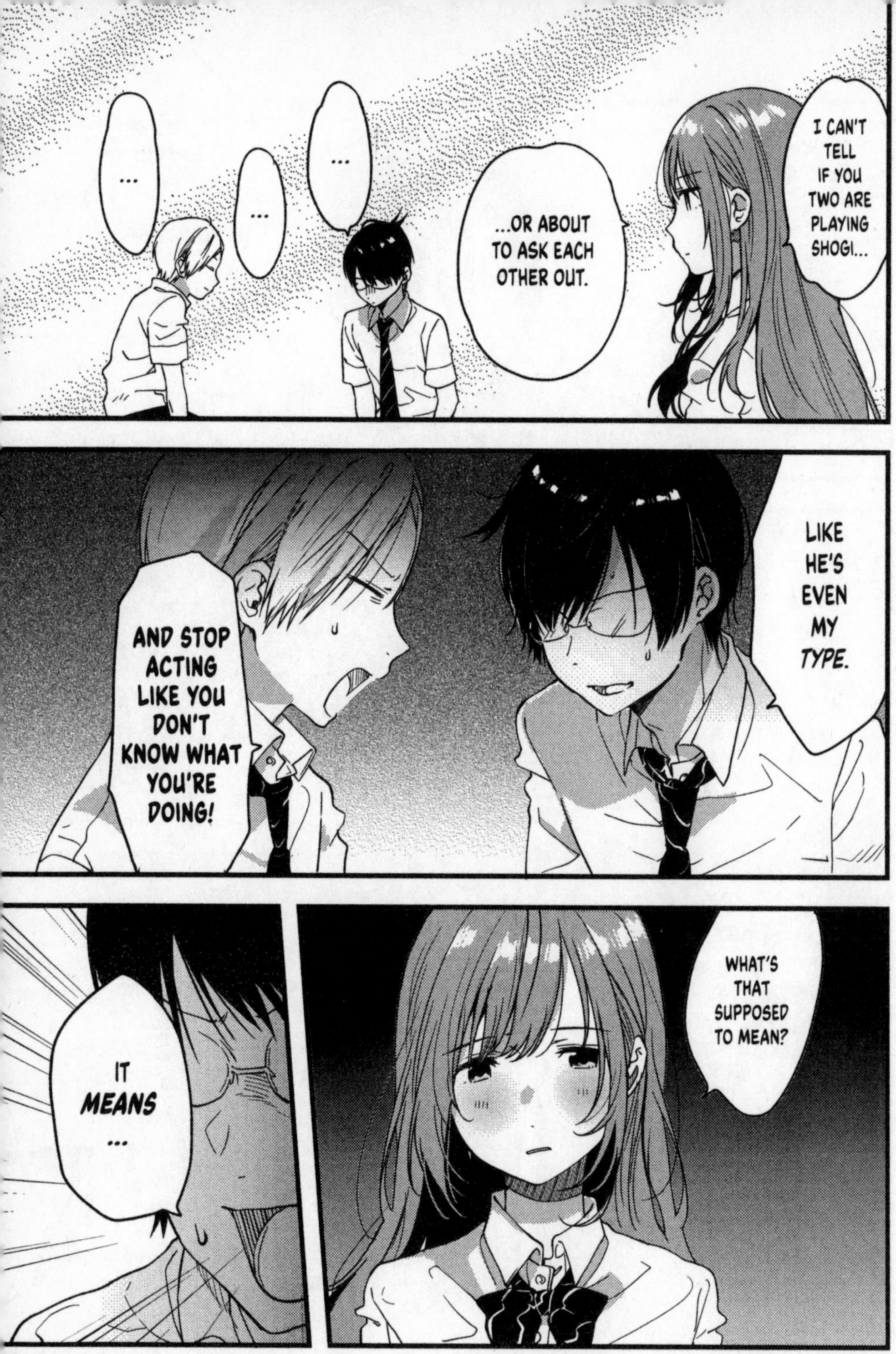
I CAN'T TELL IF YOU TWO ARE PLAYING SHOGI...
...OR ABOUT TO ASK EACH OTHER OUT.
...
...
...
LIKE HE'S EVEN MY *TYPE*.
AND STOP ACTING LIKE YOU DON'T KNOW WHAT YOU'RE DOING!
WHAT'S THAT SUPPOSED TO MEAN?
IT *MEANS* ...

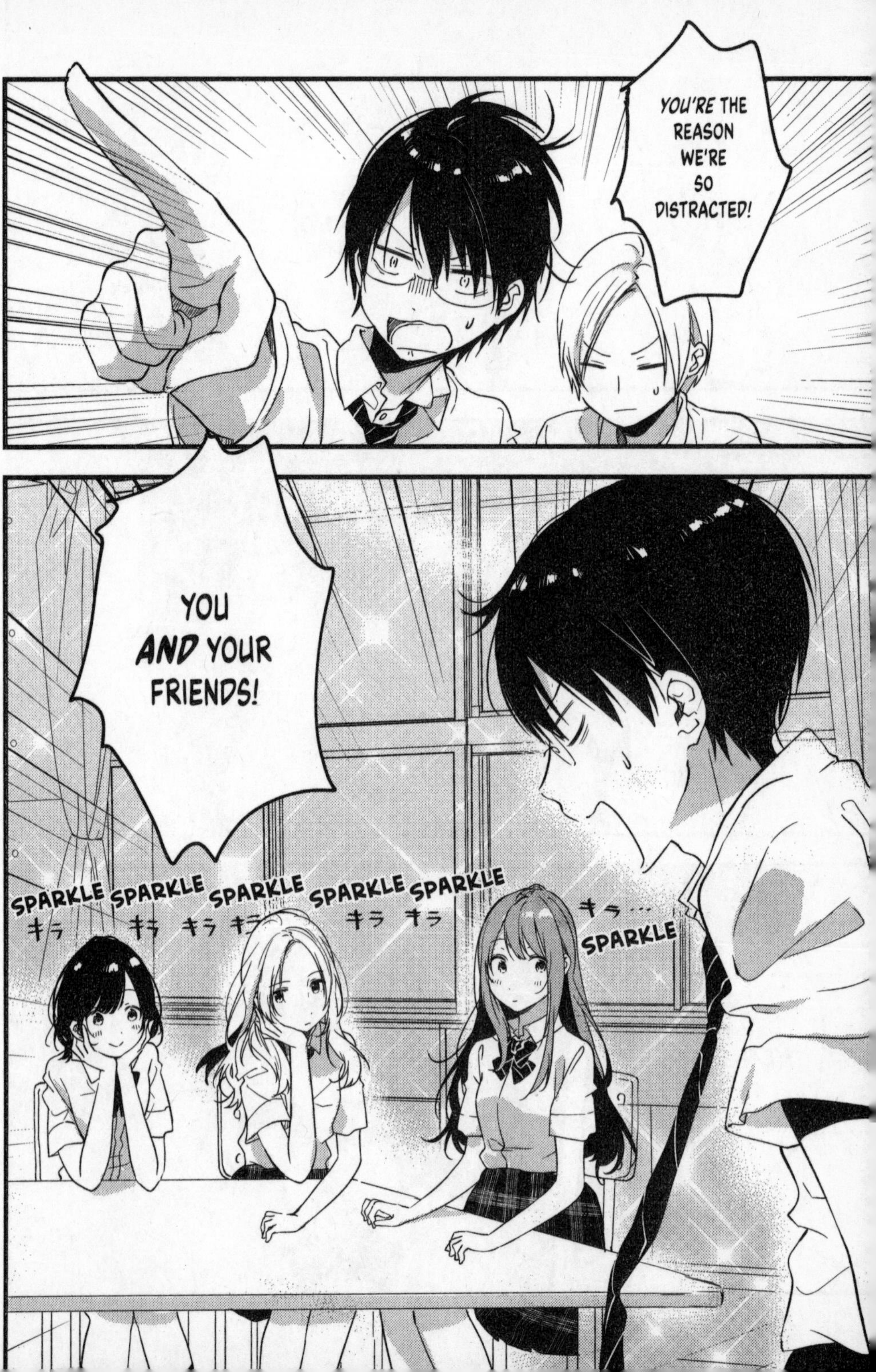
YOU'RE THE REASON WE'RE SO DISTRACTED!
YOU AND YOUR FRIENDS!
キラ…
SPARKLE
SPARKLE
キラ
SPARKLE
キラ
SPARKLE
キラ キラ
SPARKLE
キラ
SPARKLE
キラ

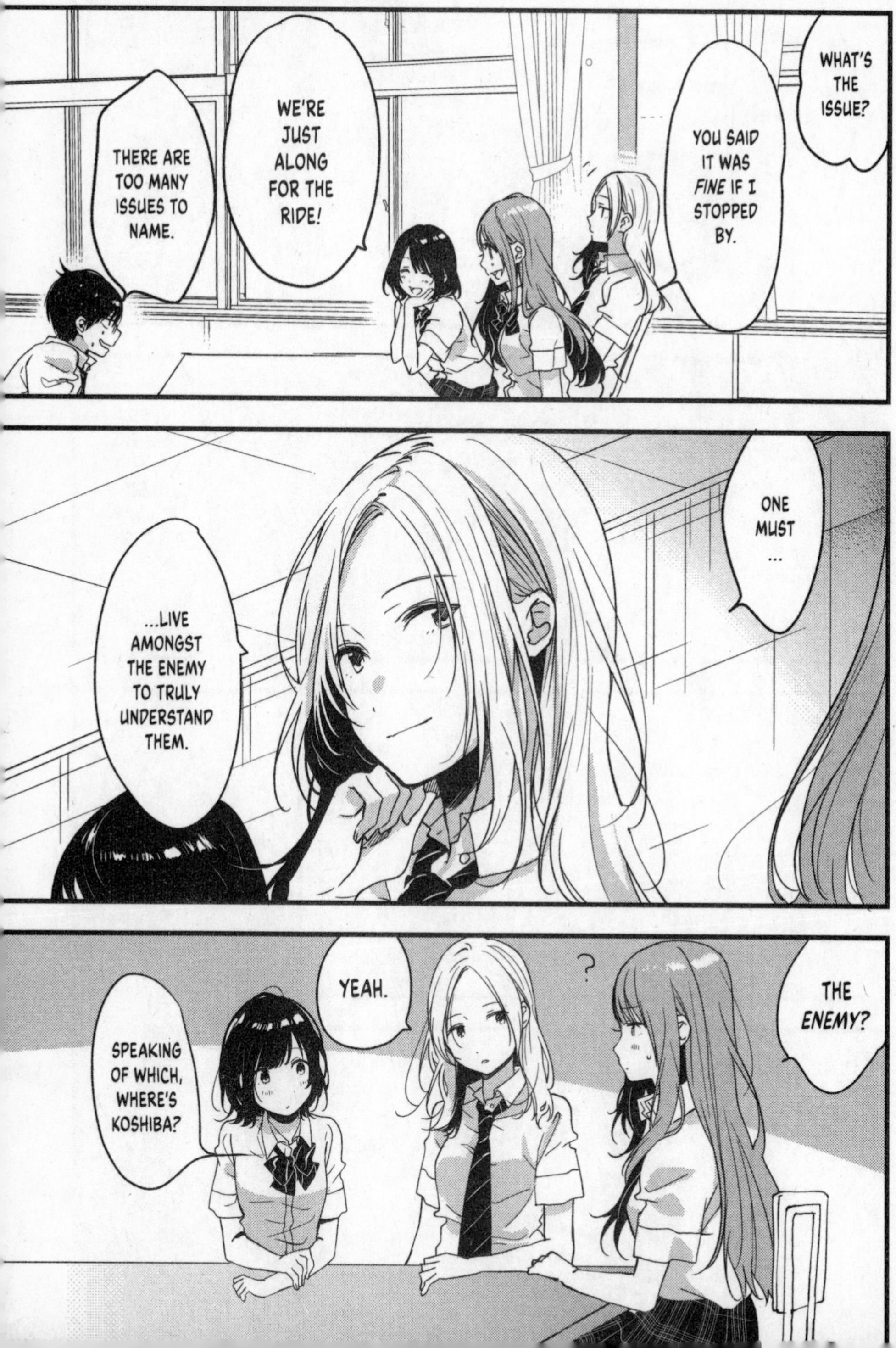
WHAT'S THE ISSUE?
YOU SAID IT WAS *FINE* IF I STOPPED BY.
WE'RE JUST ALONG FOR THE RIDE!
THERE ARE TOO MANY ISSUES TO NAME.
ONE MUST ...
...LIVE AMONGST THE ENEMY TO TRULY UNDERSTAND THEM.
THE *ENEMY?*
?
YEAH.
SPEAKING OF WHICH, WHERE'S KOSHIBA?

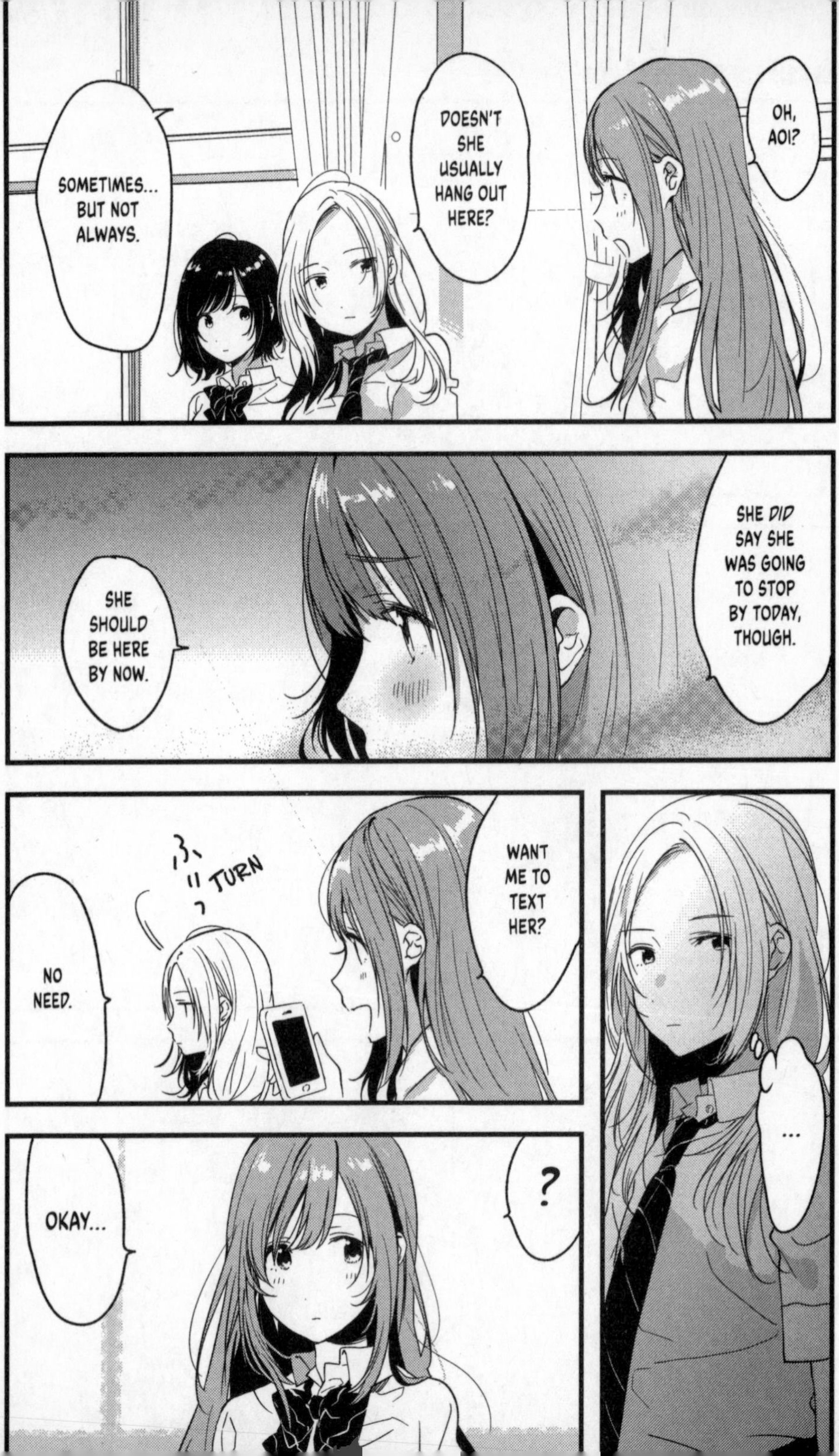
OH, AOI?
DOESN'T SHE USUALLY HANG OUT HERE?
SOMETIMES... BUT NOT ALWAYS.
SHE *DID* SAY SHE WAS GOING TO STOP BY TODAY, THOUGH.
SHE SHOULD BE HERE BY NOW.
...
WANT ME TO TEXT HER?
TURN
NO NEED.
?
OKAY...

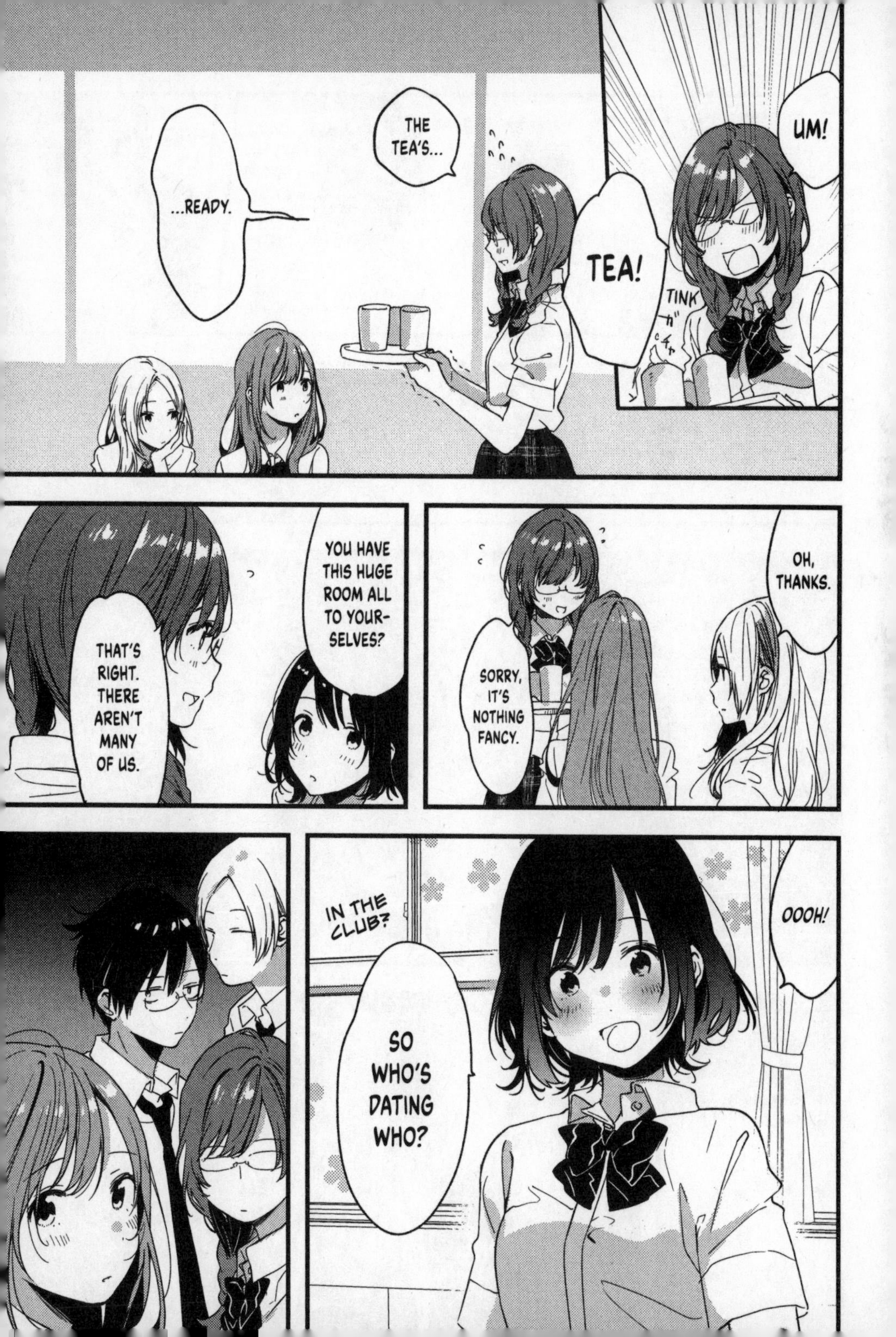
UM!
TEA!
TINK
THE TEA'S...
...READY.
OH, THANKS.
SORRY, IT'S NOTHING FANCY.
YOU HAVE THIS HUGE ROOM ALL TO YOUR-SELVES?
THAT'S RIGHT. THERE AREN'T MANY OF US.
OOOH!
SO WHO'S DATING WHO?
IN THE CLUB?

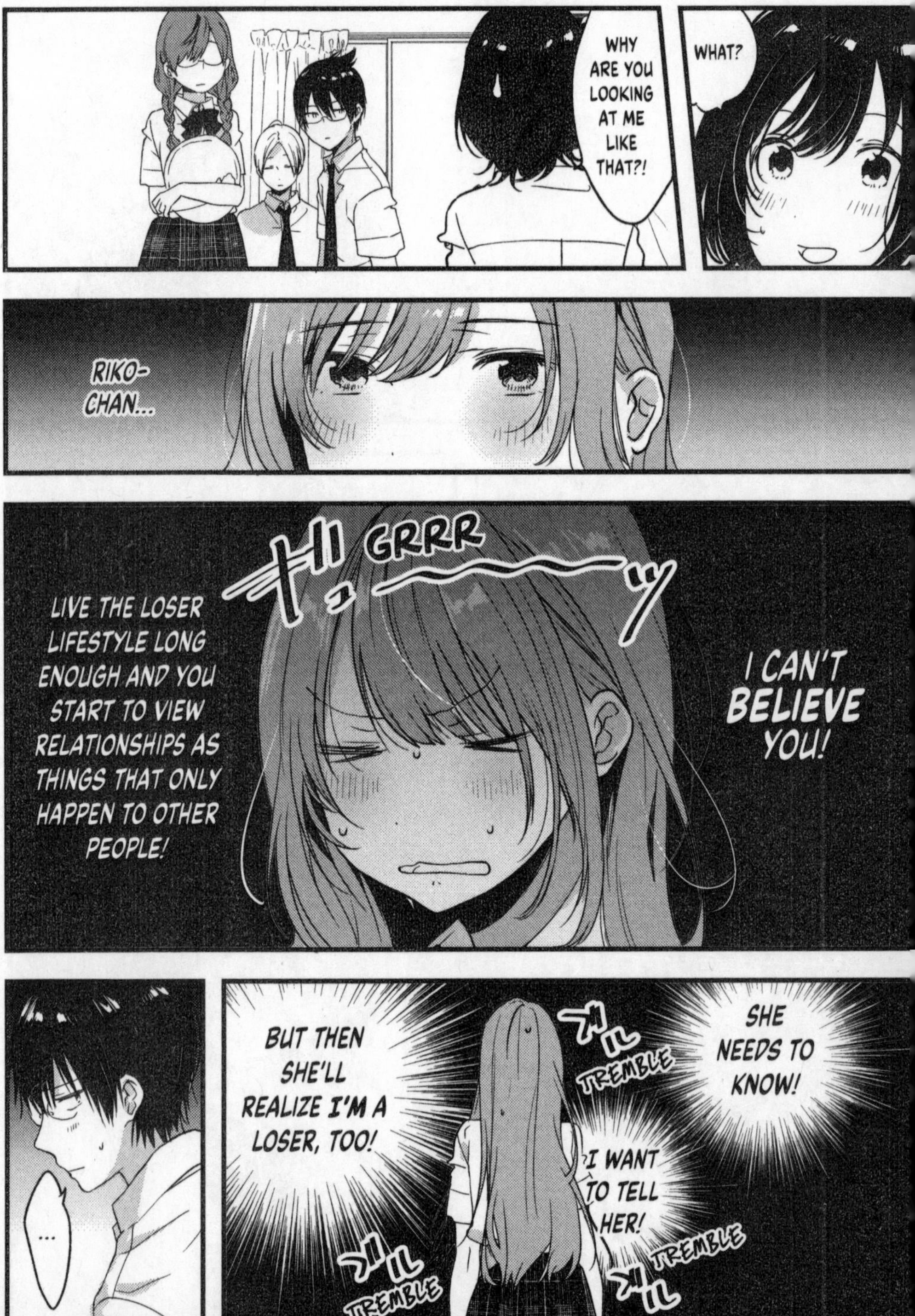
WHAT?
WHY ARE YOU LOOKING AT ME LIKE THAT?!
RIKO-CHAN...
GRRR
I CAN'T BELIEVE YOU!
LIVE THE LOSER LIFESTYLE LONG ENOUGH AND YOU START TO VIEW RELATIONSHIPS AS THINGS THAT ONLY HAPPEN TO OTHER PEOPLE!
SHE NEEDS TO KNOW!
TREMBLE
I WANT TO TELL HER!
TREMBLE
BUT THEN SHE'LL REALIZE I'M A LOSER, TOO!
TREMBLE
...

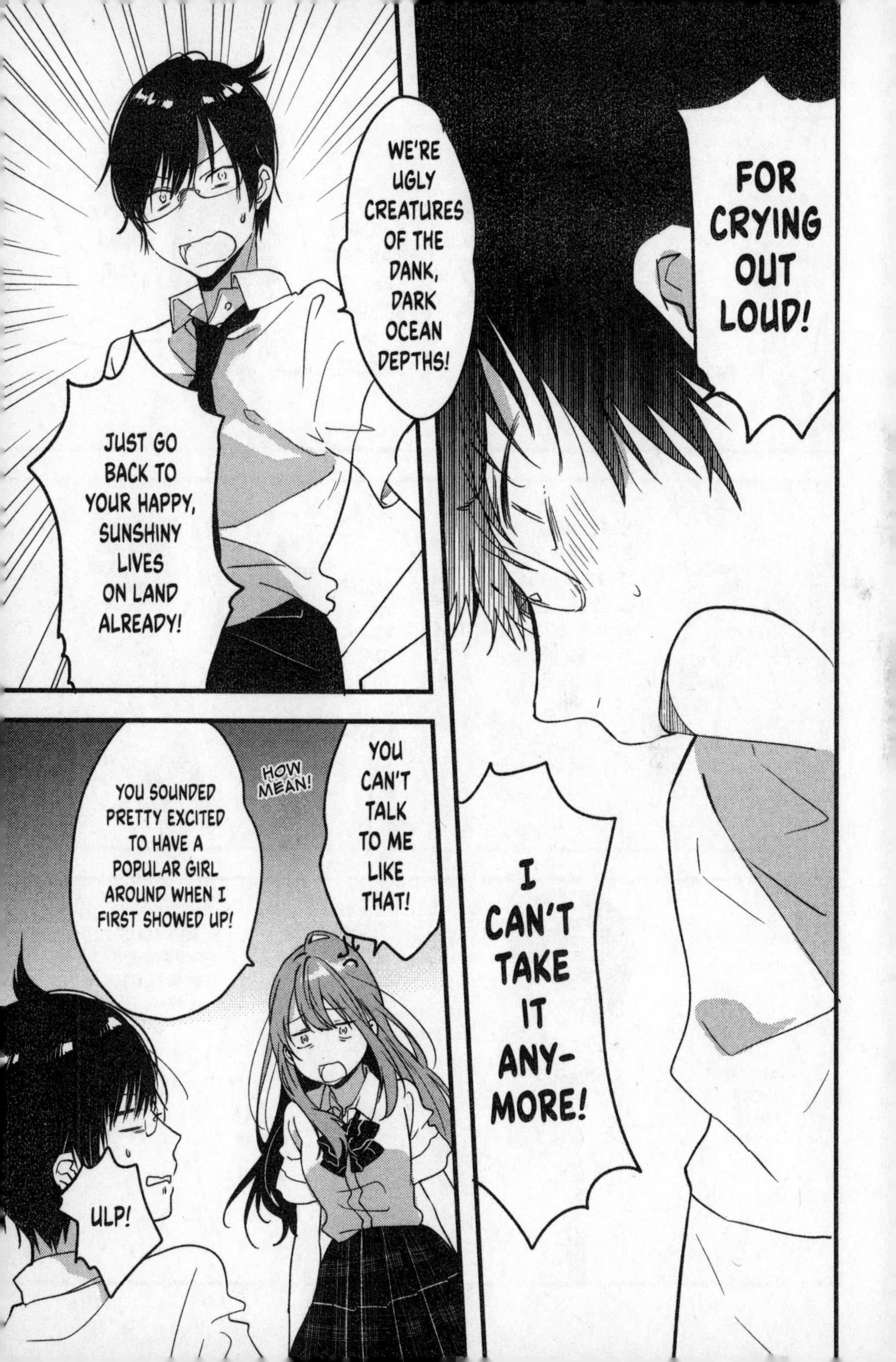
FOR CRYING OUT LOUD!
I CAN'T TAKE IT ANY-MORE!
WE'RE UGLY CREATURES OF THE DANK, DARK OCEAN DEPTHS!
JUST GO BACK TO YOUR HAPPY, SUNSHINY LIVES ON LAND ALREADY!
YOU CAN'T TALK TO ME LIKE THAT!
HOW MEAN!
YOU SOUNDED PRETTY EXCITED TO HAVE A POPULAR GIRL AROUND WHEN I FIRST SHOWED UP!
ULP!

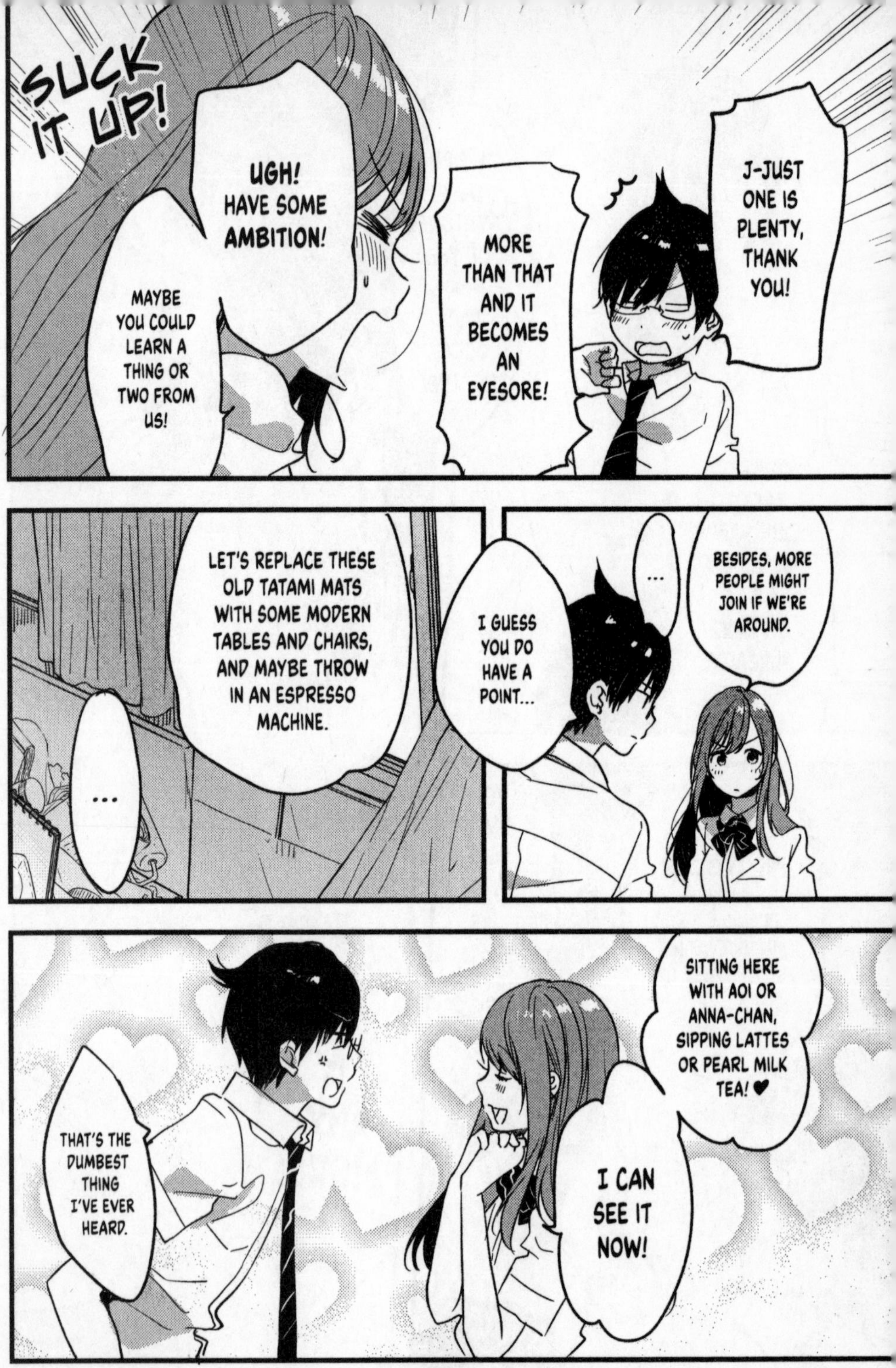
J-JUST ONE IS PLENTY, THANK YOU!
MORE THAN THAT AND IT BECOMES AN EYESORE!
UGH! HAVE SOME AMBITION!
SUCK IT UP!
MAYBE YOU COULD LEARN A THING OR TWO FROM US!
BESIDES, MORE PEOPLE MIGHT JOIN IF WE'RE AROUND.
...
I GUESS YOU DO HAVE A POINT...
LET'S REPLACE THESE OLD TATAMI MATS WITH SOME MODERN TABLES AND CHAIRS, AND MAYBE THROW IN AN ESPRESSO MACHINE.
...
SITTING HERE WITH AOI OR ANNA-CHAN, SIPPING LATTES OR PEARL MILK TEA! ♥
I CAN SEE IT NOW!
THAT'S THE DUMBEST THING I'VE EVER HEARD.

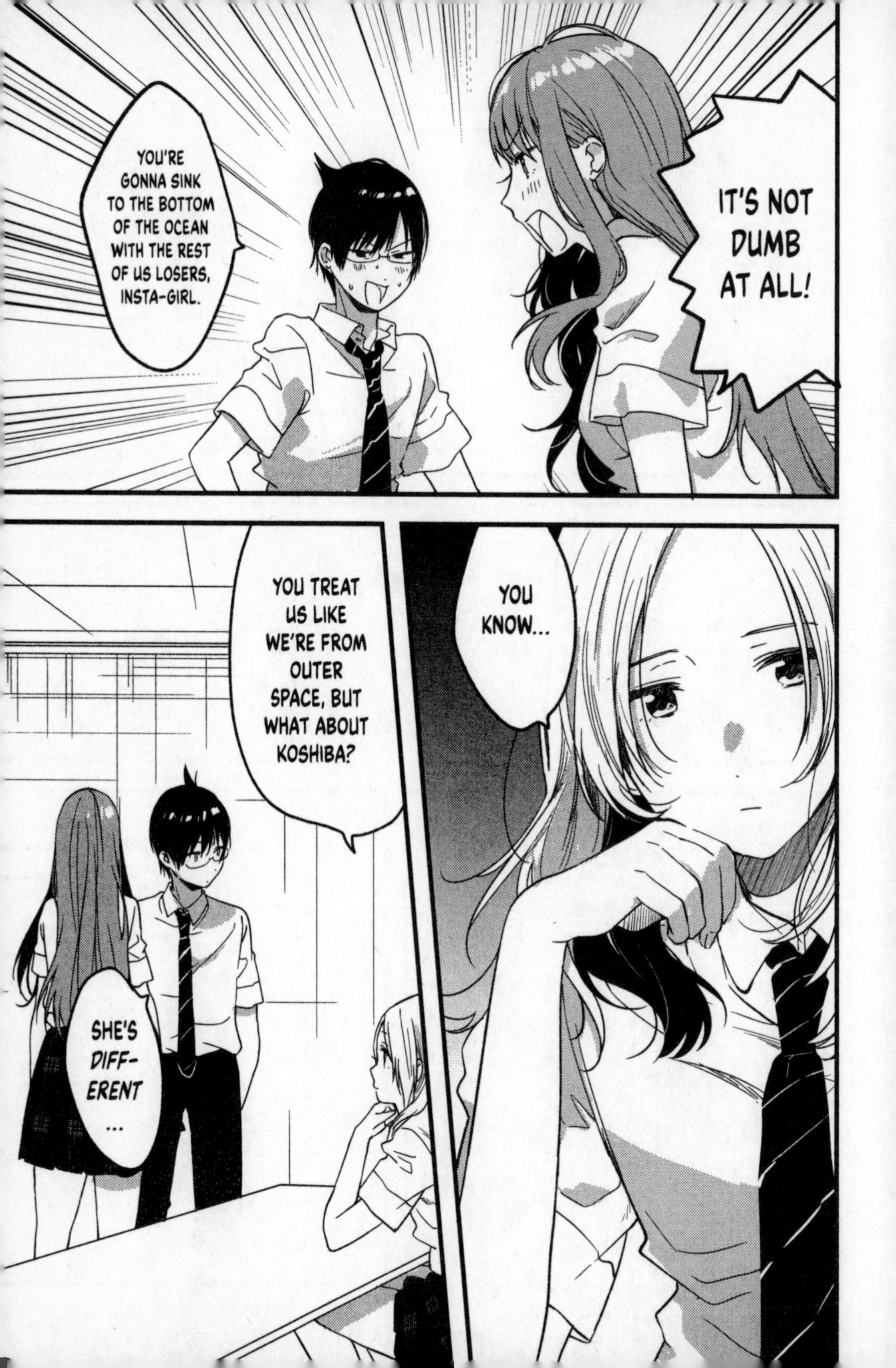
IT'S NOT DUMB AT ALL!
YOU'RE GONNA SINK TO THE BOTTOM OF THE OCEAN WITH THE REST OF US LOSERS, INSTA-GIRL.
YOU KNOW...
YOU TREAT US LIKE WE'RE FROM OUTER SPACE, BUT WHAT ABOUT KOSHIBA?
SHE'S DIFF-ERENT ...

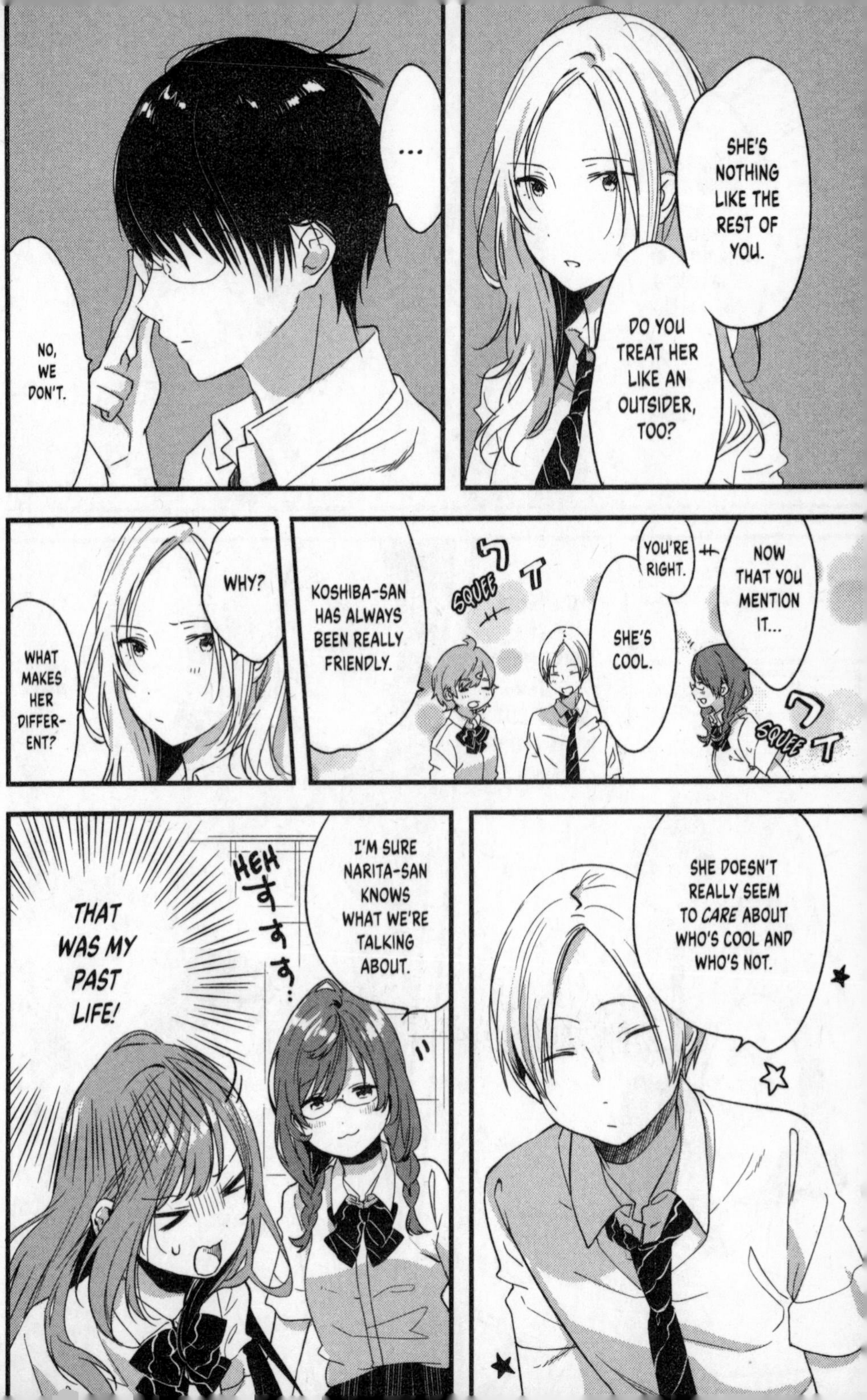
SHE'S NOTHING LIKE THE REST OF YOU.
DO YOU TREAT HER LIKE AN OUTSIDER, TOO?
...
NO, WE DON'T.
NOW THAT YOU MENTION IT...
YOU'RE RIGHT.
SQUEE
SHE'S COOL.
SQUEE
KOSHIBA-SAN HAS ALWAYS BEEN REALLY FRIENDLY.
WHY?
WHAT MAKES HER DIFFERENT?
SHE DOESN'T REALLY SEEM TO *CARE* ABOUT WHO'S COOL AND WHO'S NOT.
I'M SURE NARITA-SAN KNOWS WHAT WE'RE TALKING ABOUT.
HEH すすす
THAT WAS MY PAST LIFE!

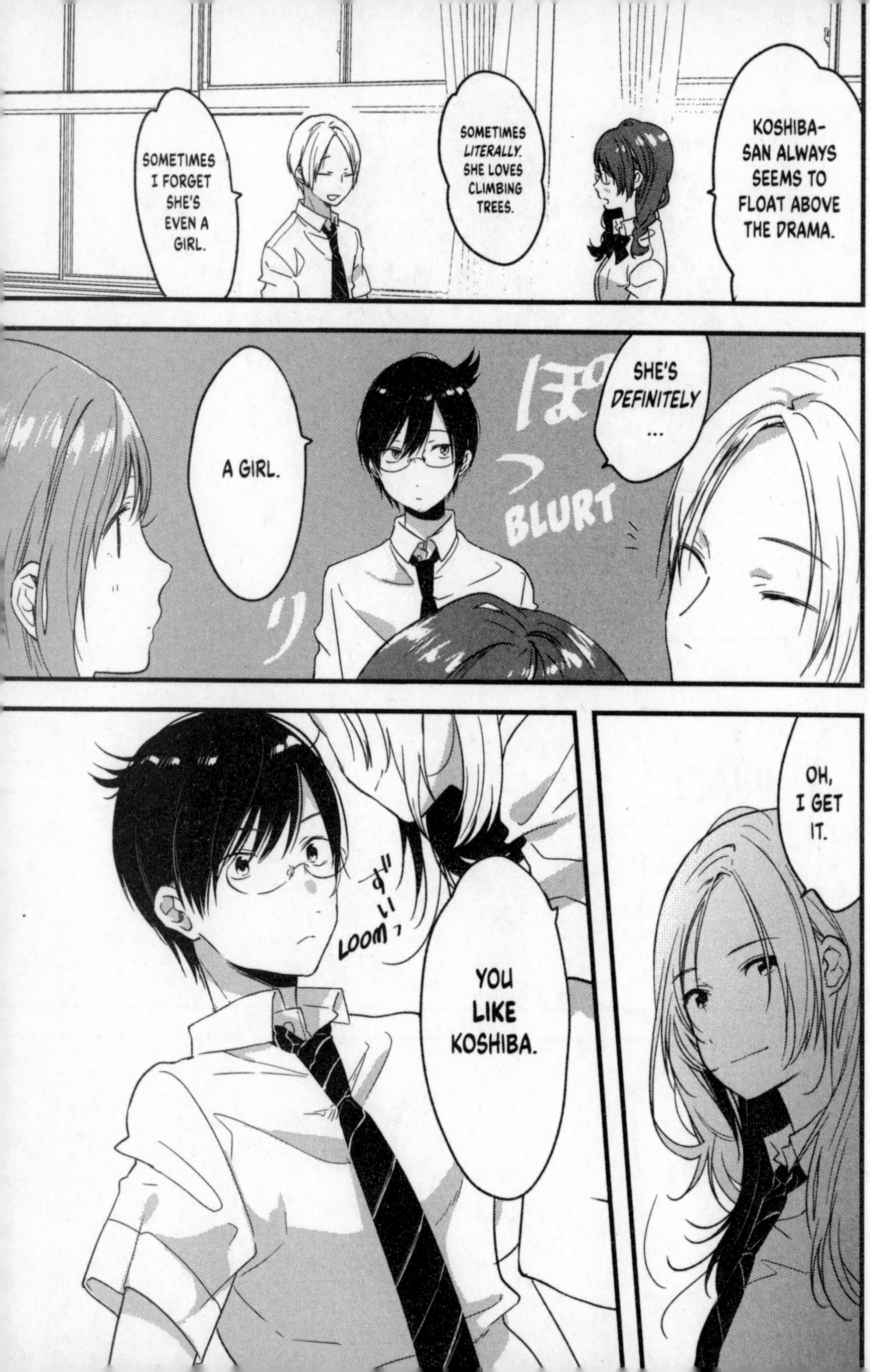
KOSHIBA-SAN ALWAYS SEEMS TO FLOAT ABOVE THE DRAMA.
SOMETIMES LITERALLY. SHE LOVES CLIMBING TREES.
SOMETIMES I FORGET SHE'S EVEN A GIRL.
SHE'S DEFINITELY ...
BLURT
A GIRL.
OH, I GET IT.
YOU LIKE KOSHIBA.
LOOM

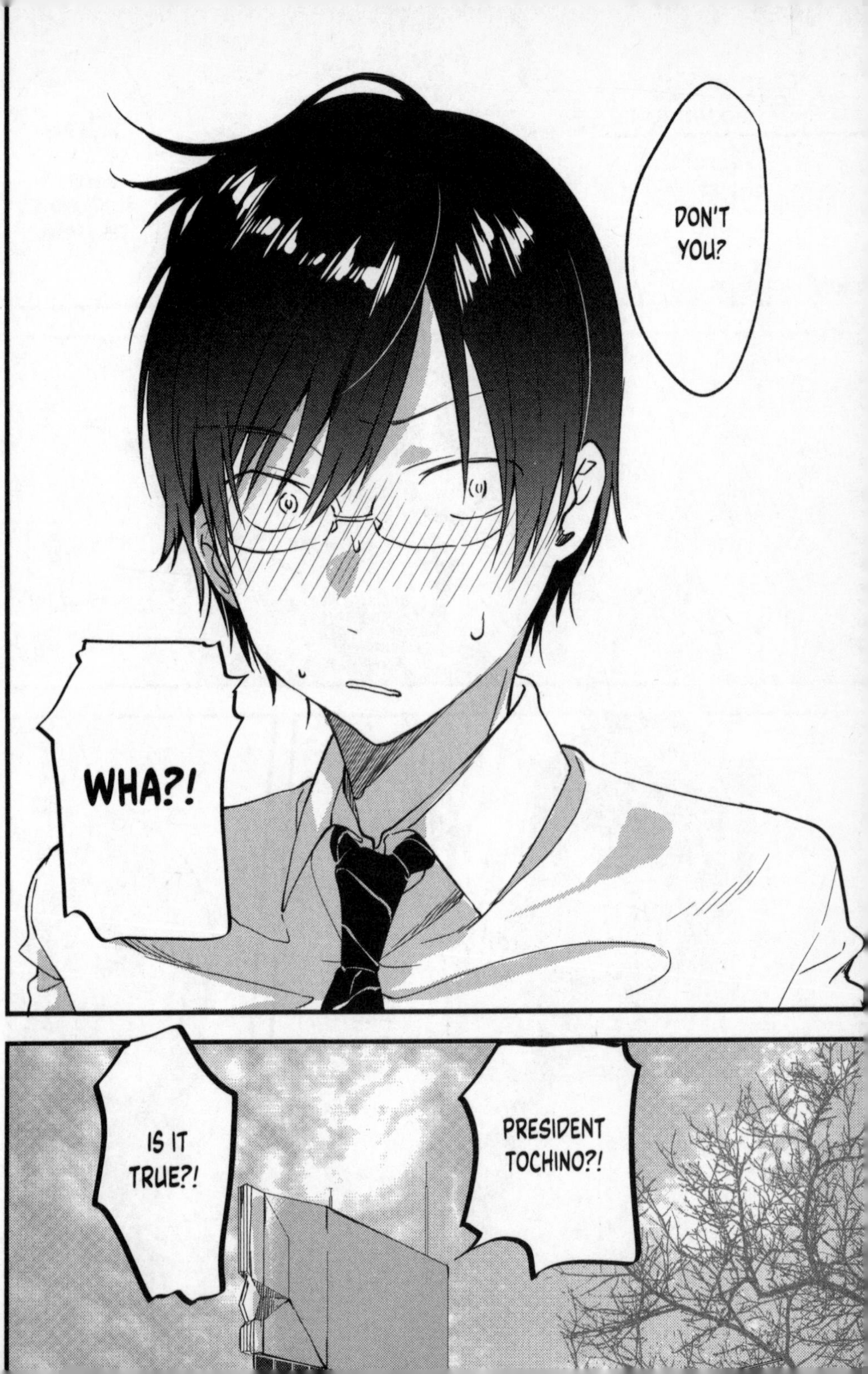
DON'T YOU?
WHA?!
PRESIDENT TOCHINO?!
IS IT TRUE?!

Chapter 12:
Oil and Vinegar 2

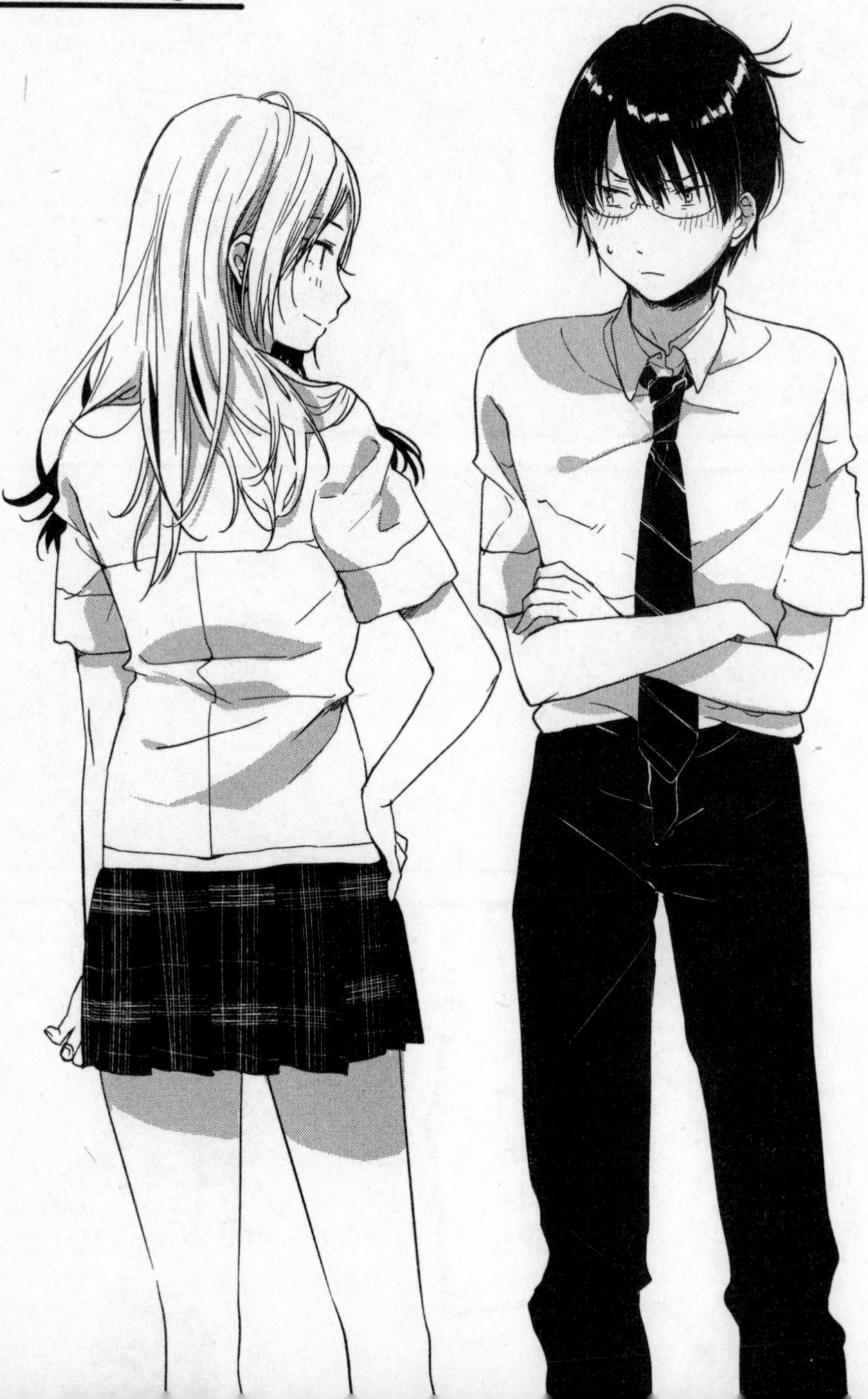

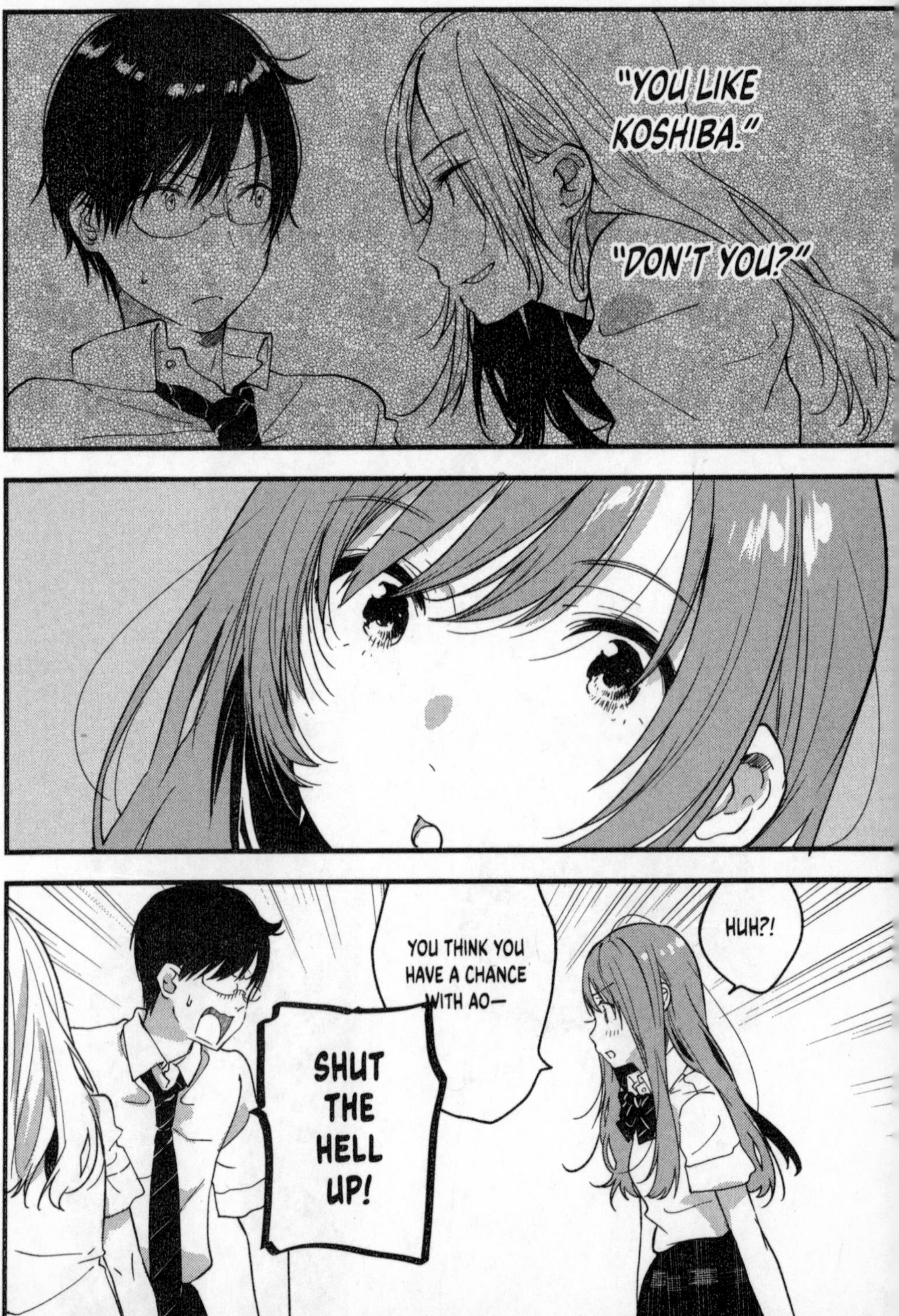
"YOU LIKE KOSHIBA."
"DON'T YOU?"
HUH?!
YOU THINK YOU HAVE A CHANCE WITH AO—
SHUT THE HELL UP!

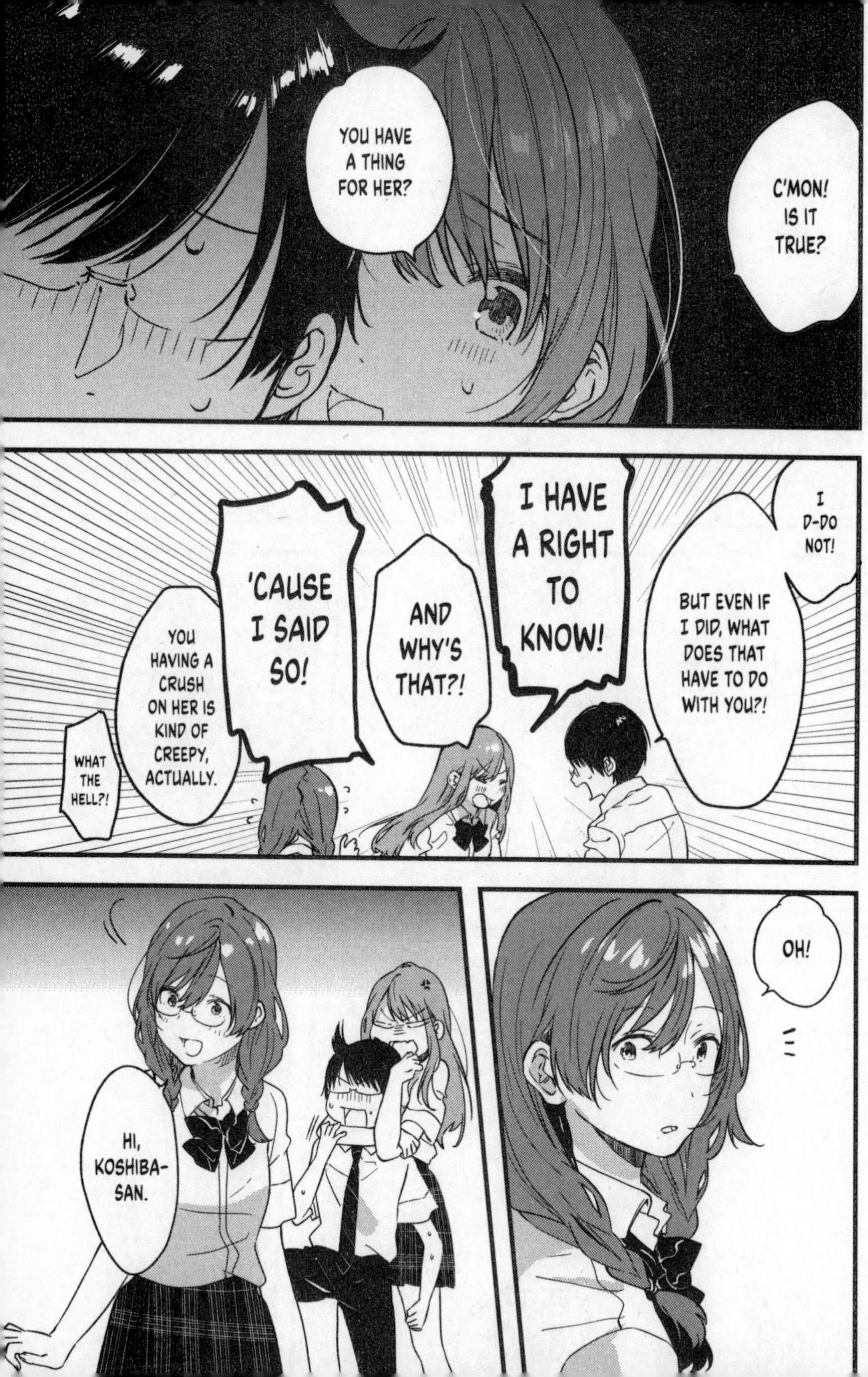
C'MON! IS IT TRUE?
YOU HAVE A THING FOR HER?
I D-DO NOT!
BUT EVEN IF I DID, WHAT DOES THAT HAVE TO DO WITH YOU?!
I HAVE A RIGHT TO KNOW!
AND WHY'S THAT?!
'CAUSE I SAID SO!
YOU HAVING A CRUSH ON HER IS KIND OF CREEPY, ACTUALLY.
WHAT THE HELL?!
OH!
HI, KOSHIBA-SAN.

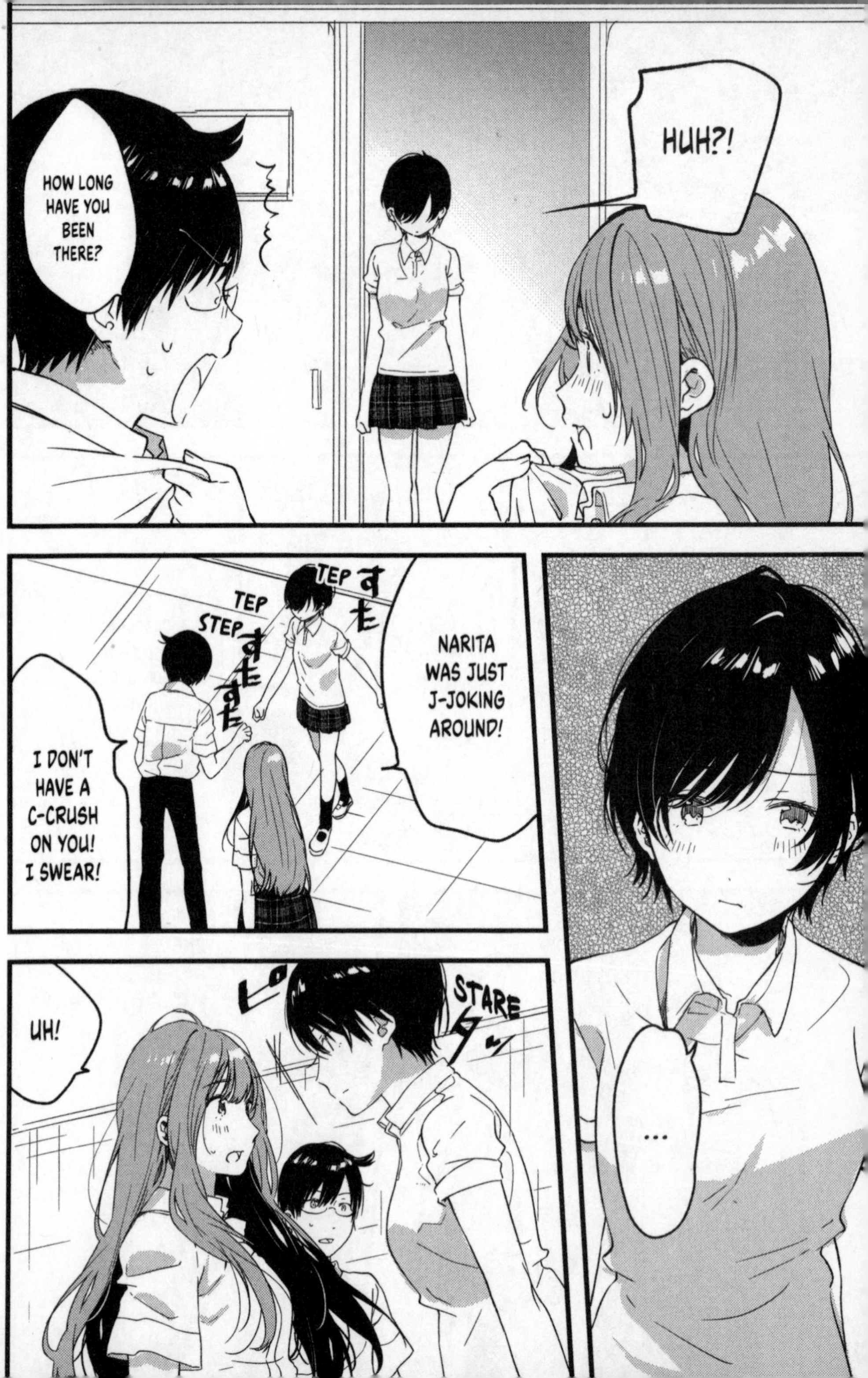
HUH?!
HOW LONG HAVE YOU BEEN THERE?
...
TEP
TEP
STEP
NARITA WAS JUST J-JOKING AROUND!
I DON'T HAVE A C-CRUSH ON YOU! I SWEAR!
STARE
UH!

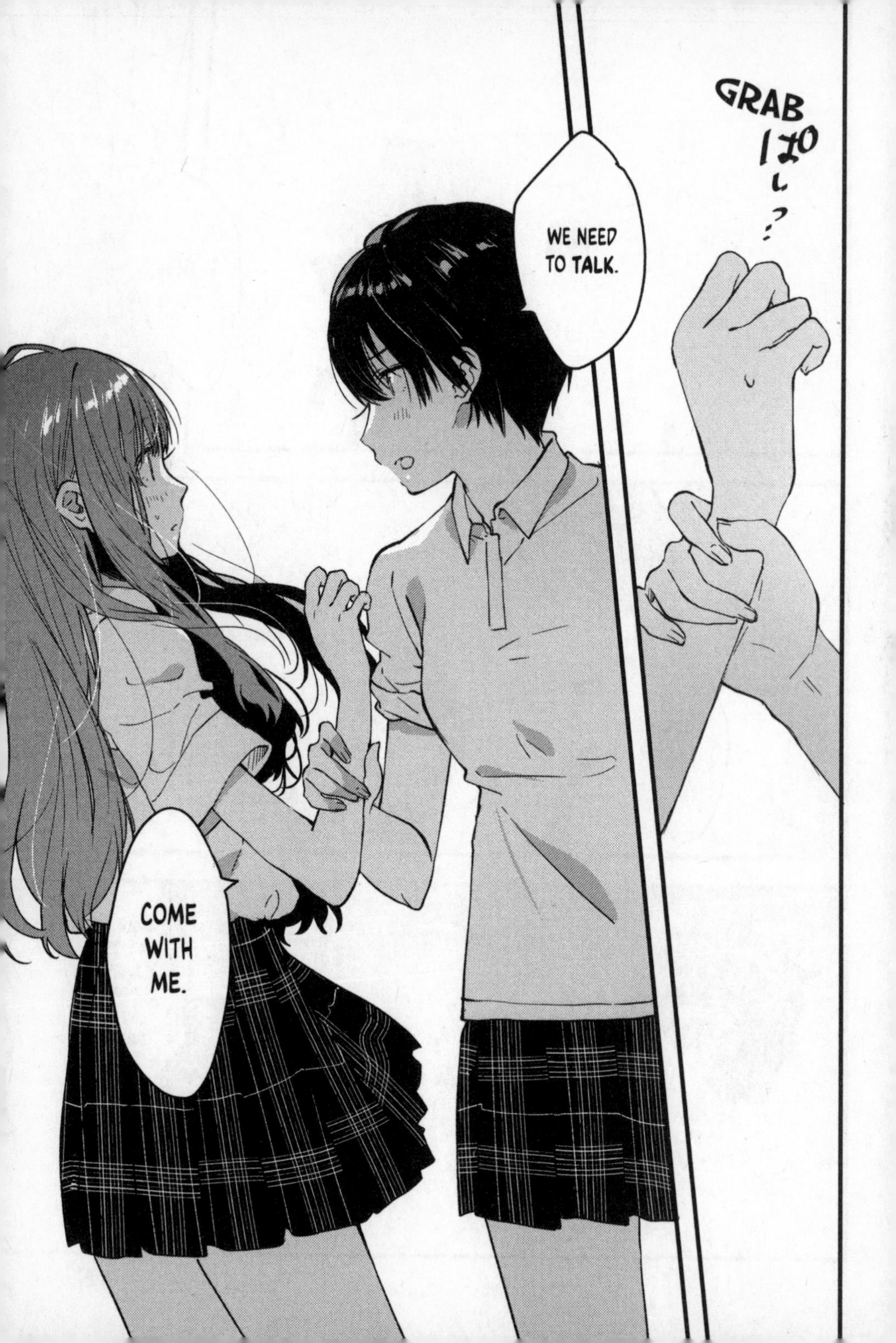
GRAB
ぱしっ
WE NEED TO TALK.
COME WITH ME.

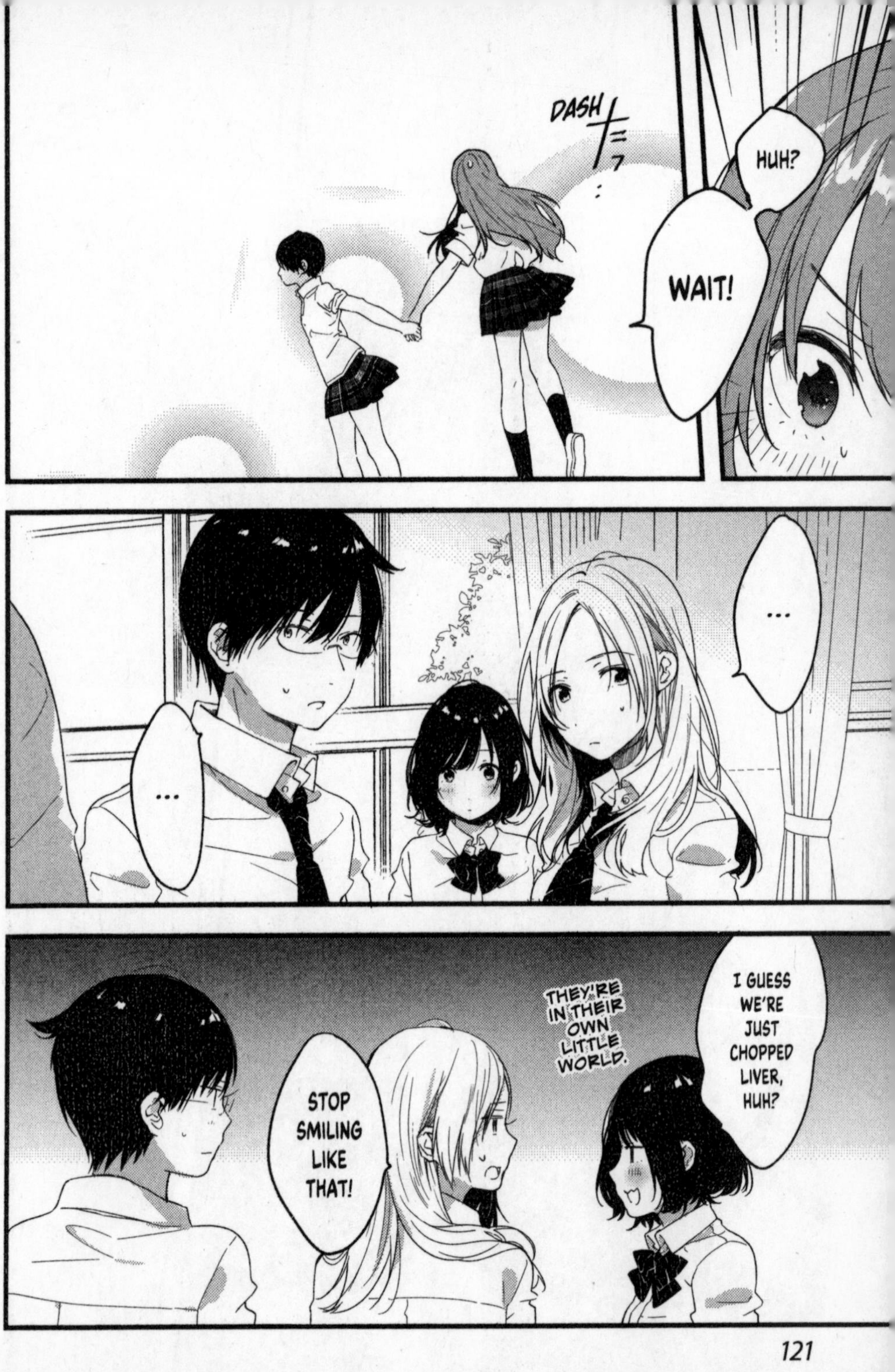
HUH?
WAIT!
DASH
...
...
I GUESS WE'RE JUST CHOPPED LIVER, HUH?
THEY'RE IN THEIR OWN LITTLE WORLD.
STOP SMILING LIKE THAT!

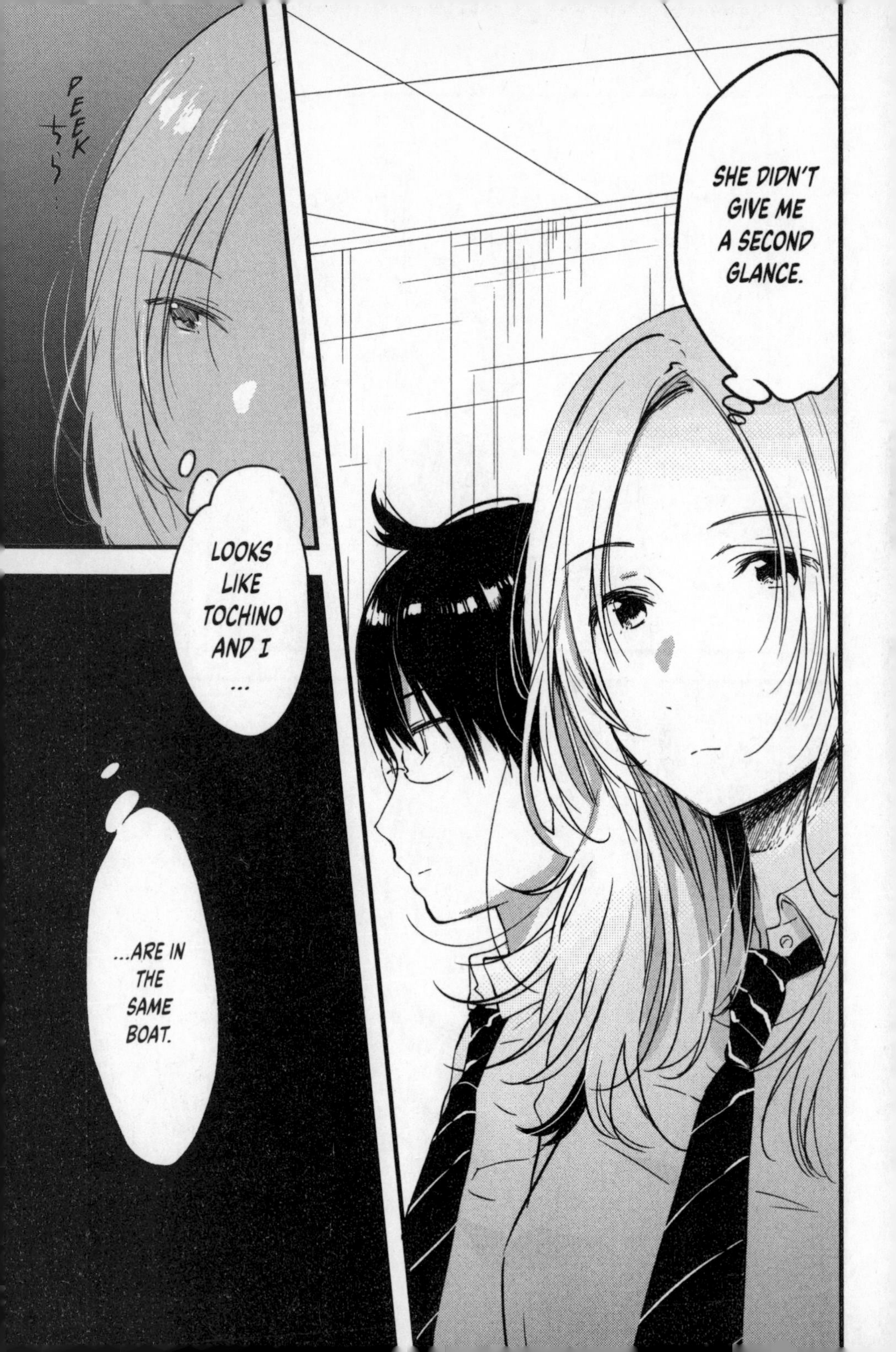
SHE DIDN'T GIVE ME A SECOND GLANCE.
PEEK
LOOKS LIKE TOCHINO AND I ...
...ARE IN THE SAME BOAT.

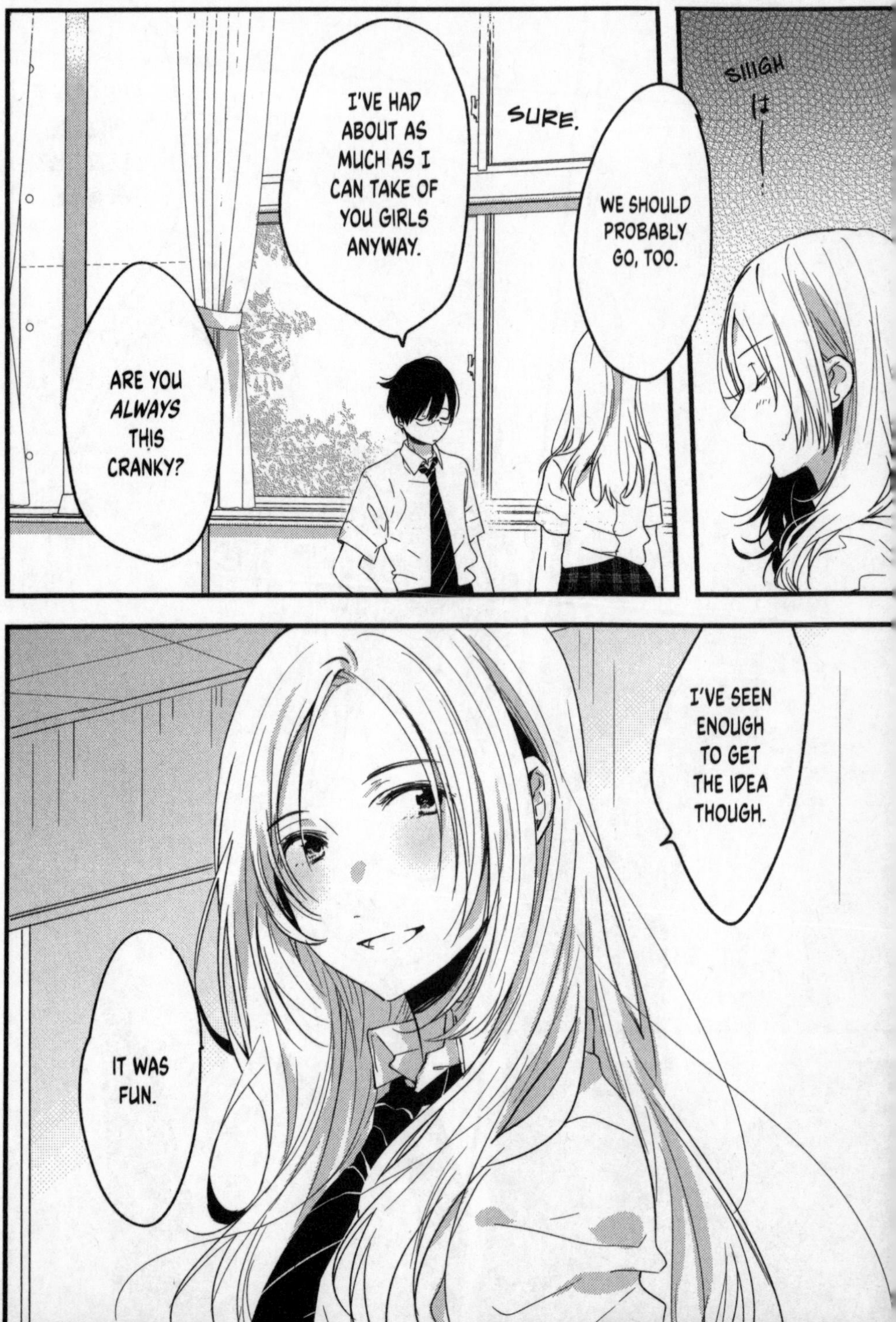
SIIIGH
は—
WE SHOULD PROBABLY GO, TOO.
SURE.
I'VE HAD ABOUT AS MUCH AS I CAN TAKE OF YOU GIRLS ANYWAY.
ARE YOU *ALWAYS* THIS CRANKY?
I'VE SEEN ENOUGH TO GET THE IDEA THOUGH.
IT WAS FUN.

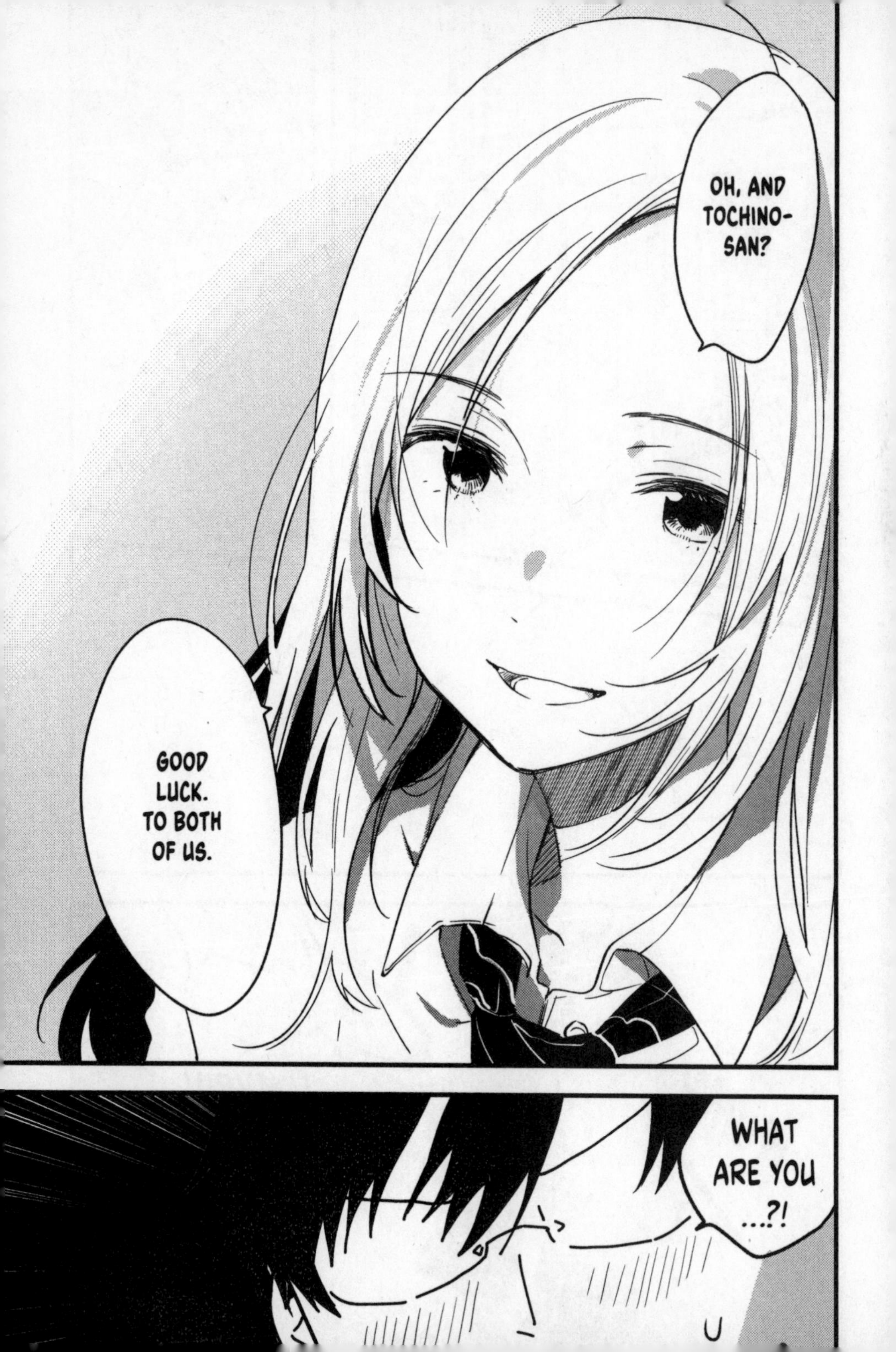
OH, AND TOCHINO-SAN?
GOOD LUCK. TO BOTH OF US.
WHAT ARE YOU ...?!

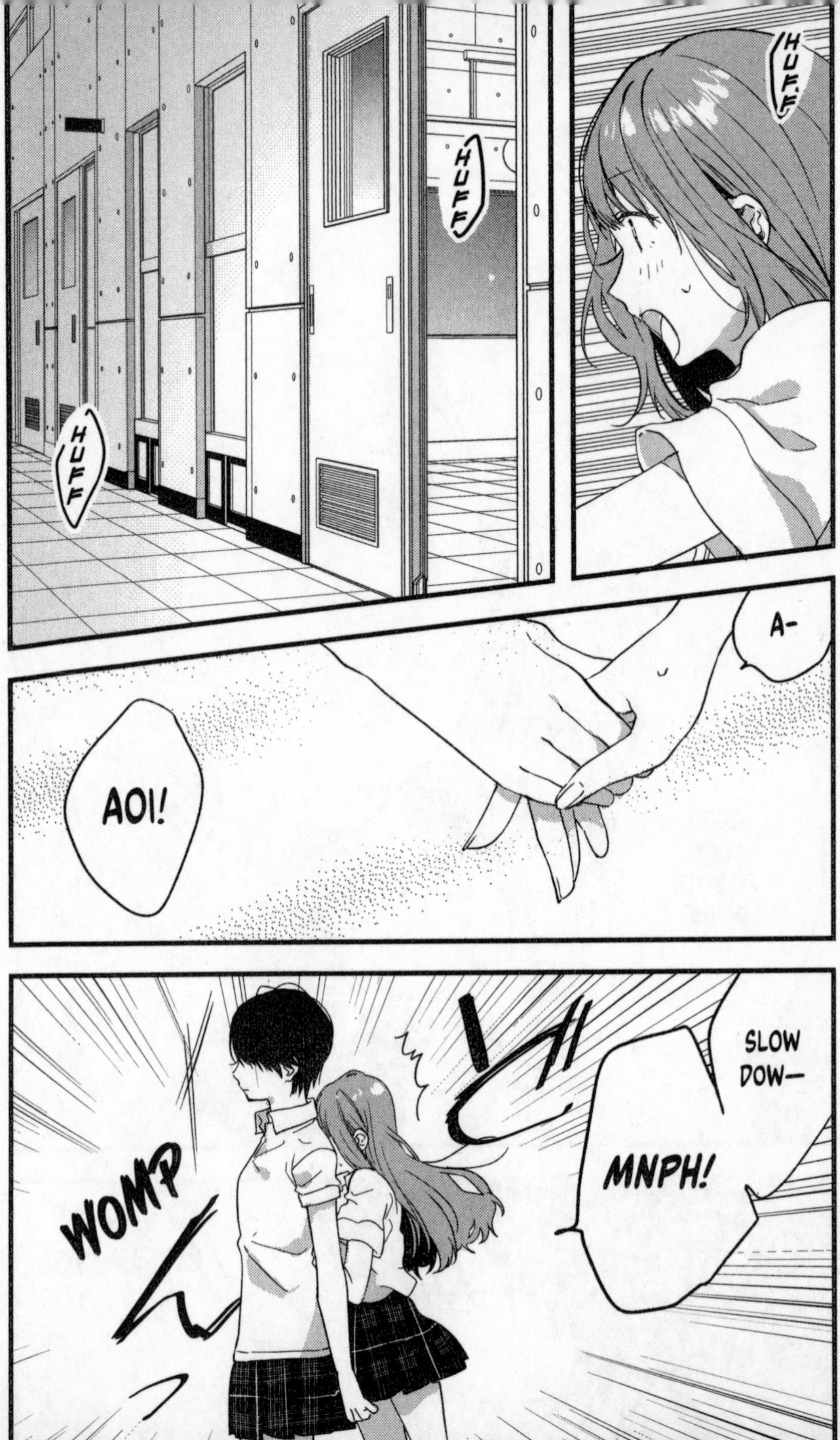
HUFF
HUFF
HUFF
HUFF
A-
AOI!
SLOW DOW—
MNPH!
WOMP

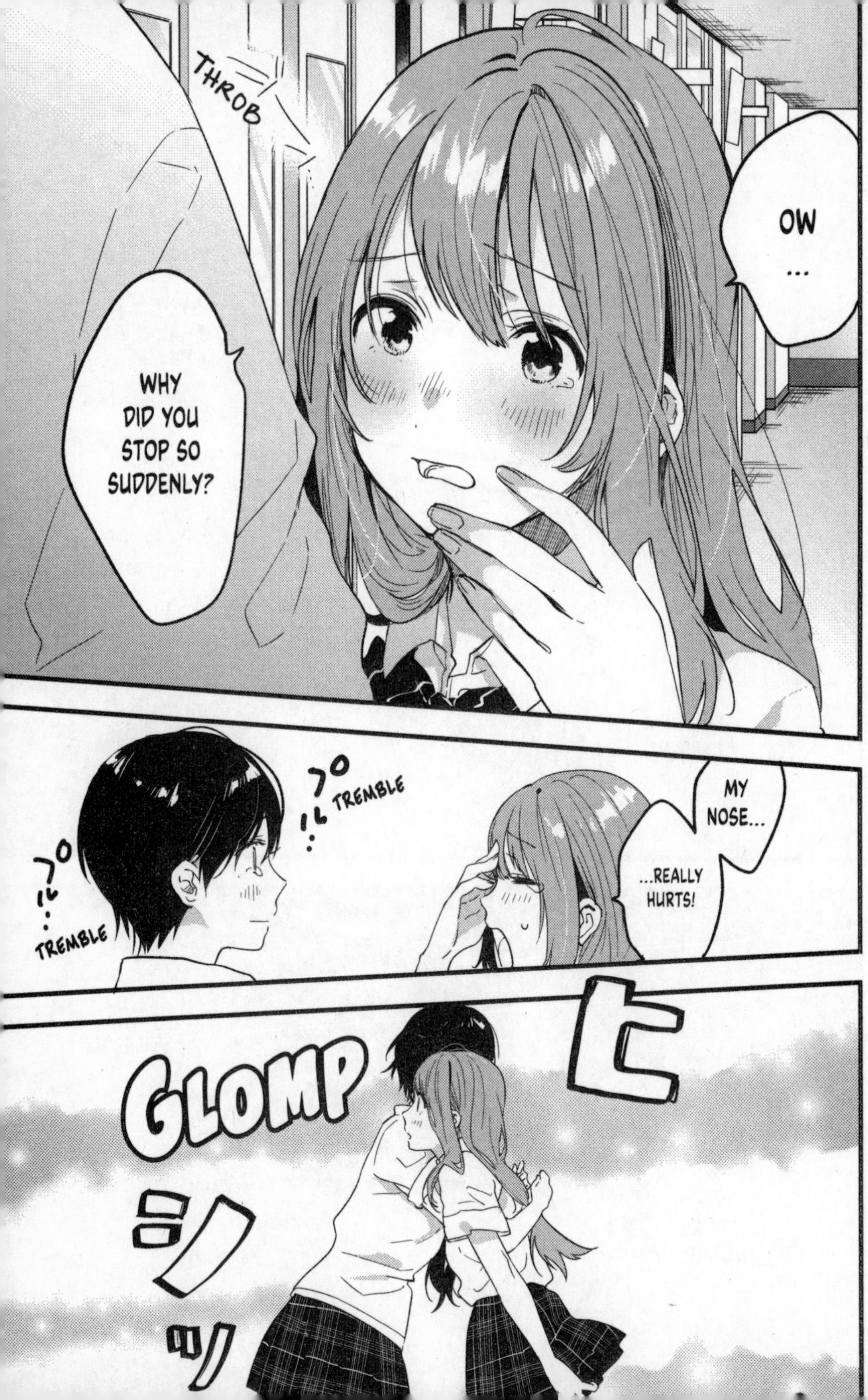
OW ...
THROB
WHY DID YOU STOP SO SUDDENLY?
MY NOSE...
...REALLY HURTS!
TREMBLE
TREMBLE
GLOMP

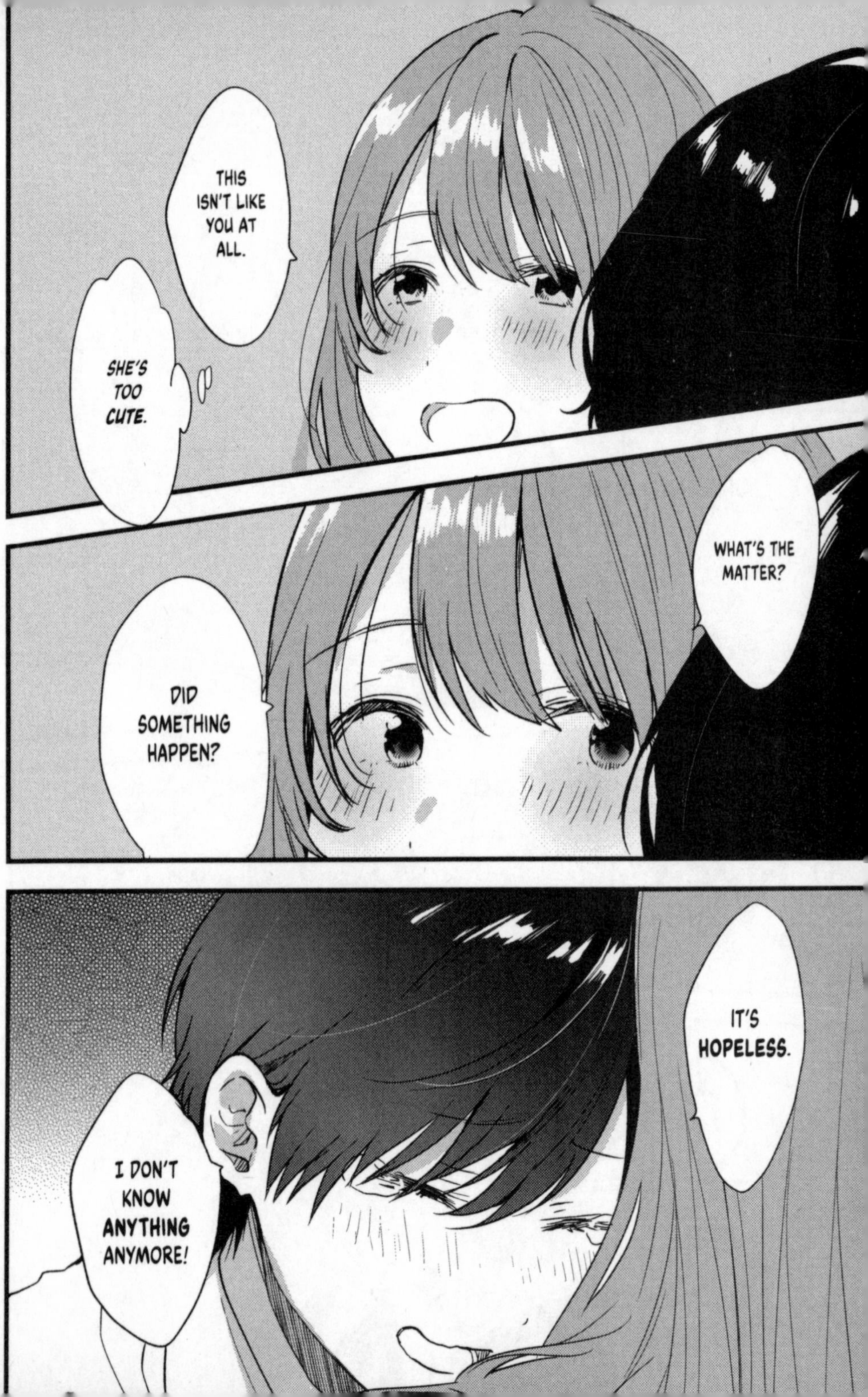
THIS ISN'T LIKE YOU AT ALL.
SHE'S TOO CUTE.
WHAT'S THE MATTER?
DID SOMETHING HAPPEN?
IT'S HOPELESS.
I DON'T KNOW ANYTHING ANYMORE!

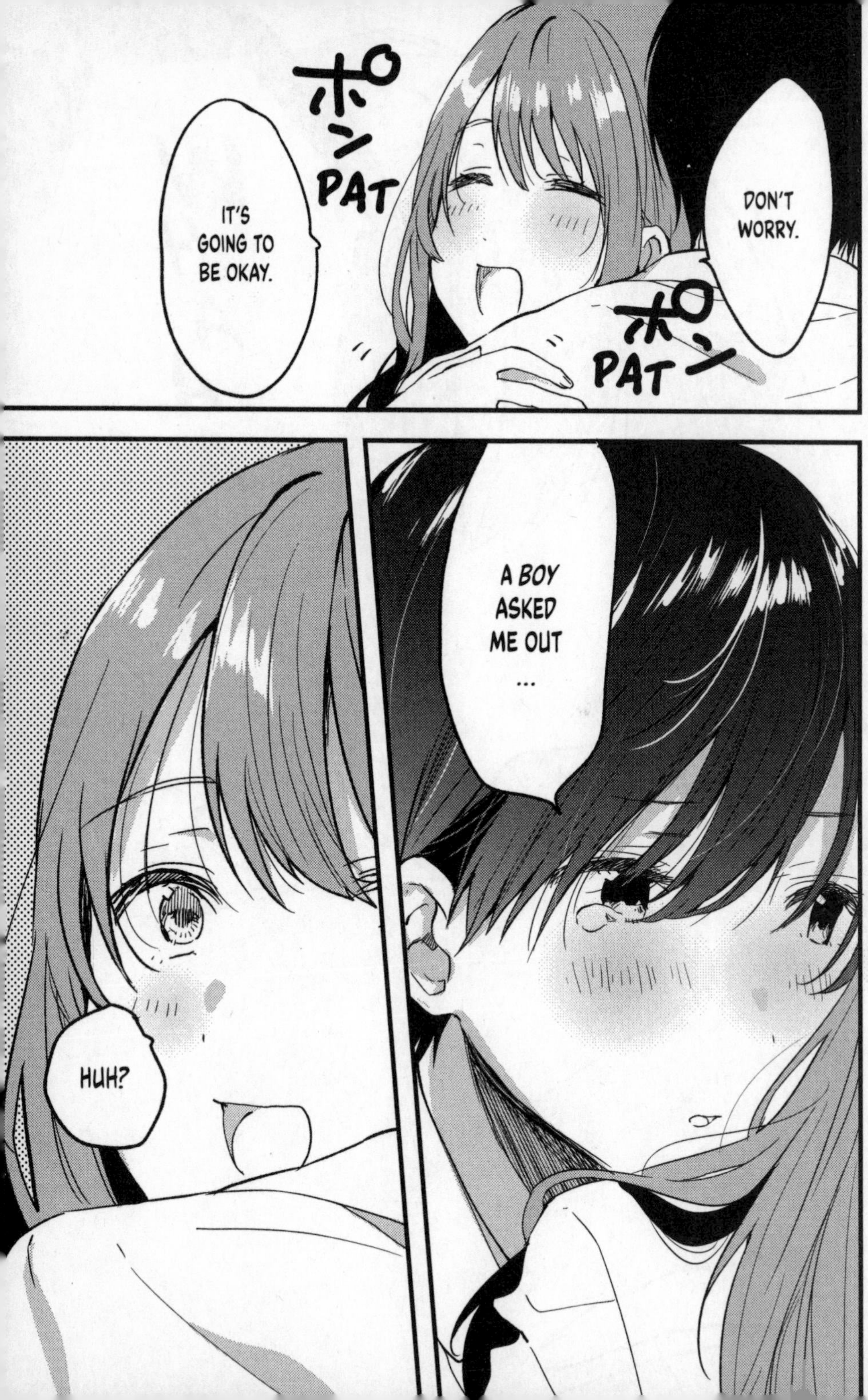
DON'T WORRY.
ポン PAT
ポン PAT
IT'S GOING TO BE OKAY.
A BOY ASKED ME OUT ...
HUH?

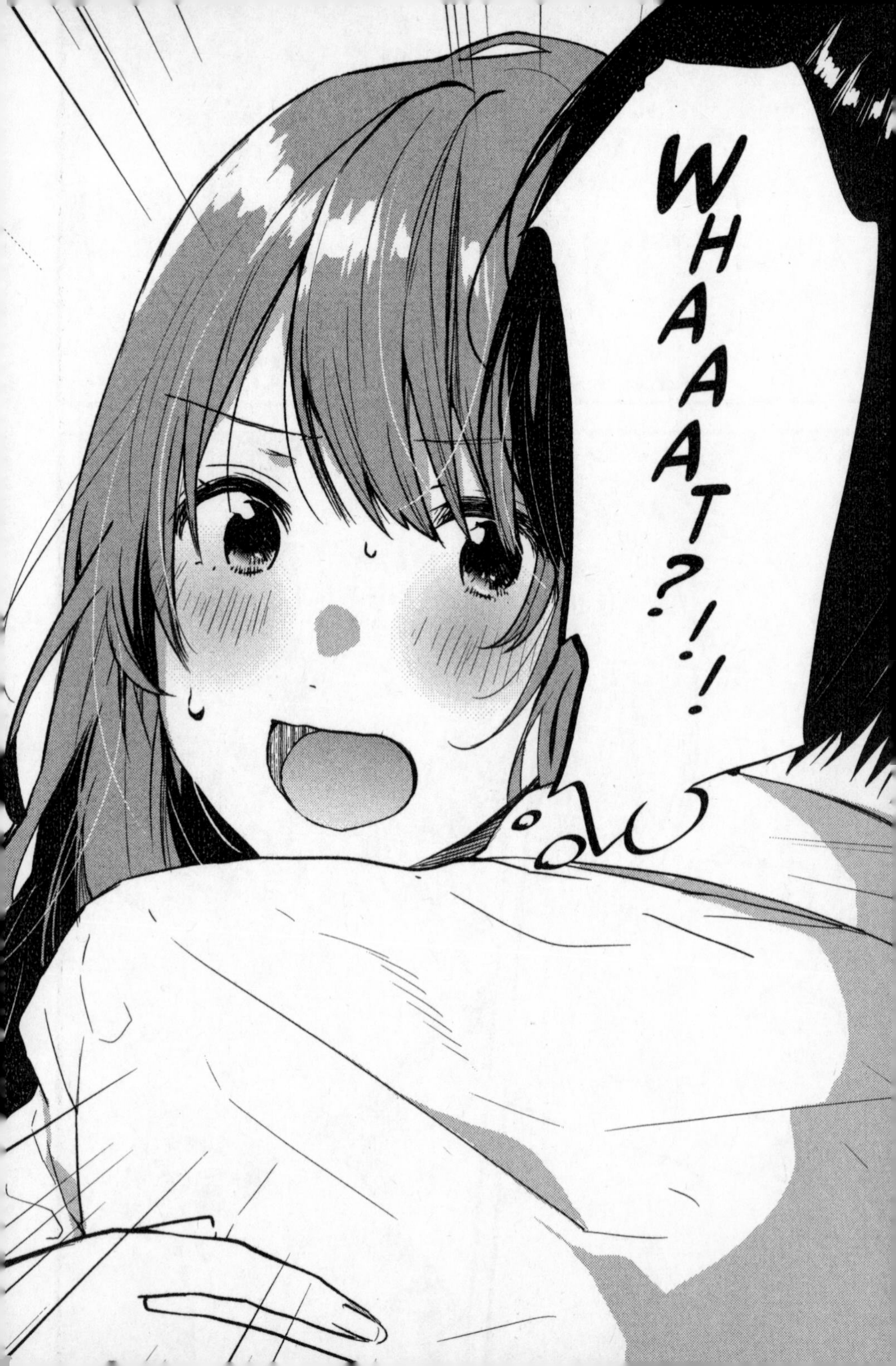
WHAAAT?!!

Chapter 13:
It's a Date?

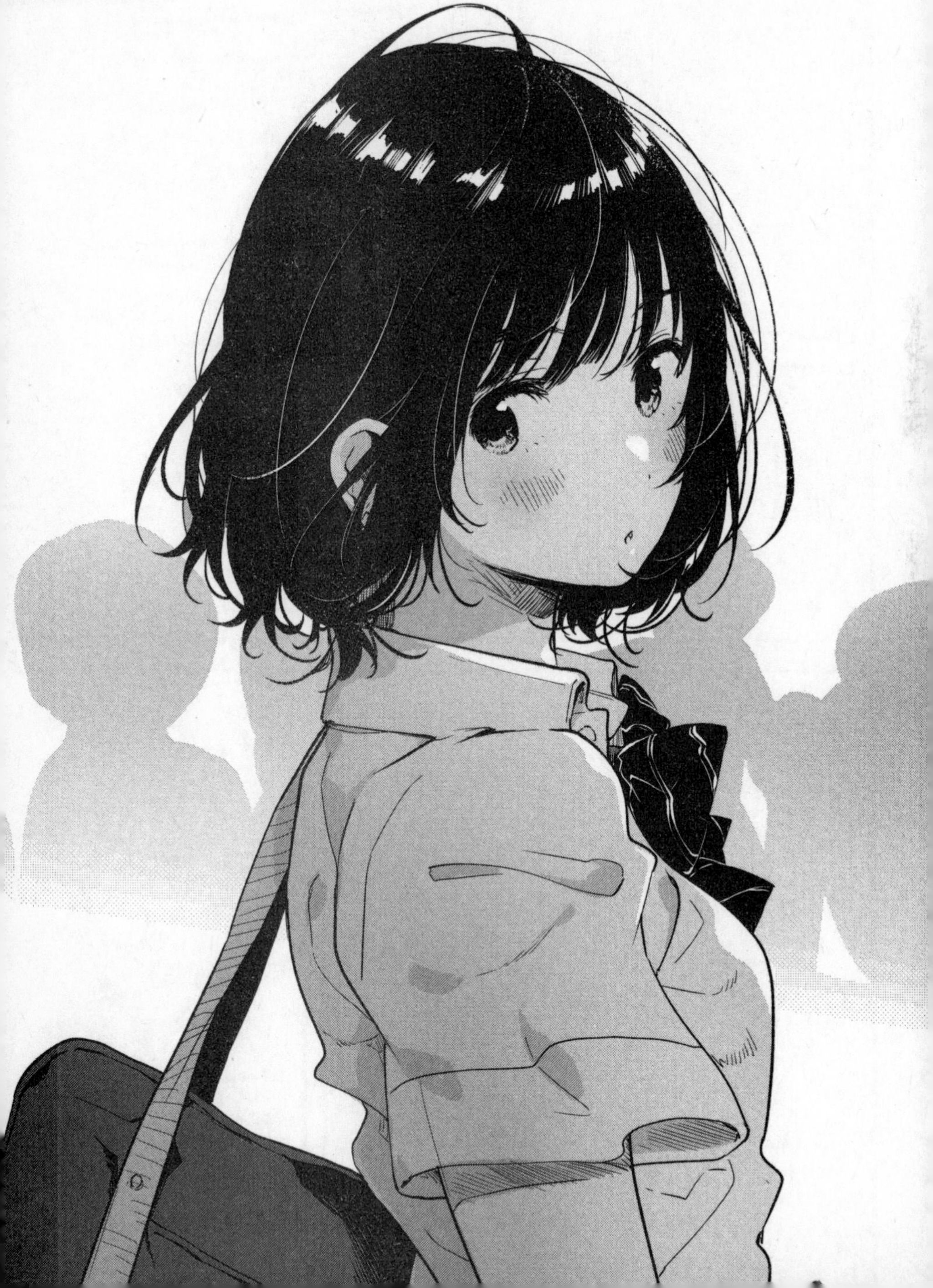

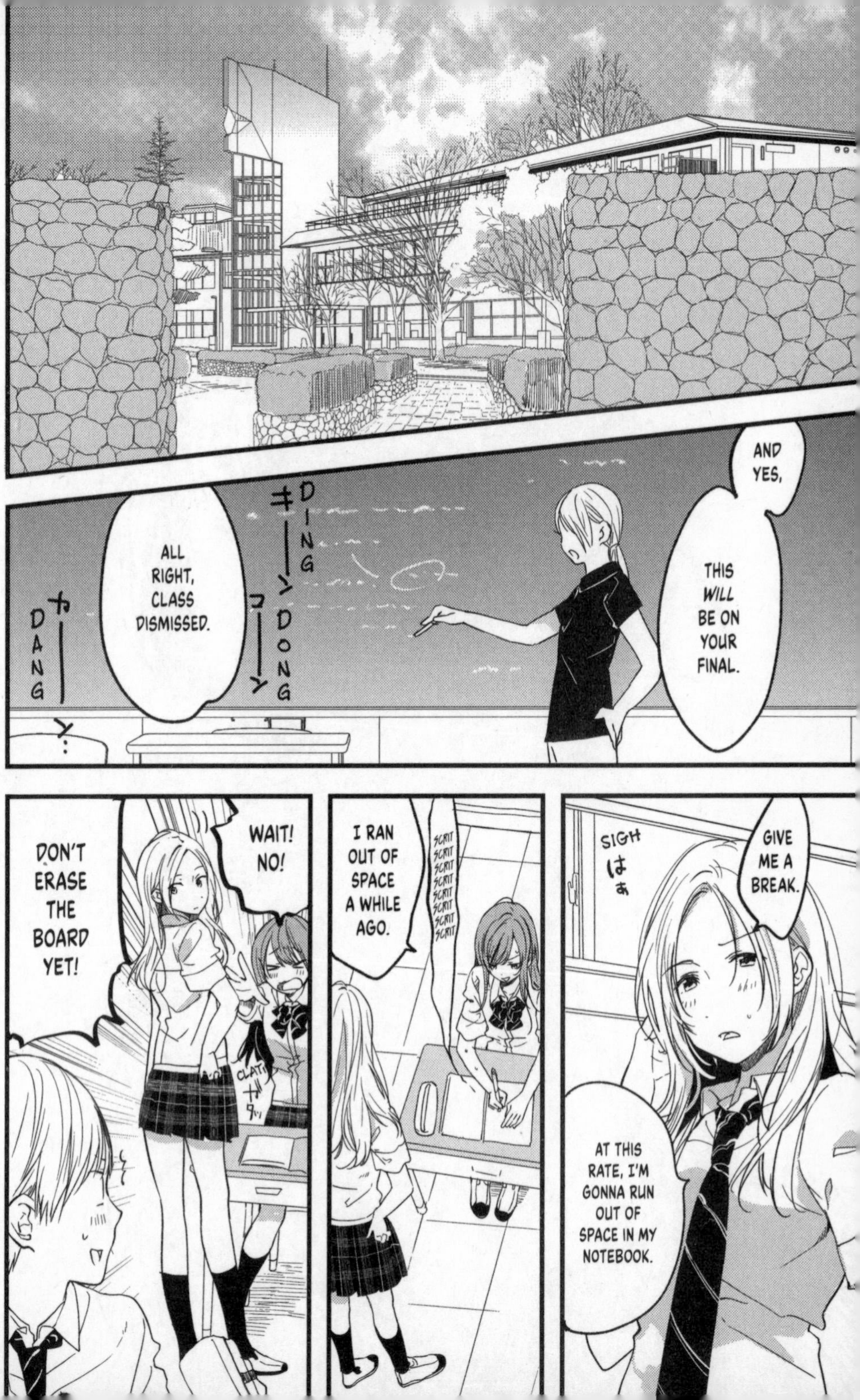

AND YES,
THIS WILL BE ON YOUR FINAL.
DING DONG
ALL RIGHT, CLASS DISMISSED.
DANG
GIVE ME A BREAK.
SIGH
AT THIS RATE, I'M GONNA RUN OUT OF SPACE IN MY NOTEBOOK.
SCRIT SCRIT SCRIT SCRIT SCRIT SCRIT SCRIT SCRIT
I RAN OUT OF SPACE A WHILE AGO.
WAIT! NO!
DON'T ERASE THE BOARD YET!
CLATT

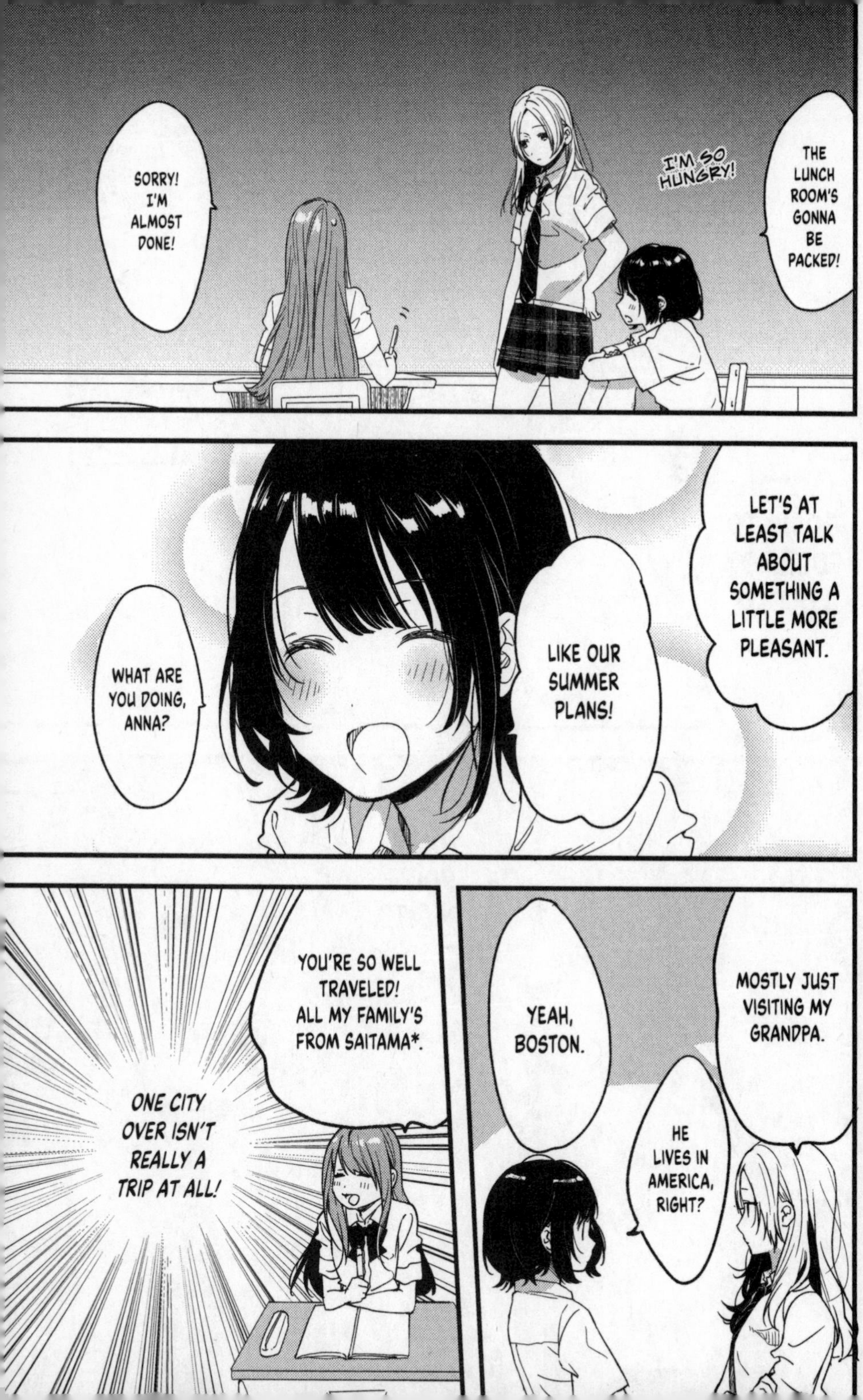
THE LUNCH ROOM'S GONNA BE PACKED!
I'M SO HUNGRY!
SORRY! I'M ALMOST DONE!
LET'S AT LEAST TALK ABOUT SOMETHING A LITTLE MORE PLEASANT.
LIKE OUR SUMMER PLANS!
WHAT ARE YOU DOING, ANNA?
MOSTLY JUST VISITING MY GRANDPA.
YEAH, BOSTON.
HE LIVES IN AMERICA, RIGHT?
YOU'RE SO WELL TRAVELED! ALL MY FAMILY'S FROM SAITAMA*.
ONE CITY OVER ISN'T REALLY A TRIP AT ALL!

*SAITAMA IS A PREFECTURE DIRECTLY NORTH OF TOKYO. A LOT OF PEOPLE WHO WORK IN TOKYO COMMUTE FROM SAITAMA.

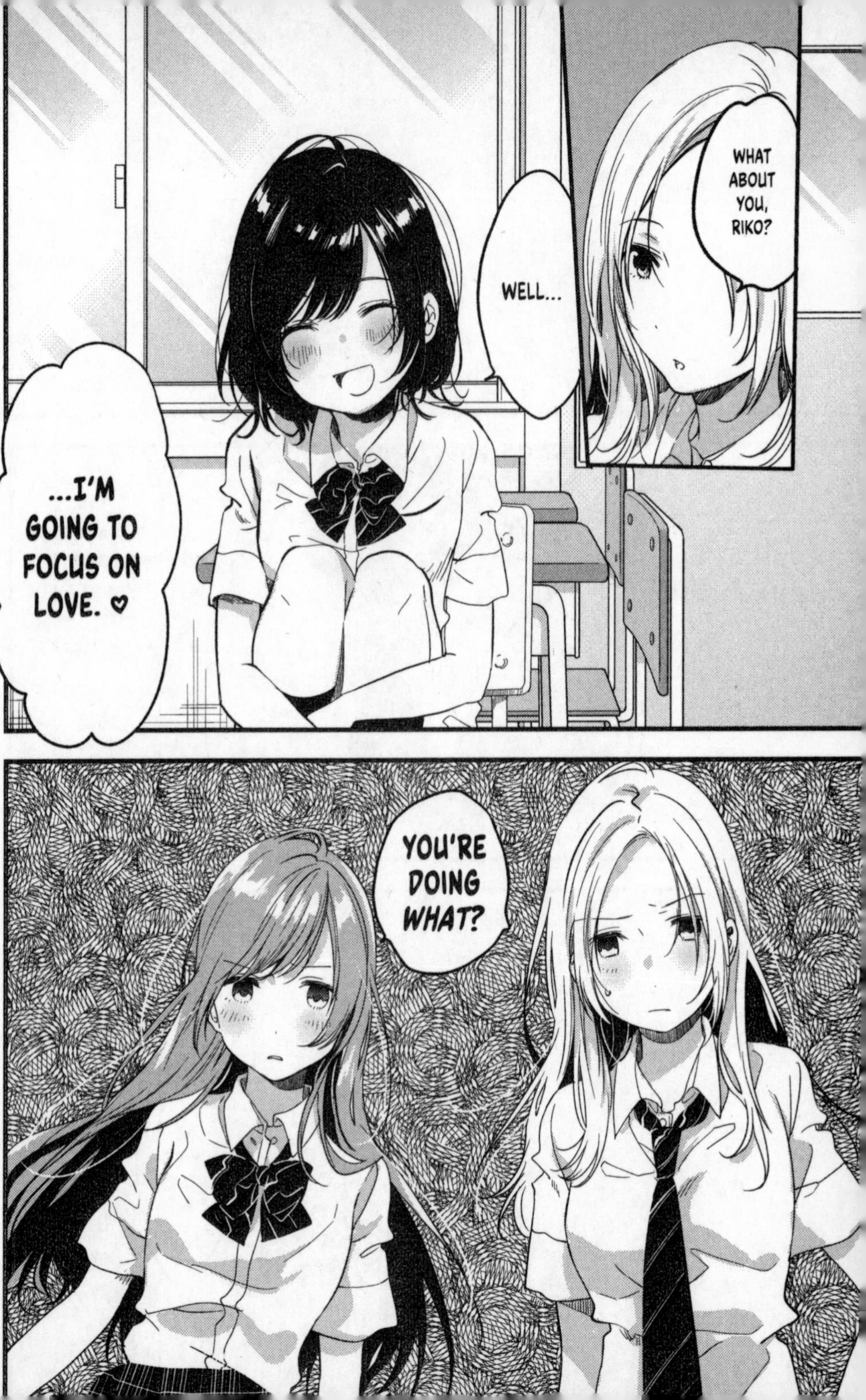
WHAT ABOUT YOU, RIKO?
WELL...
...I'M GOING TO FOCUS ON LOVE. ♡
YOU'RE DOING WHAT?

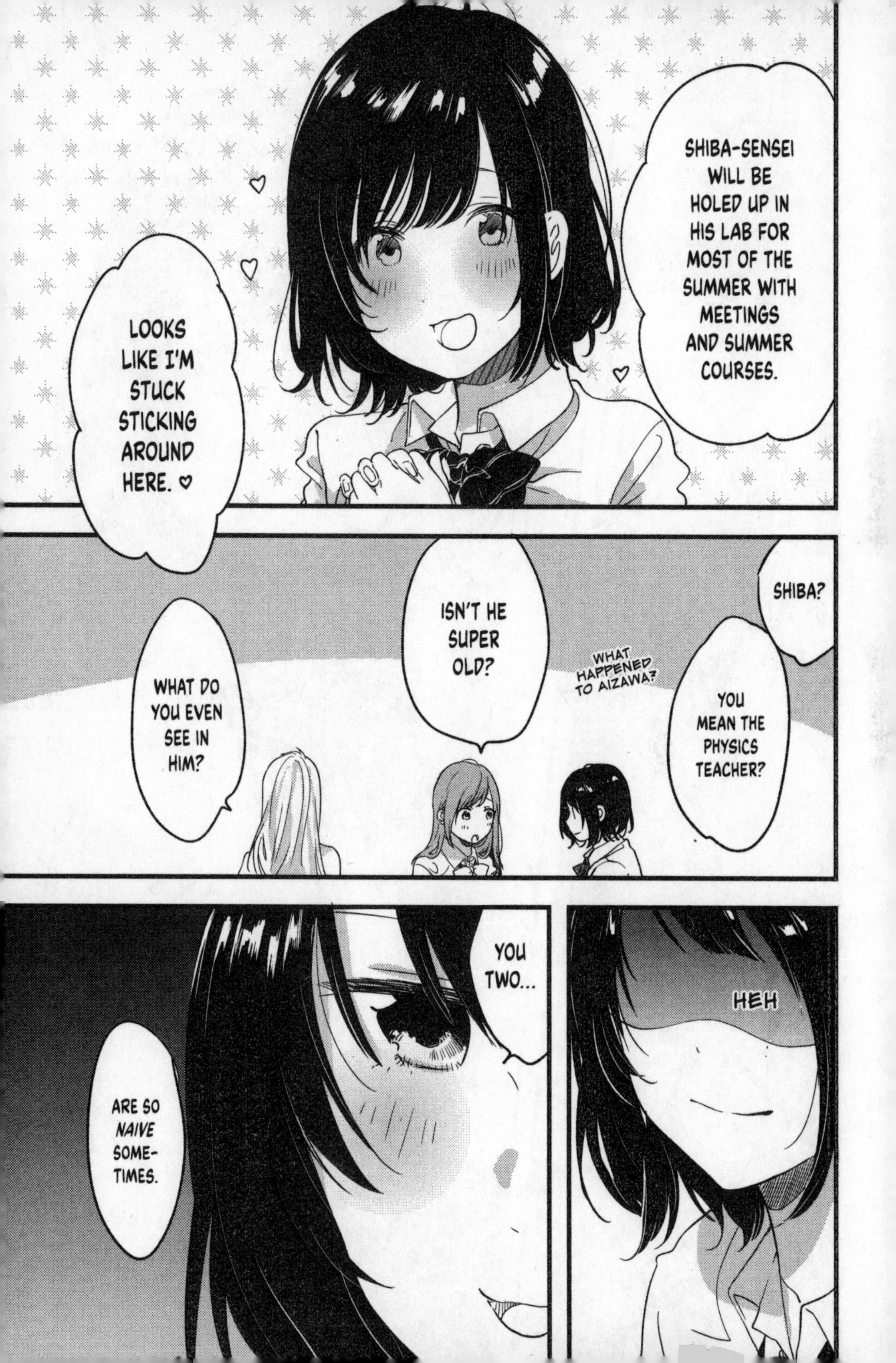
SHIBA-SENSEI WILL BE HOLED UP IN HIS LAB FOR MOST OF THE SUMMER WITH MEETINGS AND SUMMER COURSES.
LOOKS LIKE I'M STUCK STICKING AROUND HERE. ♡
SHIBA?
YOU MEAN THE PHYSICS TEACHER?
WHAT HAPPENED TO AIZAWA?
ISN'T HE SUPER OLD?
WHAT DO YOU EVEN SEE IN HIM?
HEH
YOU TWO...
ARE SO *NAIVE* SOME-TIMES.

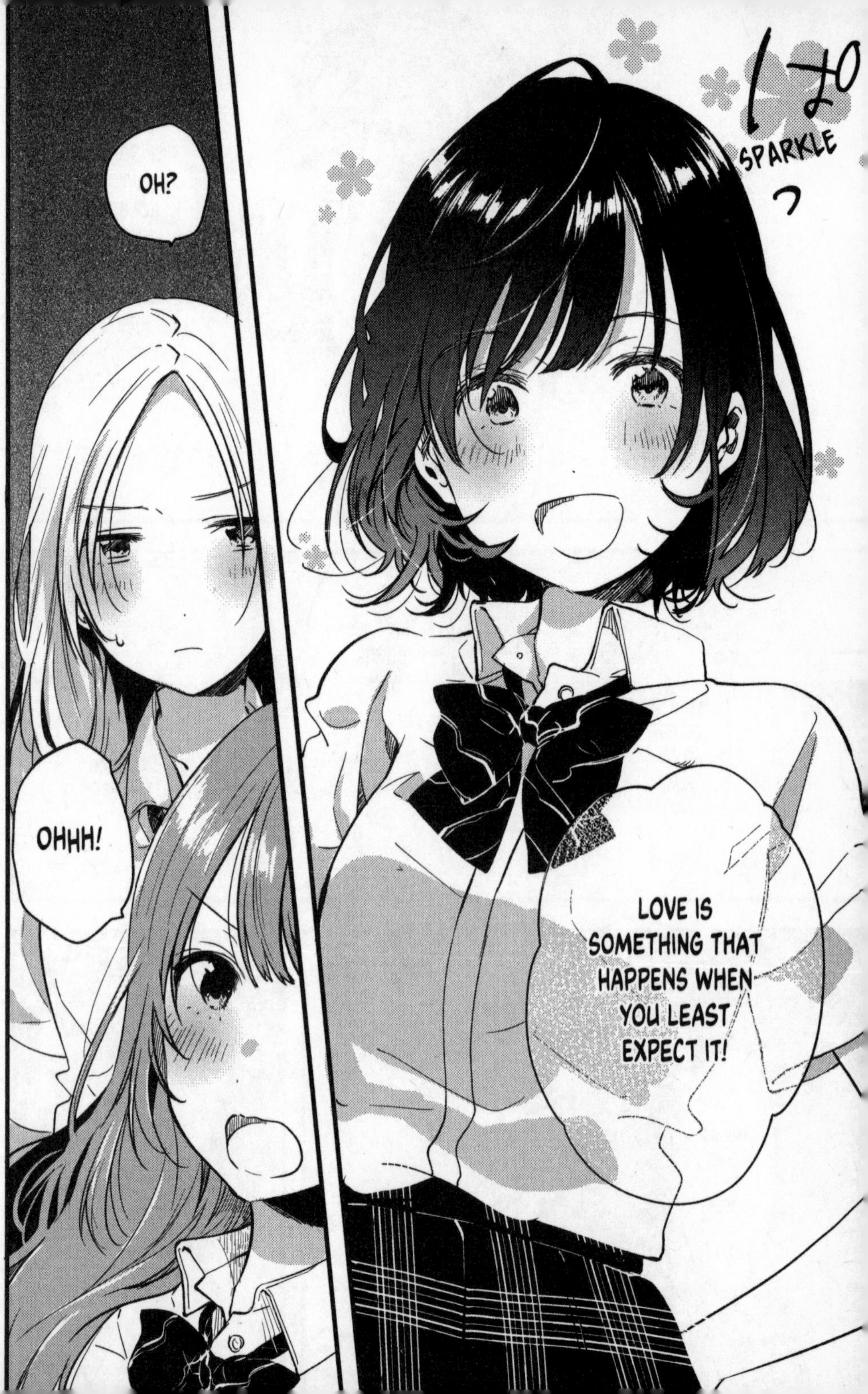
SPARKLE
LOVE IS SOMETHING THAT HAPPENS WHEN YOU LEAST EXPECT IT!
OH?
OHHH!

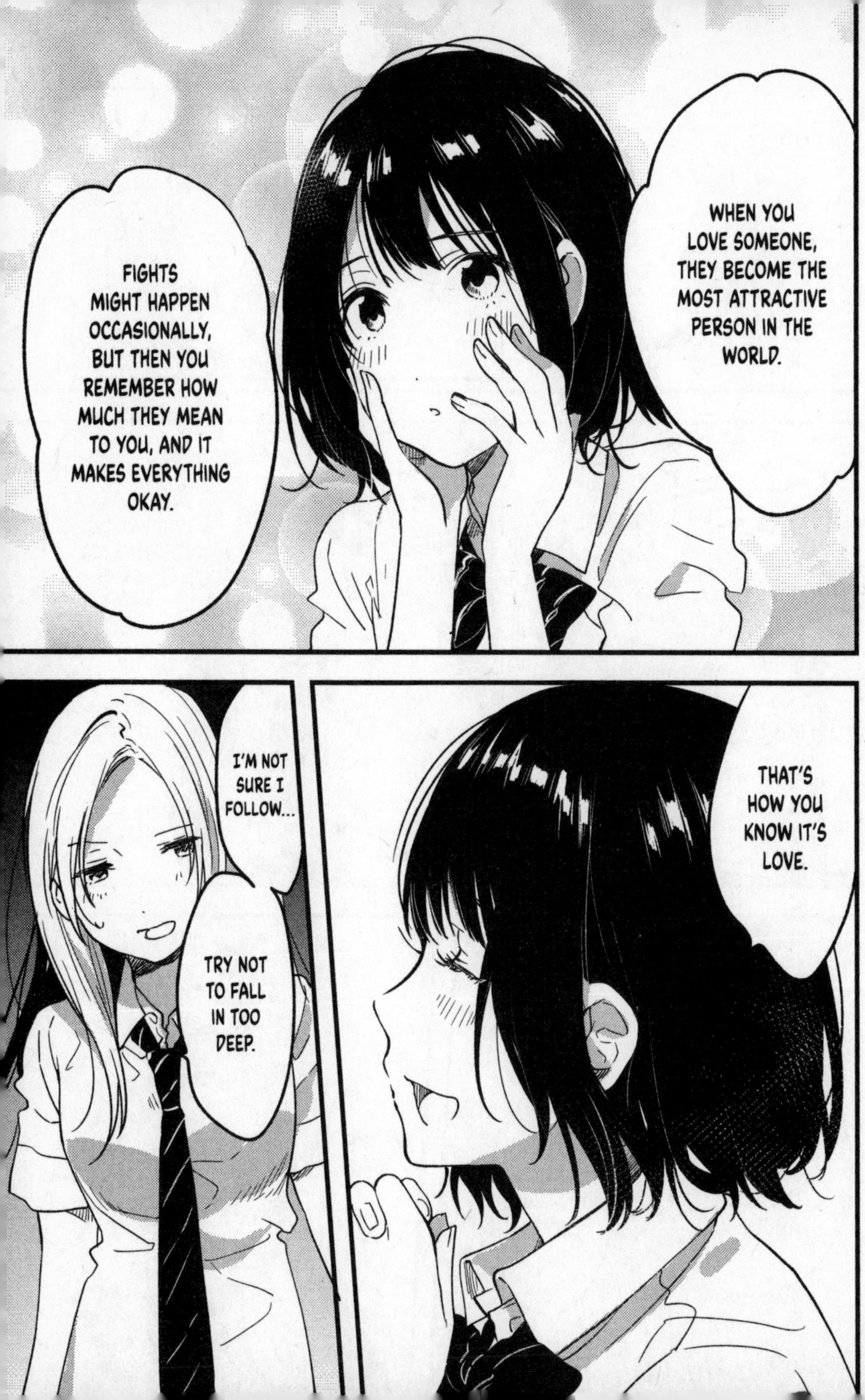
WHEN YOU LOVE SOMEONE, THEY BECOME THE MOST ATTRACTIVE PERSON IN THE WORLD.
FIGHTS MIGHT HAPPEN OCCASIONALLY, BUT THEN YOU REMEMBER HOW MUCH THEY MEAN TO YOU, AND IT MAKES EVERYTHING OKAY.
THAT'S HOW YOU KNOW IT'S LOVE.
I'M NOT SURE I FOLLOW...
TRY NOT TO FALL IN TOO DEEP.

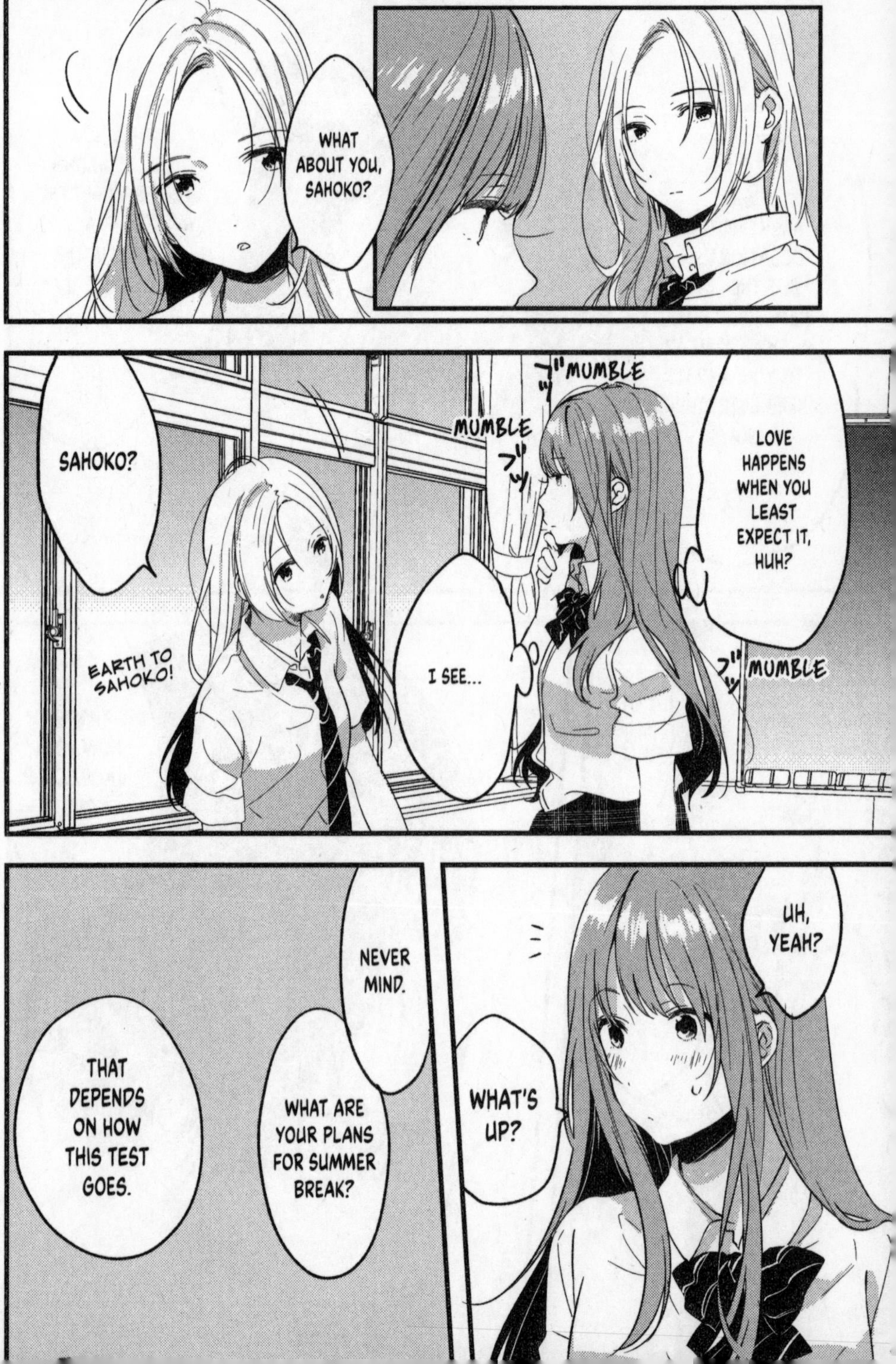
WHAT ABOUT YOU, SAHOKO?
LOVE HAPPENS WHEN YOU LEAST EXPECT IT, HUH?
MUMBLE
MUMBLE
MUMBLE
I SEE...
SAHOKO?
EARTH TO SAHOKO!
UH, YEAH?
WHAT'S UP?
NEVER MIND.
WHAT ARE YOUR PLANS FOR SUMMER BREAK?
THAT DEPENDS ON HOW THIS TEST GOES.

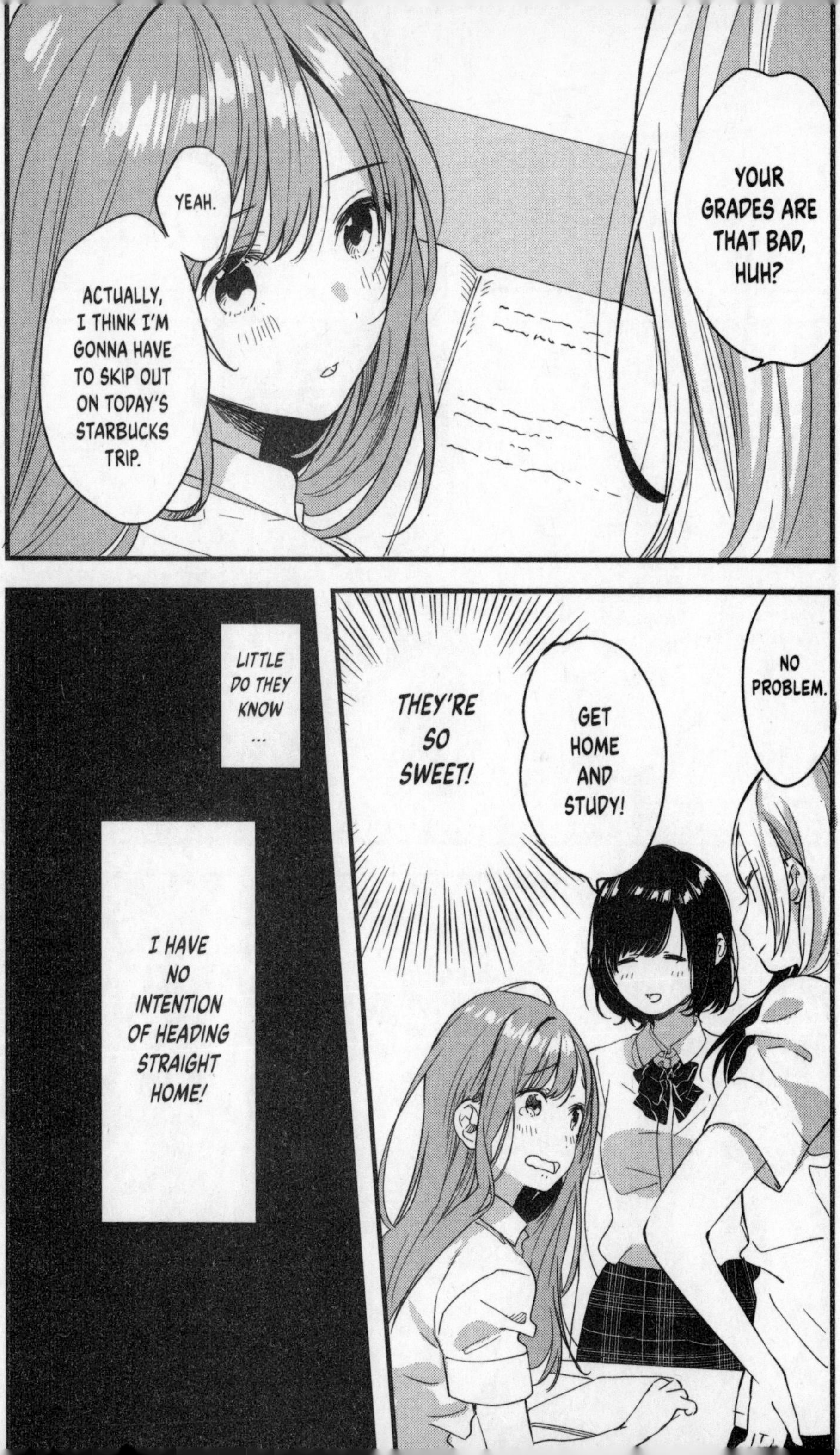
YOUR GRADES ARE THAT BAD, HUH?
YEAH.
ACTUALLY, I THINK I'M GONNA HAVE TO SKIP OUT ON TODAY'S STARBUCKS TRIP.
NO PROBLEM.
GET HOME AND STUDY!
THEY'RE SO SWEET!
LITTLE DO THEY KNOW ...
I HAVE NO INTENTION OF HEADING STRAIGHT HOME!

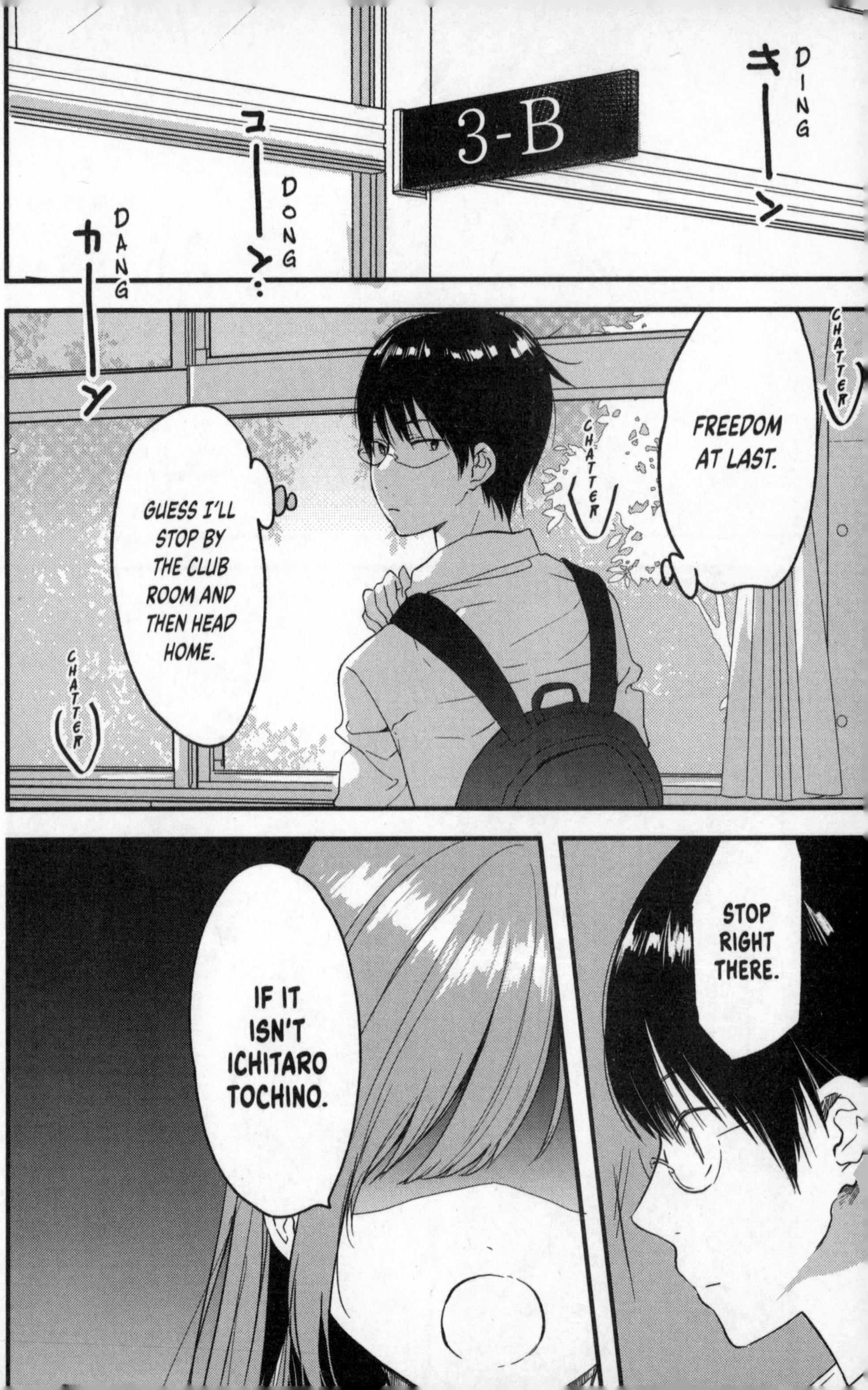
キーン
DING
コーン‥
DONG
カーン
DANG
CHATTER
FREEDOM AT LAST.
CHATTER
GUESS I'LL STOP BY THE CLUB ROOM AND THEN HEAD HOME.
CHATTER
STOP RIGHT THERE.
IF IT ISN'T ICHITARO TOCHINO.

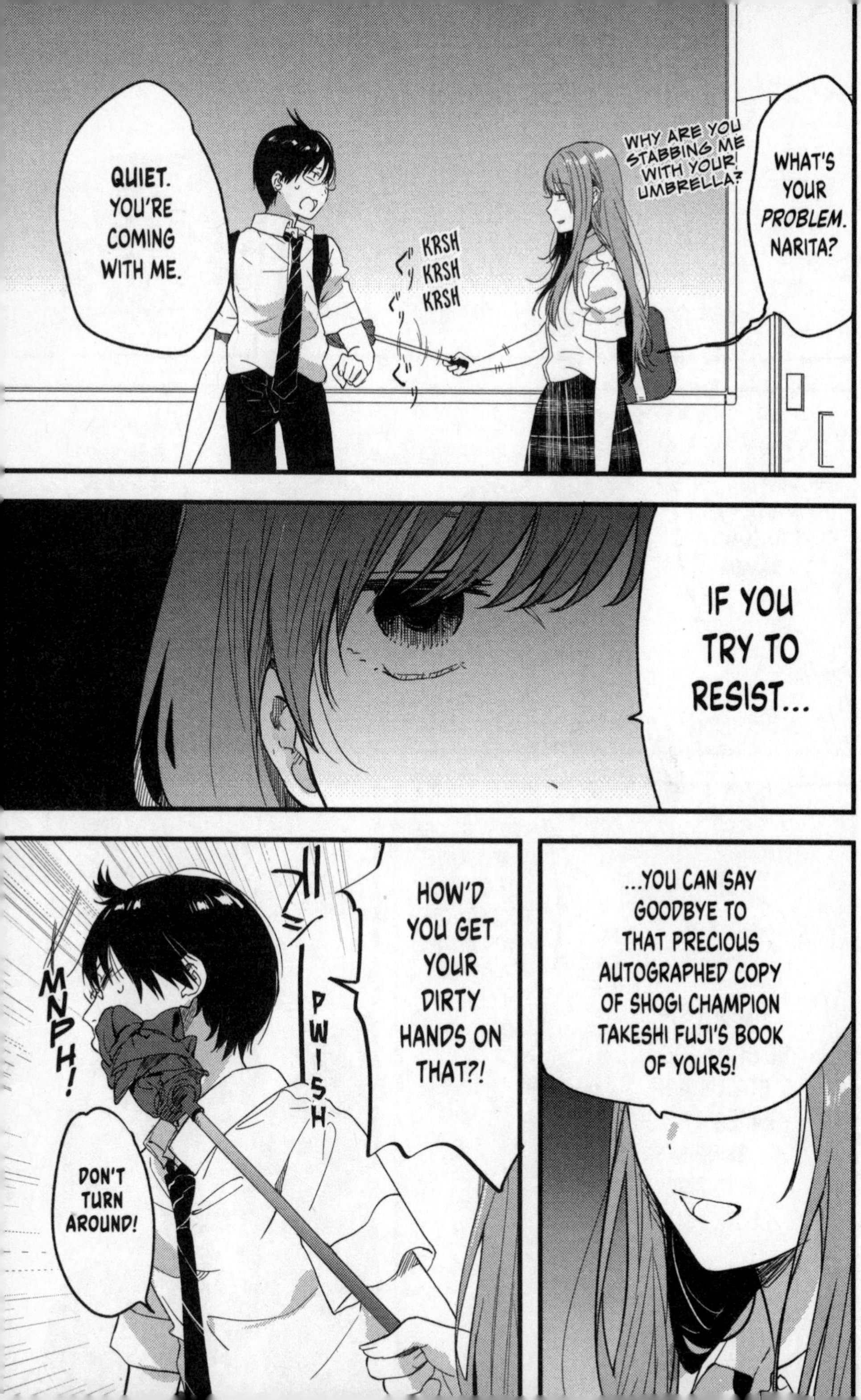
WHAT'S YOUR *PROBLEM*. NARITA?
WHY ARE YOU STABBING ME WITH YOUR UMBRELLA?
KRSH KRSH KRSH
QUIET. YOU'RE COMING WITH ME.
IF YOU TRY TO RESIST...
...YOU CAN SAY GOODBYE TO THAT PRECIOUS AUTOGRAPHED COPY OF SHOGI CHAMPION TAKESHI FUJI'S BOOK OF YOURS!
HOW'D YOU GET YOUR DIRTY HANDS ON THAT?!
PWISH
MNPH!
DON'T TURN AROUND!

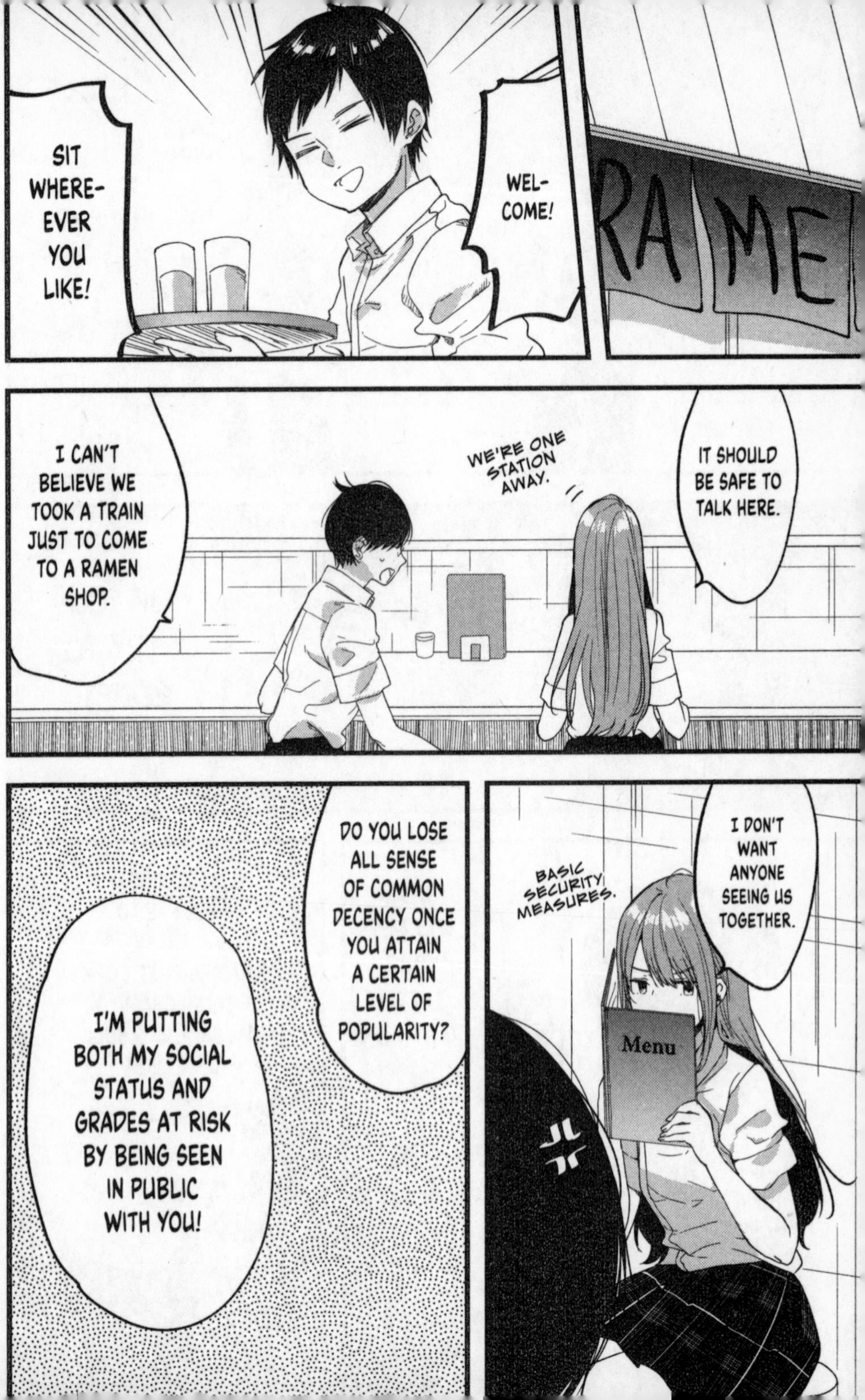
RAME
WEL-COME!
SIT WHERE-EVER YOU LIKE!
IT SHOULD BE SAFE TO TALK HERE.
WE'RE ONE STATION AWAY.
I CAN'T BELIEVE WE TOOK A TRAIN JUST TO COME TO A RAMEN SHOP.
I DON'T WANT ANYONE SEEING US TOGETHER.
BASIC SECURITY MEASURES.
Menu
DO YOU LOSE ALL SENSE OF COMMON DECENCY ONCE YOU ATTAIN A CERTAIN LEVEL OF POPULARITY?
I'M PUTTING BOTH MY SOCIAL STATUS AND GRADES AT RISK BY BEING SEEN IN PUBLIC WITH YOU!

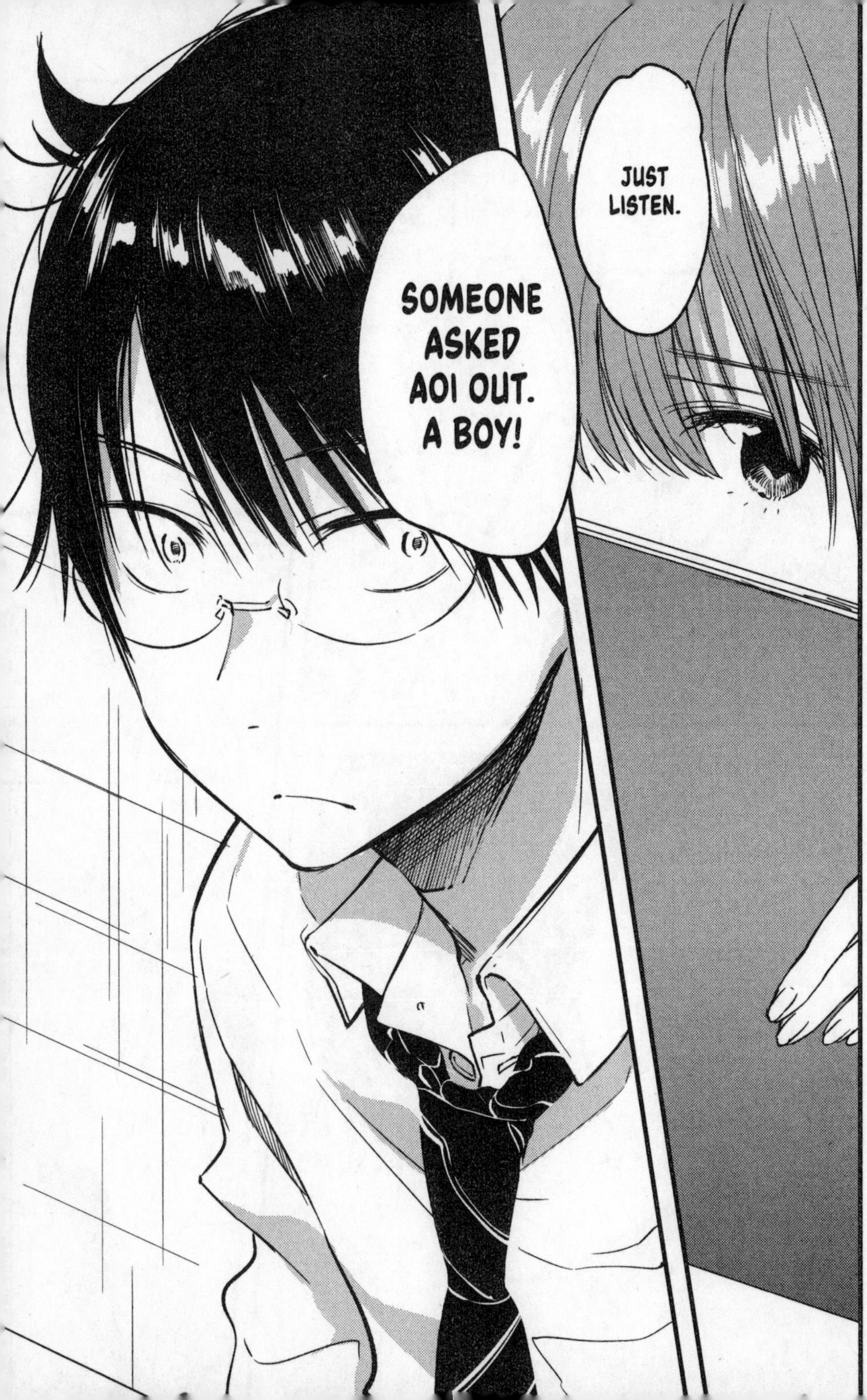
JUST LISTEN.
SOMEONE ASKED AOI OUT. A BOY!

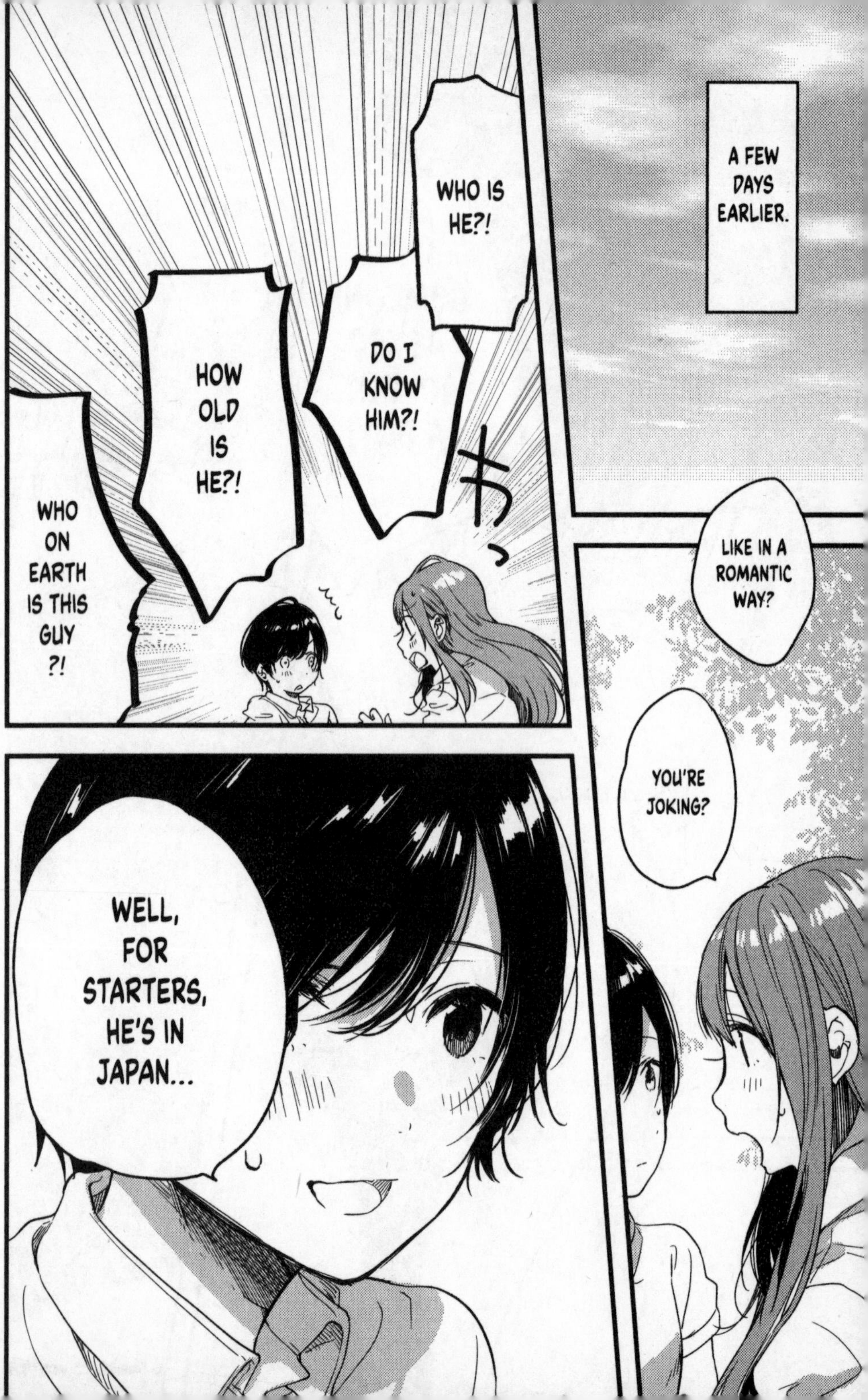
A FEW DAYS EARLIER.
LIKE IN A ROMANTIC WAY?
YOU'RE JOKING?
WHO IS HE?!
DO I KNOW HIM?!
HOW OLD IS HE?!
WHO ON EARTH IS THIS GUY ?!
WELL, FOR STARTERS, HE'S IN JAPAN...

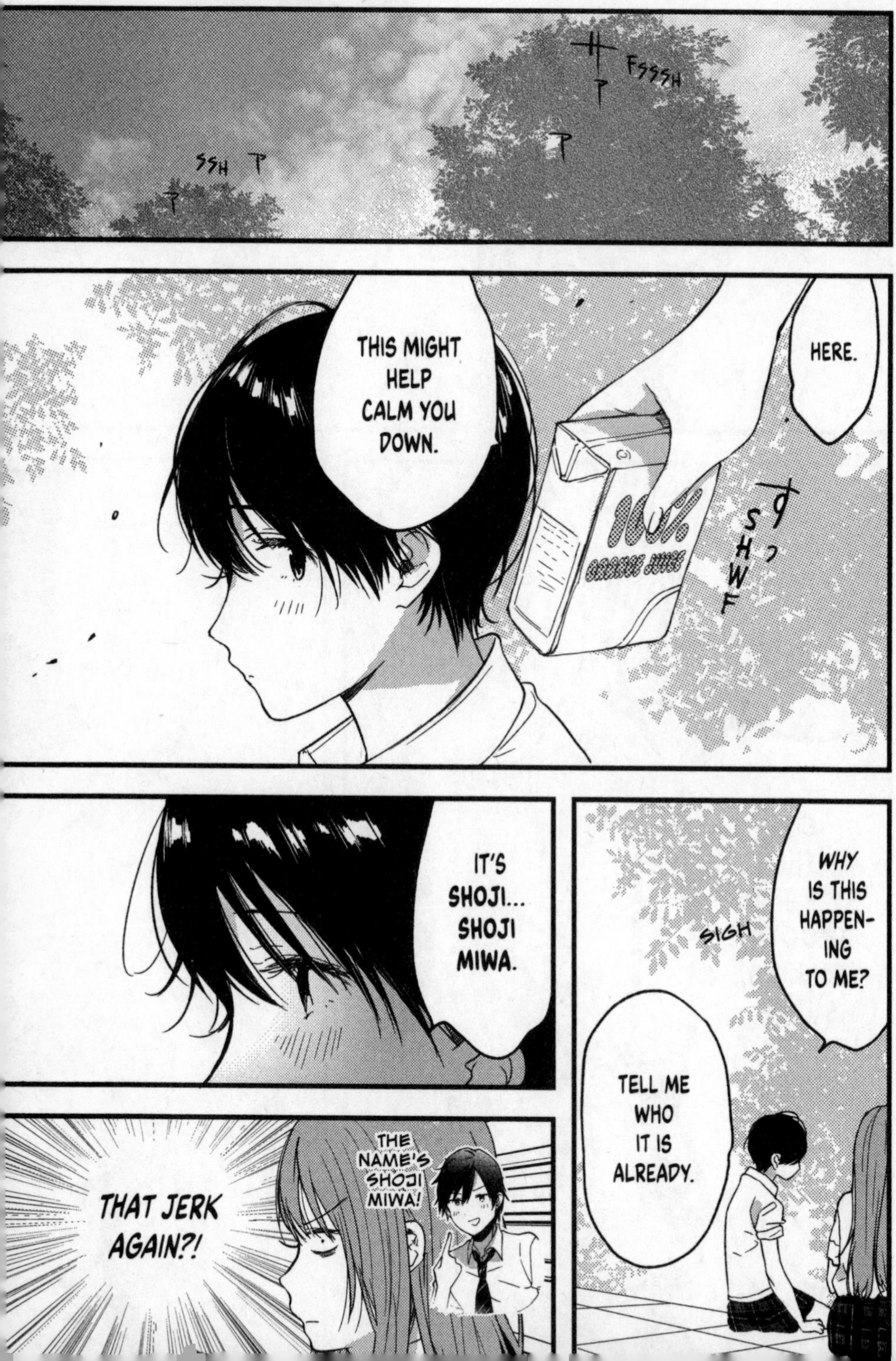
FSSSH
SSH
HERE.
THIS MIGHT HELP CALM YOU DOWN.
SHWF
WHY IS THIS HAPPEN-ING TO ME?
SIGH
TELL ME WHO IT IS ALREADY.
IT'S SHOJI... SHOJI MIWA.
THE NAME'S SHOJI MIWA!
THAT JERK AGAIN?!

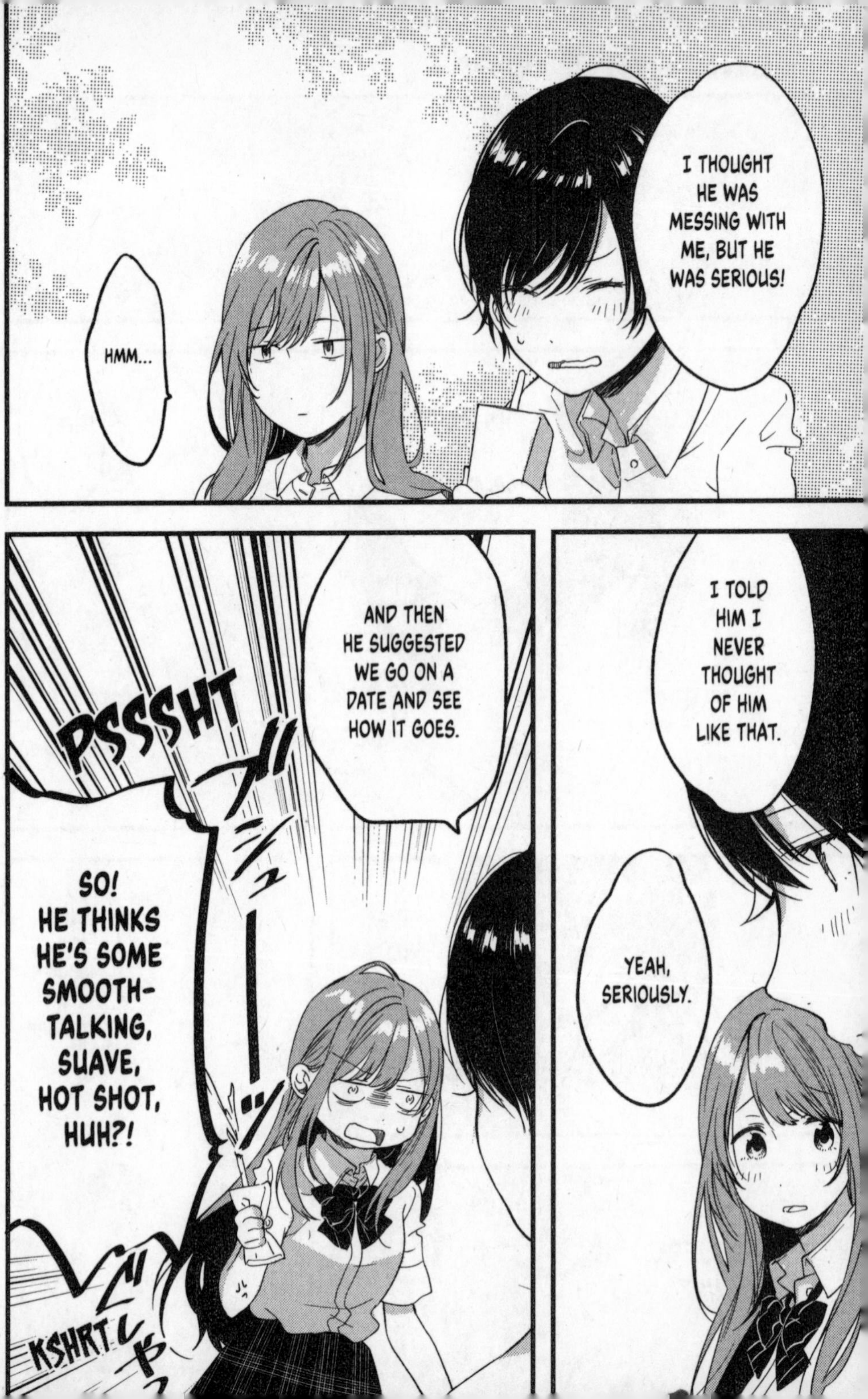
I THOUGHT HE WAS MESSING WITH ME, BUT HE WAS SERIOUS!
HMM...
I TOLD HIM I NEVER THOUGHT OF HIM LIKE THAT.
YEAH, SERIOUSLY.
AND THEN HE SUGGESTED WE GO ON A DATE AND SEE HOW IT GOES.
PSSSHT
SO! HE THINKS HE'S SOME SMOOTH-TALKING, SUAVE, HOT SHOT, HUH?!
KSHRT

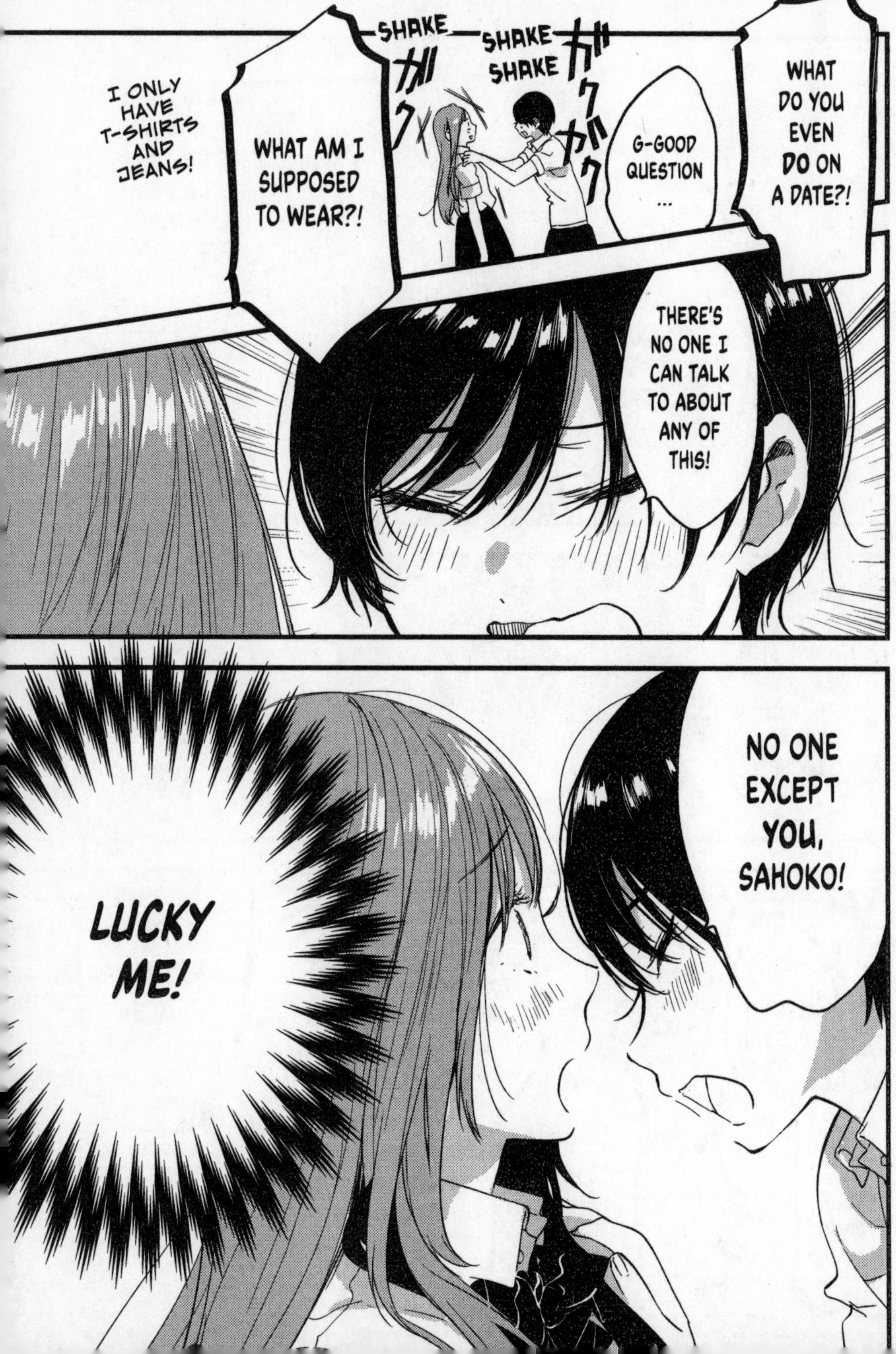
WHAT DO YOU EVEN DO ON A DATE?!
G-GOOD QUESTION ...
SHAKE SHAKE
SHAKE
WHAT AM I SUPPOSED TO WEAR?!
I ONLY HAVE T-SHIRTS AND JEANS!
THERE'S NO ONE I CAN TALK TO ABOUT ANY OF THIS!
NO ONE EXCEPT YOU, SAHOKO!
LUCKY ME!

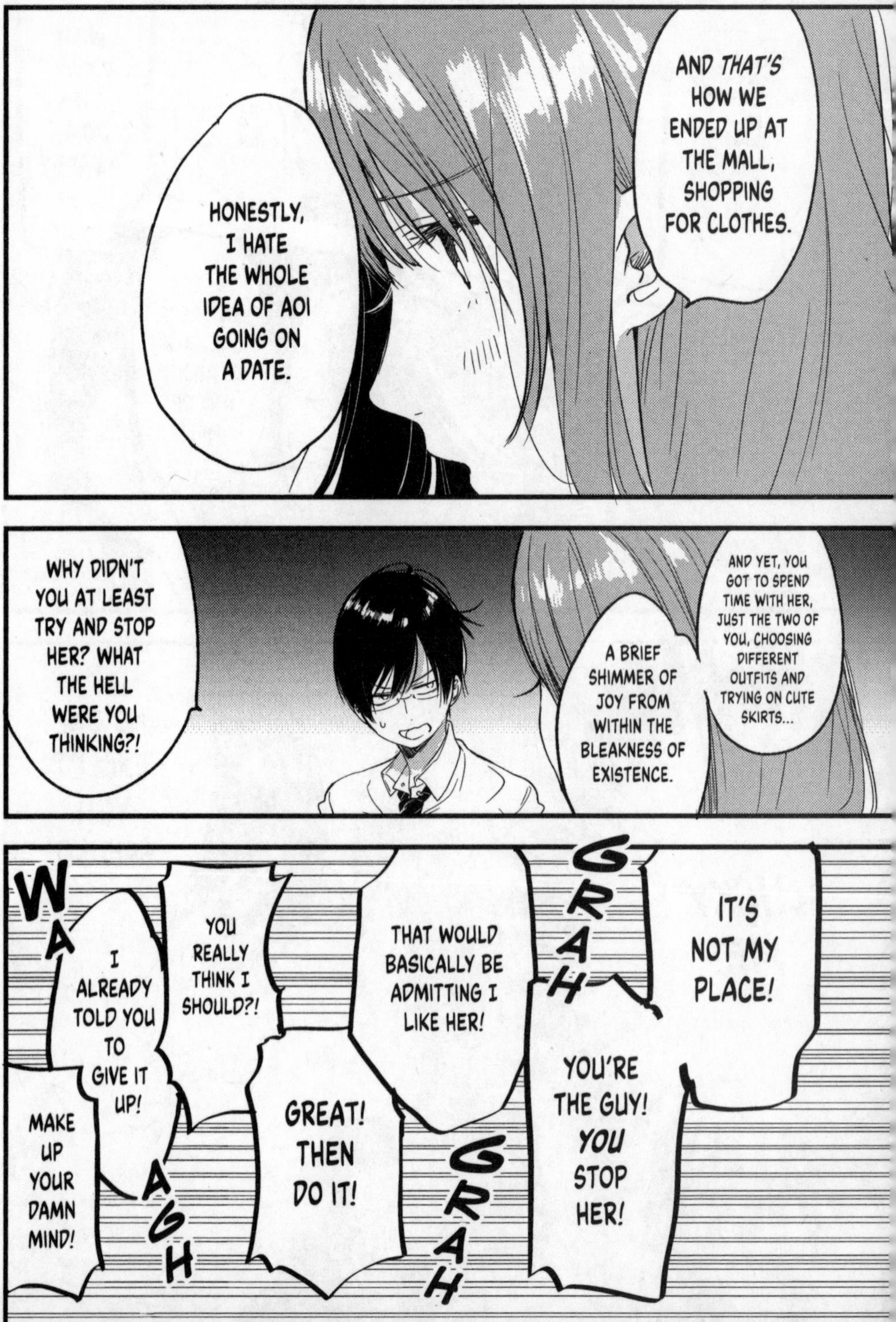
AND THAT'S HOW WE ENDED UP AT THE MALL, SHOPPING FOR CLOTHES.
HONESTLY, I HATE THE WHOLE IDEA OF AOI GOING ON A DATE.
AND YET, YOU GOT TO SPEND TIME WITH HER, JUST THE TWO OF YOU, CHOOSING DIFFERENT OUTFITS AND TRYING ON CUTE SKIRTS...
A BRIEF SHIMMER OF JOY FROM WITHIN THE BLEAKNESS OF EXISTENCE.
WHY DIDN'T YOU AT LEAST TRY AND STOP HER? WHAT THE HELL WERE YOU THINKING?!
GRAH
IT'S NOT MY PLACE!
YOU'RE THE GUY! YOU STOP HER!
THAT WOULD BASICALLY BE ADMITTING I LIKE HER!
GRAH
GREAT! THEN DO IT!
YOU REALLY THINK I SHOULD?!
WA
I ALREADY TOLD YOU TO GIVE IT UP!
AGH
MAKE UP YOUR DAMN MIND!

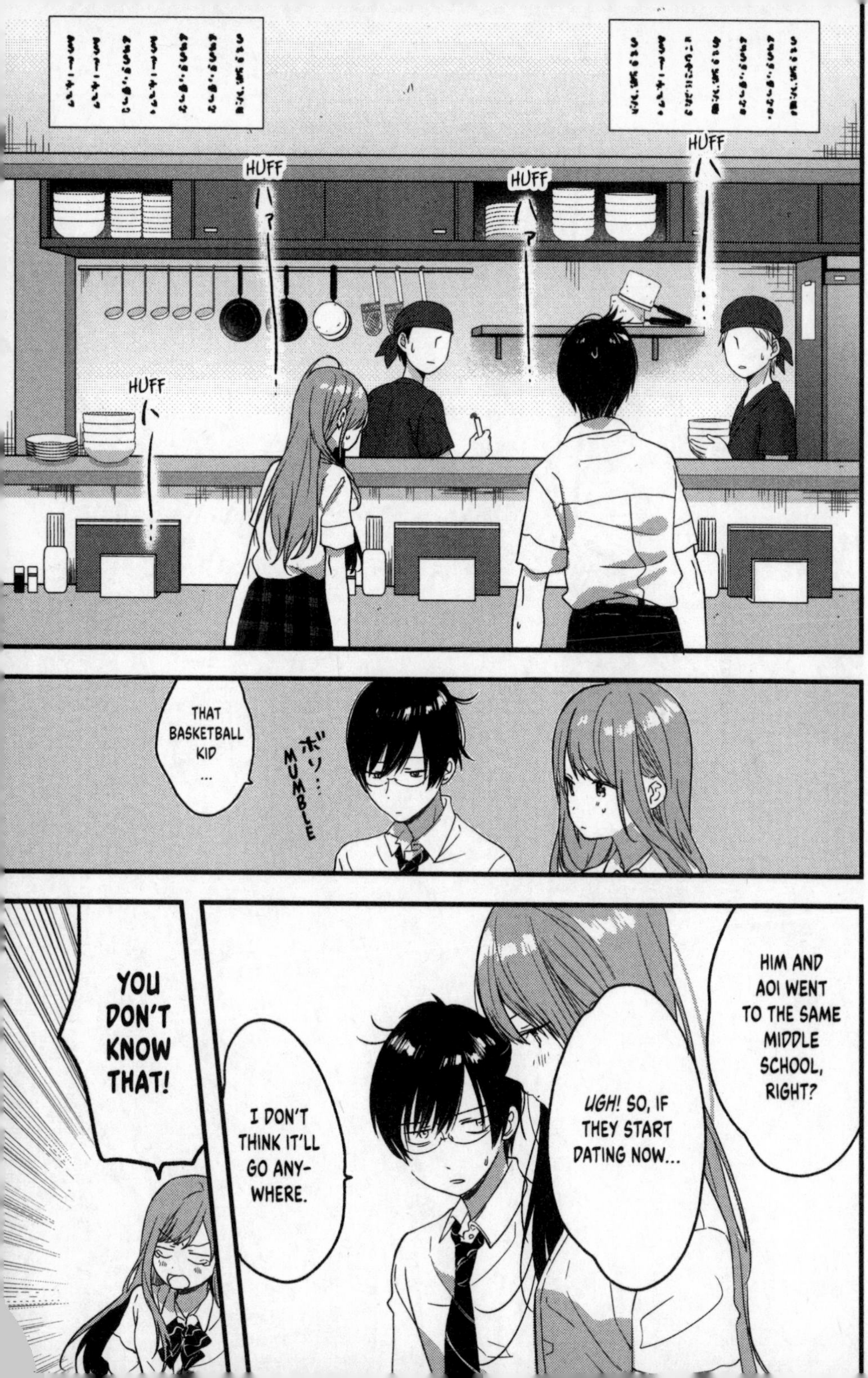
HUFF
ハー
HUFF
ハー
HUFF
ハー
HUFF
ハー
ボソ…
MUMBLE
THAT BASKETBALL KID ...
HIM AND AOI WENT TO THE SAME MIDDLE SCHOOL, RIGHT?
UGH! SO, IF THEY START DATING NOW...
I DON'T THINK IT'LL GO ANY-WHERE.
YOU DON'T KNOW THAT!

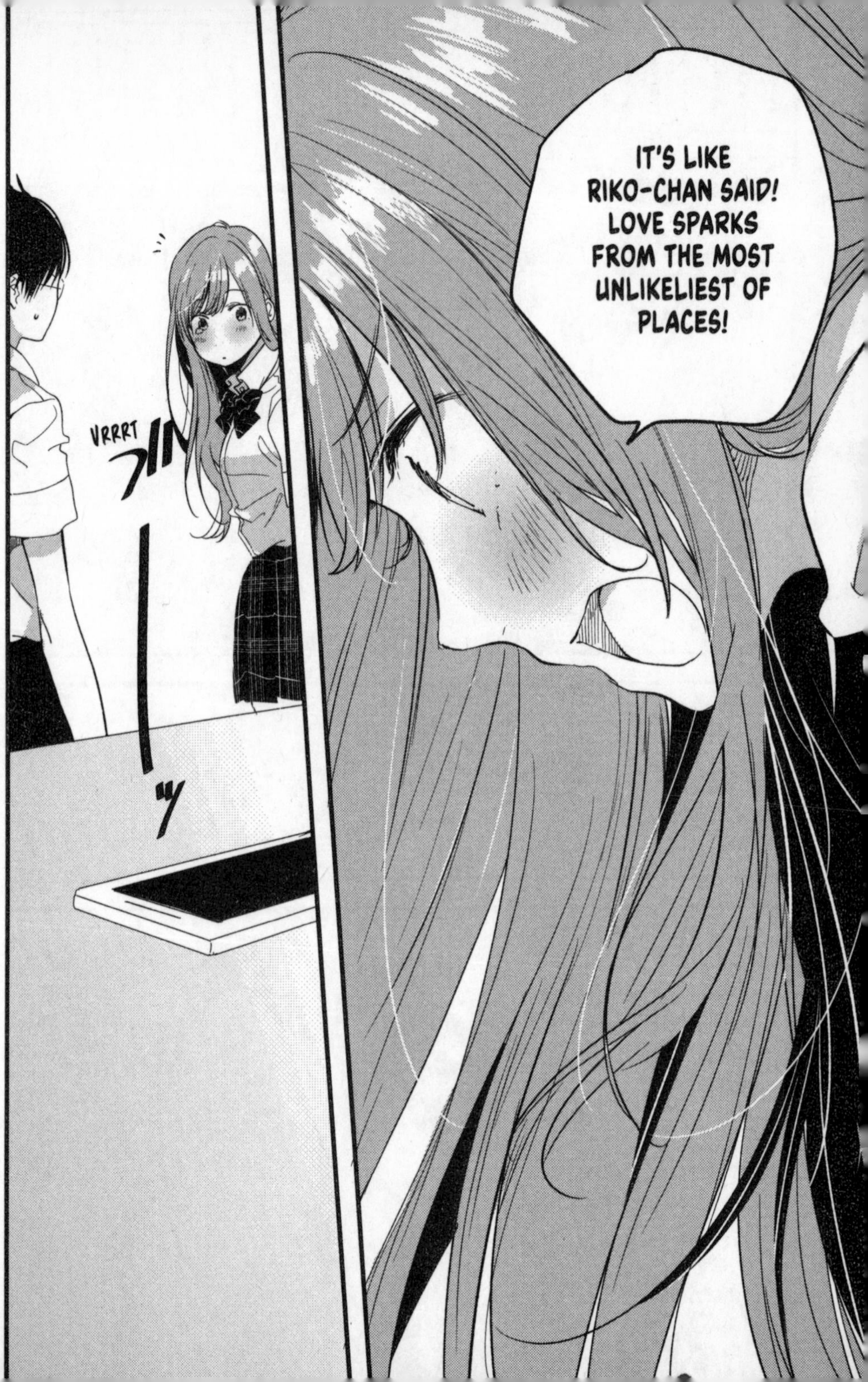
IT'S LIKE RIKO-CHAN SAID! LOVE SPARKS FROM THE MOST UNLIKELIEST OF PLACES!
VRRRT

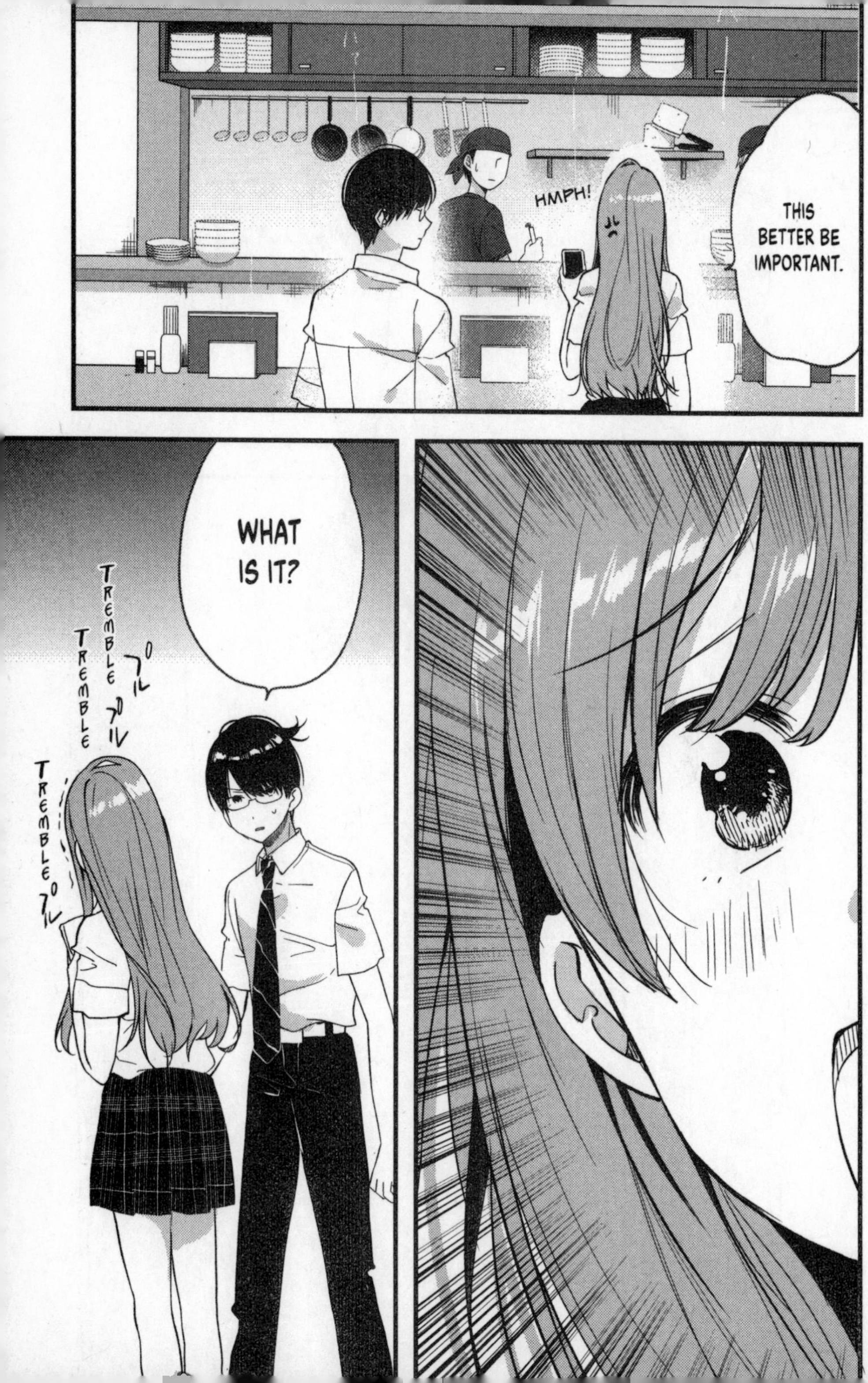
THIS BETTER BE IMPORTANT.
HMPH!
WHAT IS IT?
TREMBLE ブル
TREMBLE ブル
TREMBLE ブル

SHWF

す?

LOOK.

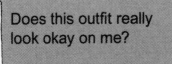

Does this outfit really look okay on me?

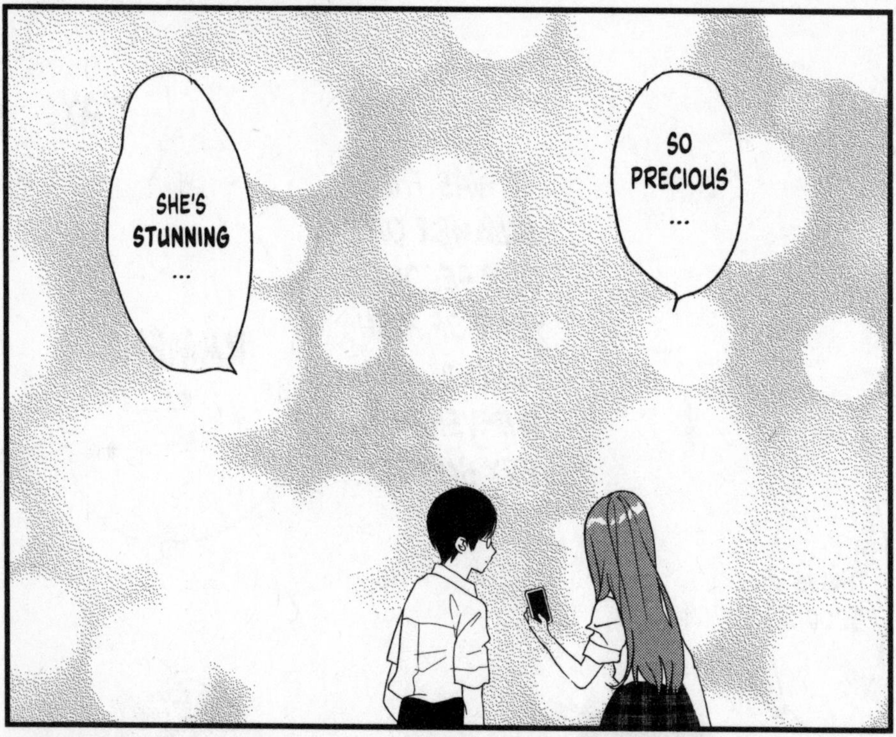
SO PRECIOUS ...
SHE'S STUNNING ...

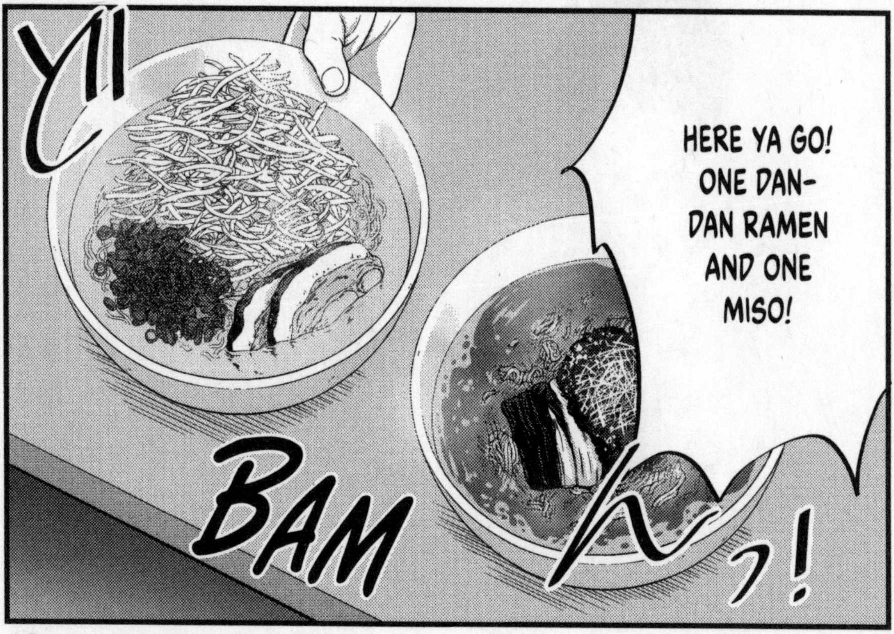
HERE YA GO! ONE DAN-DAN RAMEN AND ONE MISO!
YI
BAM

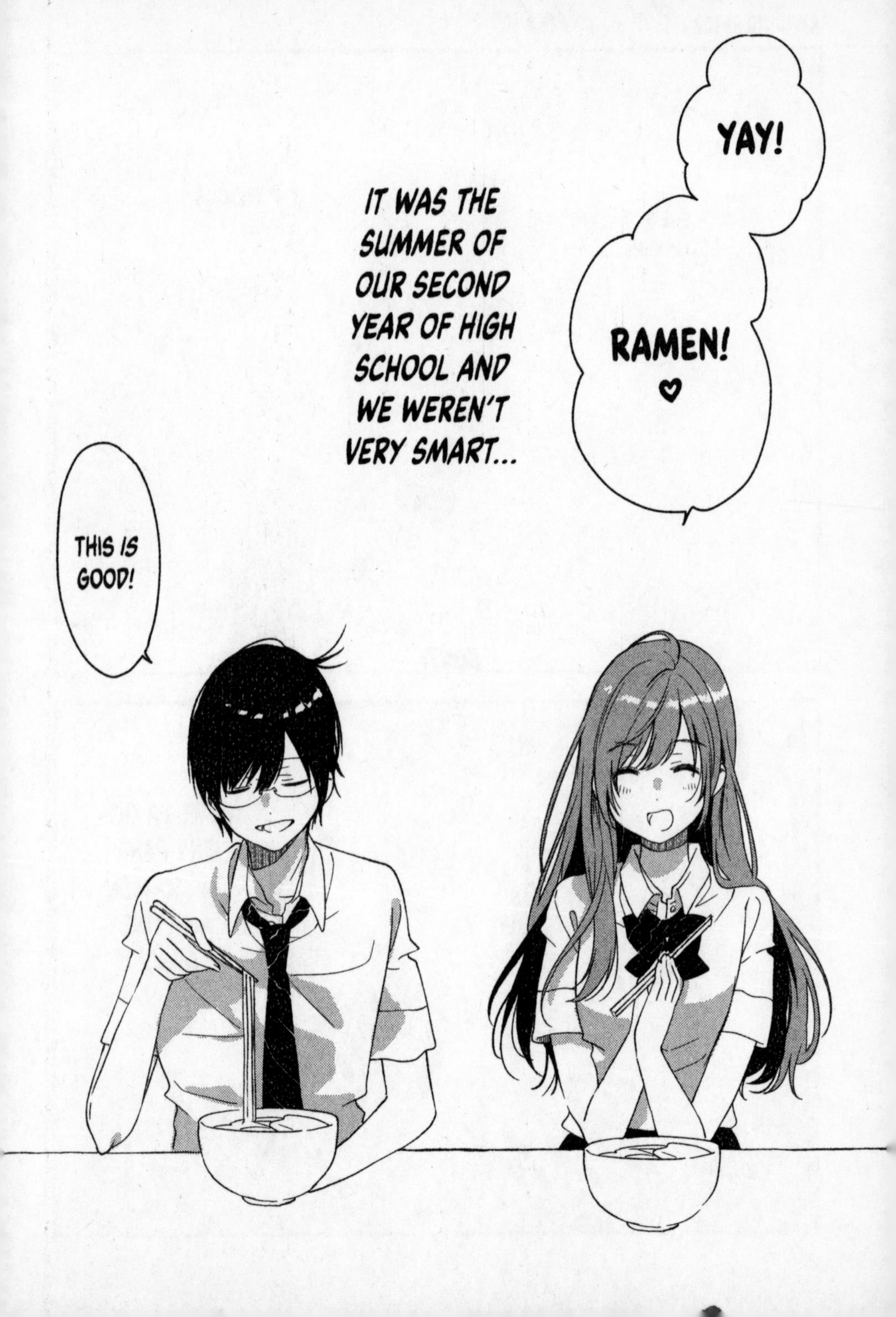
YAY! RAMEN! ♡
IT WAS THE SUMMER OF OUR SECOND YEAR OF HIGH SCHOOL AND WE WEREN'T VERY SMART...
THIS IS GOOD!

Chapter 14:
Crossroads 1

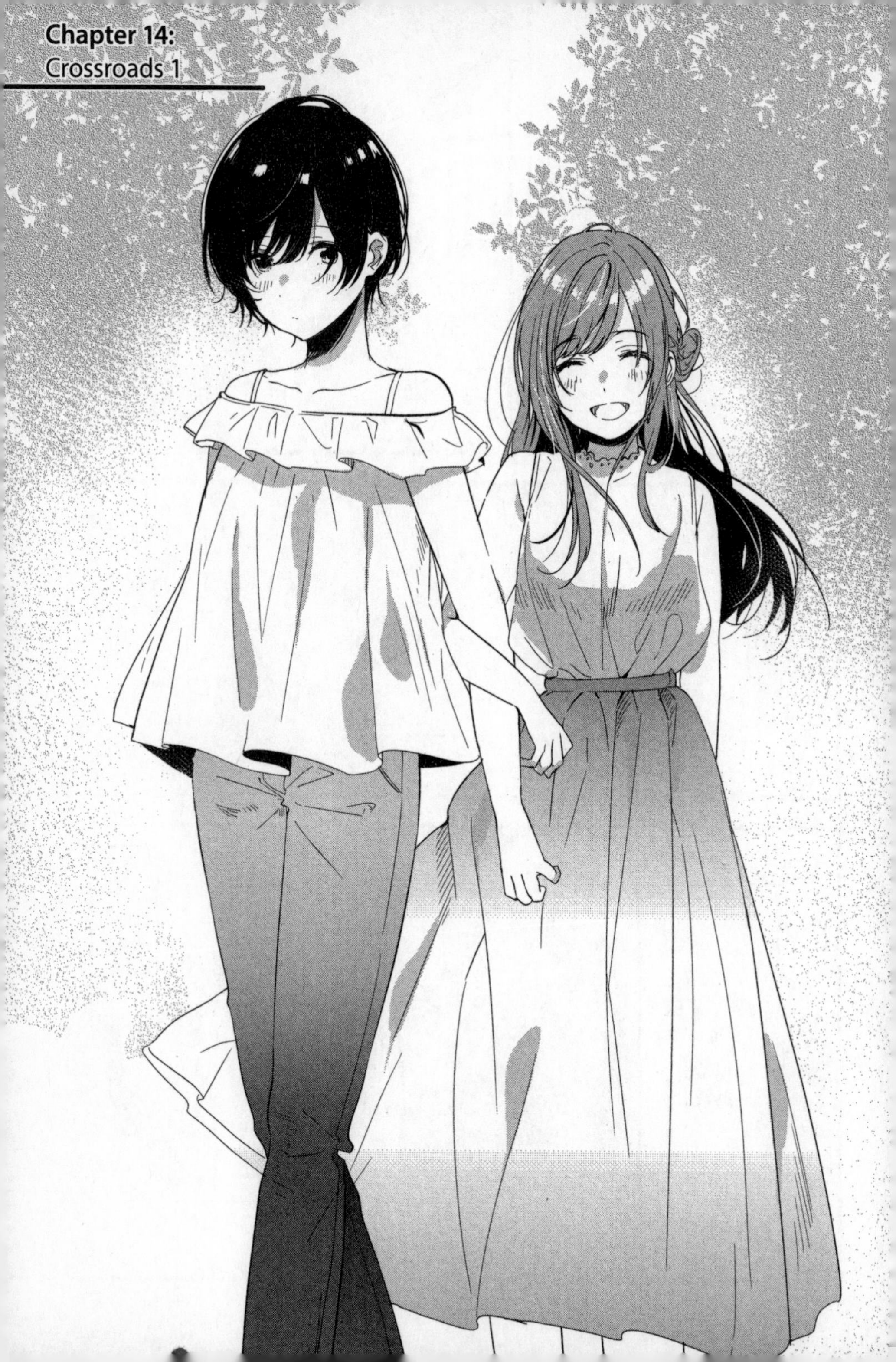

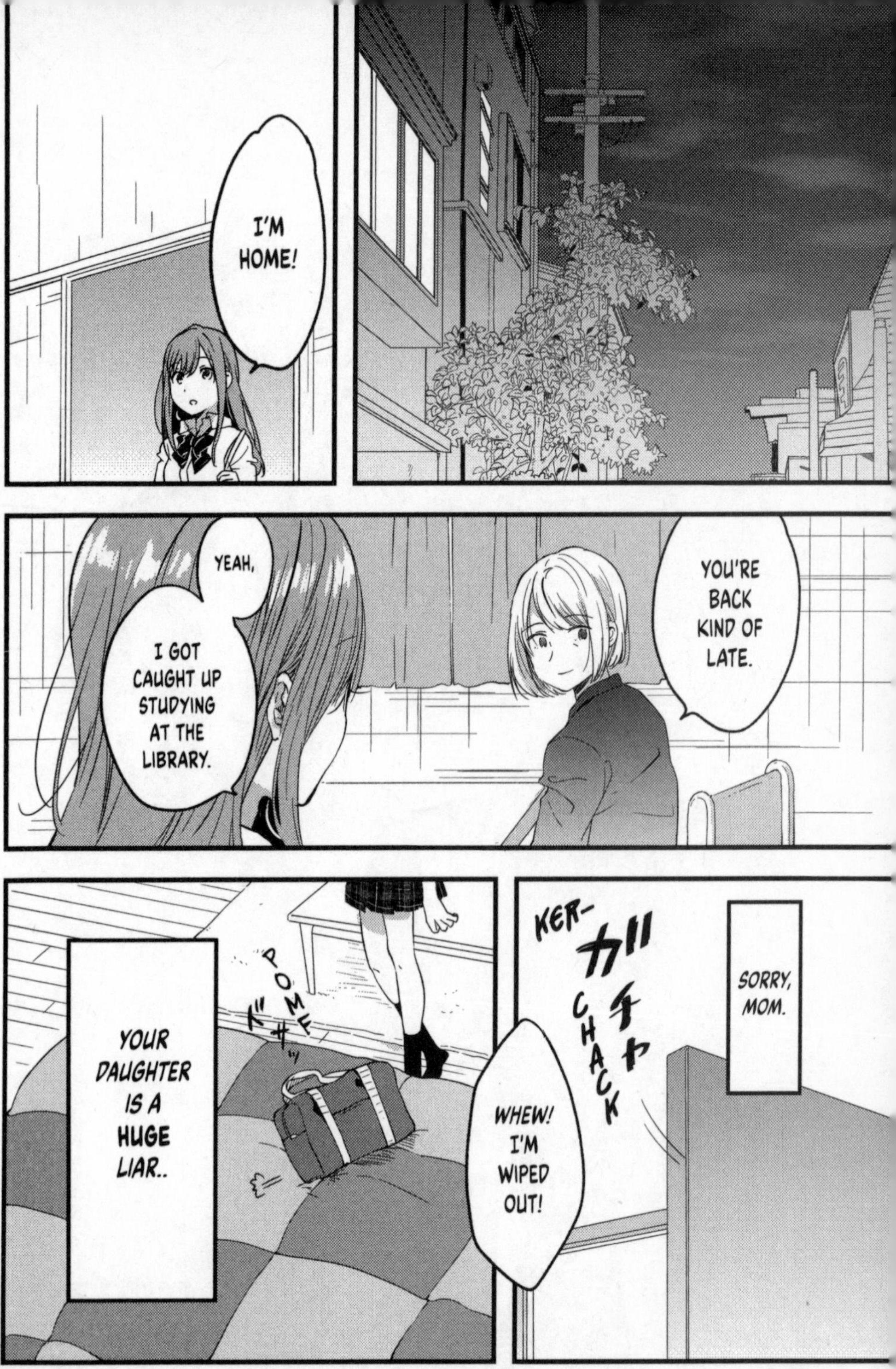
I'M HOME!
YOU'RE BACK KIND OF LATE.
YEAH,
I GOT CAUGHT UP STUDYING AT THE LIBRARY.
SORRY, MOM.
KER-
ガチャ
CHACK
WHEW! I'M WIPED OUT!
POMF
ドサッ
YOUR DAUGHTER IS A HUGE LIAR..

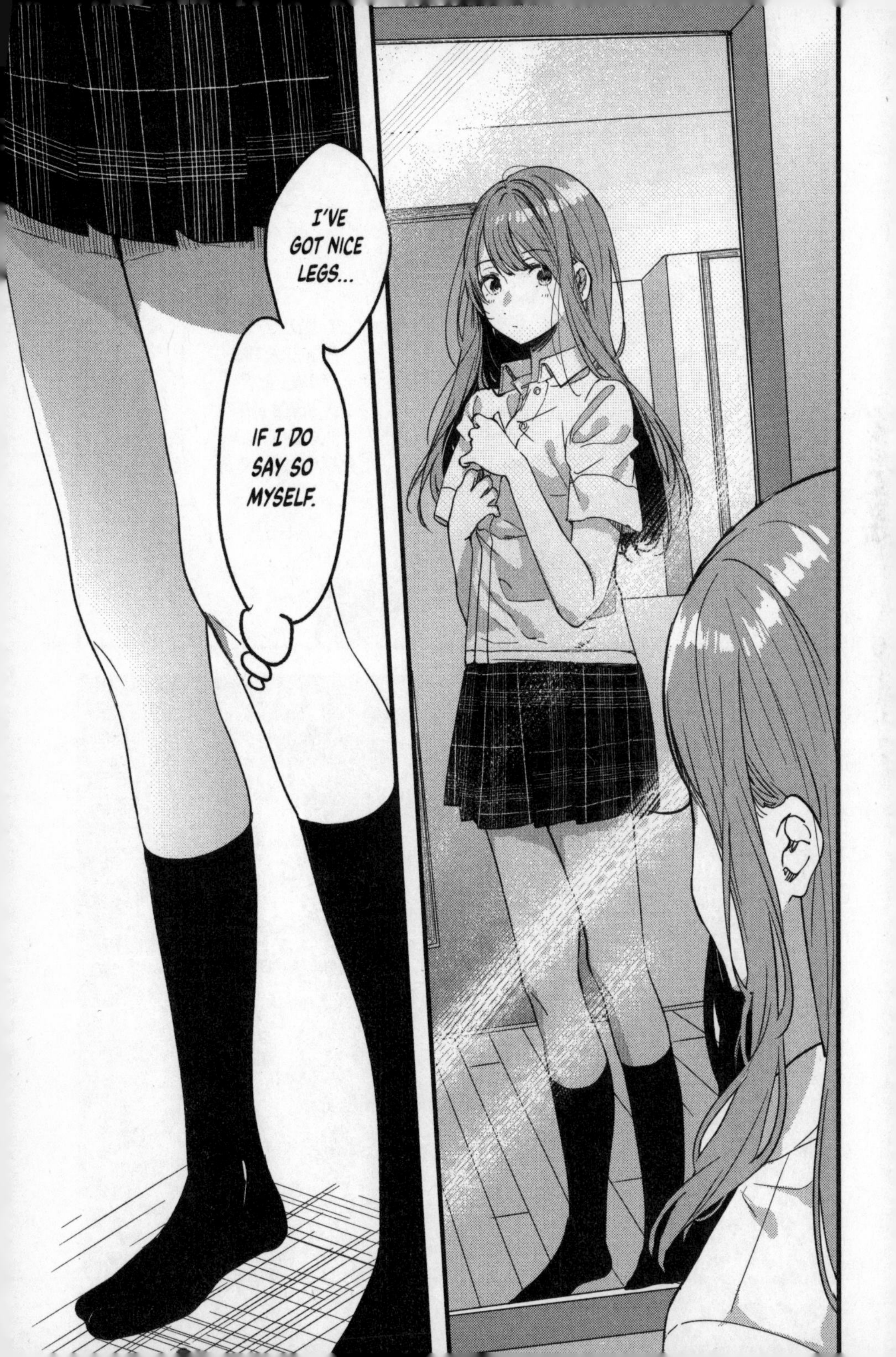
I'VE GOT NICE LEGS...
IF I DO SAY SO MYSELF.

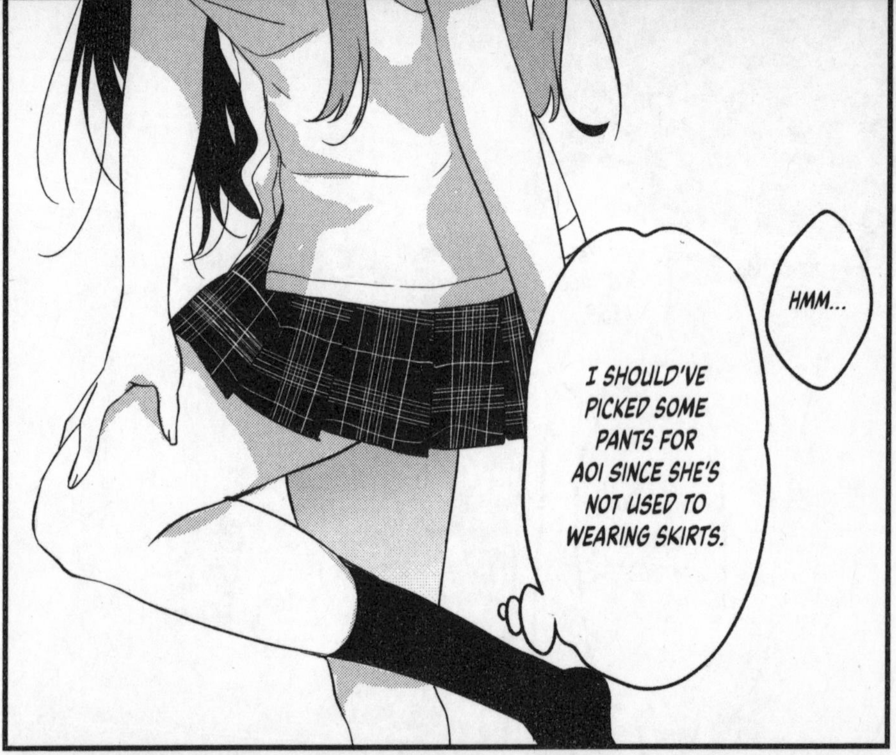
HMM...
I SHOULD'VE PICKED SOME PANTS FOR AOI SINCE SHE'S NOT USED TO WEARING SKIRTS.

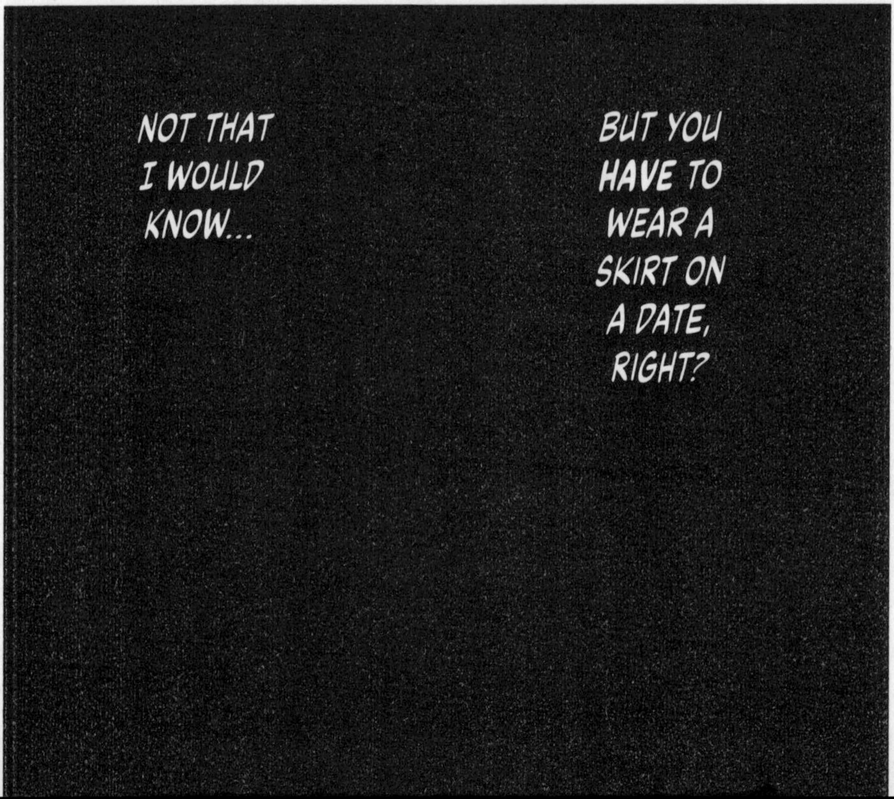
BUT YOU HAVE TO WEAR A SKIRT ON A DATE, RIGHT?
NOT THAT I WOULD KNOW...

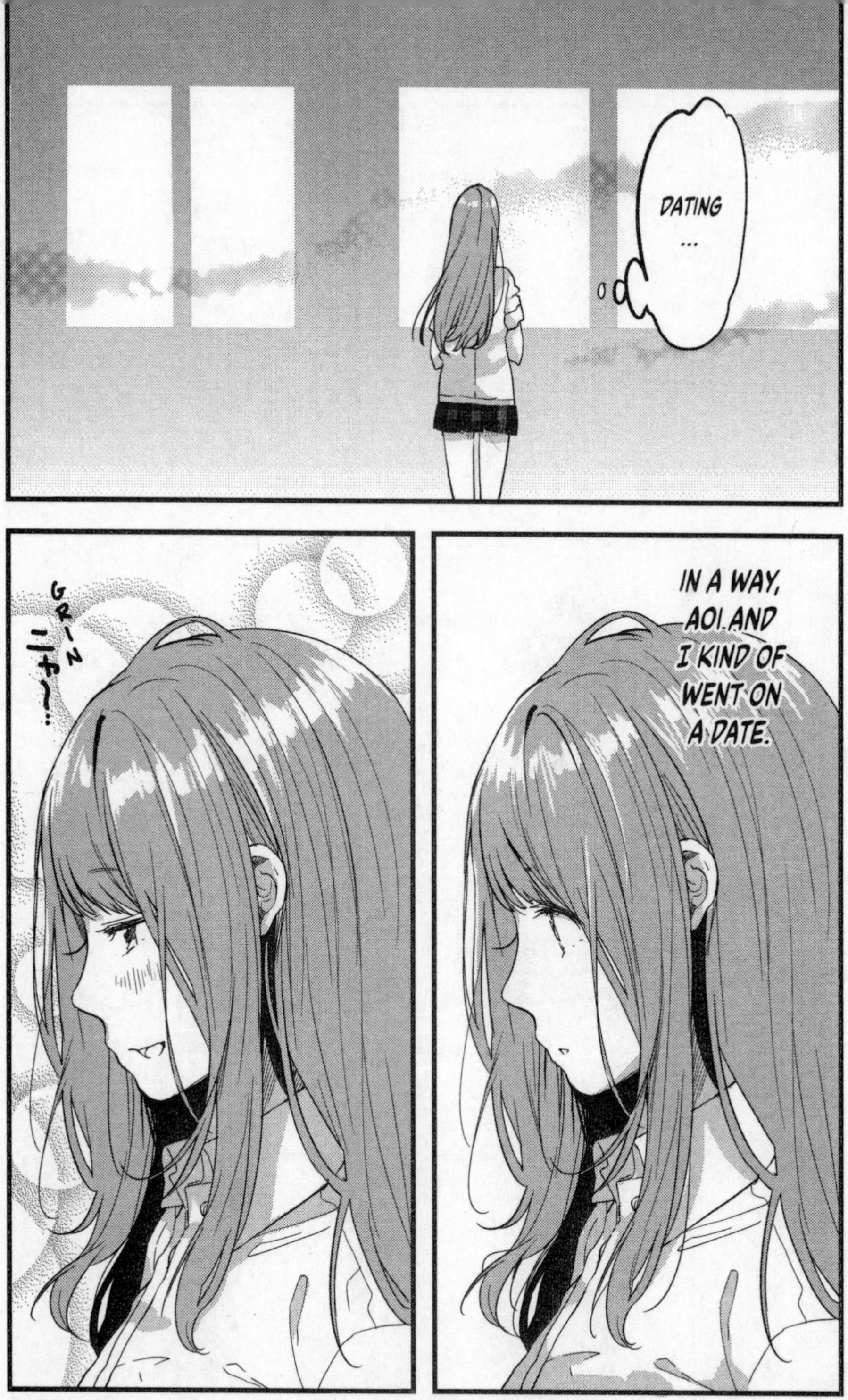
DATING
...
IN A WAY, AOI AND I KIND OF WENT ON A DATE.
GRIN
ニヤ〜…

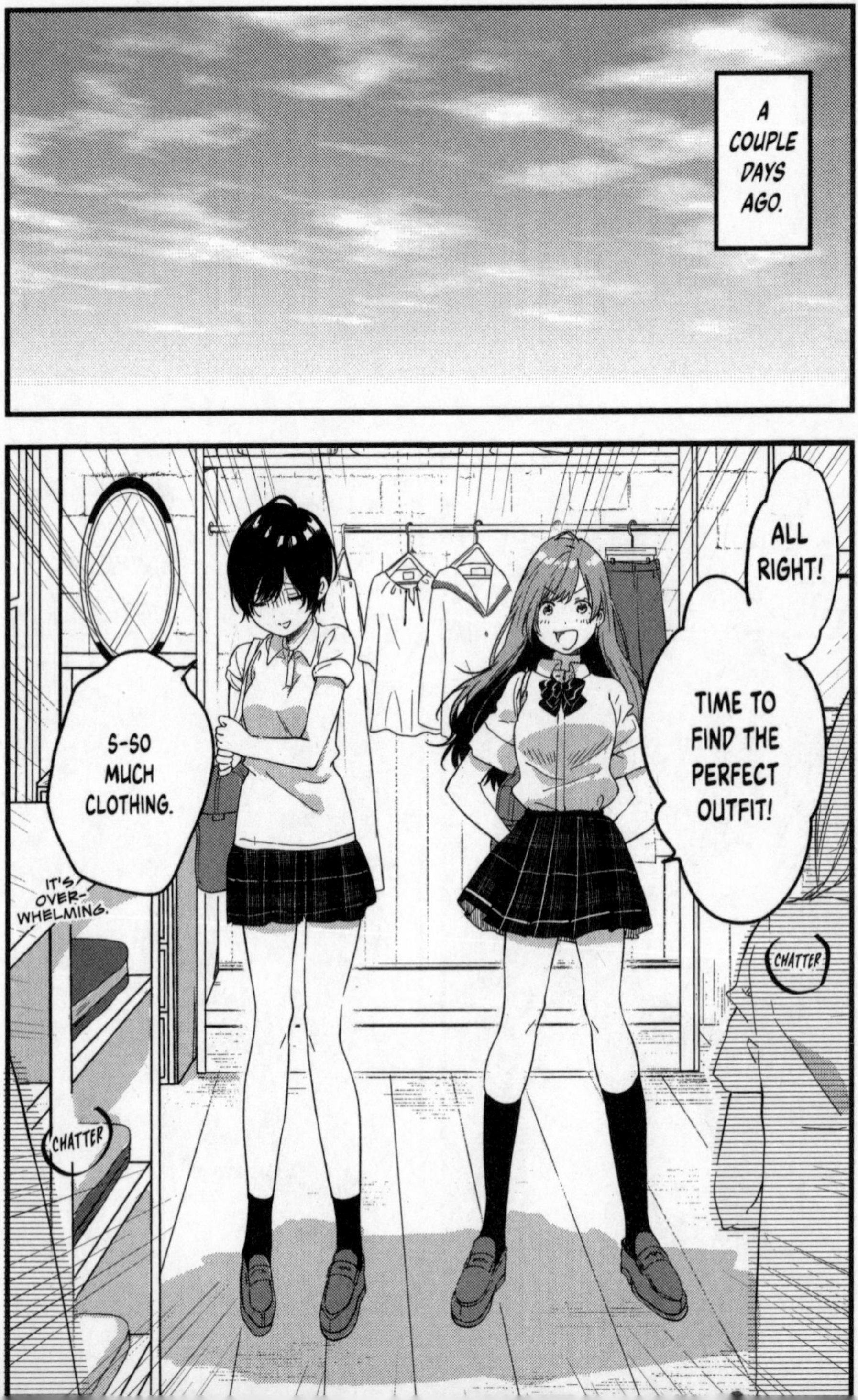
A COUPLE DAYS AGO.
ALL RIGHT!
TIME TO FIND THE PERFECT OUTFIT!
S-SO MUCH CLOTHING.
IT'S OVER-WHELMING.
CHATTER
CHATTER

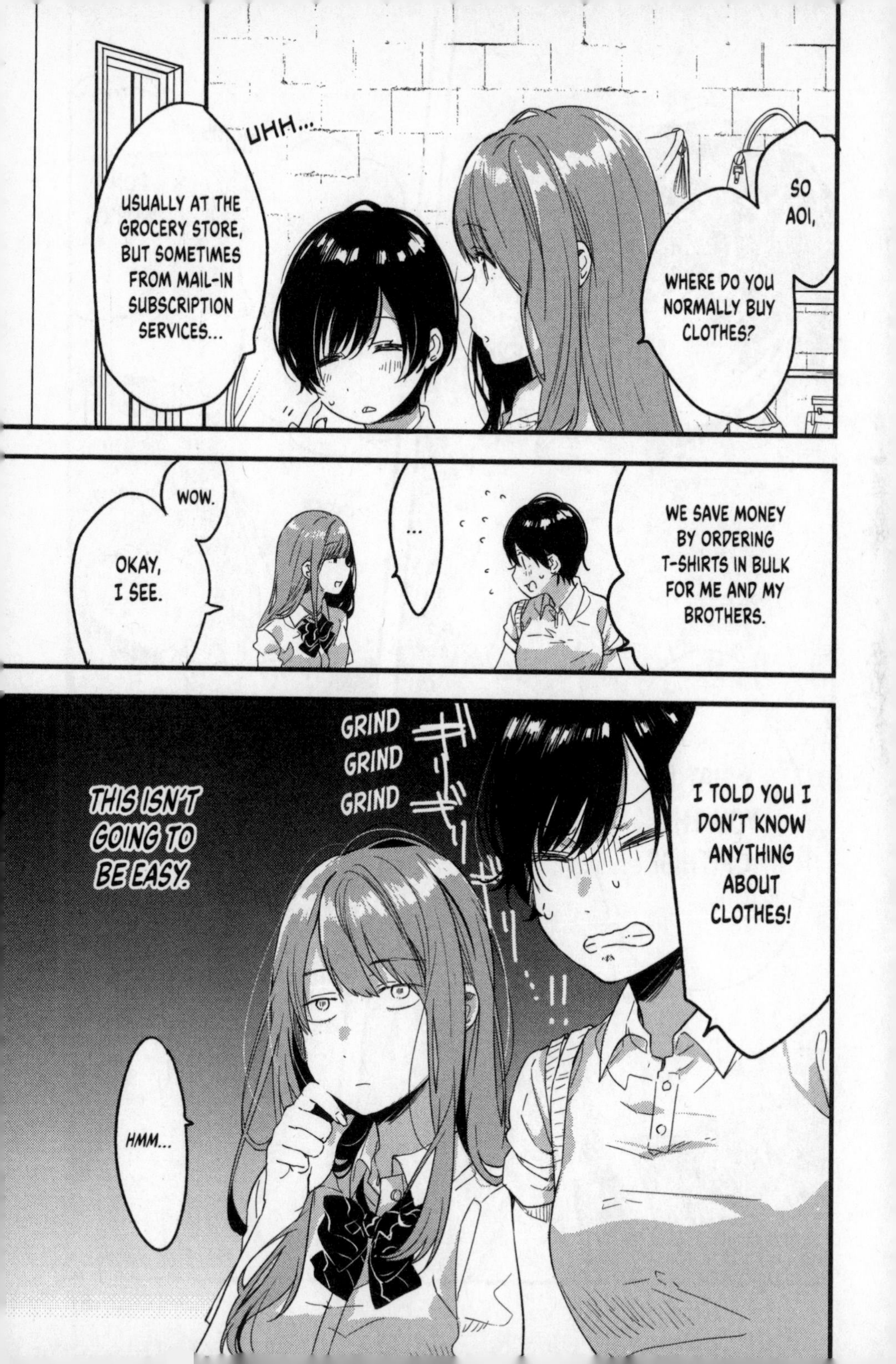
SO AOI,
WHERE DO YOU NORMALLY BUY CLOTHES?
UHH...
USUALLY AT THE GROCERY STORE, BUT SOMETIMES FROM MAIL-IN SUBSCRIPTION SERVICES...
WE SAVE MONEY BY ORDERING T-SHIRTS IN BULK FOR ME AND MY BROTHERS.
...
WOW.
OKAY, I SEE.
I TOLD YOU I DON'T KNOW ANYTHING ABOUT CLOTHES!
GRIND GRIND GRIND
THIS ISN'T GOING TO BE EASY.
HMM...

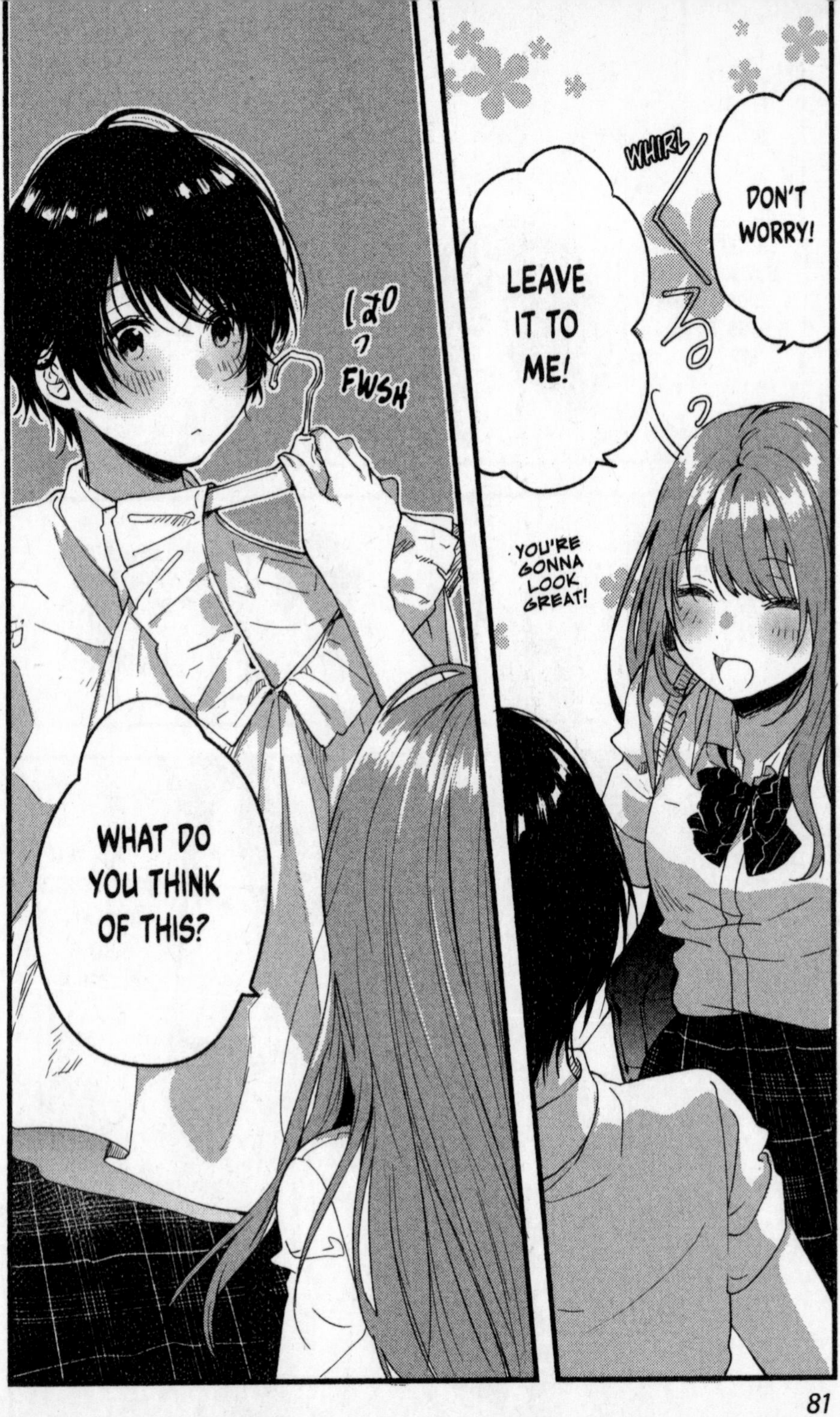
WHIRL
くるっ
DON'T WORRY!
LEAVE IT TO ME!
YOU'RE GONNA LOOK GREAT!
ぱっ
FWSH
WHAT DO YOU THINK OF THIS?

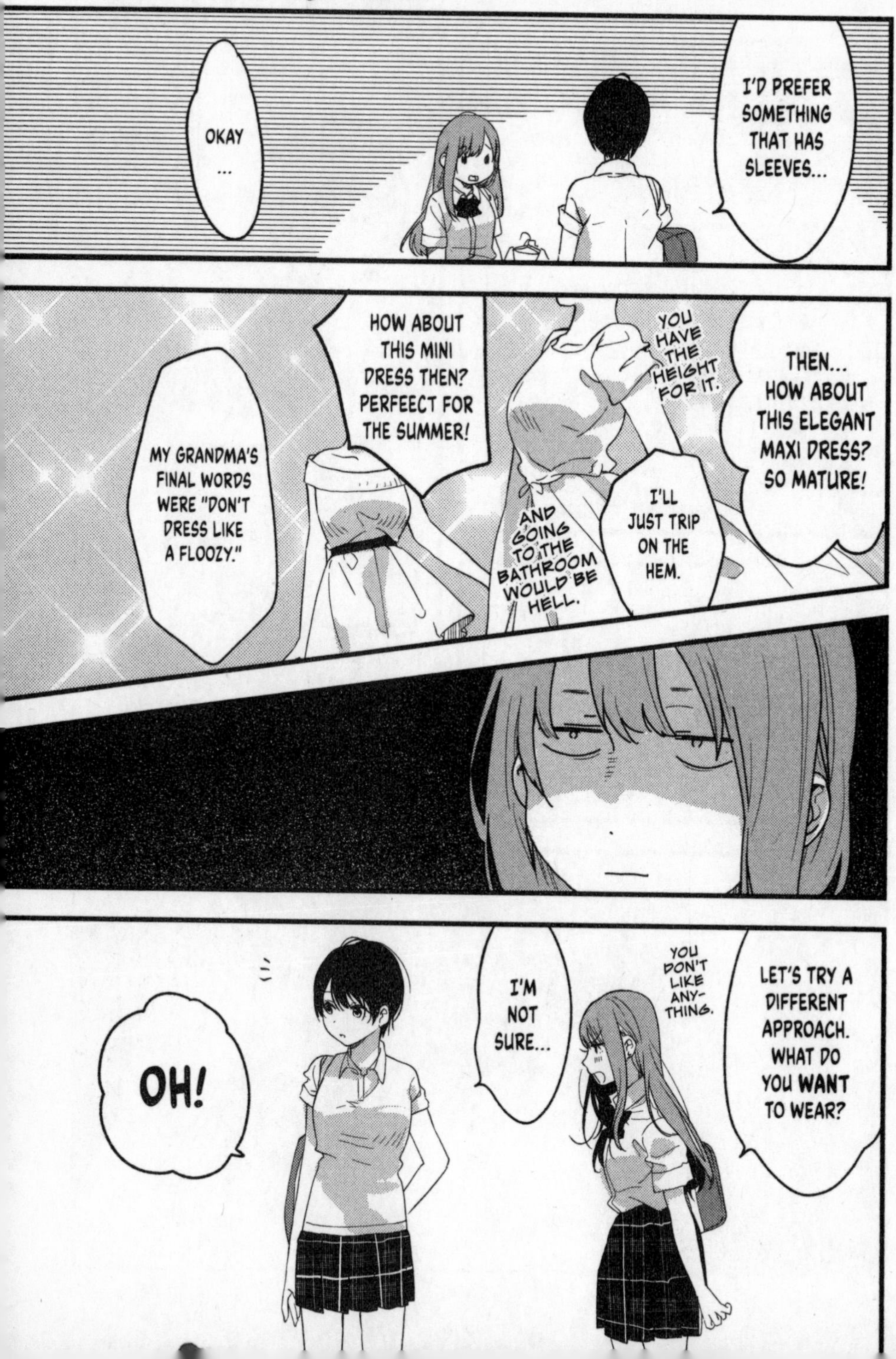
I'D PREFER SOMETHING THAT HAS SLEEVES...
OKAY ...
THEN... HOW ABOUT THIS ELEGANT MAXI DRESS? SO MATURE!
YOU HAVE THE HEIGHT FOR IT.
I'LL JUST TRIP ON THE HEM.
AND GOING TO THE BATHROOM WOULD BE HELL.
HOW ABOUT THIS MINI DRESS THEN? PERFEECT FOR THE SUMMER!
MY GRANDMA'S FINAL WORDS WERE "DON'T DRESS LIKE A FLOOZY."
LET'S TRY A DIFFERENT APPROACH. WHAT DO YOU WANT TO WEAR?
YOU DON'T LIKE ANY-THING.
I'M NOT SURE...
OH!

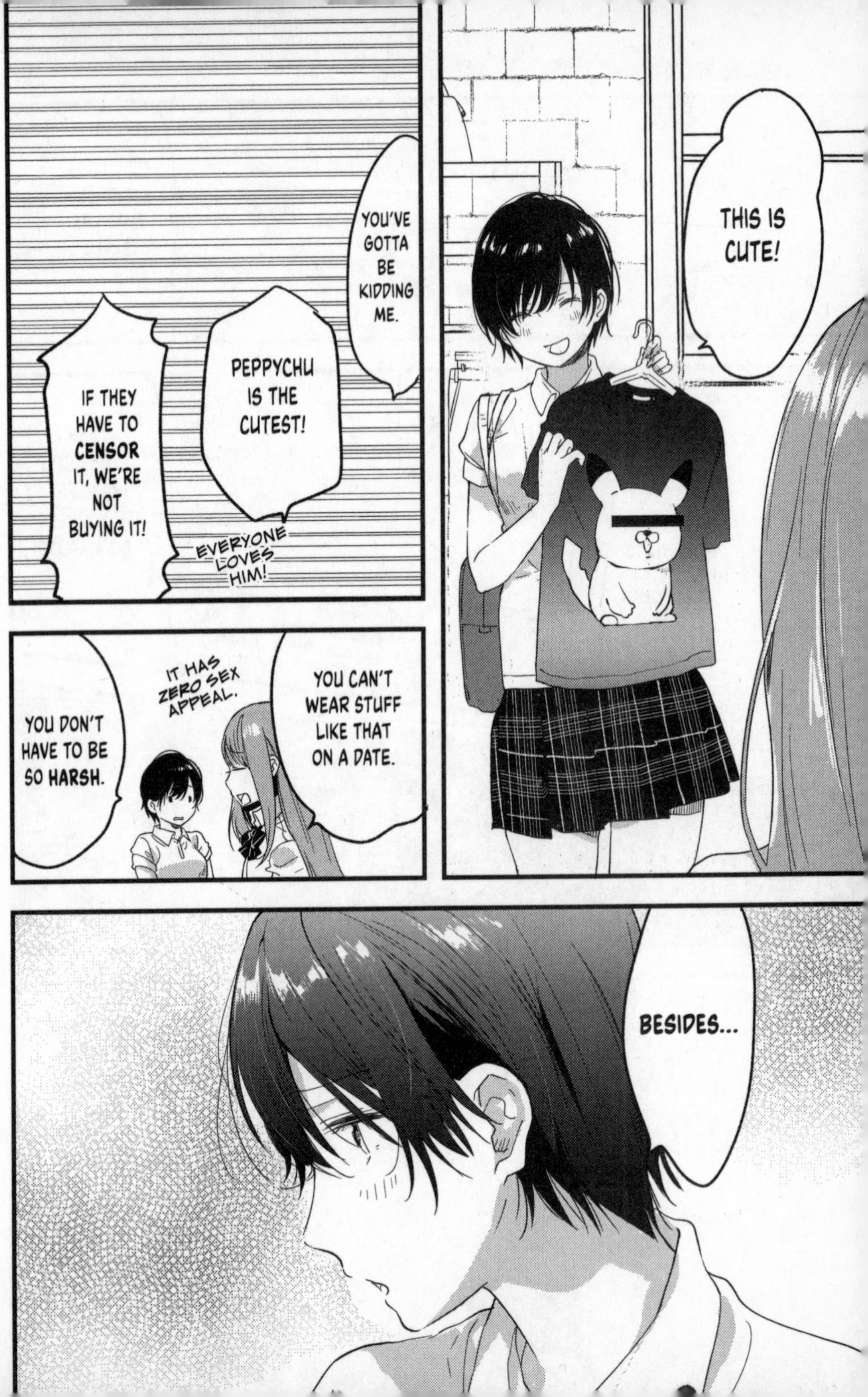
THIS IS CUTE!
YOU'VE GOTTA BE KIDDING ME.
PEPPYCHU IS THE CUTEST!
EVERYONE LOVES HIM!
IF THEY HAVE TO CENSOR IT, WE'RE NOT BUYING IT!
YOU CAN'T WEAR STUFF LIKE THAT ON A DATE.
IT HAS ZERO SEX APPEAL.
YOU DON'T HAVE TO BE SO HARSH.
BESIDES...

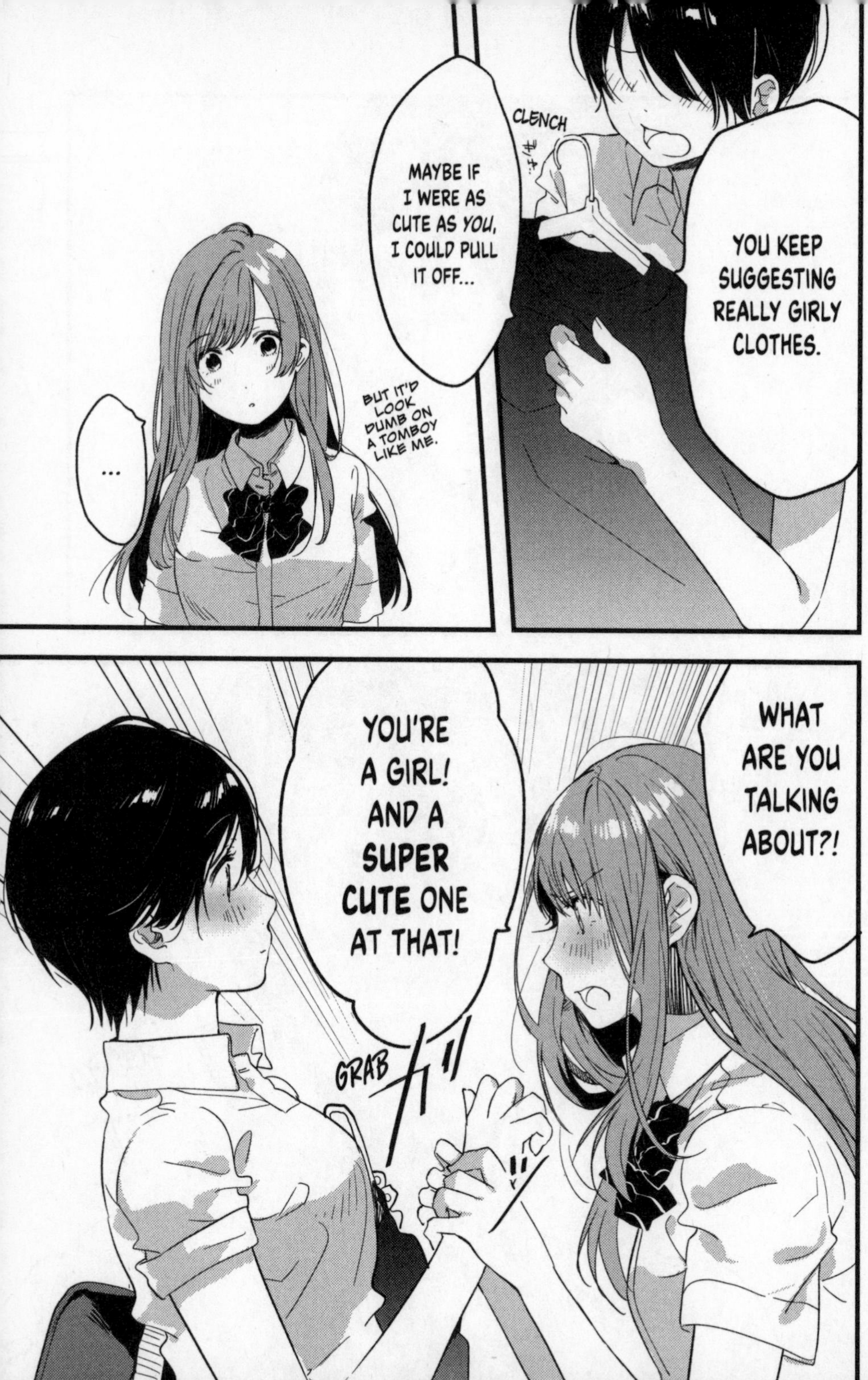
YOU KEEP SUGGESTING REALLY GIRLY CLOTHES.
CLENCH
MAYBE IF I WERE AS CUTE AS *YOU*, I COULD PULL IT OFF...
BUT IT'D LOOK DUMB ON A TOMBOY LIKE ME.
...
WHAT ARE YOU TALKING ABOUT?!
YOU'RE A GIRL! AND A **SUPER CUTE** ONE AT THAT!
GRAB
!!

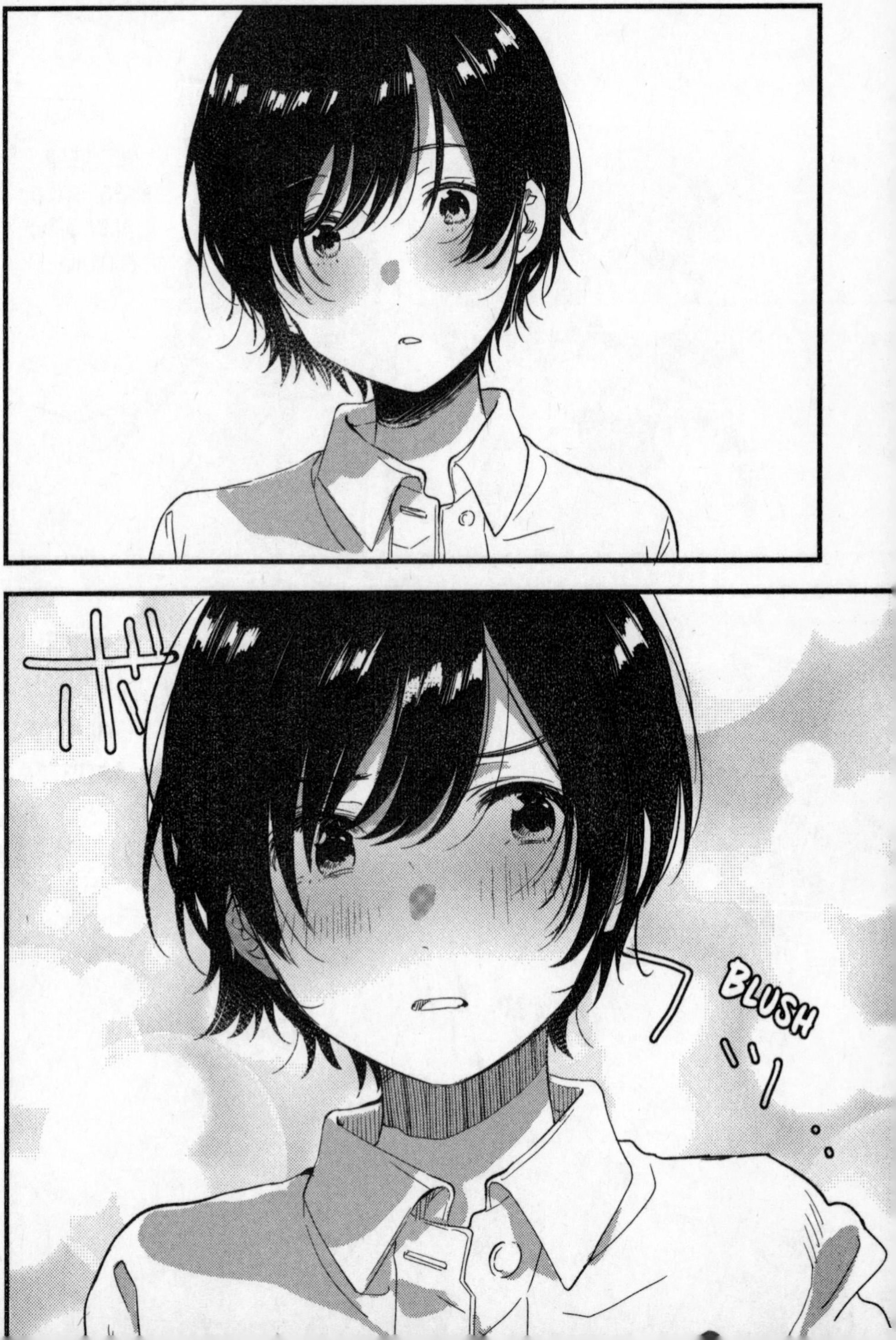
BLUSH

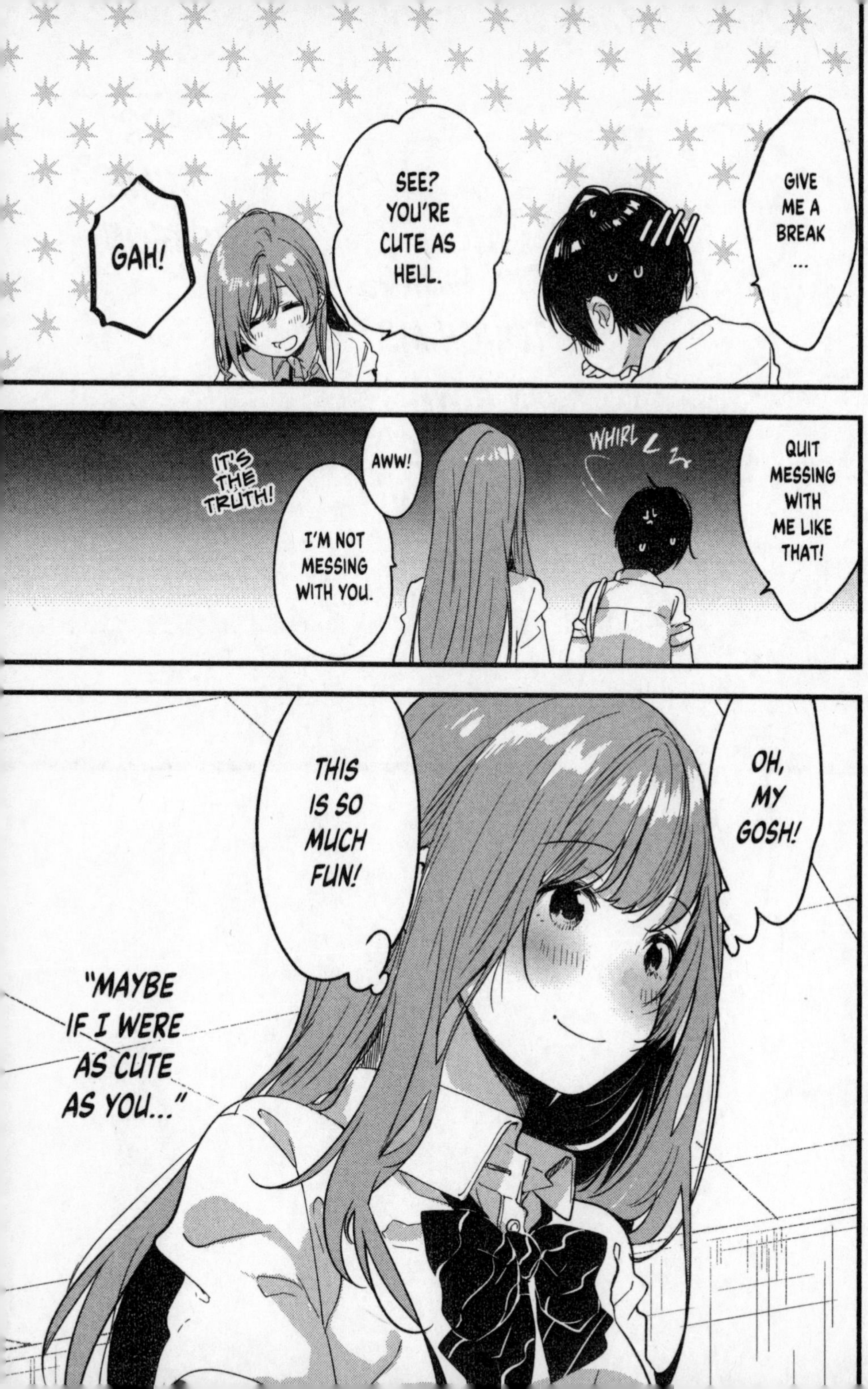
GIVE ME A BREAK ...
SEE? YOU'RE CUTE AS HELL.
GAH!
QUIT MESSING WITH ME LIKE THAT!
WHIRL
AWW!
I'M NOT MESSING WITH YOU.
IT'S THE TRUTH!
OH, MY GOSH!
THIS IS SO MUCH FUN!
"MAYBE IF I WERE AS CUTE AS YOU..."

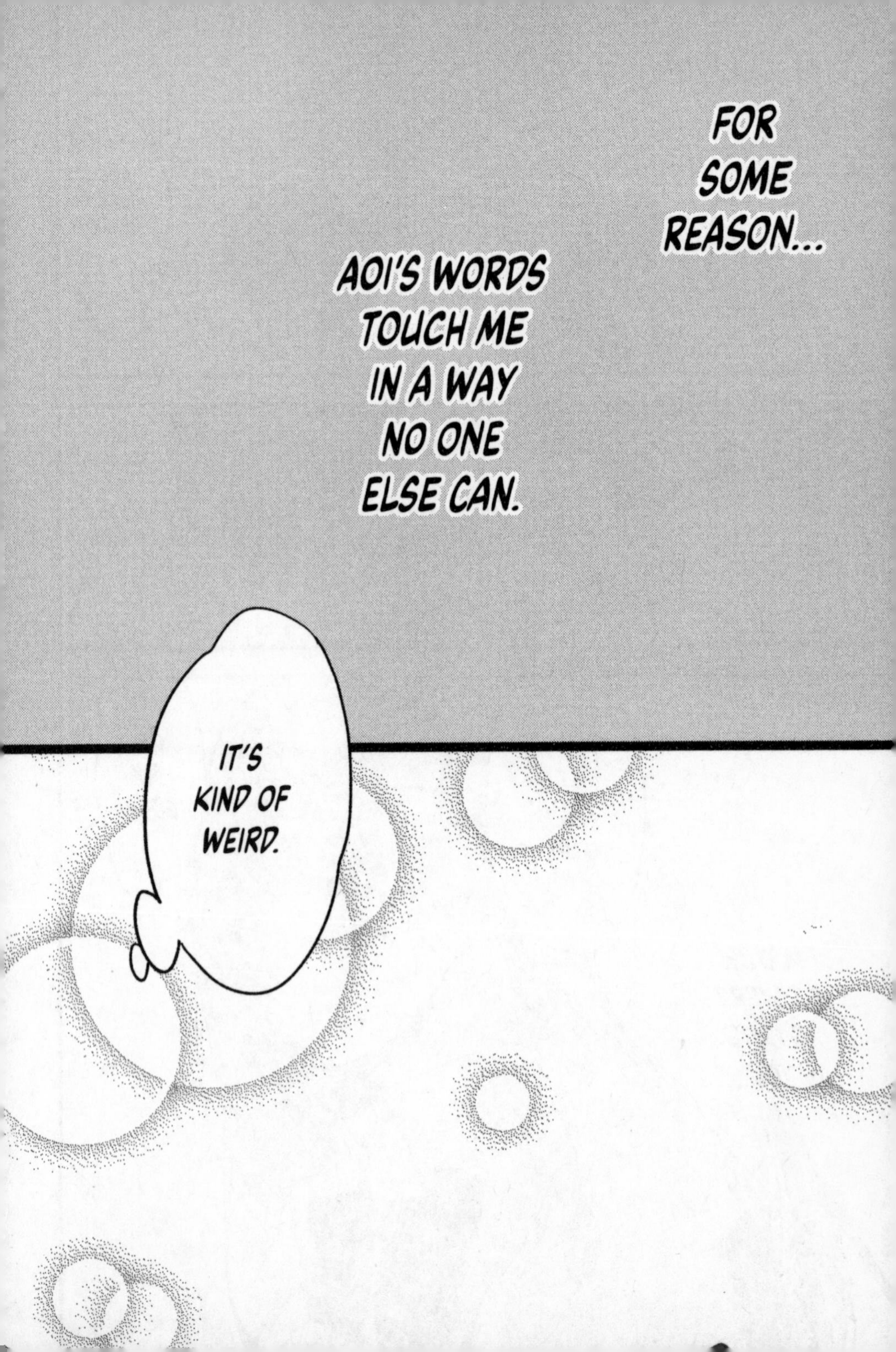
FOR SOME REASON...
AOI'S WORDS TOUCH ME IN A WAY NO ONE ELSE CAN.
IT'S KIND OF WEIRD.

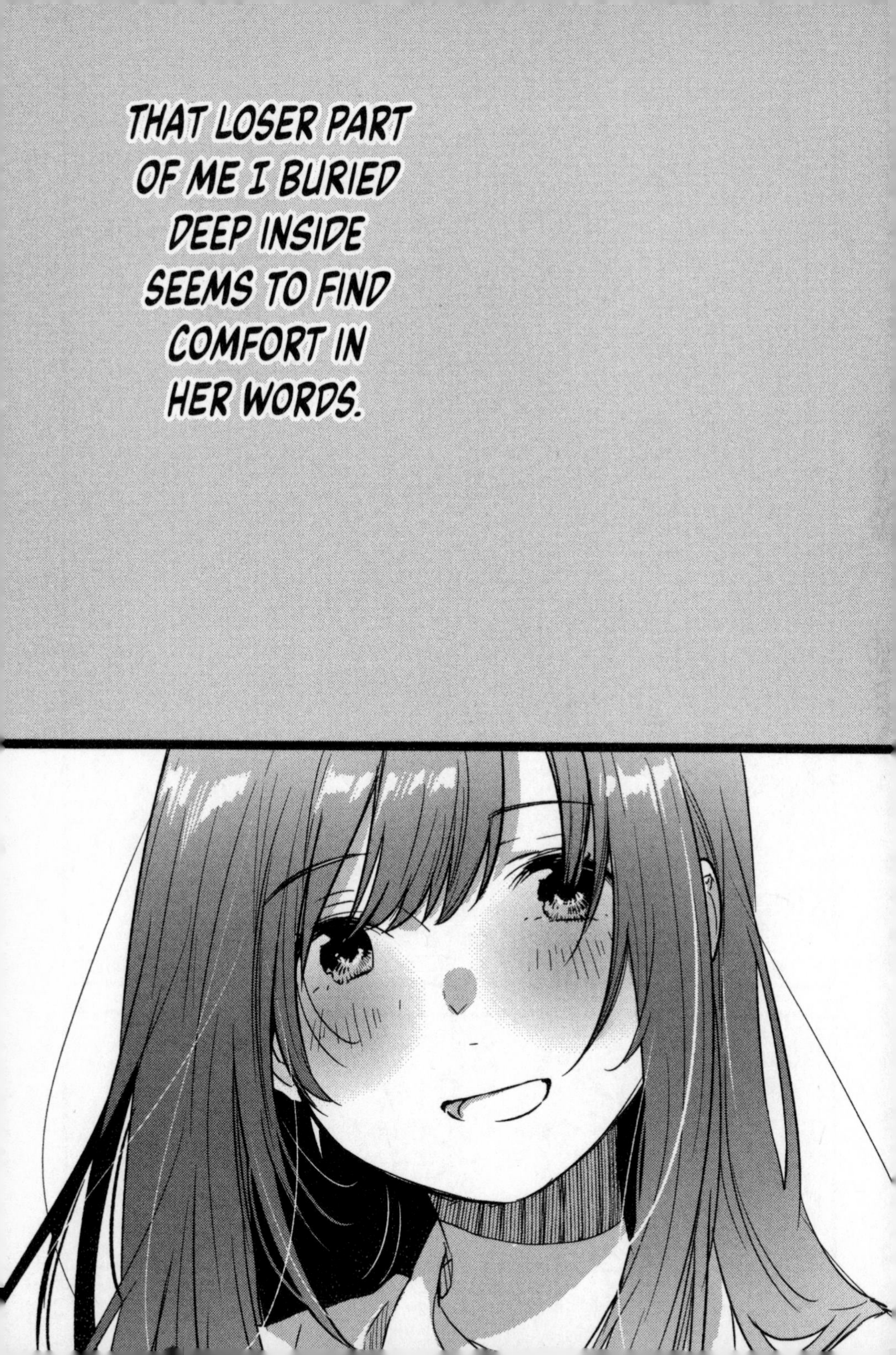
THAT LOSER PART OF ME I BURIED DEEP INSIDE SEEMS TO FIND COMFORT IN HER WORDS.

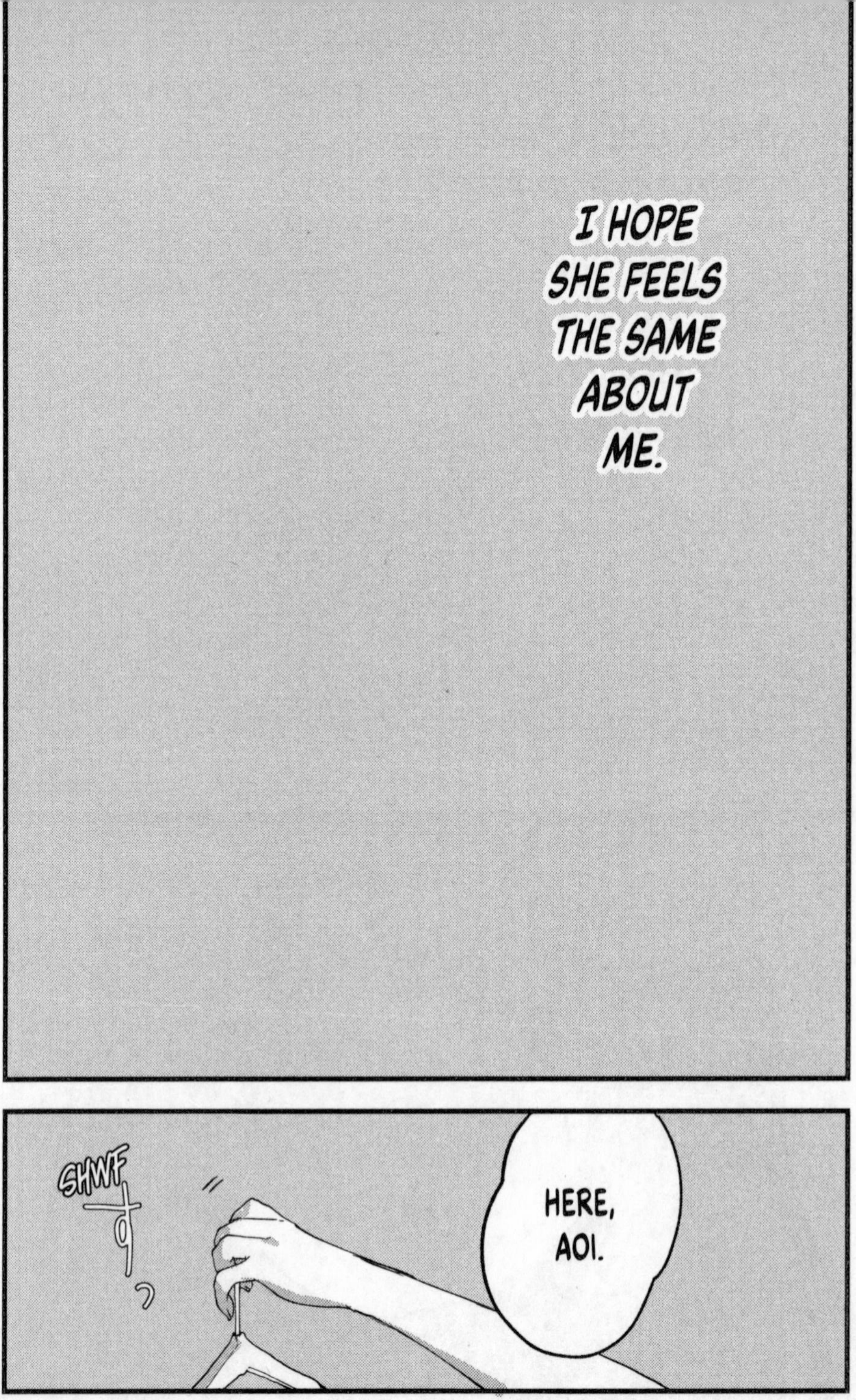
I HOPE SHE FEELS THE SAME ABOUT ME.
HERE, AOI.
SHWF
すっ

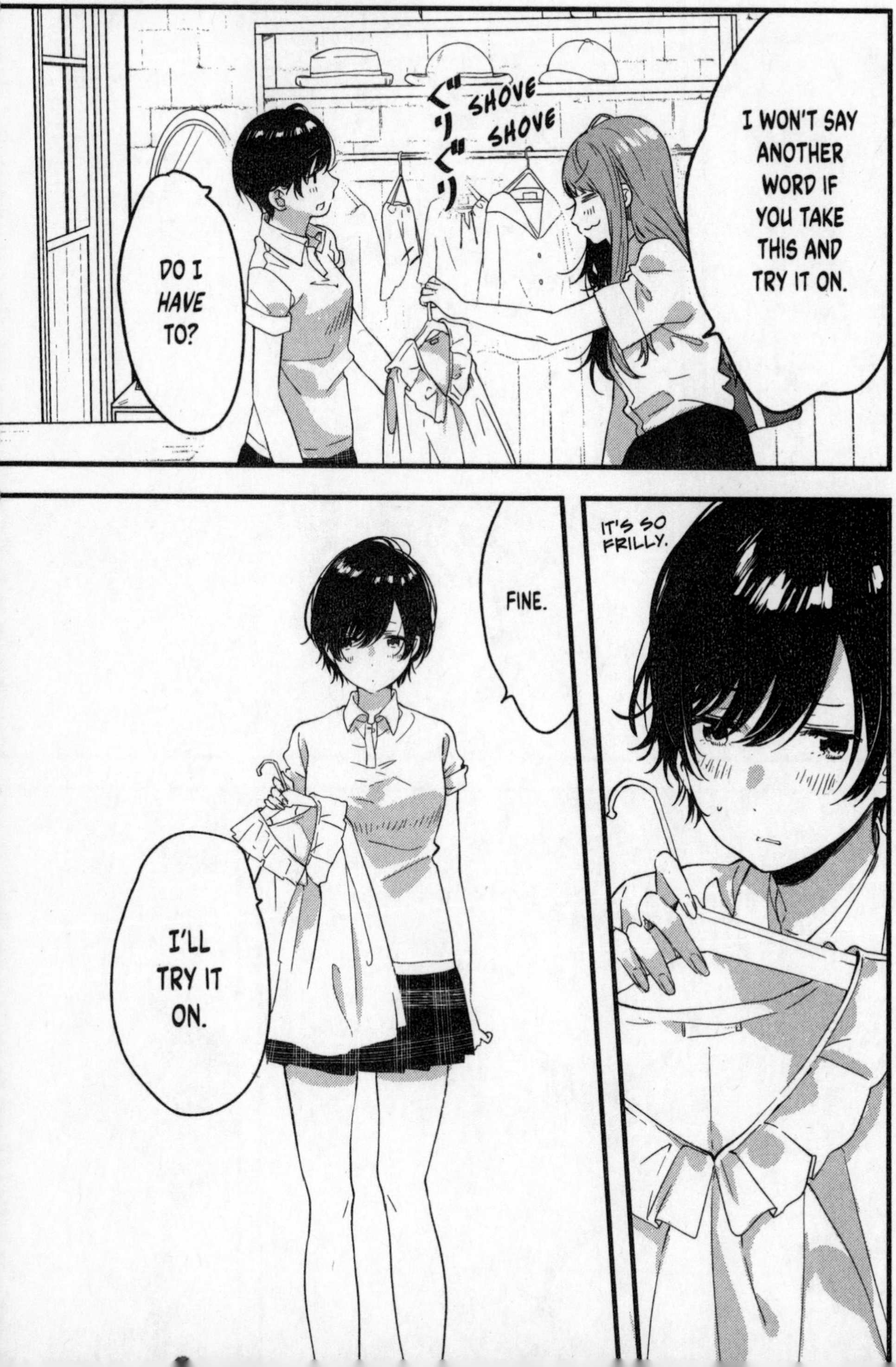
I WON'T SAY ANOTHER WORD IF YOU TAKE THIS AND TRY IT ON.
ぐりぐり
SHOVE SHOVE
DO I HAVE TO?
IT'S SO FRILLY.
FINE.
I'LL TRY IT ON.

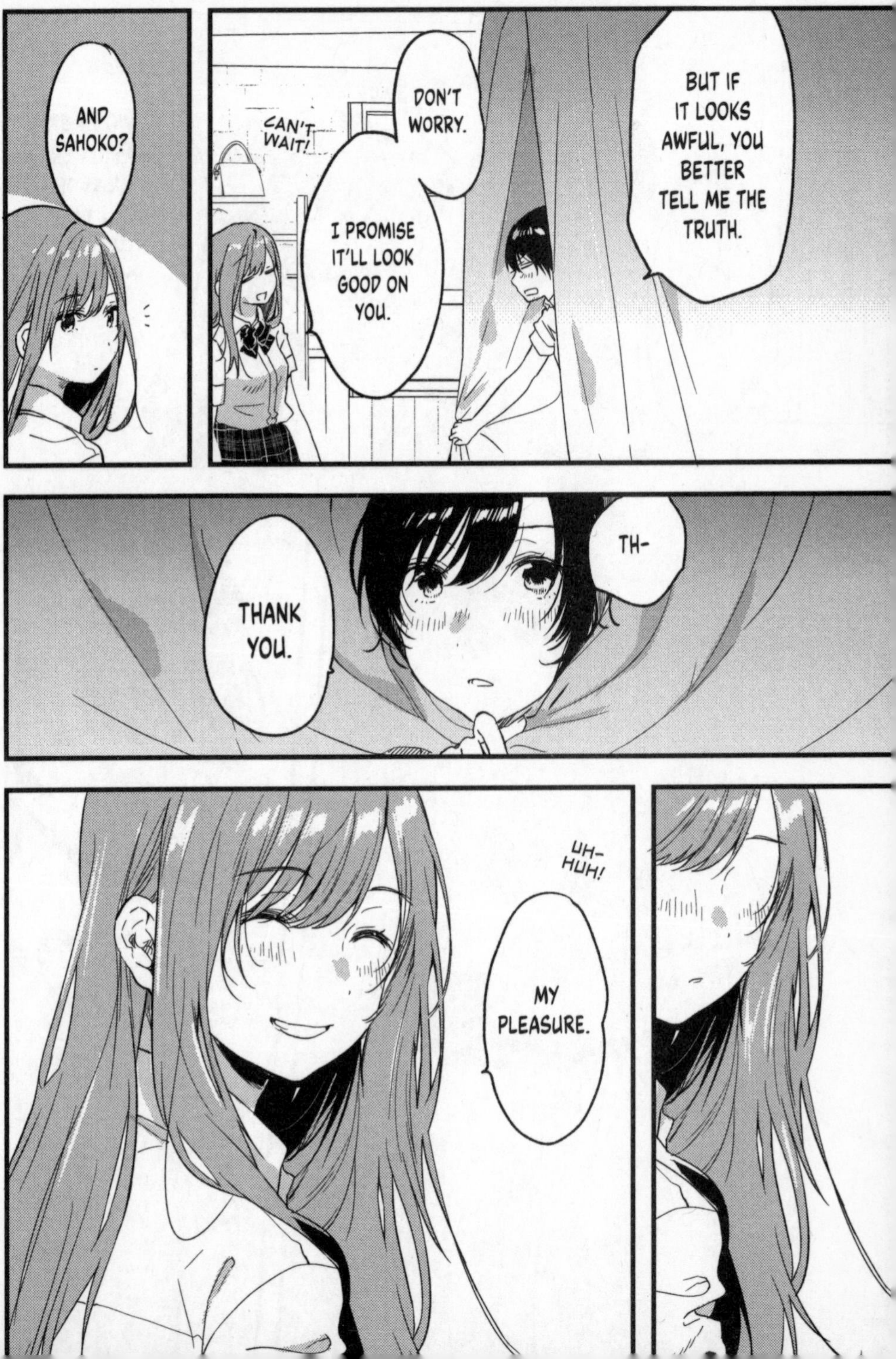
BUT IF IT LOOKS AWFUL, YOU BETTER TELL ME THE TRUTH.
DON'T WORRY.
CAN'T WAIT!
I PROMISE IT'LL LOOK GOOD ON YOU.
AND SAHOKO?
TH-
THANK YOU.
UH-HUH!
MY PLEASURE.

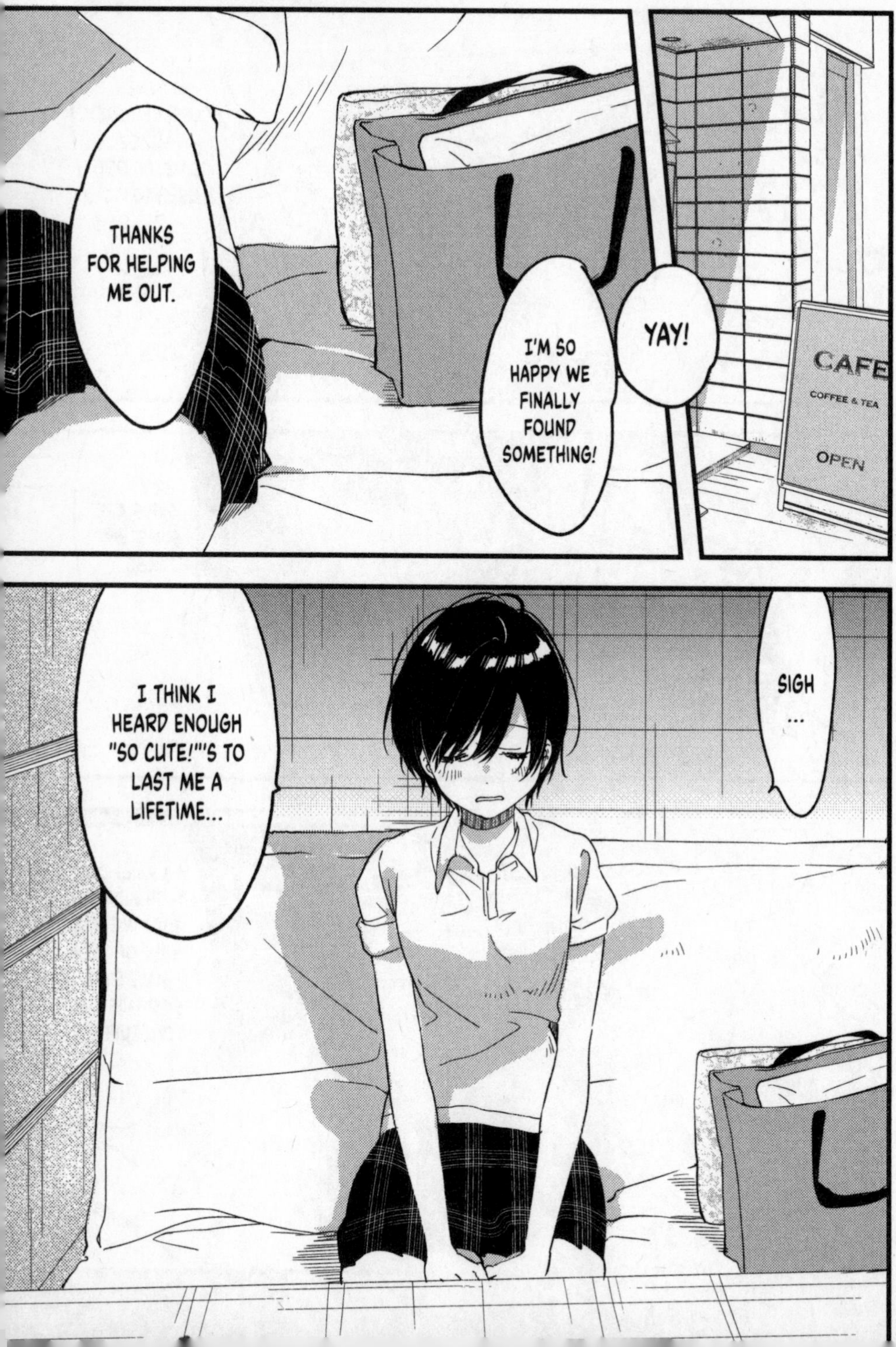
CAFE
COFFEE & TEA
OPEN
YAY!
I'M SO HAPPY WE FINALLY FOUND SOMETHING!
THANKS FOR HELPING ME OUT.
SIGH ...
I THINK I HEARD ENOUGH "SO CUTE!"'S TO LAST ME A LIFETIME...

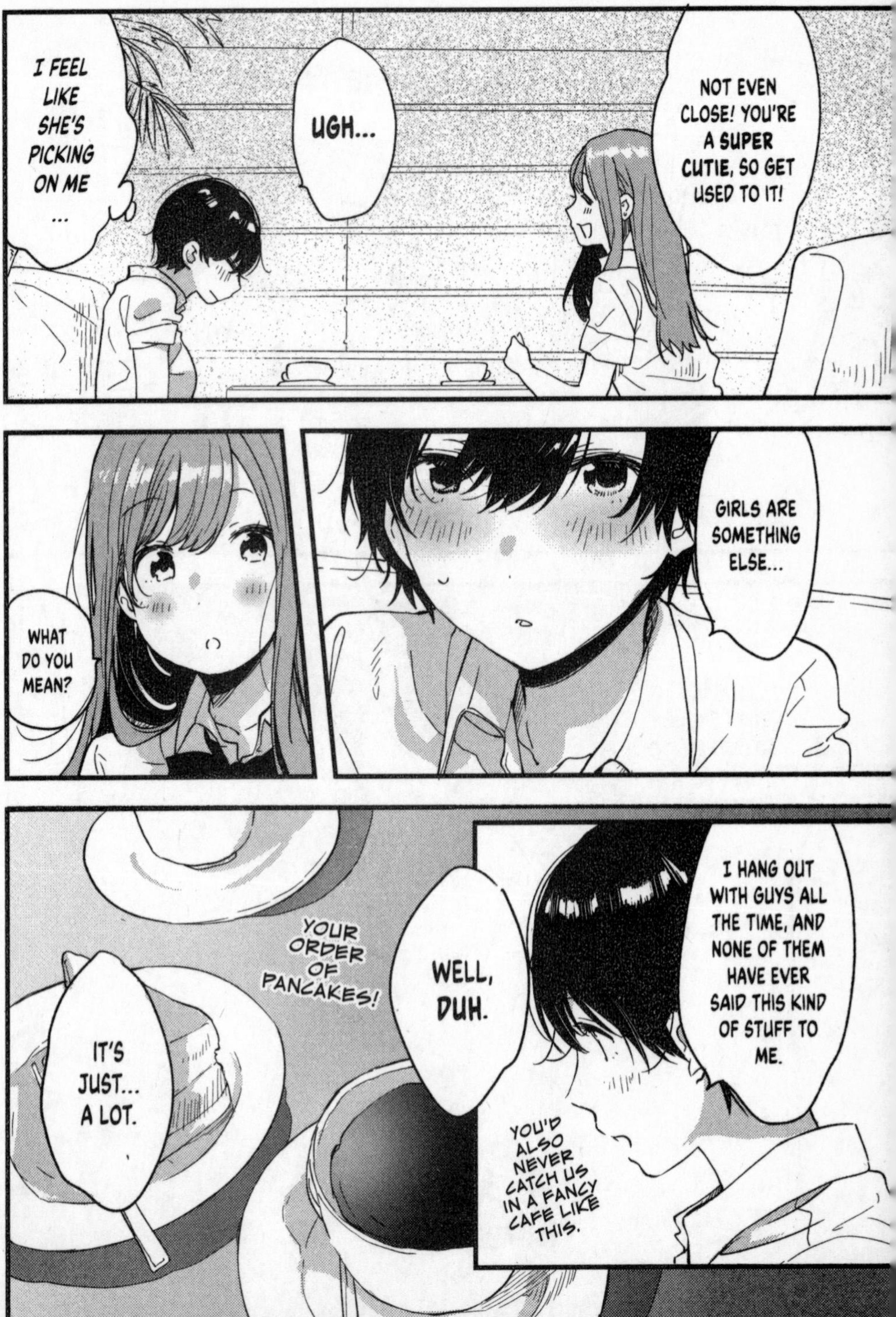
NOT EVEN CLOSE! YOU'RE A SUPER CUTIE, SO GET USED TO IT!
UGH...
I FEEL LIKE SHE'S PICKING ON ME ...
GIRLS ARE SOMETHING ELSE...
WHAT DO YOU MEAN?
I HANG OUT WITH GUYS ALL THE TIME, AND NONE OF THEM HAVE EVER SAID THIS KIND OF STUFF TO ME.
YOU'D ALSO NEVER CATCH US IN A FANCY CAFE LIKE THIS.
WELL, DUH.
YOUR ORDER OF PANCAKES!
IT'S JUST... A LOT.

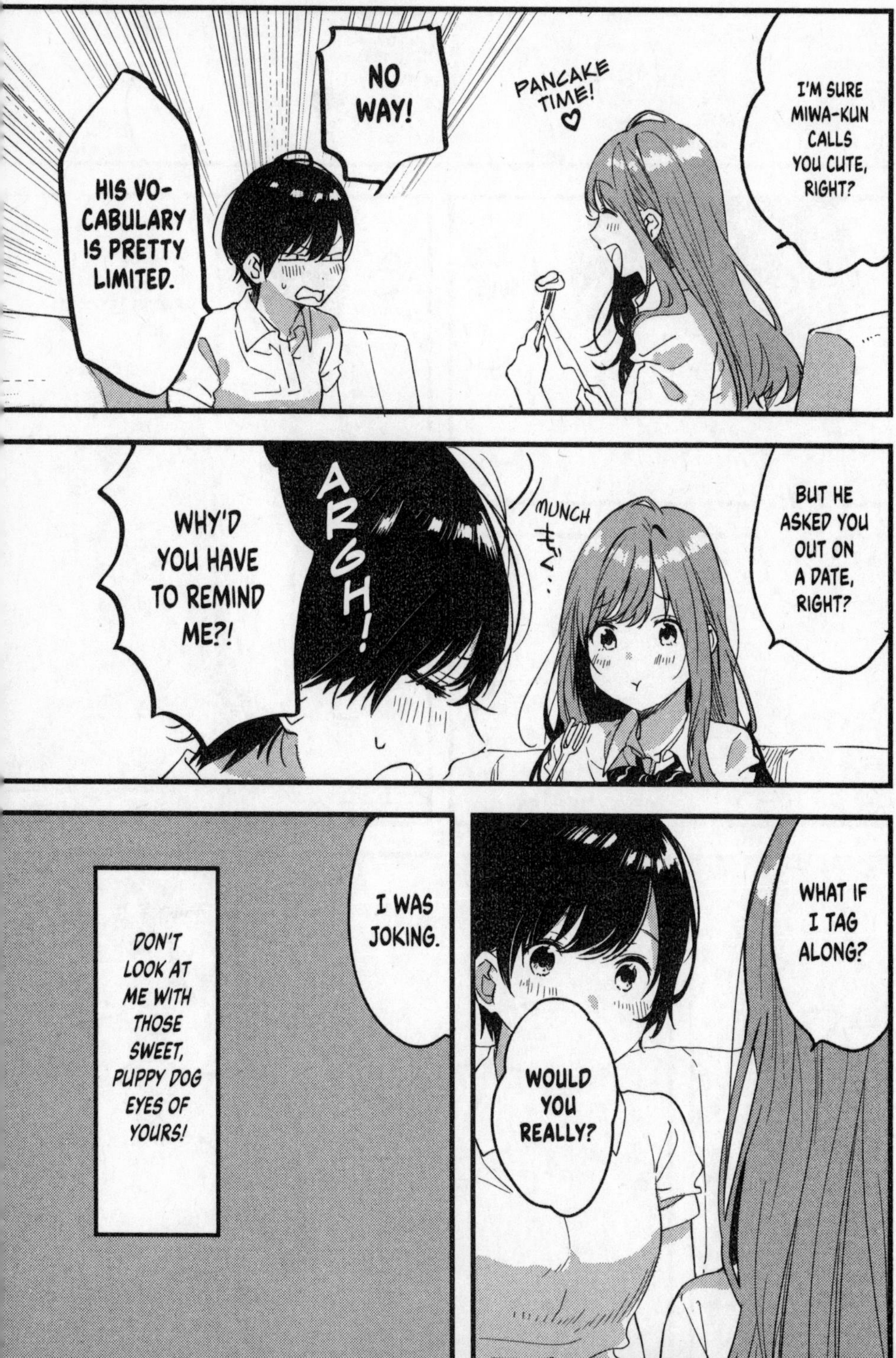
I'M SURE MIWA-KUN CALLS YOU CUTE, RIGHT?
PANCAKE TIME! ♡
NO WAY!
HIS VO-CABULARY IS PRETTY LIMITED.
BUT HE ASKED YOU OUT ON A DATE, RIGHT?
MUNCH
もぐ…
ARGH!
WHY'D YOU HAVE TO REMIND ME?!
WHAT IF I TAG ALONG?
WOULD YOU REALLY?
I WAS JOKING.
DON'T LOOK AT ME WITH THOSE SWEET, PUPPY DOG EYES OF YOURS!

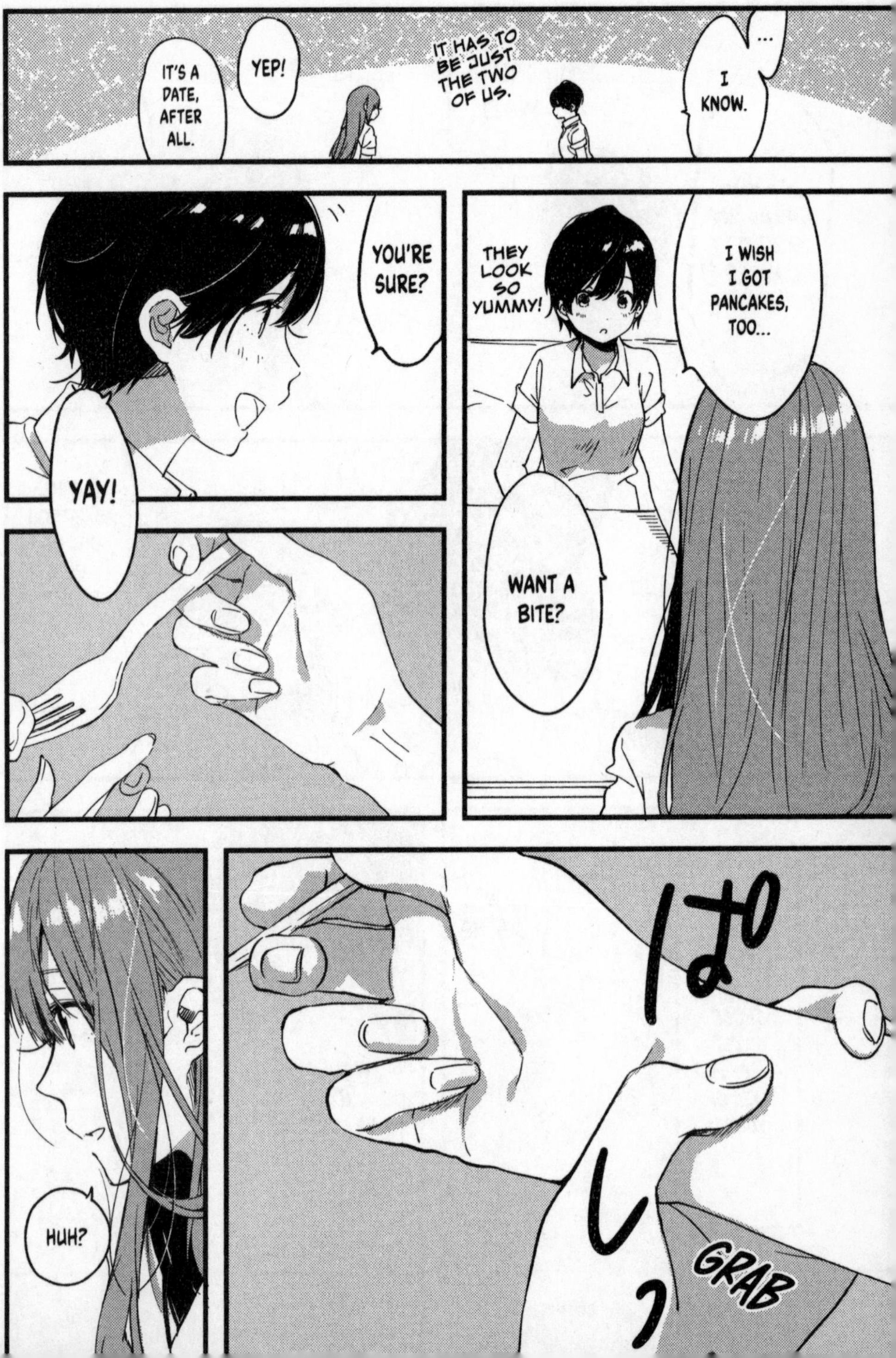
...
I KNOW.
IT HAS TO BE JUST THE TWO OF US.
YEP!
IT'S A DATE, AFTER ALL.
I WISH I GOT PANCAKES, TOO...
THEY LOOK SO YUMMY!
WANT A BITE?
YOU'RE SURE?
YAY!
ぱしっ
GRAB
HUH?

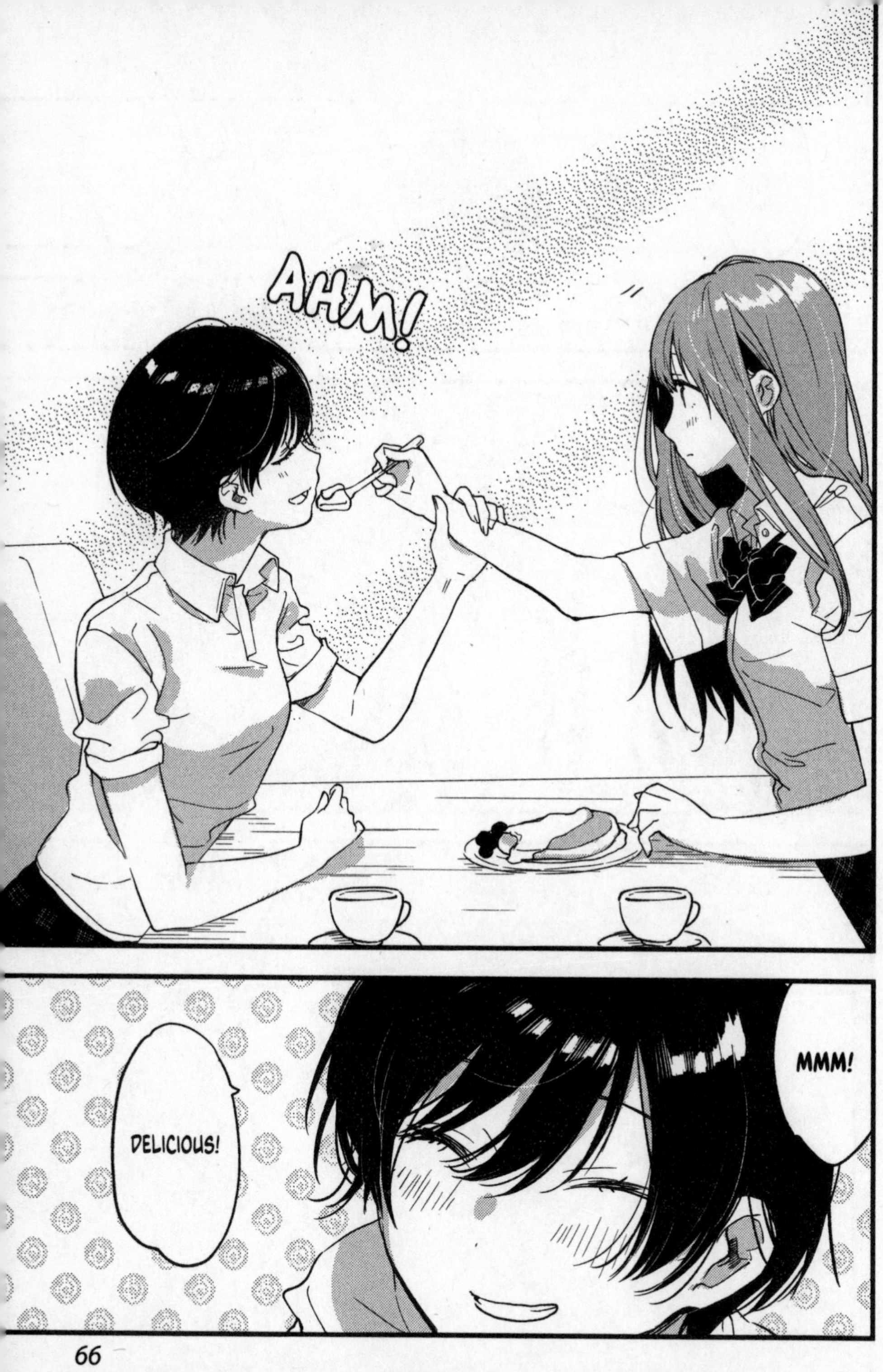
AHM!
MMM!
DELICIOUS!

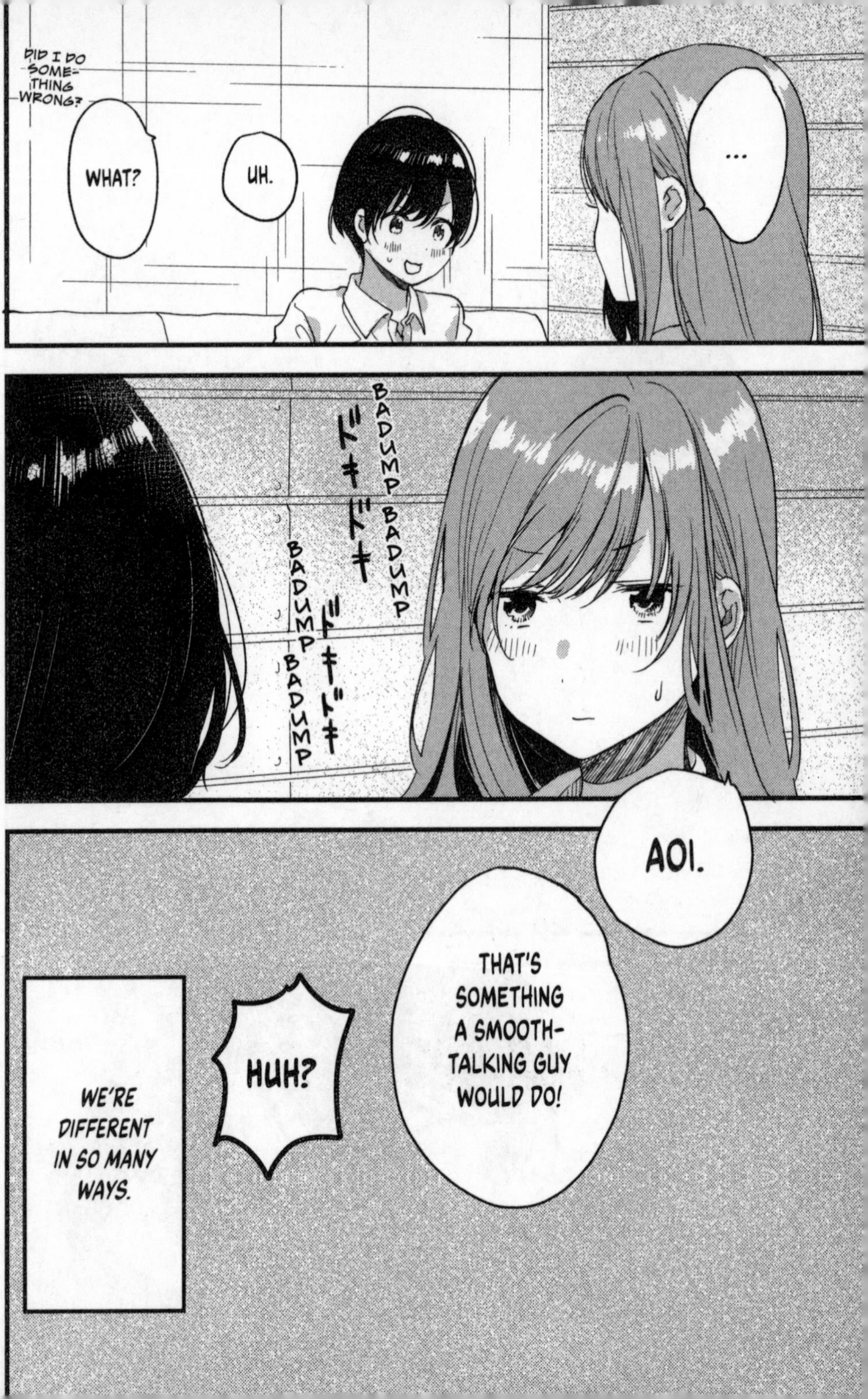
...
UH.
WHAT?
DID I DO SOMETHING WRONG?
BADUMP BADUMP BADUMP
BADUMP BADUMP BADUMP
AOI.
THAT'S SOMETHING A SMOOTH-TALKING GUY WOULD DO!
HUH?
WE'RE DIFFERENT IN SO MANY WAYS.

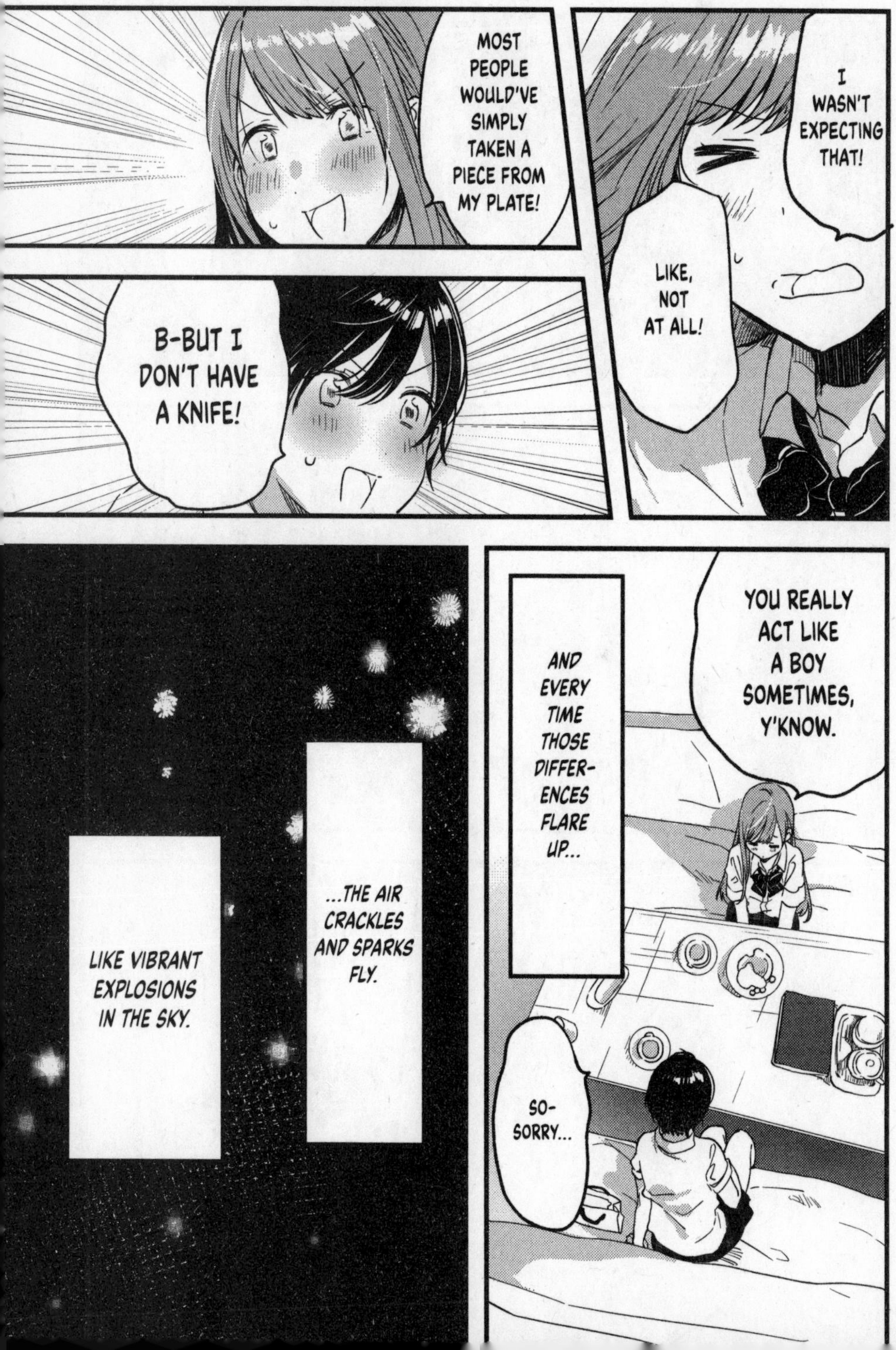
I WASN'T EXPECTING THAT!
LIKE, NOT AT ALL!
MOST PEOPLE WOULD'VE SIMPLY TAKEN A PIECE FROM MY PLATE!
B-BUT I DON'T HAVE A KNIFE!
YOU REALLY ACT LIKE A BOY SOMETIMES, Y'KNOW.
AND EVERY TIME THOSE DIFFER-ENCES FLARE UP...
SO-SORRY...
...THE AIR CRACKLES AND SPARKS FLY.
LIKE VIBRANT EXPLOSIONS IN THE SKY.

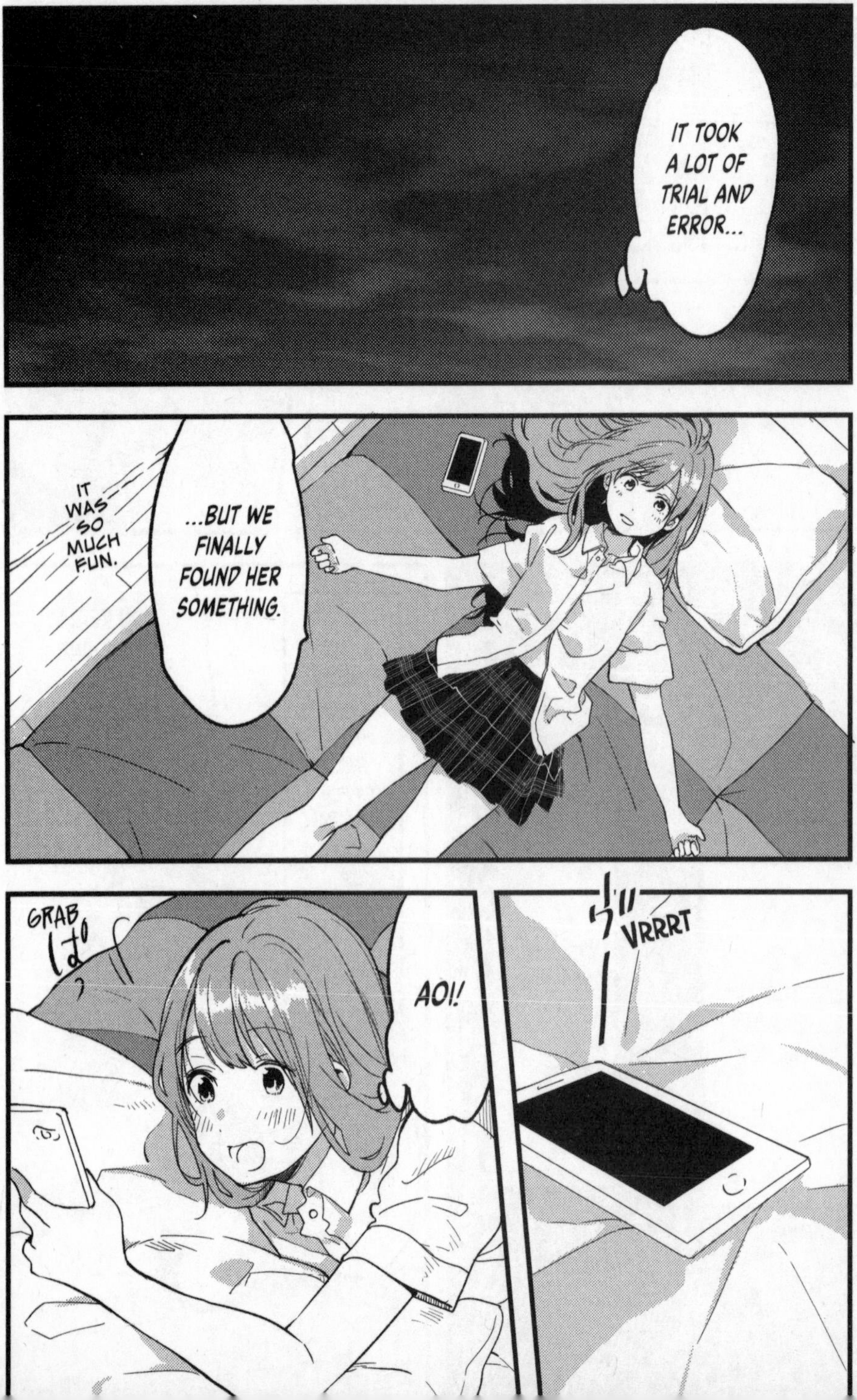
IT TOOK A LOT OF TRIAL AND ERROR...
...BUT WE FINALLY FOUND HER SOMETHING.
IT WAS SO MUCH FUN.
ヴッ VRRRT
GRAB ぱ
AOI!

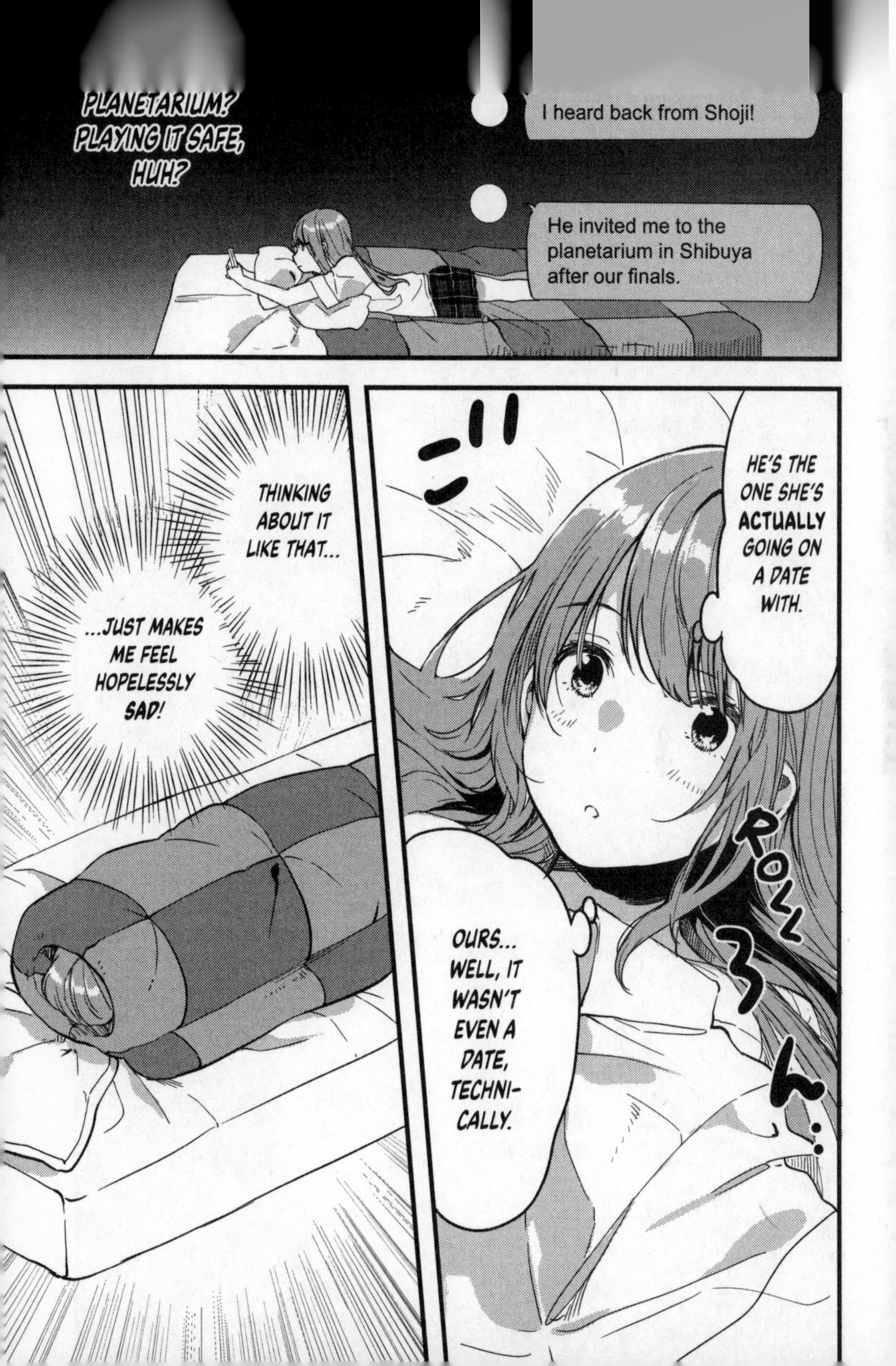

I heard back from Shoji!
He invited me to the planetarium in Shibuya after our finals.
PLANETARIUM? PLAYING IT SAFE, HUH?
HE'S THE ONE SHE'S ACTUALLY GOING ON A DATE WITH.
ROLL
OURS... WELL, IT WASN'T EVEN A DATE, TECHNICALLY.
THINKING ABOUT IT LIKE THAT...
...JUST MAKES ME FEEL HOPELESSLY SAD!

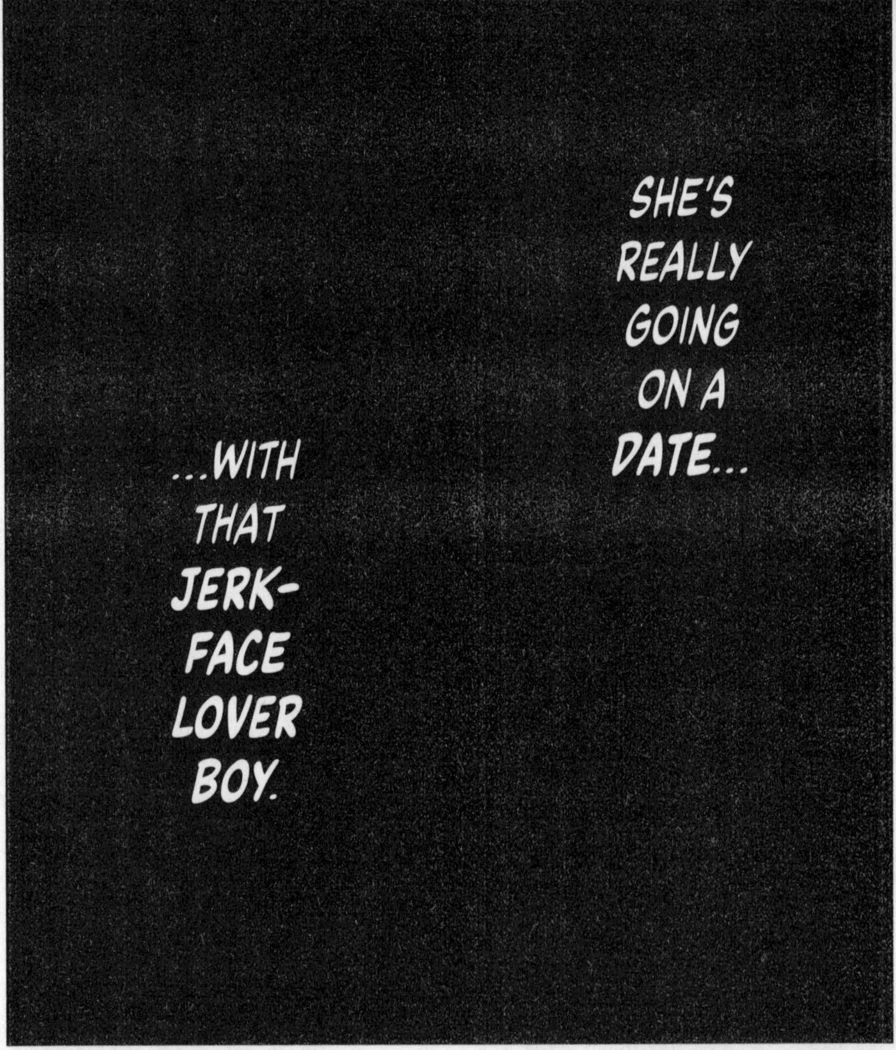
SHE'S REALLY GOING ON A DATE...
...WITH THAT JERK-FACE LOVER BOY.

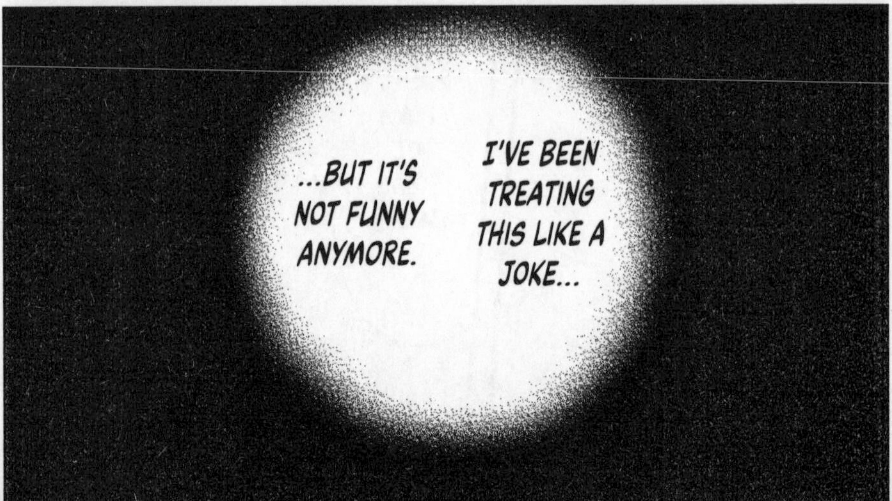
I'VE BEEN TREATING THIS LIKE A JOKE...
...BUT IT'S NOT FUNNY ANYMORE.

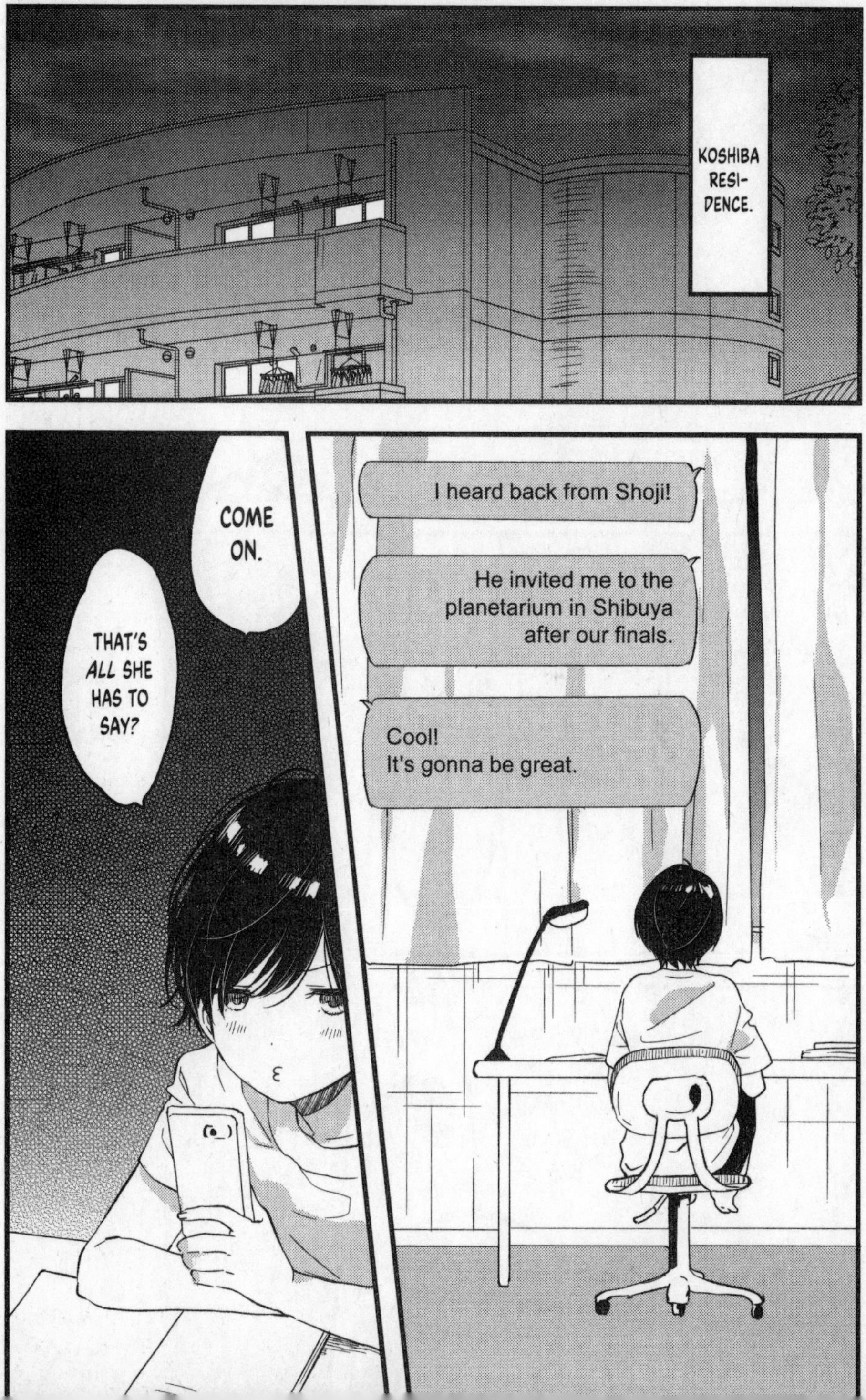
KOSHIBA RESI- DENCE.
I heard back from Shoji!
He invited me to the planetarium in Shibuya after our finals.
Cool! It's gonna be great.
COME ON.
THAT'S *ALL* SHE HAS TO SAY?

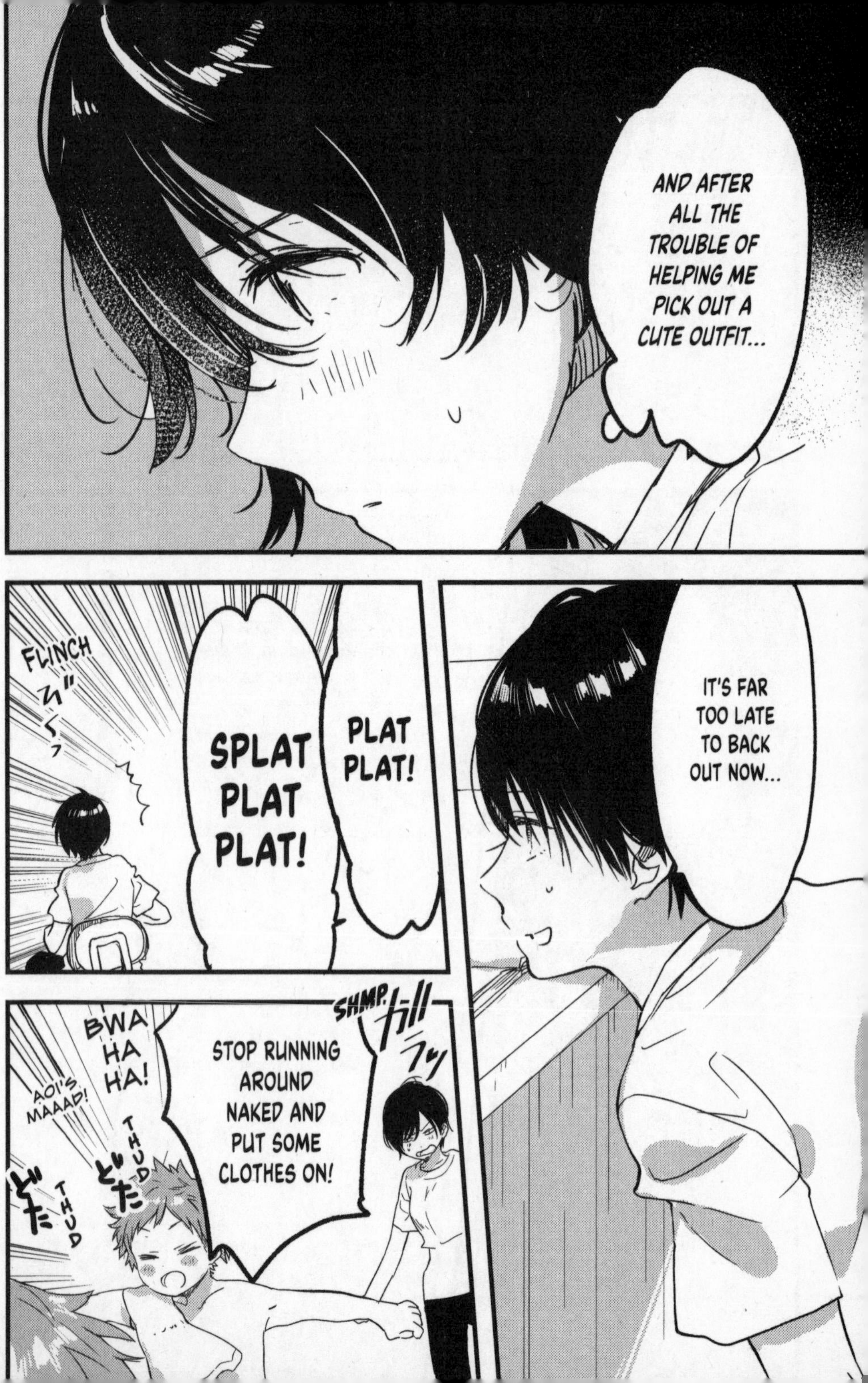

AND AFTER ALL THE TROUBLE OF HELPING ME PICK OUT A CUTE OUTFIT...
IT'S FAR TOO LATE TO BACK OUT NOW...
PLAT PLAT!
SPLAT PLAT PLAT!
FLINCH
びくっ
SHMP.
STOP RUNNING AROUND NAKED AND PUT SOME CLOTHES ON!
BWA HA HA!
AOI'S MAAAD!
THUD
どた
THUD
どた

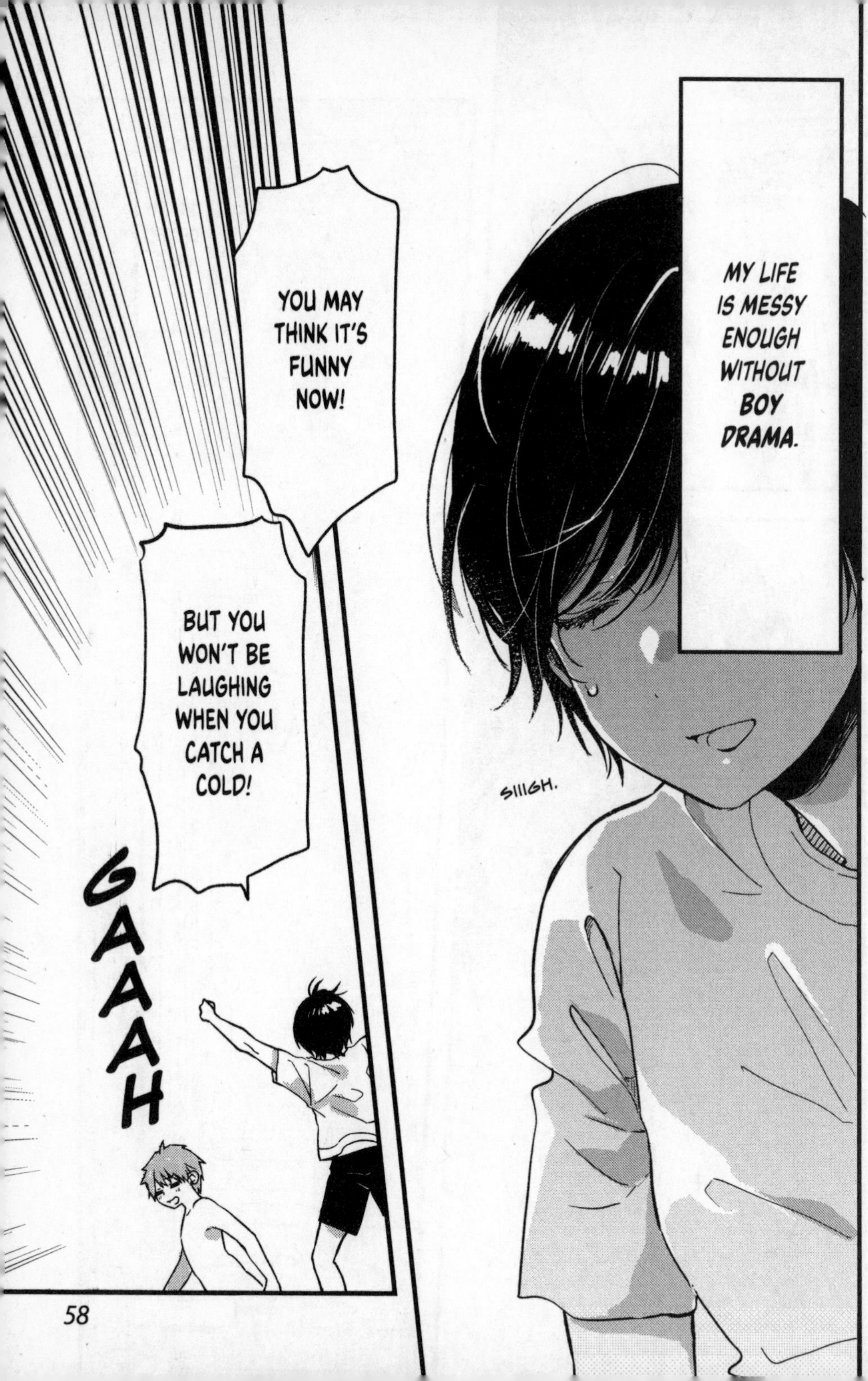
MY LIFE IS MESSY ENOUGH WITHOUT BOY DRAMA.
SIIIGH.
YOU MAY THINK IT'S FUNNY NOW!
BUT YOU WON'T BE LAUGHING WHEN YOU CATCH A COLD!
GAAAH

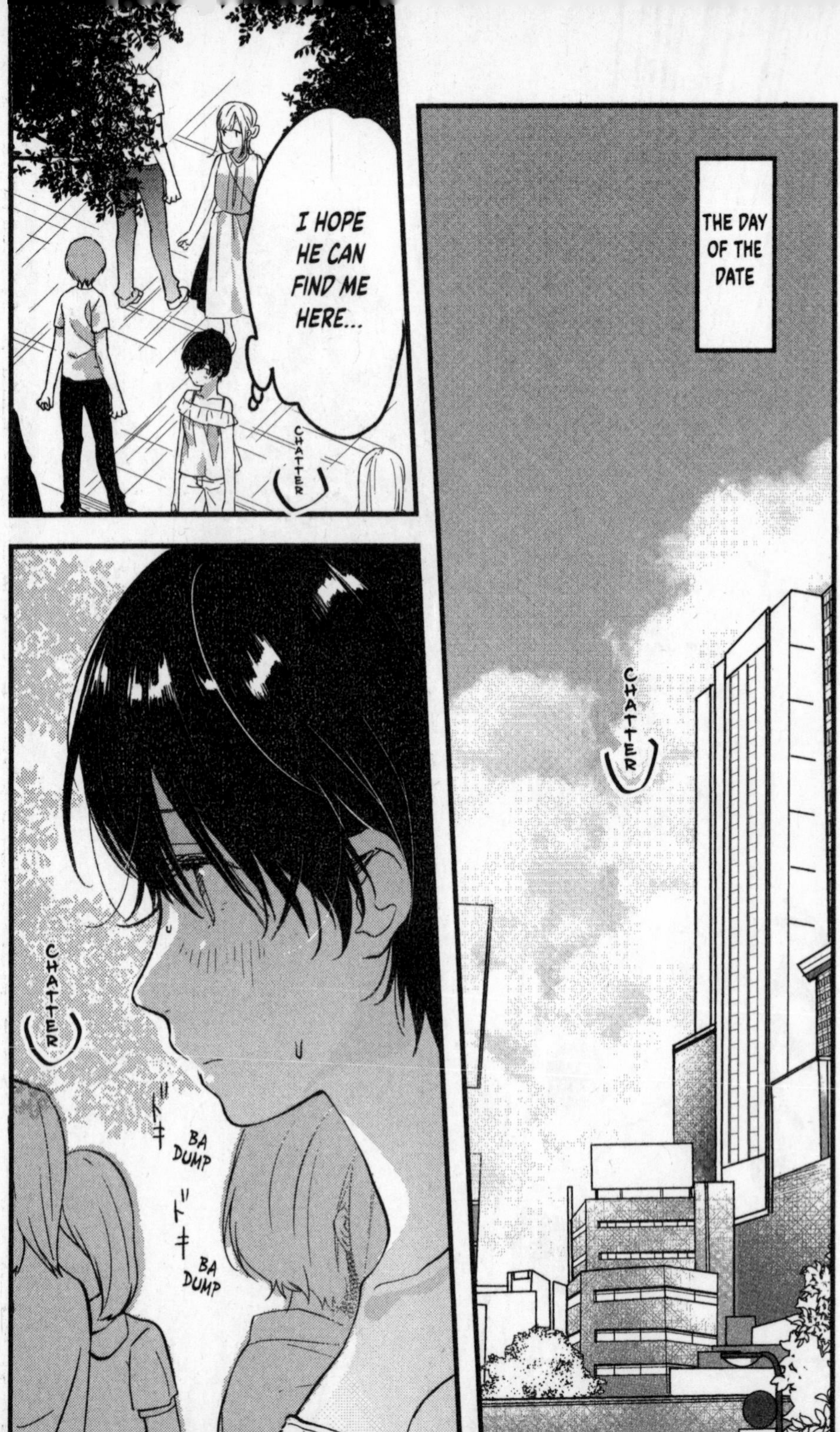
THE DAY OF THE DATE
CHATTER
I HOPE HE CAN FIND ME HERE...
CHATTER
CHATTER
ドキ
BA DUMP
ドキ
BA DUMP

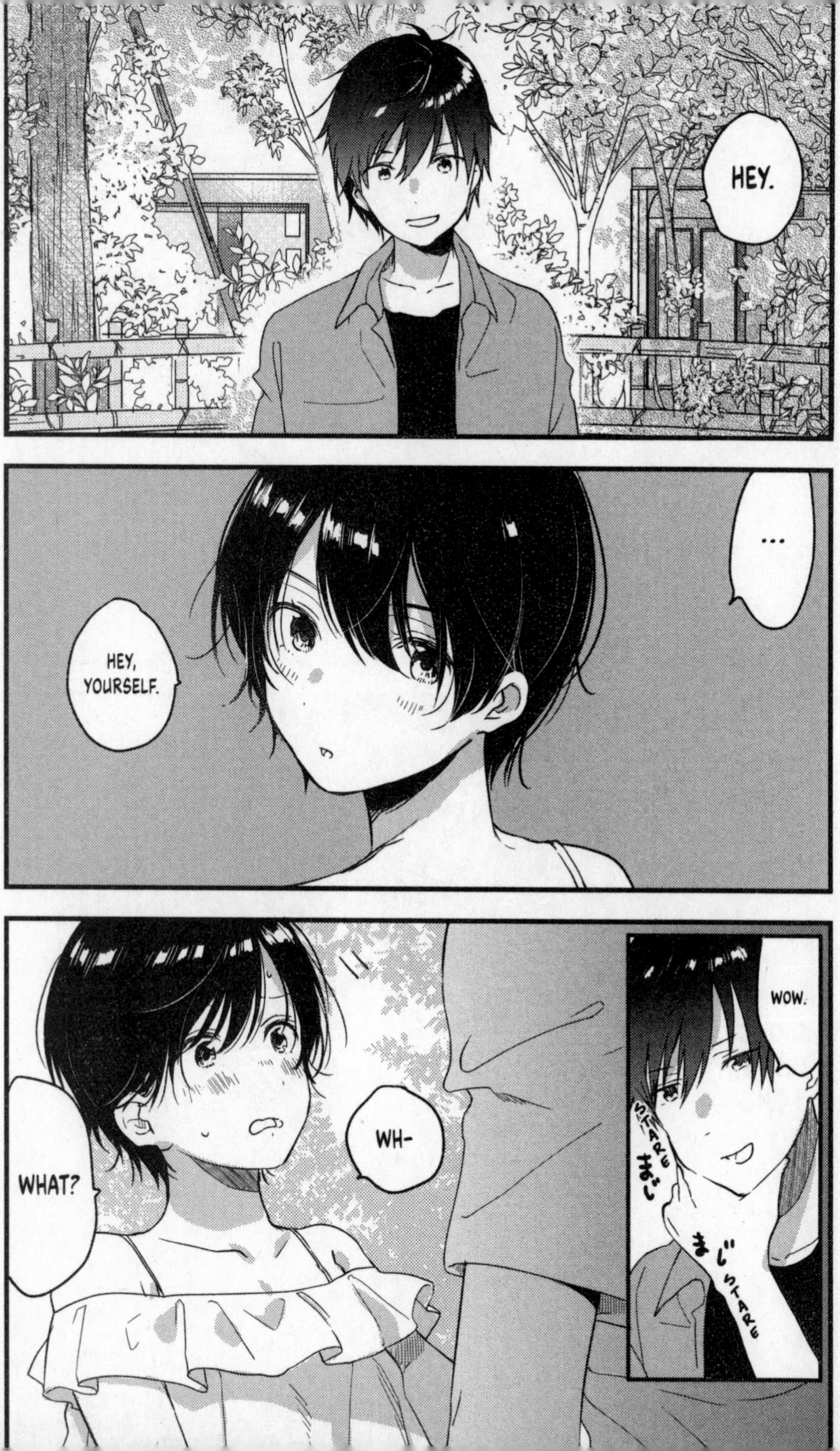
HEY.
...
HEY, YOURSELF.
WOW.
STARE まじ
まじ STARE
WH-
WHAT?

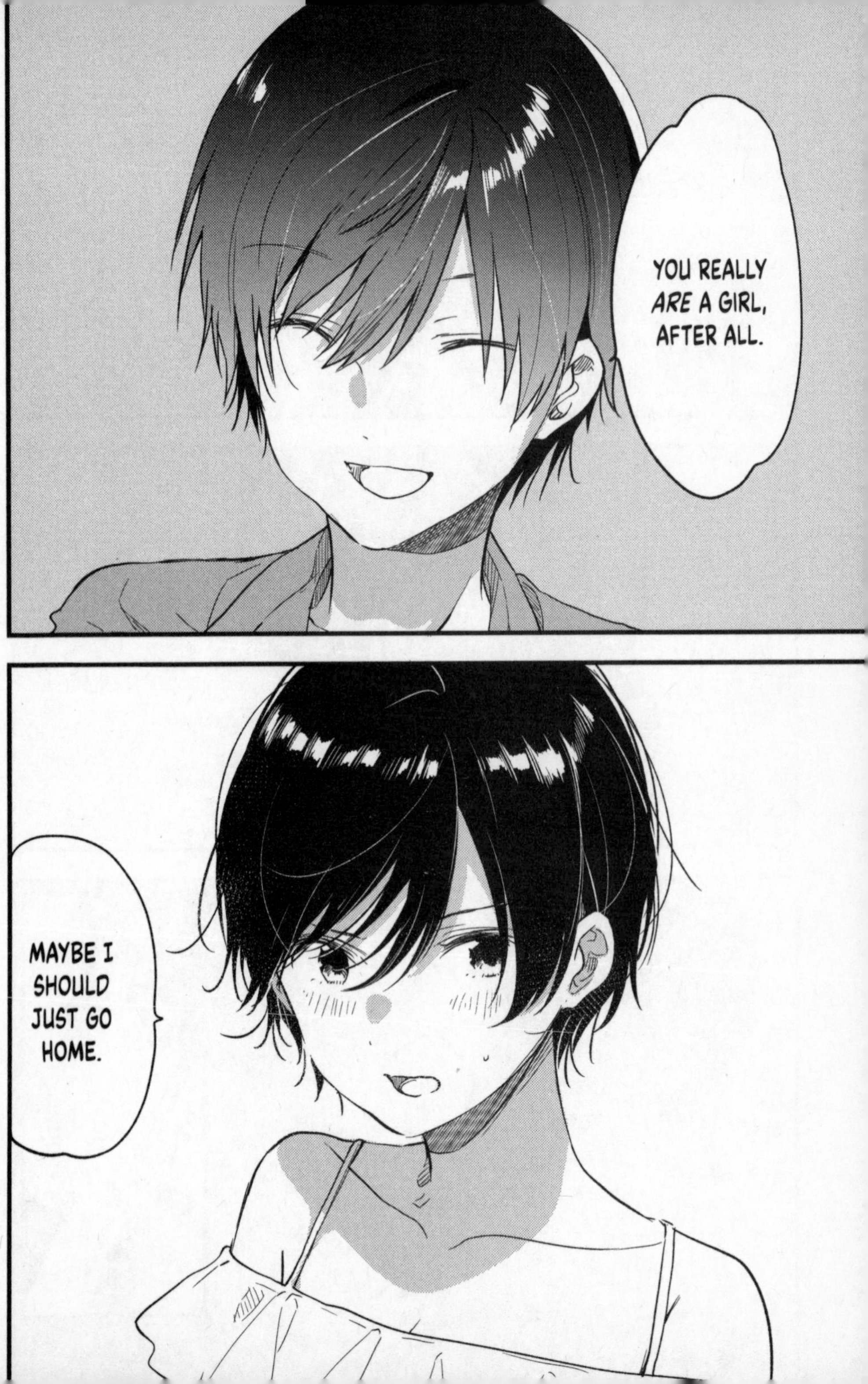
YOU REALLY *ARE* A GIRL, AFTER ALL.
MAYBE I SHOULD JUST GO HOME.

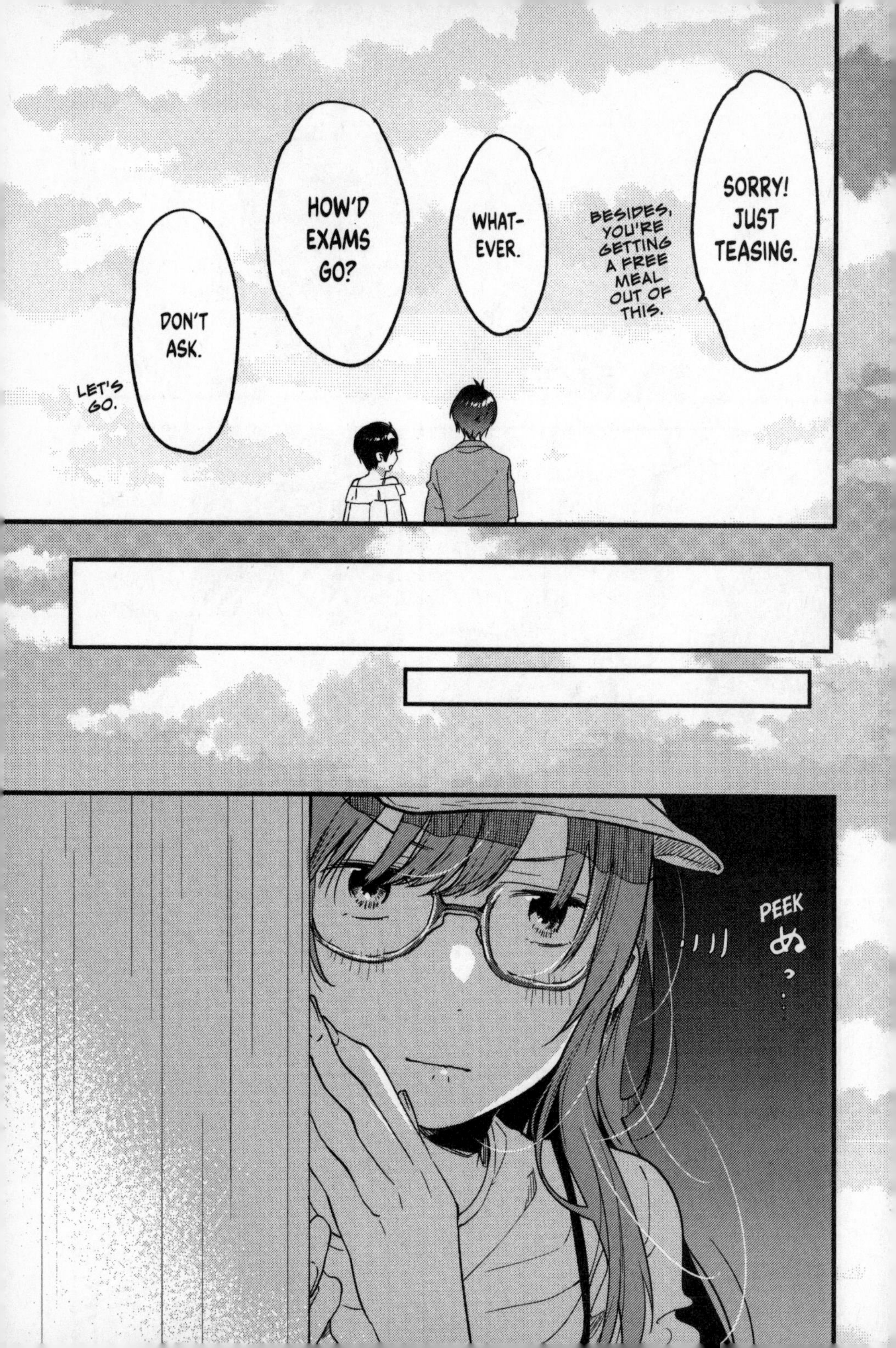
SORRY! JUST TEASING.
BESIDES, YOU'RE GETTING A FREE MEAL OUT OF THIS.
WHAT-EVER.
HOW'D EXAMS GO?
DON'T ASK.
LET'S GO.
PEEK
ぬっ

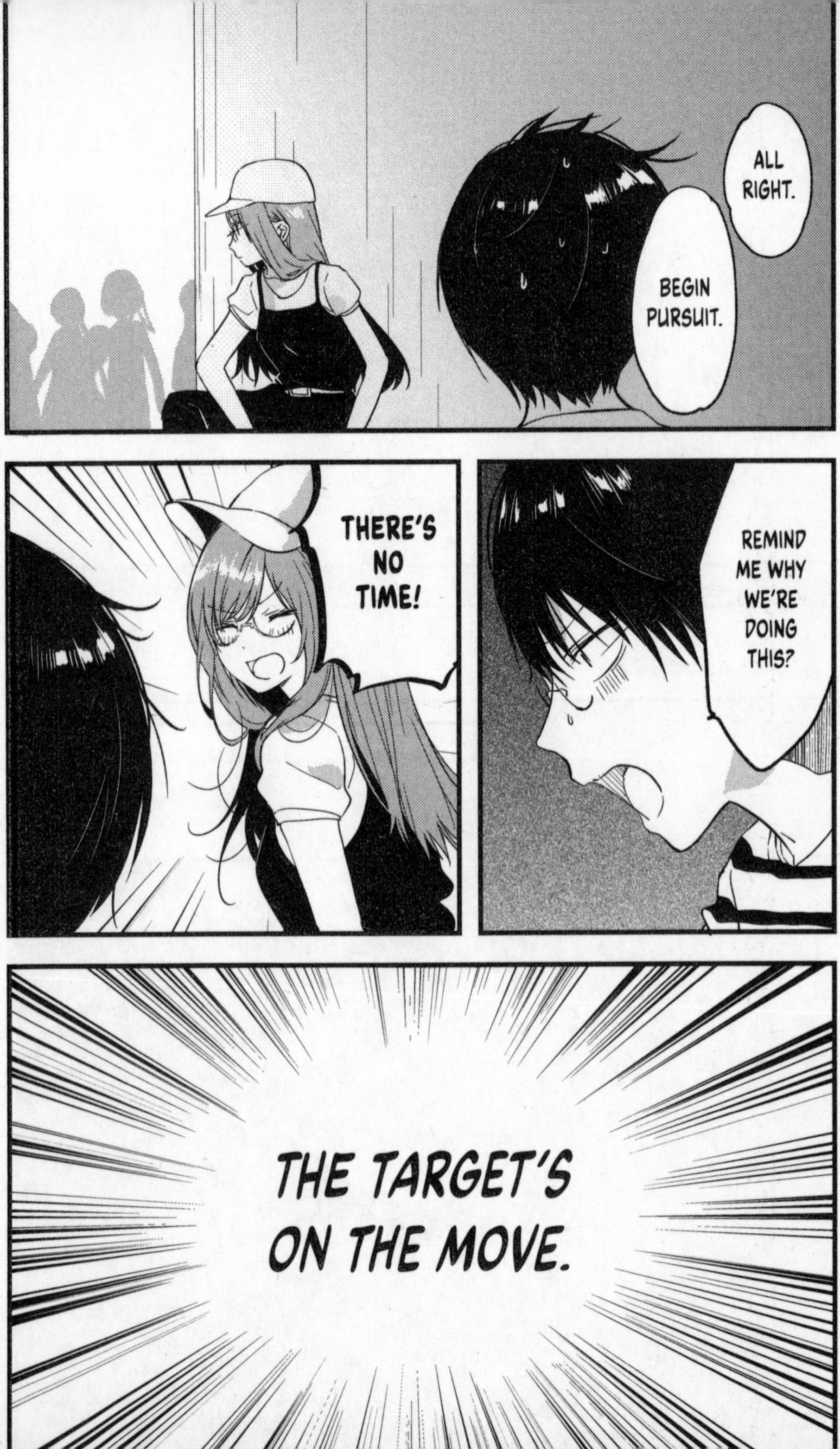
ALL RIGHT.
BEGIN PURSUIT.
REMIND ME WHY WE'RE DOING THIS?
THERE'S NO TIME!
THE TARGET'S ON THE MOVE.

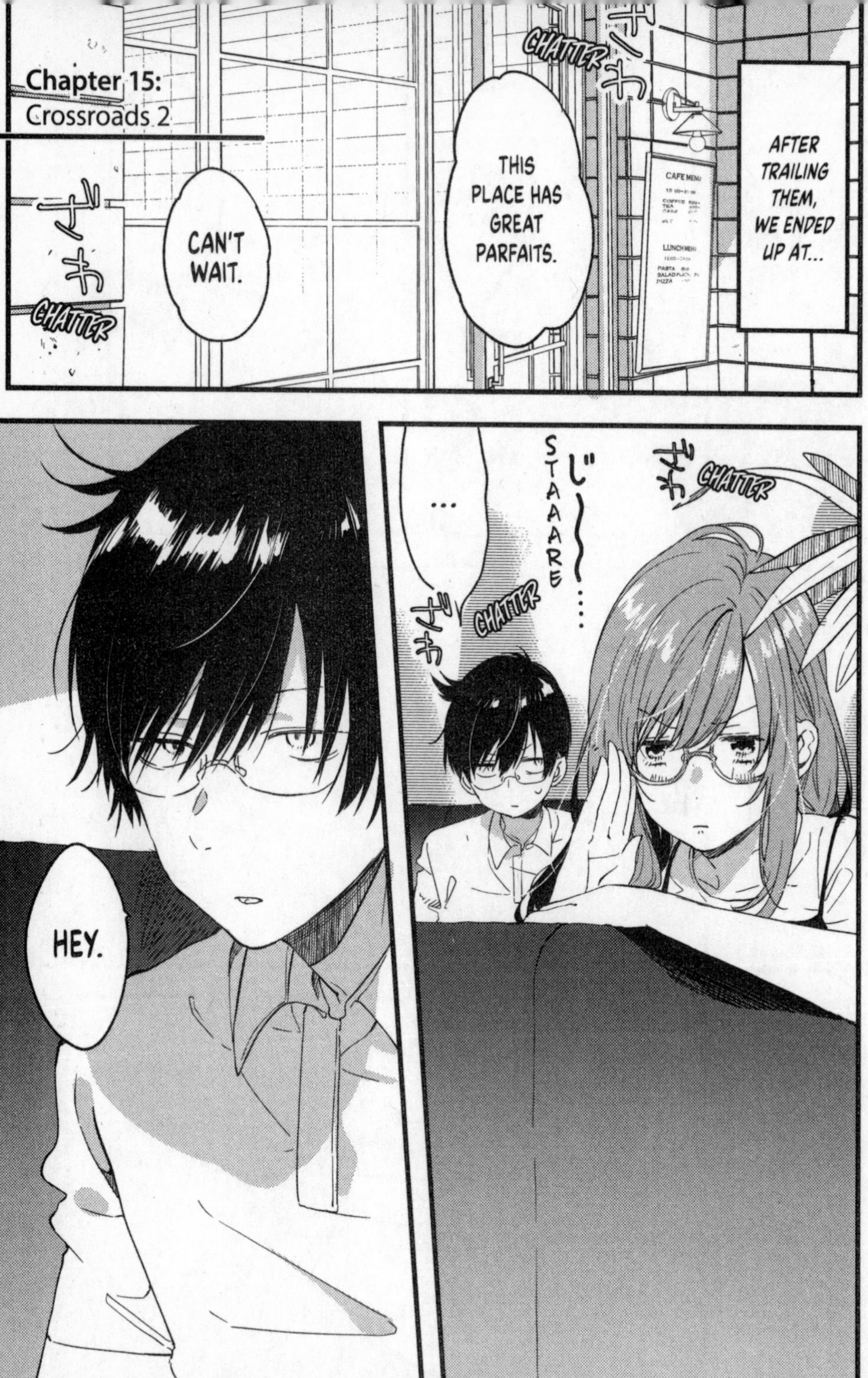
Chapter 15:
Crossroads 2
AFTER TRAILING THEM, WE ENDED UP AT...
CHATTER
THIS PLACE HAS GREAT PARFAITS.
CAN'T WAIT.
CHATTER
CHATTER
STAAAARE....
...
CHATTER
HEY.

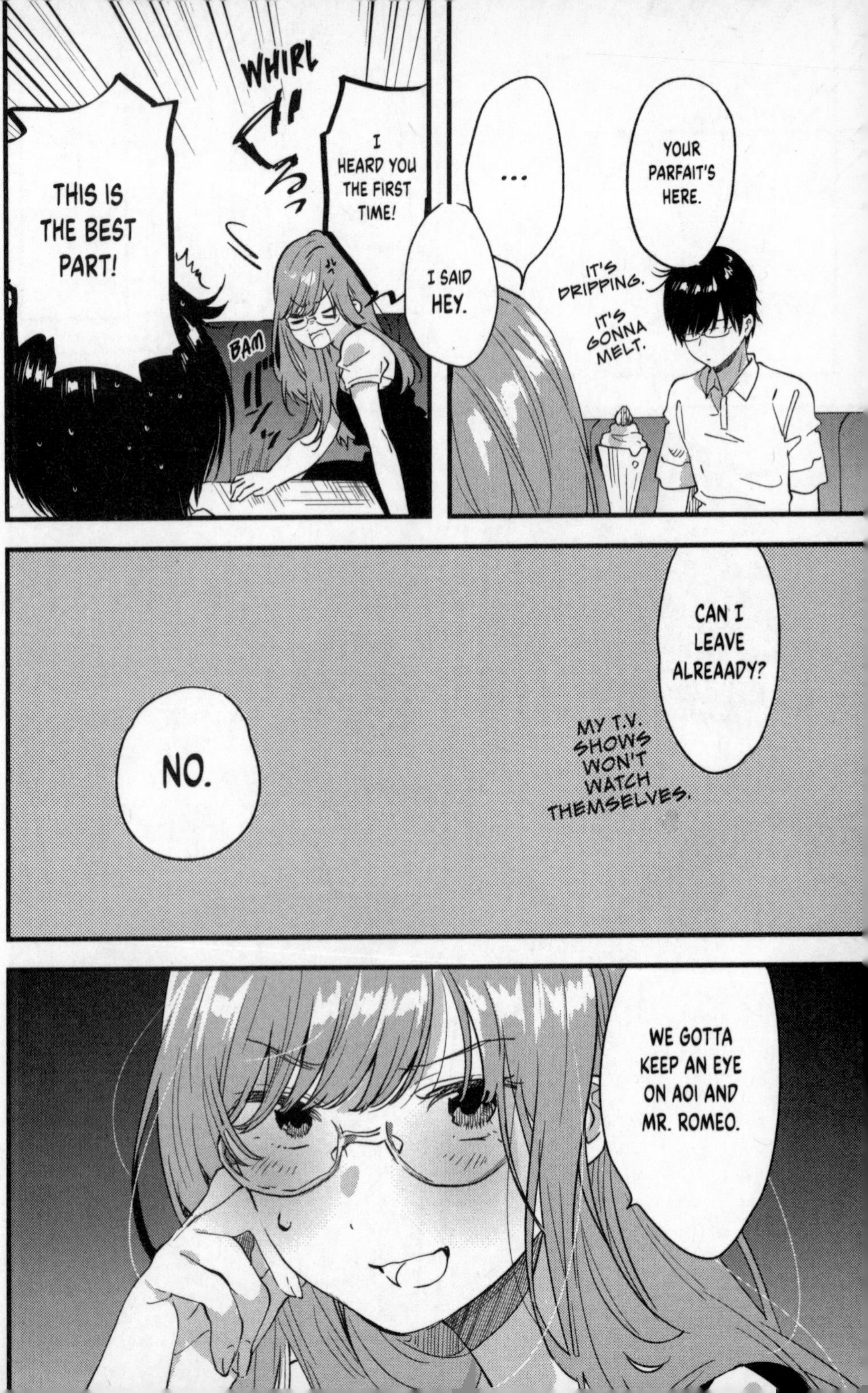
YOUR PARFAIT'S HERE.
...
IT'S DRIPPING.
IT'S GONNA MELT.
I SAID HEY.
WHIRL
I HEARD YOU THE FIRST TIME!
THIS IS THE BEST PART!
BAM
CAN I LEAVE ALREAADY?
MY T.V. SHOWS WON'T WATCH THEMSELVES.
NO.
WE GOTTA KEEP AN EYE ON AOI AND MR. ROMEO.

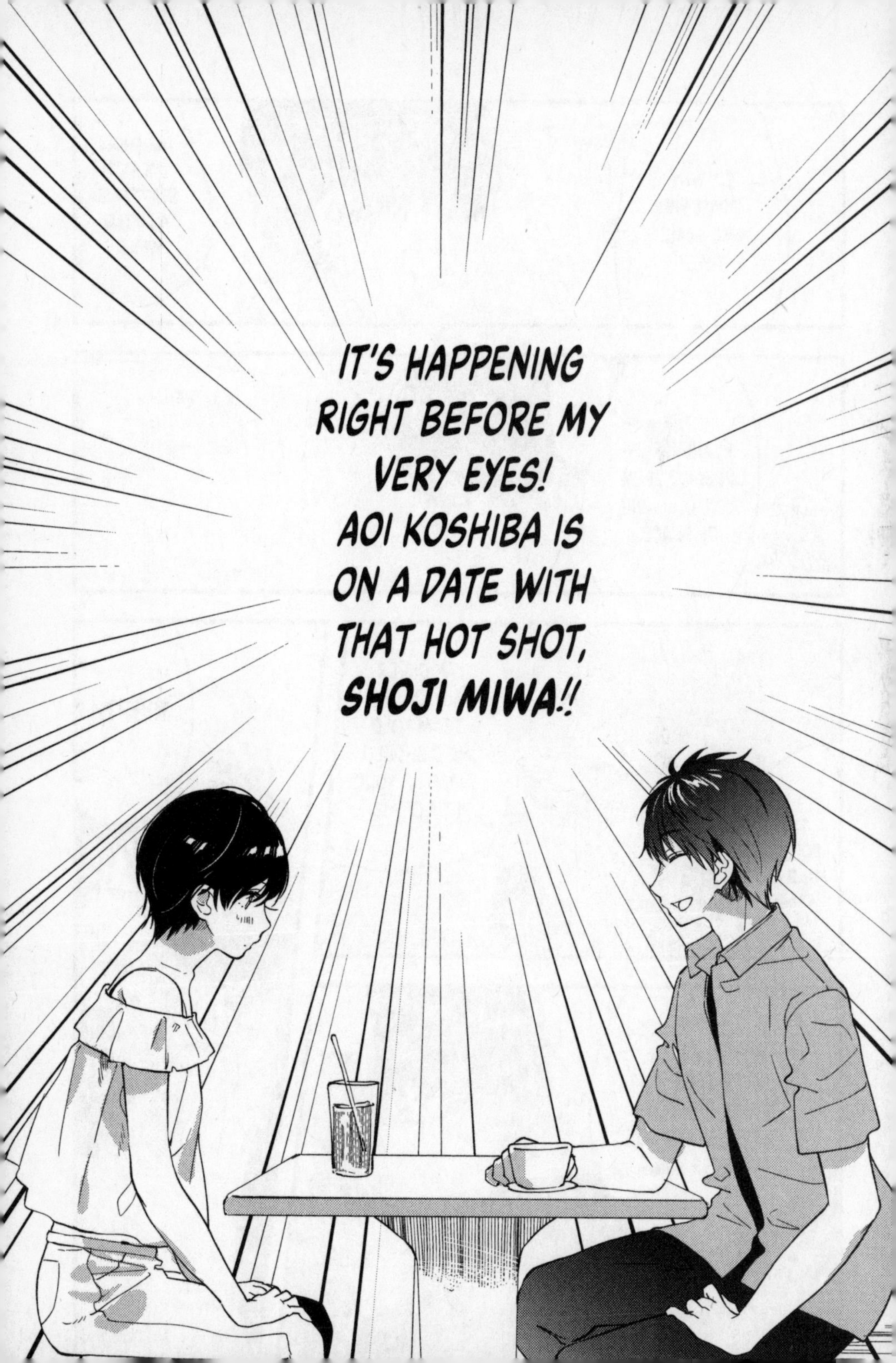
IT'S HAPPENING RIGHT BEFORE MY VERY EYES! AOI KOSHIBA IS ON A DATE WITH THAT HOT SHOT, SHOJI MIWA!!

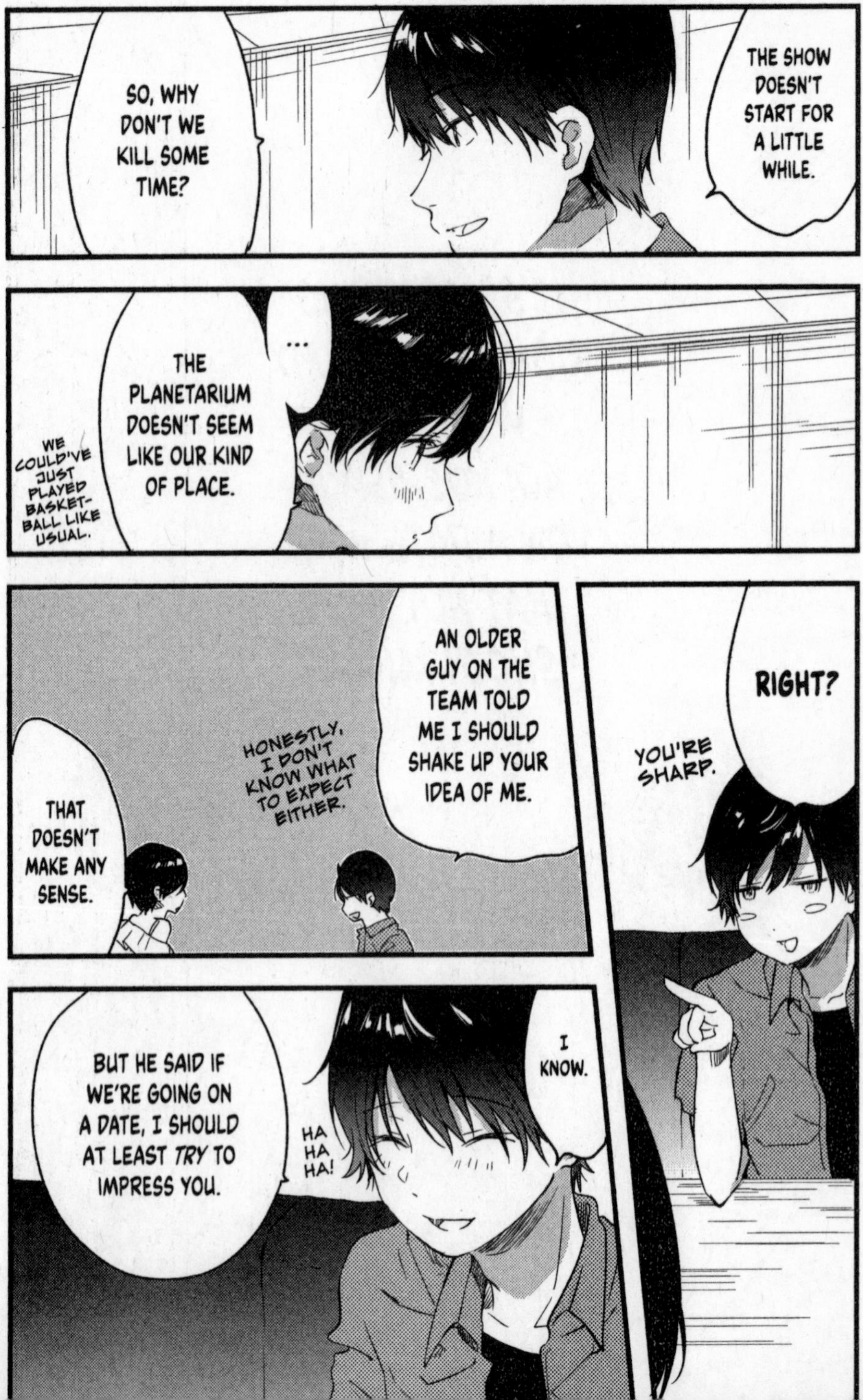
THE SHOW DOESN'T START FOR A LITTLE WHILE.
SO, WHY DON'T WE KILL SOME TIME?
...
THE PLANETARIUM DOESN'T SEEM LIKE OUR KIND OF PLACE.
WE COULD'VE JUST PLAYED BASKET-BALL LIKE USUAL.
RIGHT?
YOU'RE SHARP.
AN OLDER GUY ON THE TEAM TOLD ME I SHOULD SHAKE UP YOUR IDEA OF ME.
HONESTLY, I DON'T KNOW WHAT TO EXPECT EITHER.
THAT DOESN'T MAKE ANY SENSE.
I KNOW.
HA HA HA!
BUT HE SAID IF WE'RE GOING ON A DATE, I SHOULD AT LEAST *TRY* TO IMPRESS YOU.

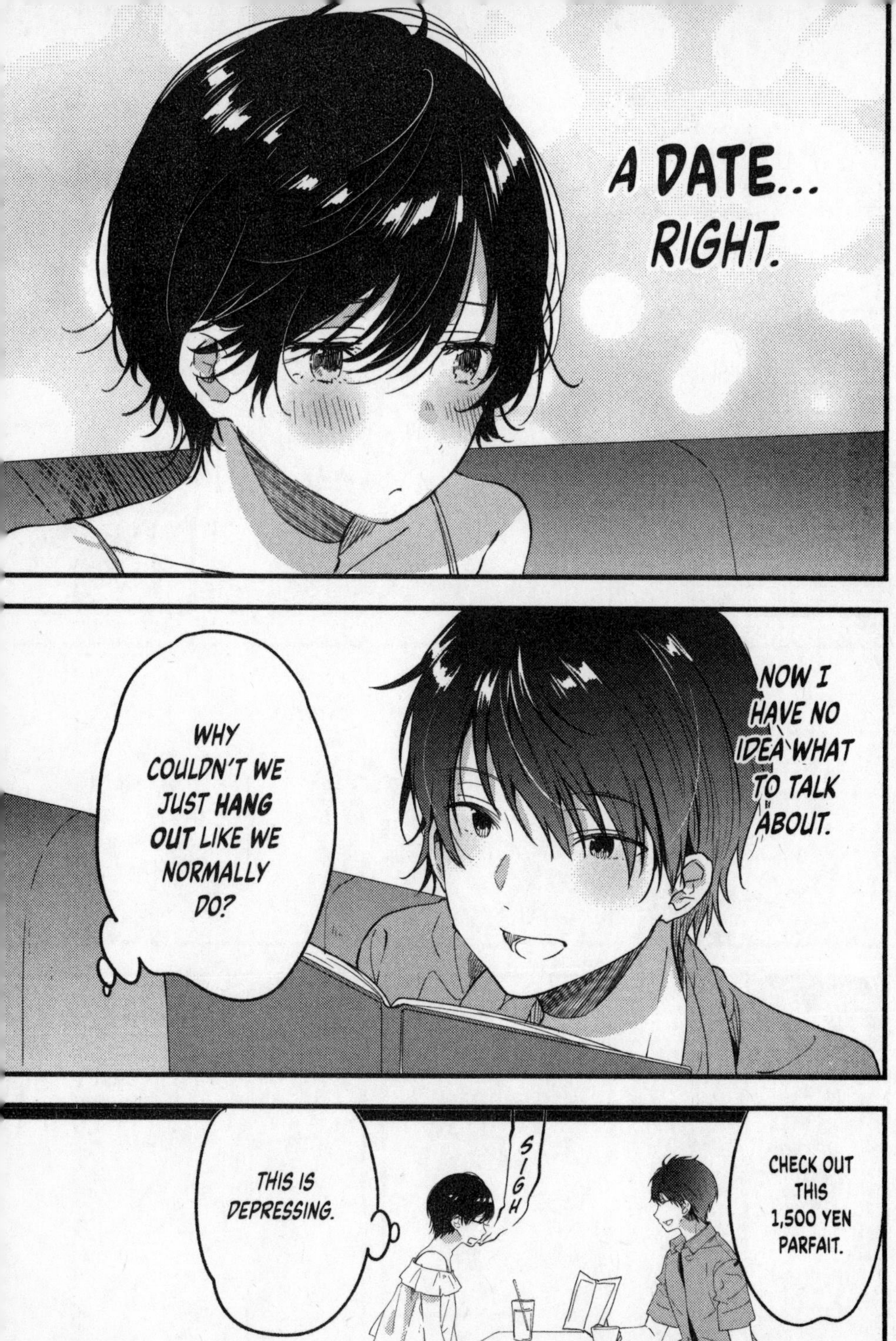
A DATE... RIGHT.
NOW I HAVE NO IDEA WHAT TO TALK ABOUT.
WHY COULDN'T WE JUST HANG OUT LIKE WE NORMALLY DO?
CHECK OUT THIS 1,500 YEN PARFAIT.
SIGH
THIS IS DEPRESSING.

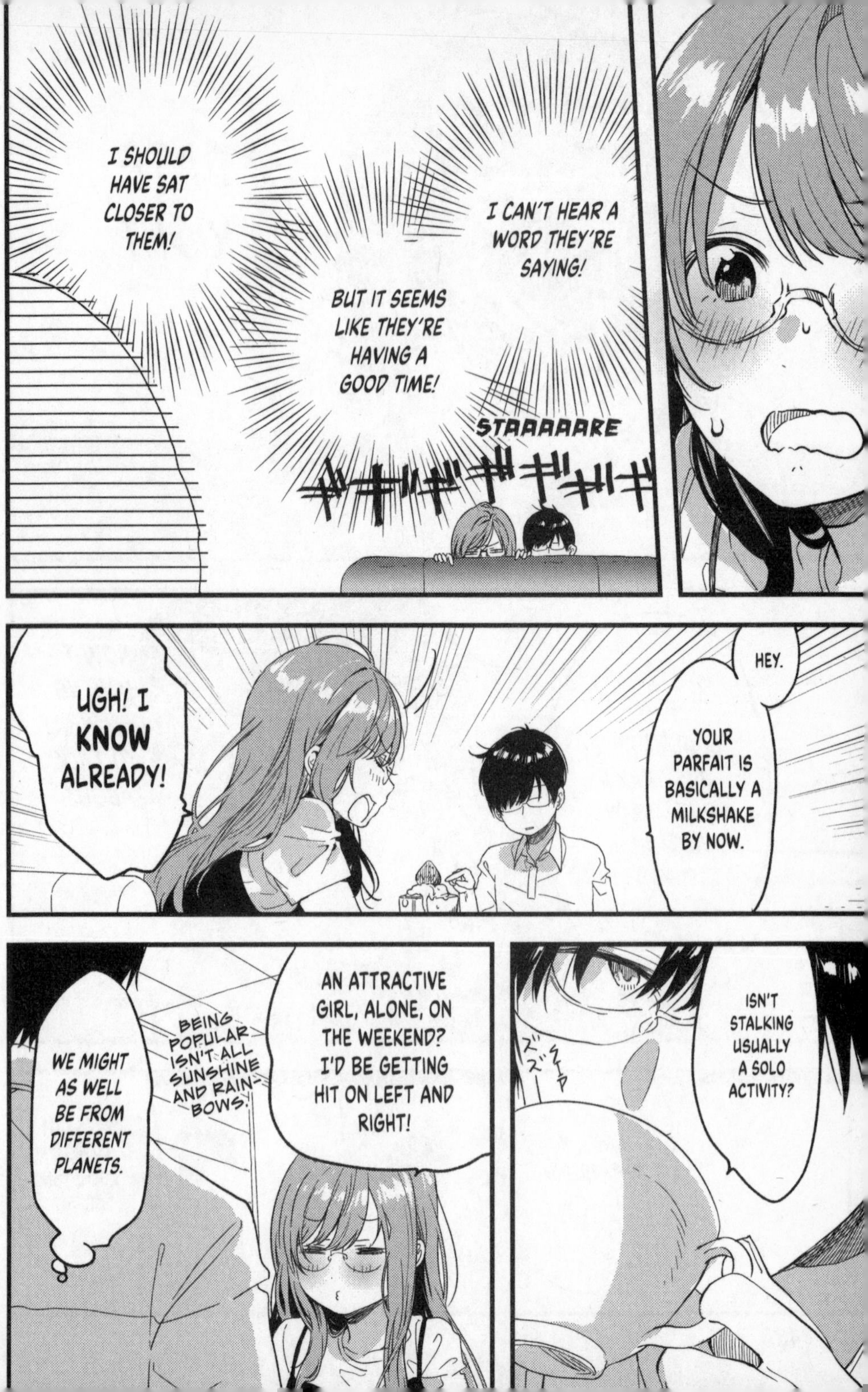
I CAN'T HEAR A WORD THEY'RE SAYING!
BUT IT SEEMS LIKE THEY'RE HAVING A GOOD TIME!
I SHOULD HAVE SAT CLOSER TO THEM!
STAAAAARE
HEY.
YOUR PARFAIT IS BASICALLY A MILKSHAKE BY NOW.
UGH! I KNOW ALREADY!
ISN'T STALKING USUALLY A SOLO ACTIVITY?
AN ATTRACTIVE GIRL, ALONE, ON THE WEEKEND? I'D BE GETTING HIT ON LEFT AND RIGHT!
BEING POPULAR ISN'T ALL SUNSHINE AND RAINBOWS.
WE MIGHT AS WELL BE FROM DIFFERENT PLANETS.

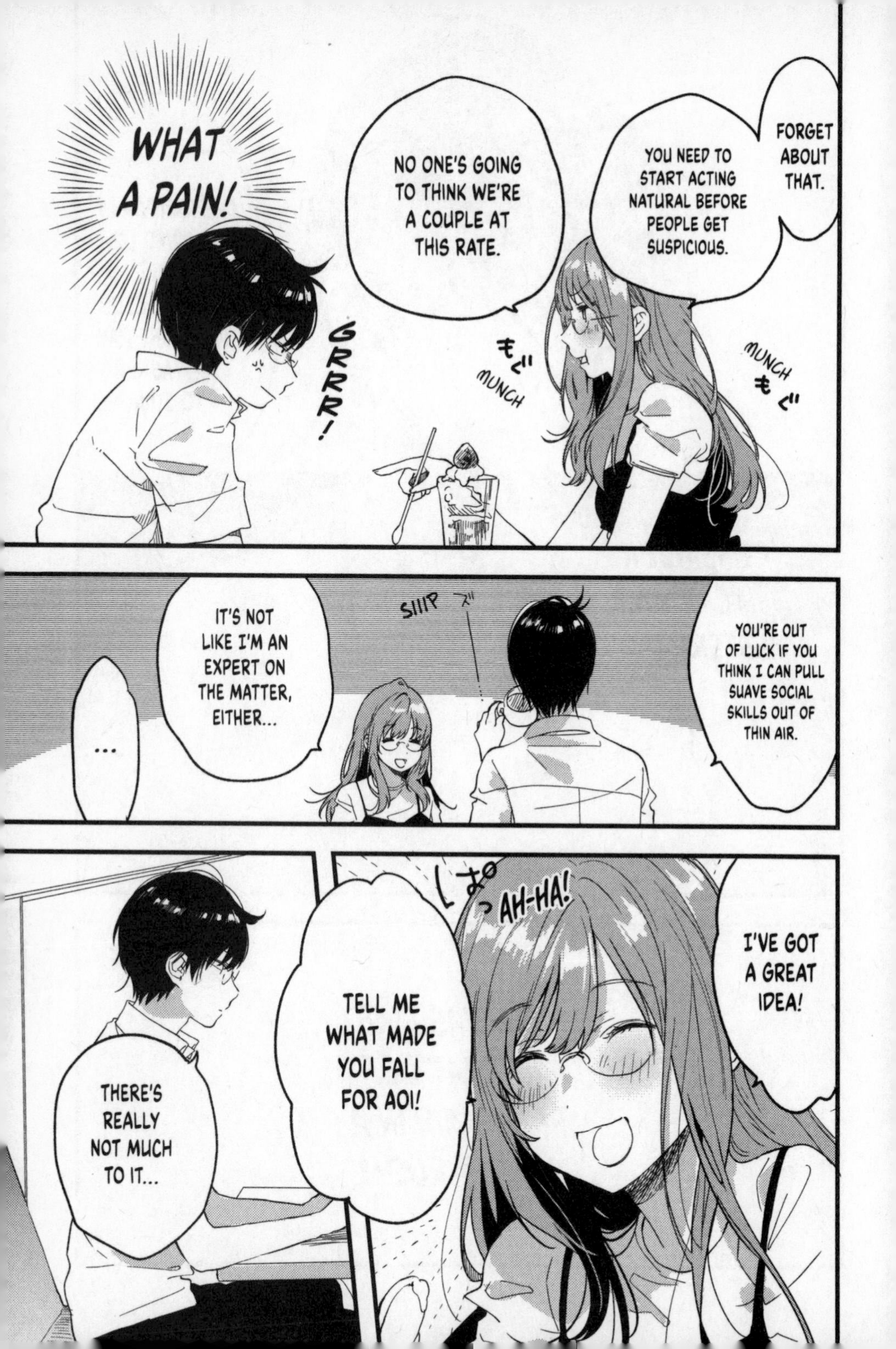
FORGET ABOUT THAT.
YOU NEED TO START ACTING NATURAL BEFORE PEOPLE GET SUSPICIOUS.
MUNCH もぐ
NO ONE'S GOING TO THINK WE'RE A COUPLE AT THIS RATE.
もぐ MUNCH
GRRR!
WHAT A PAIN!
YOU'RE OUT OF LUCK IF YOU THINK I CAN PULL SUAVE SOCIAL SKILLS OUT OF THIN AIR.
SIIIP ズ
IT'S NOT LIKE I'M AN EXPERT ON THE MATTER, EITHER...
...
I'VE GOT A GREAT IDEA!
AH-HA!
TELL ME WHAT MADE YOU FALL FOR AOI!
THERE'S REALLY NOT MUCH TO IT...

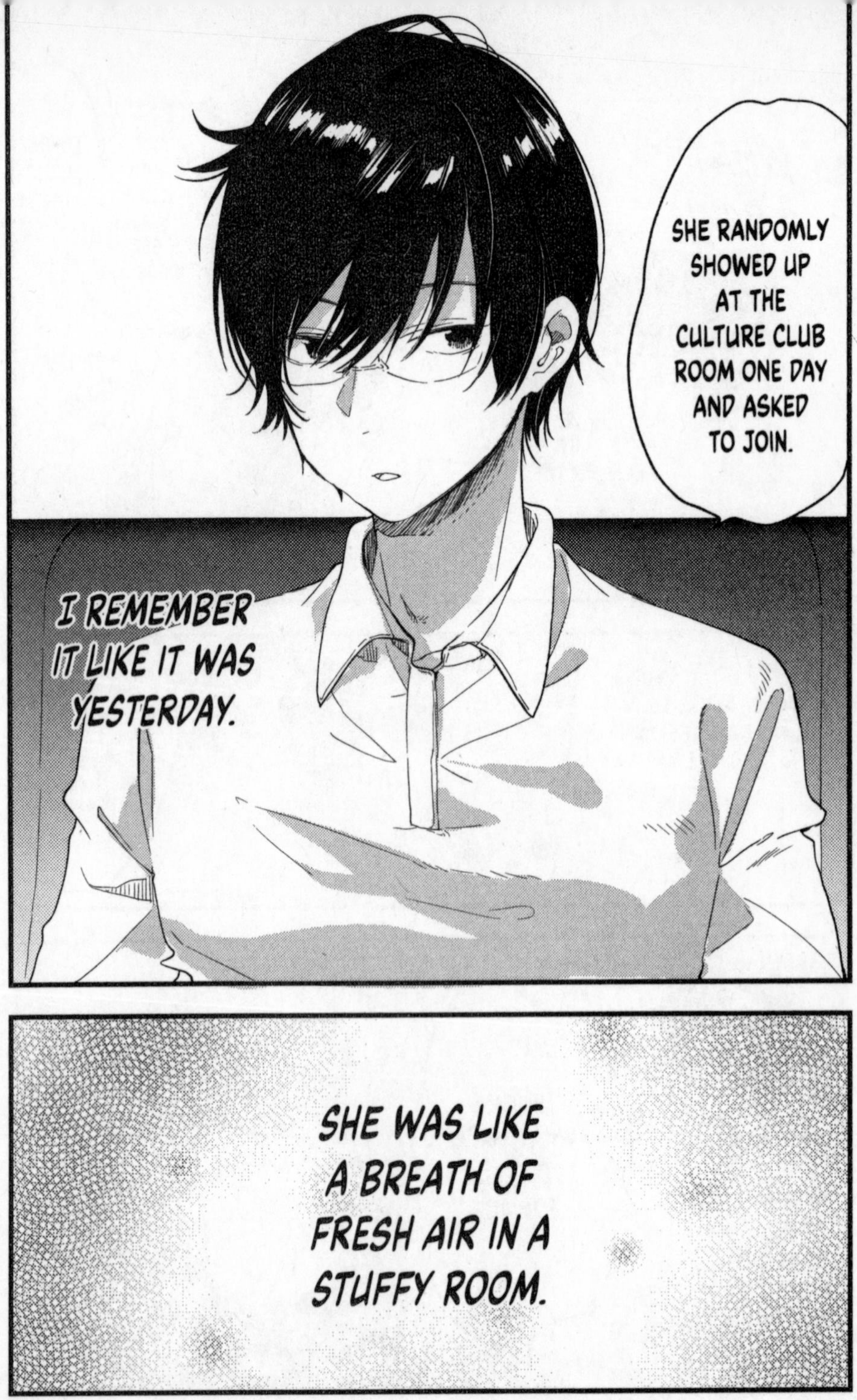
SHE RANDOMLY SHOWED UP AT THE CULTURE CLUB ROOM ONE DAY AND ASKED TO JOIN.
I REMEMBER IT LIKE IT WAS YESTERDAY.
SHE WAS LIKE A BREATH OF FRESH AIR IN A STUFFY ROOM.

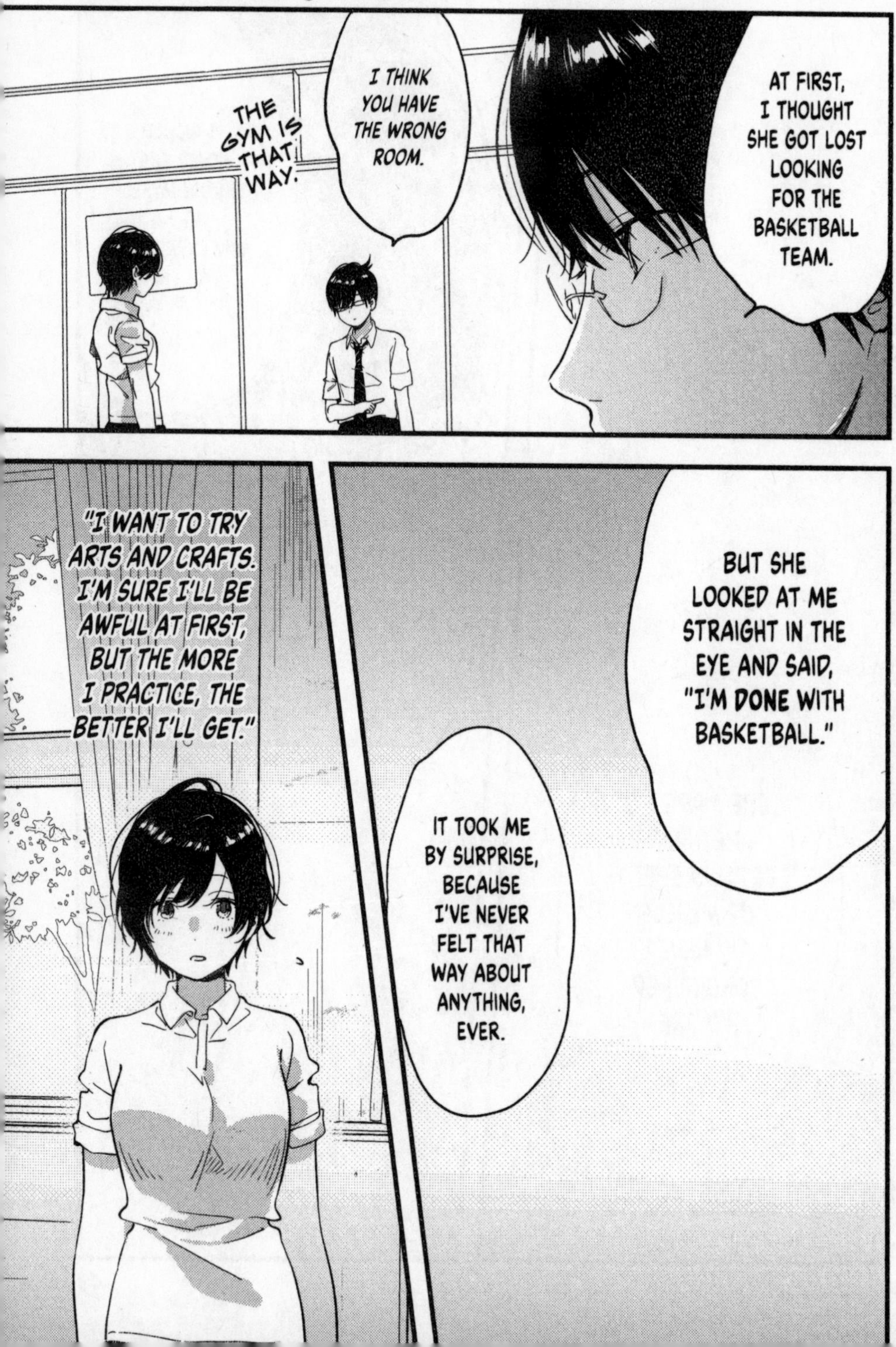
AT FIRST, I THOUGHT SHE GOT LOST LOOKING FOR THE BASKETBALL TEAM.
I THINK YOU HAVE THE WRONG ROOM.
THE GYM IS THAT WAY.
BUT SHE LOOKED AT ME STRAIGHT IN THE EYE AND SAID, "I'M DONE WITH BASKETBALL."
IT TOOK ME BY SURPRISE, BECAUSE I'VE NEVER FELT THAT WAY ABOUT ANYTHING, EVER.
"I WANT TO TRY ARTS AND CRAFTS. I'M SURE I'LL BE AWFUL AT FIRST, BUT THE MORE I PRACTICE, THE BETTER I'LL GET."

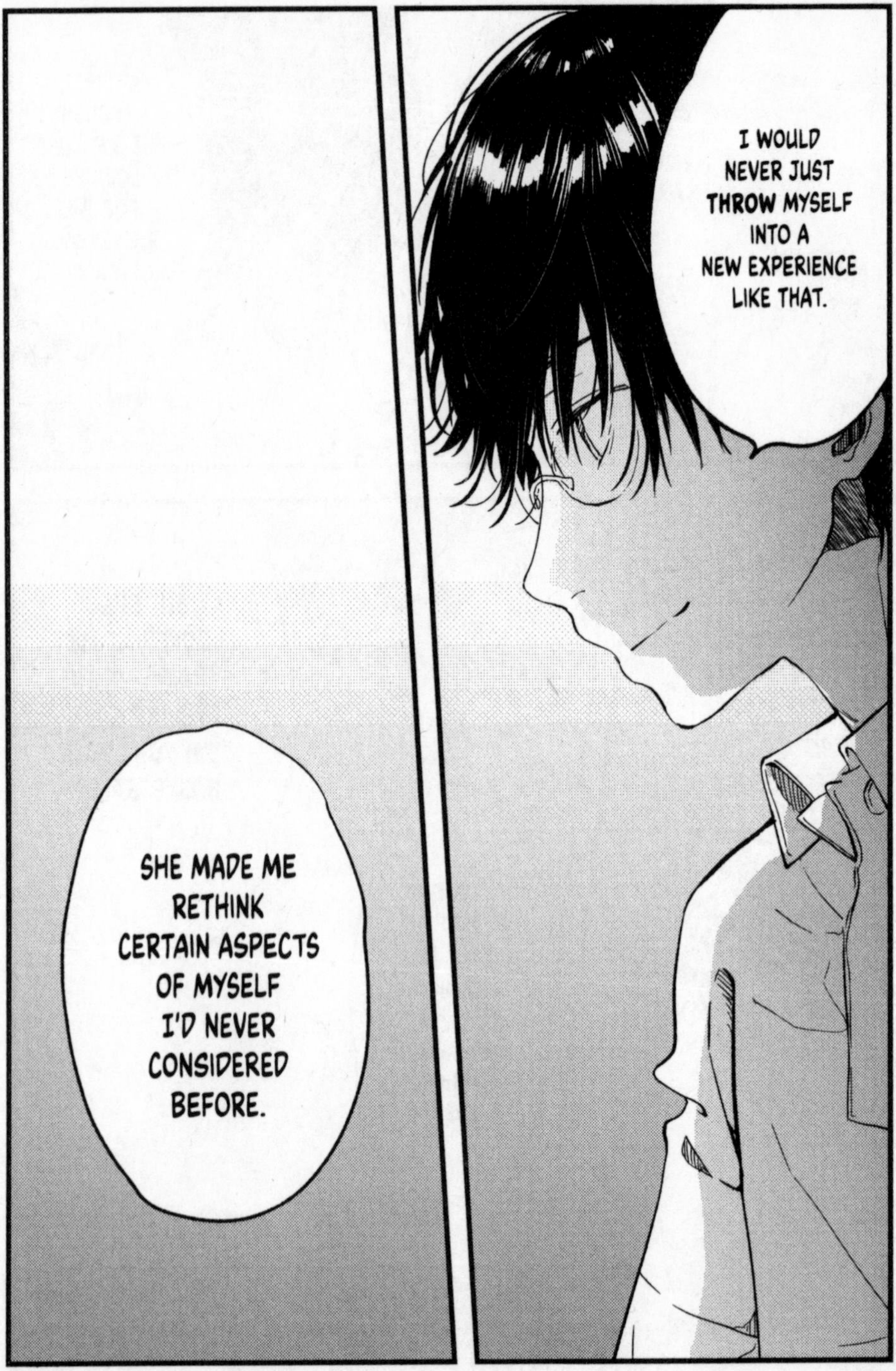
I WOULD NEVER JUST THROW MYSELF INTO A NEW EXPERIENCE LIKE THAT.
SHE MADE ME RETHINK CERTAIN ASPECTS OF MYSELF I'D NEVER CONSIDERED BEFORE.

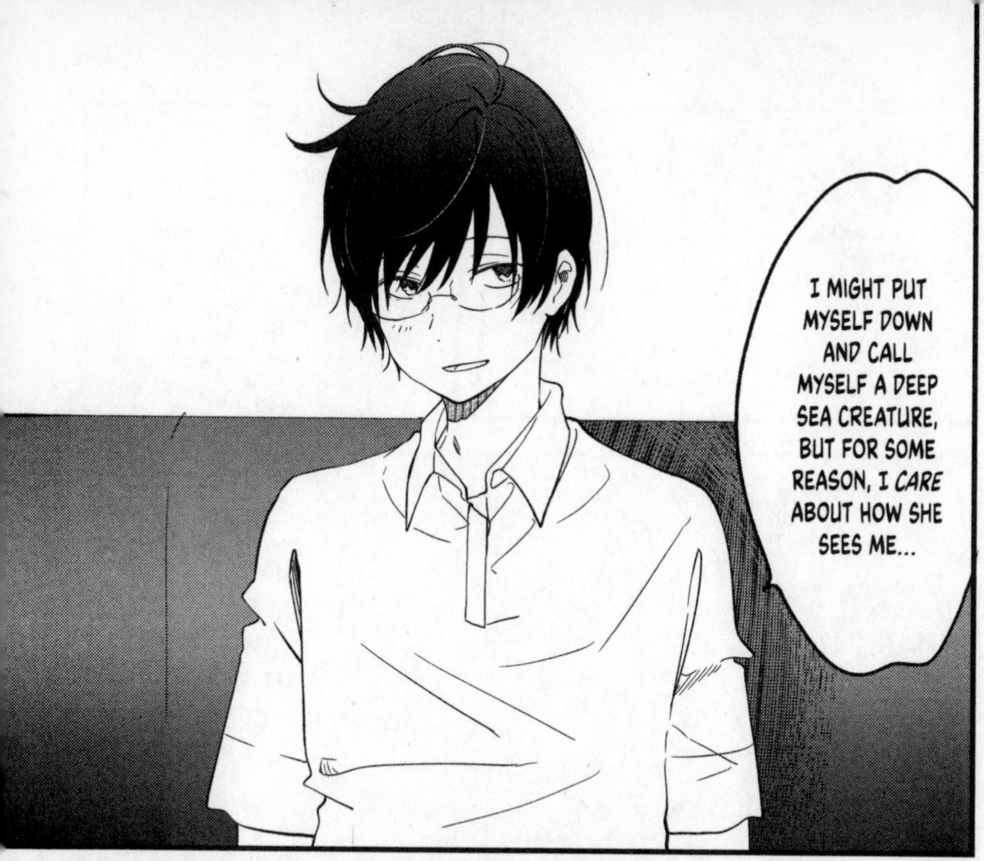
I MIGHT PUT MYSELF DOWN AND CALL MYSELF A DEEP SEA CREATURE, BUT FOR SOME REASON, I *CARE* ABOUT HOW SHE SEES ME...
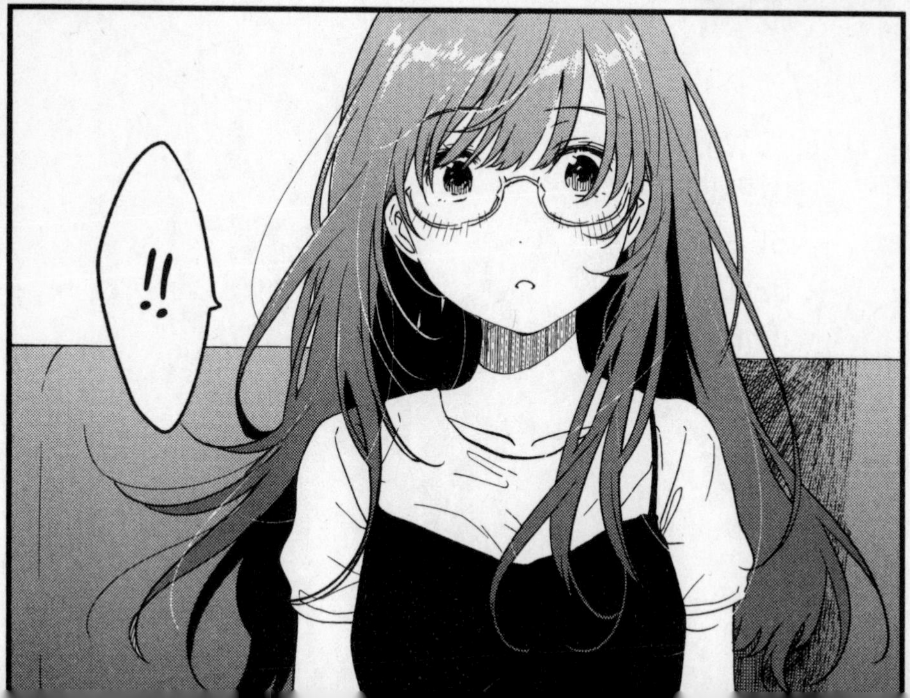
!!

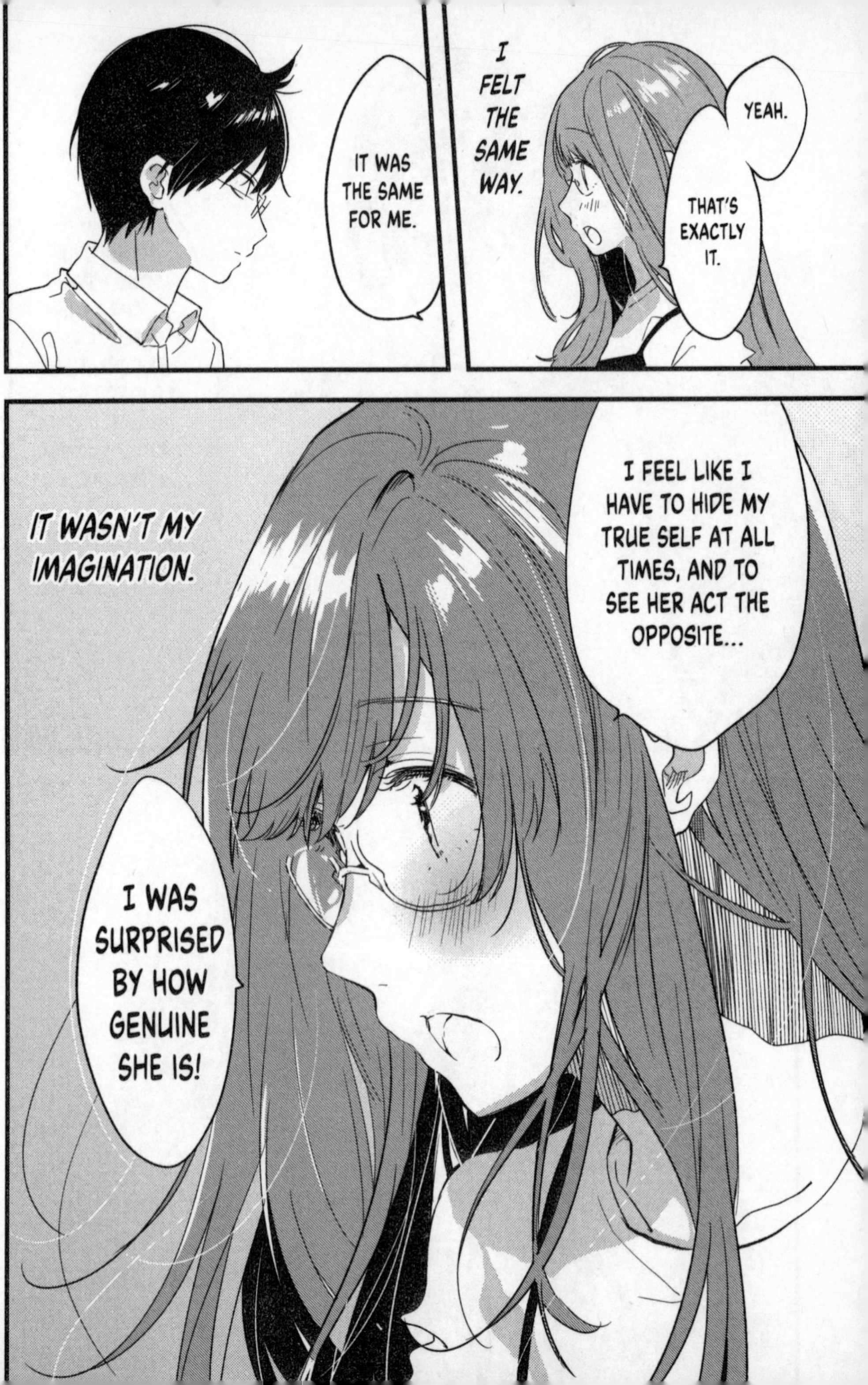
YEAH.
THAT'S EXACTLY IT.
I FELT THE SAME WAY.
IT WAS THE SAME FOR ME.
I FEEL LIKE I HAVE TO HIDE MY TRUE SELF AT ALL TIMES, AND TO SEE HER ACT THE OPPOSITE...
IT WASN'T MY IMAGINATION.
I WAS SURPRISED BY HOW GENUINE SHE IS!

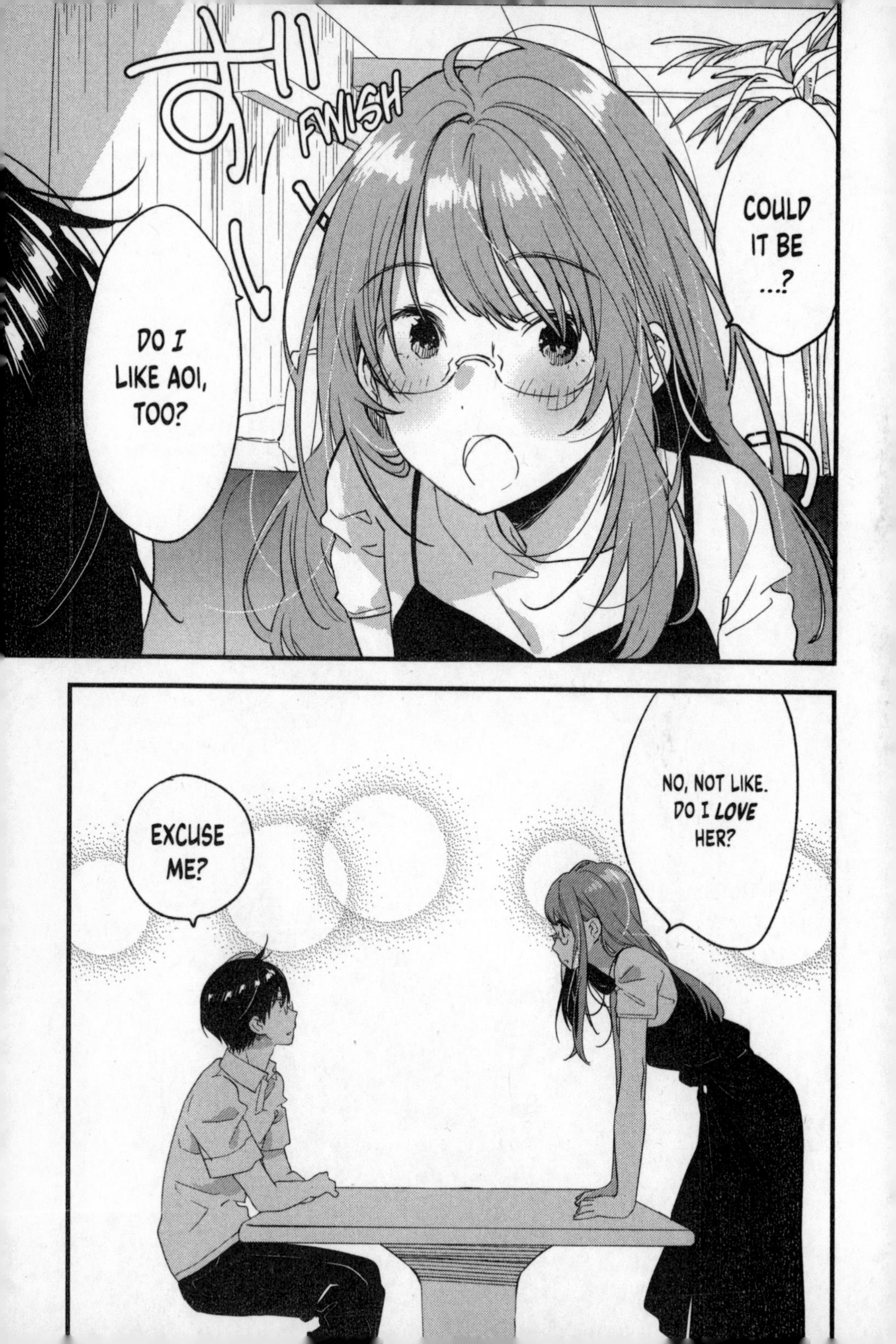
COULD IT BE ...?
FWISH
DO I LIKE AOI, TOO?
NO, NOT LIKE. DO I *LOVE* HER?
EXCUSE ME?

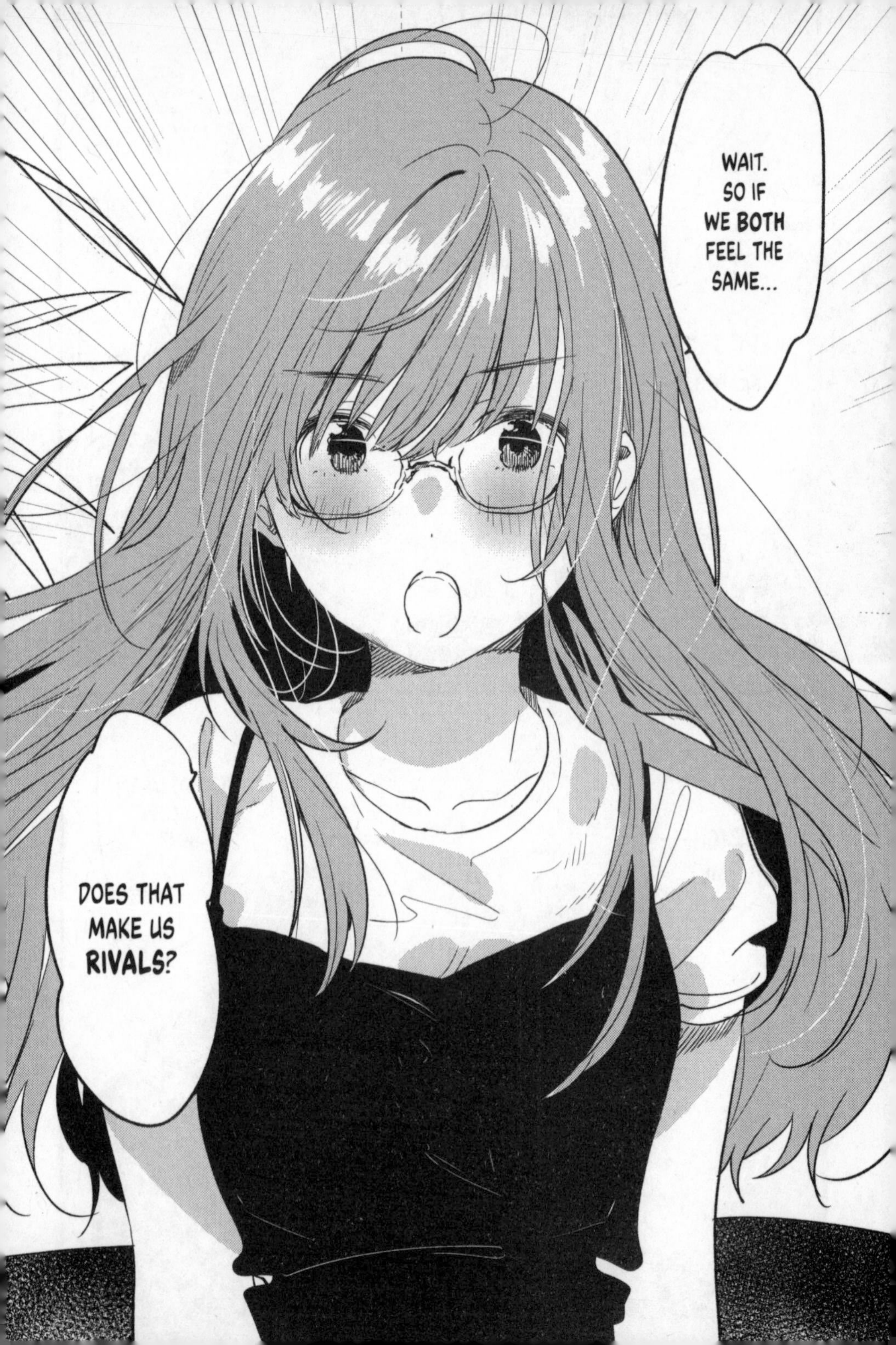
WAIT. SO IF WE BOTH FEEL THE SAME...
DOES THAT MAKE US RIVALS?

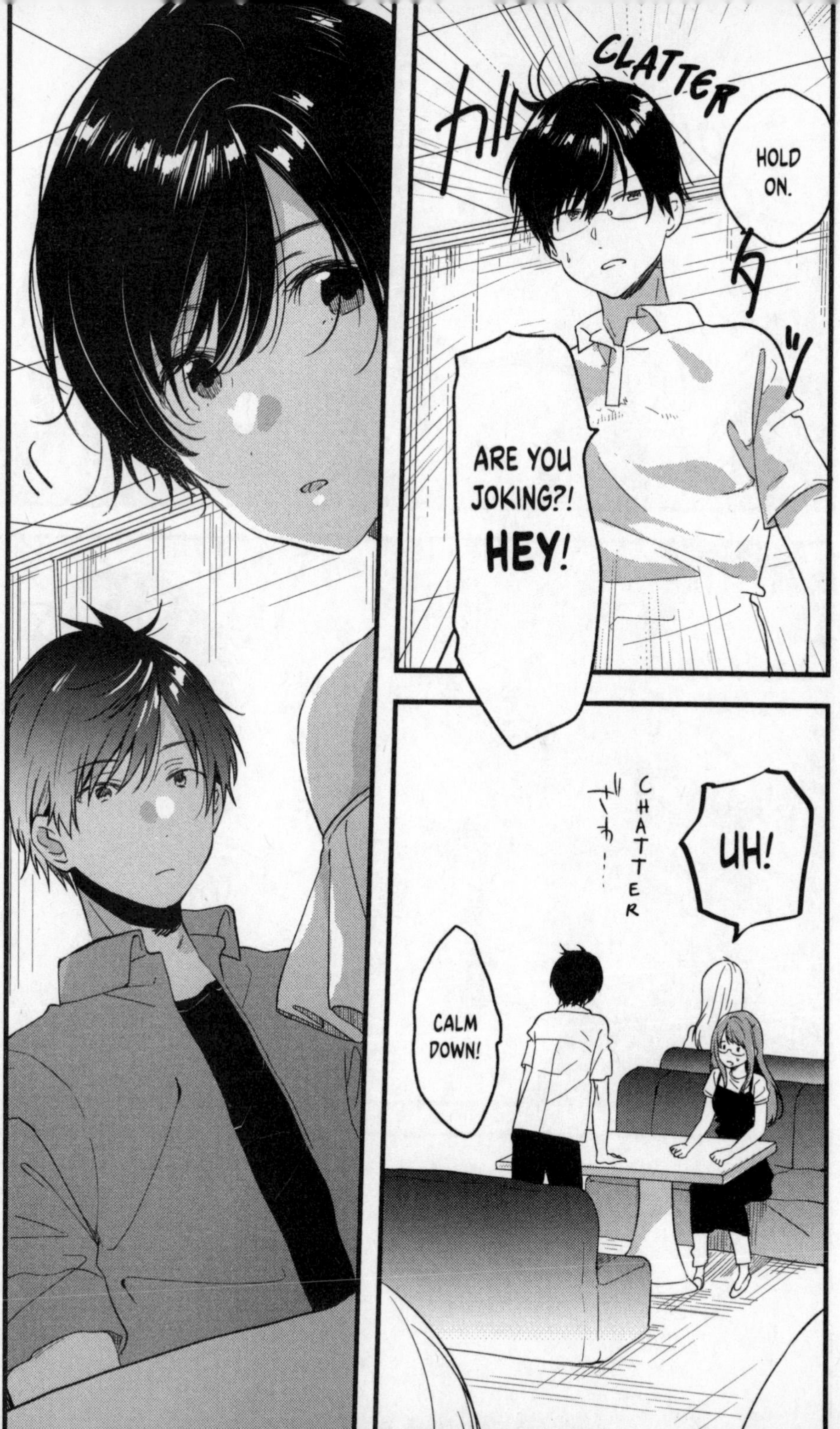
HOLD ON.
CLATTER
ARE YOU JOKING?! HEY!
UH!
CHATTER
ざわ…
CALM DOWN!

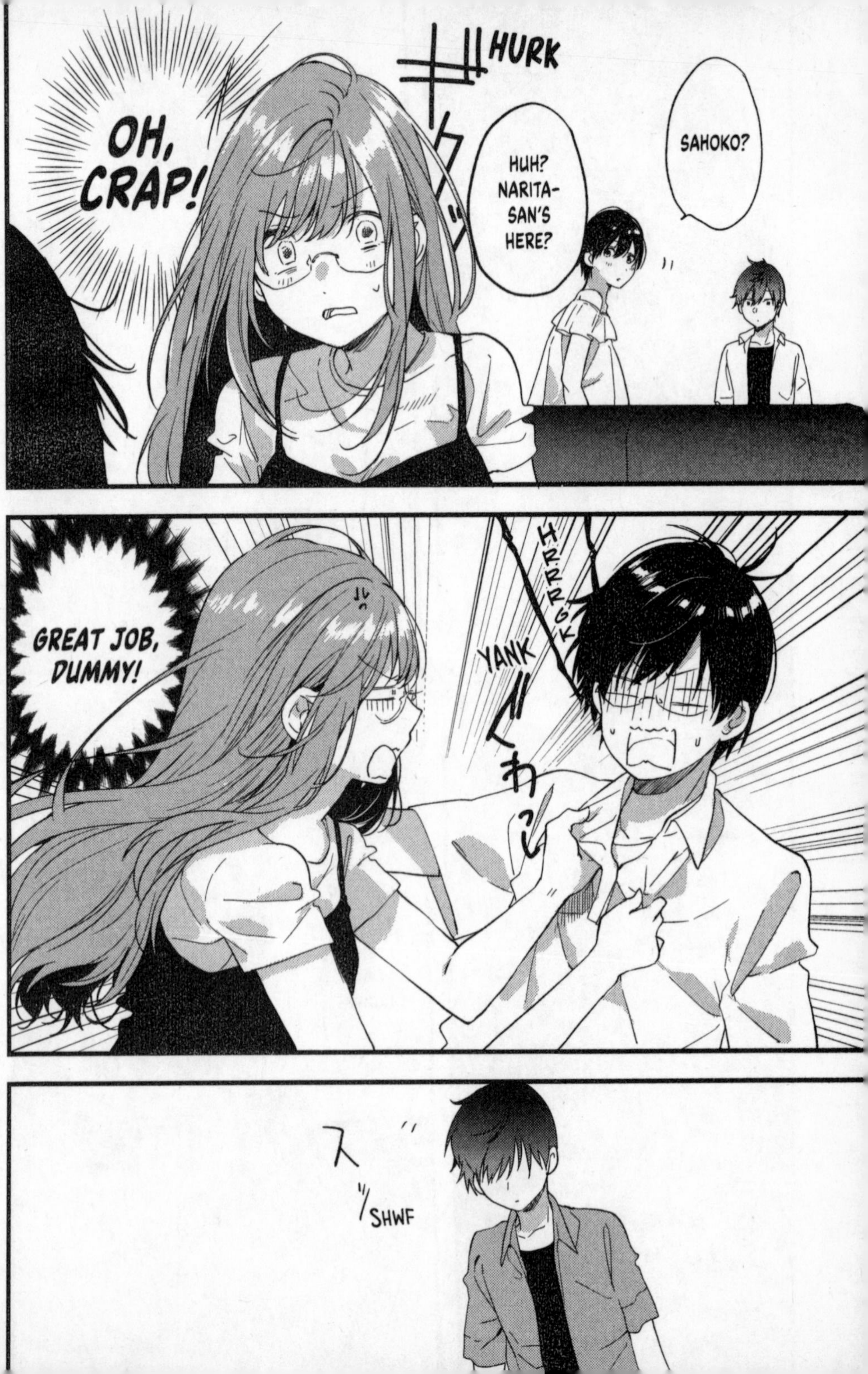
SAHOKO?
HUH? NARITA-SAN'S HERE?
HURK
OH, CRAP!
HRRRGK
YANK
GREAT JOB, DUMMY!
SHWF

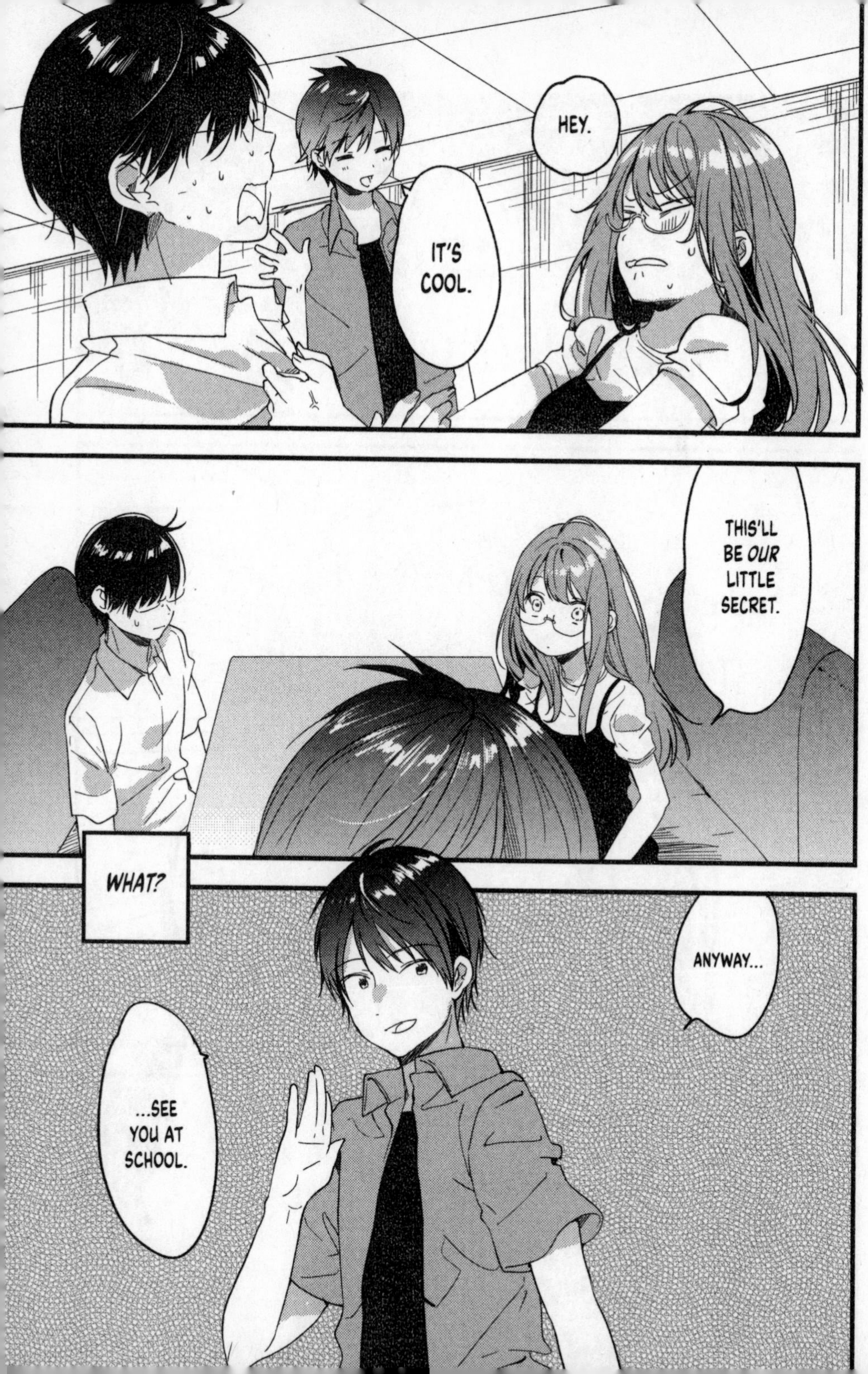
HEY.
IT'S COOL.
THIS'LL BE *OUR* LITTLE SECRET.
WHAT?
ANYWAY...
...SEE YOU AT SCHOOL.

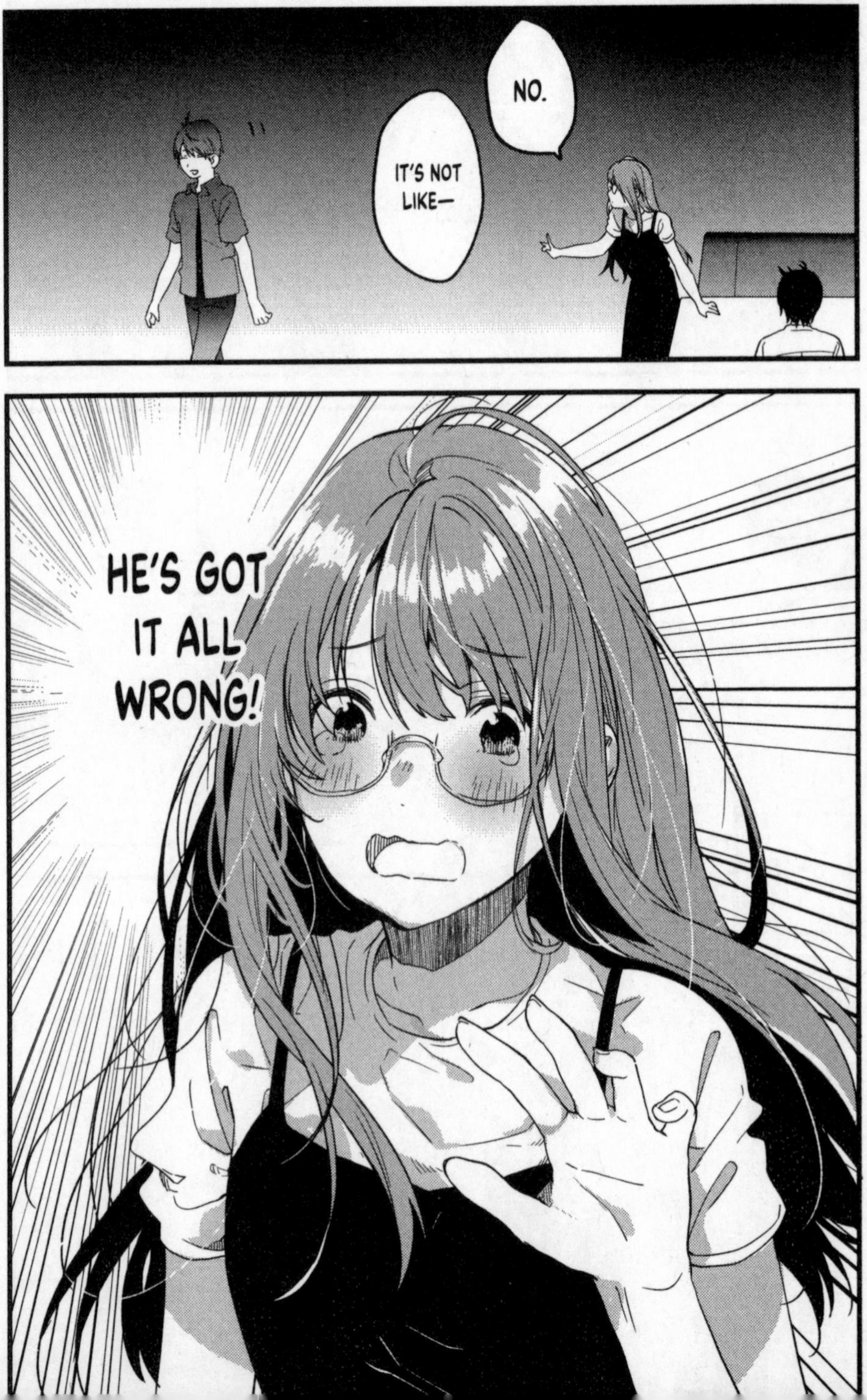
NO.
IT'S NOT LIKE—
HE'S GOT IT ALL WRONG!

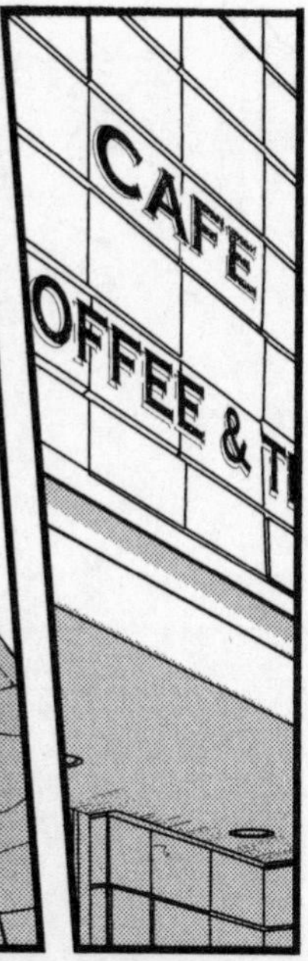
CAFE

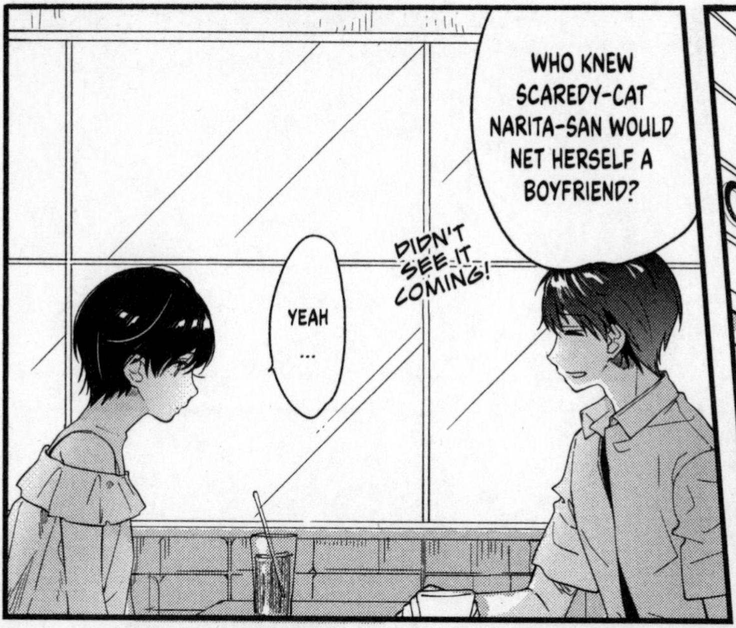
WHO KNEW SCAREDY-CAT NARITA-SAN WOULD NET HERSELF A BOYFRIEND?
DIDN'T SEE IT COMING!
YEAH ...

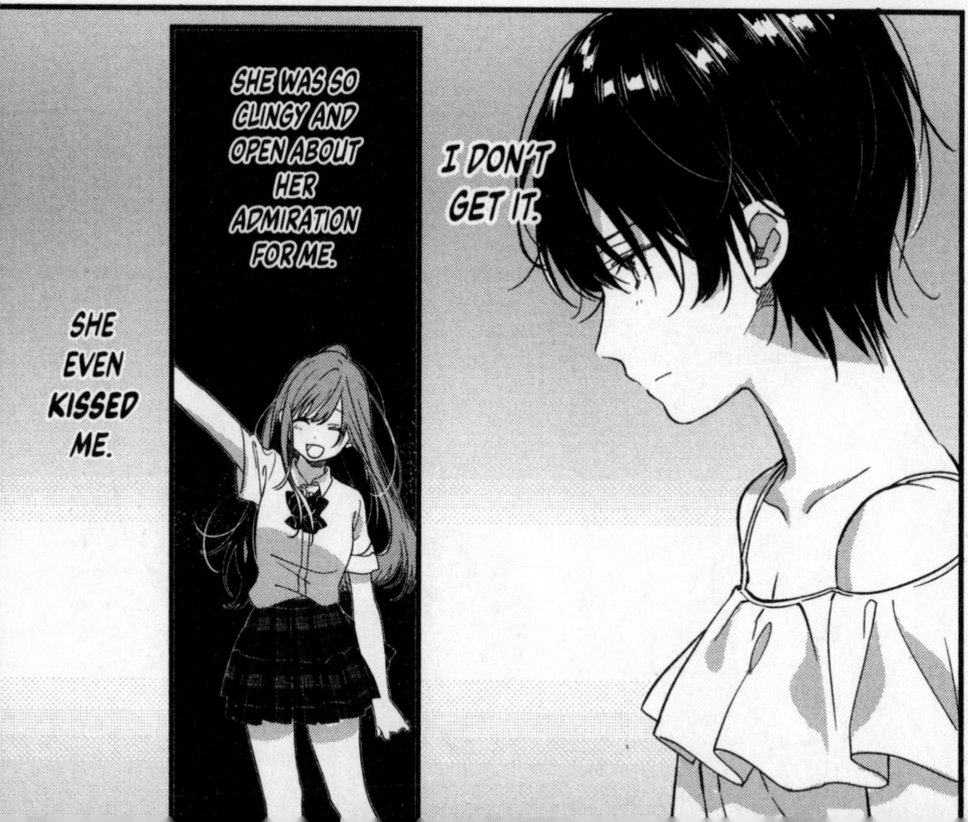
I DON'T GET IT.
SHE WAS SO CLINGY AND OPEN ABOUT HER ADMIRATION FOR ME.
SHE EVEN KISSED ME.

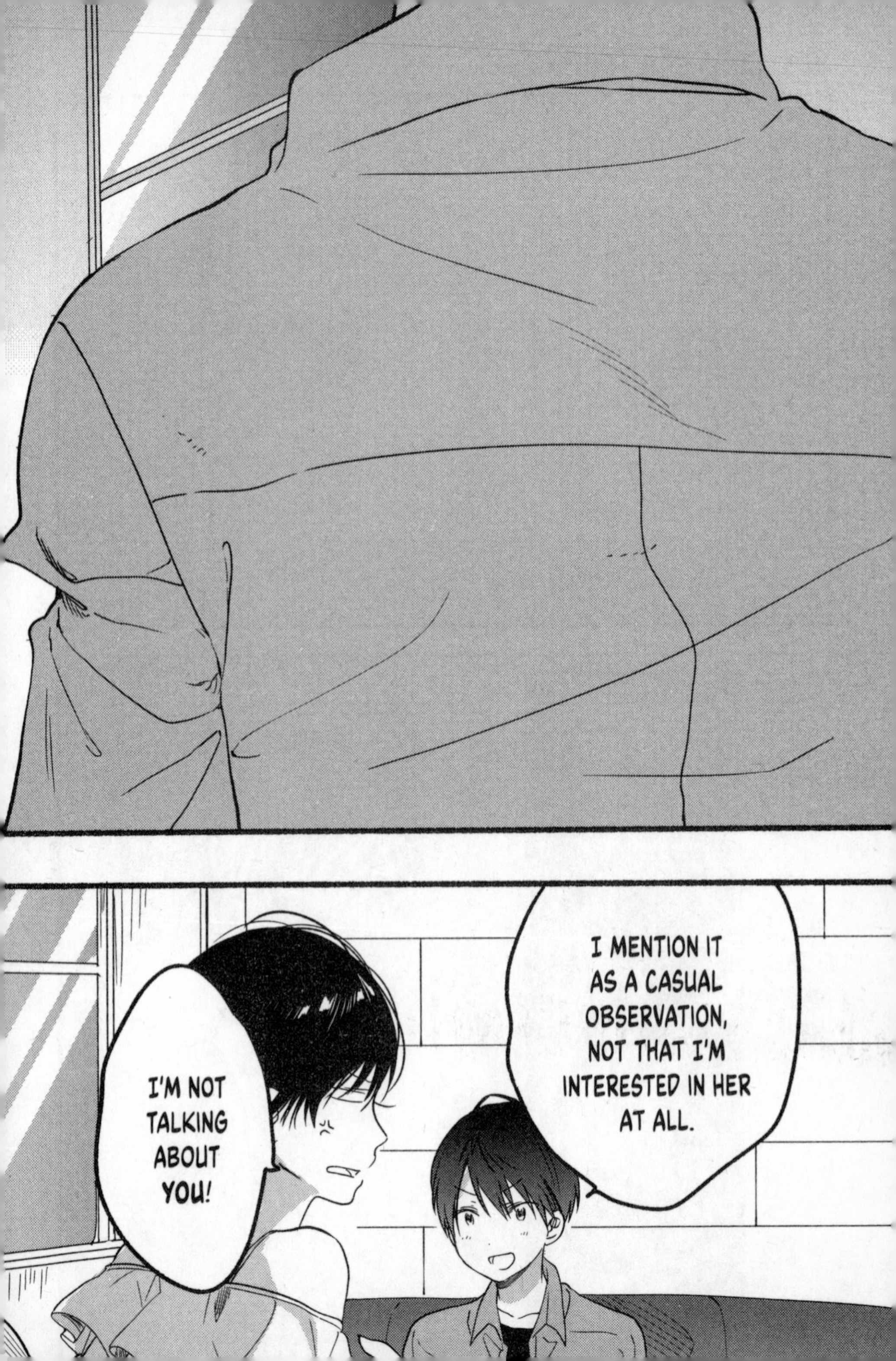
I MENTION IT AS A CASUAL OBSERVATION, NOT THAT I'M INTERESTED IN HER AT ALL.
I'M NOT TALKING ABOUT YOU!

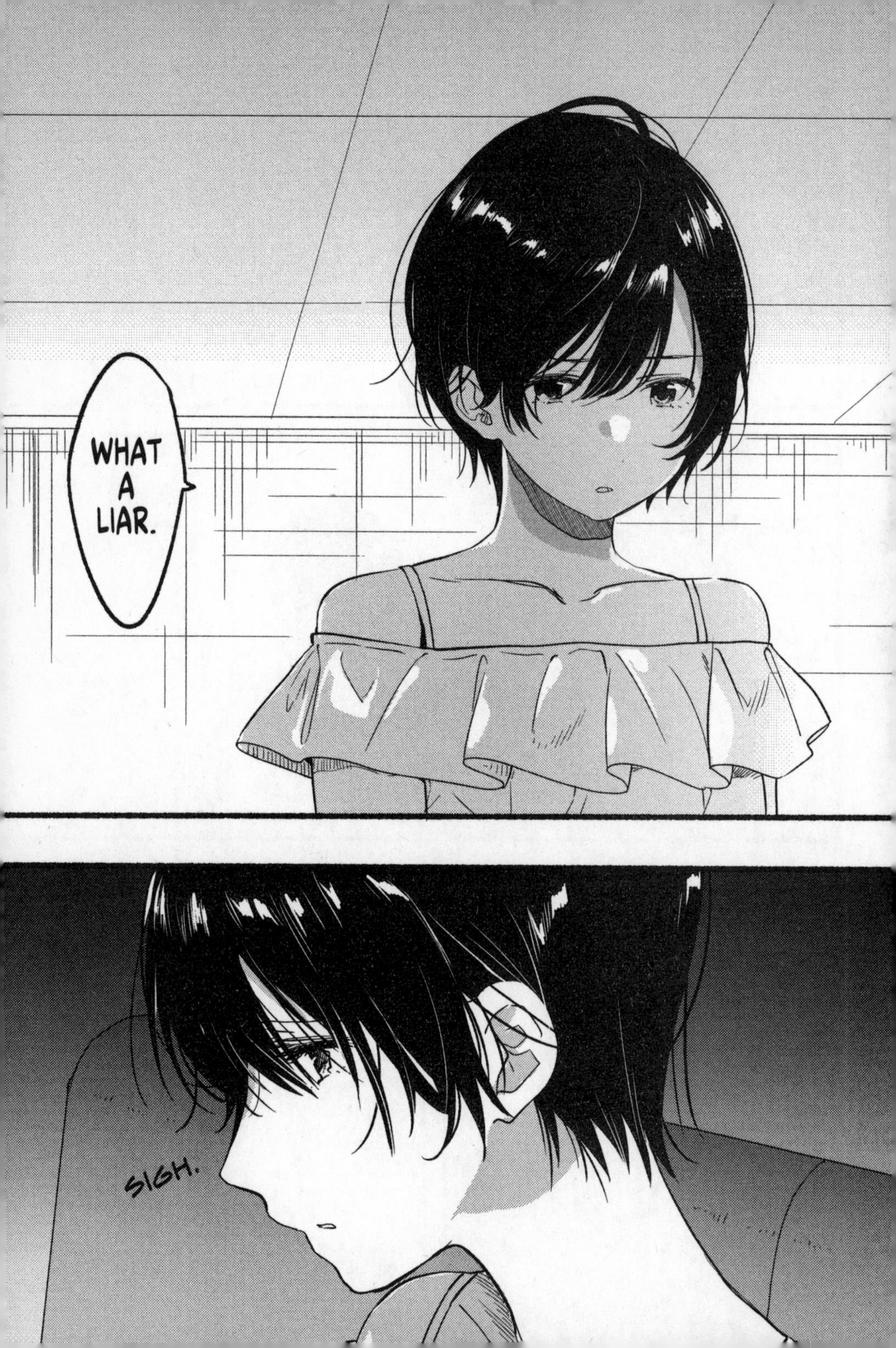
WHAT A LIAR.
SIGH.

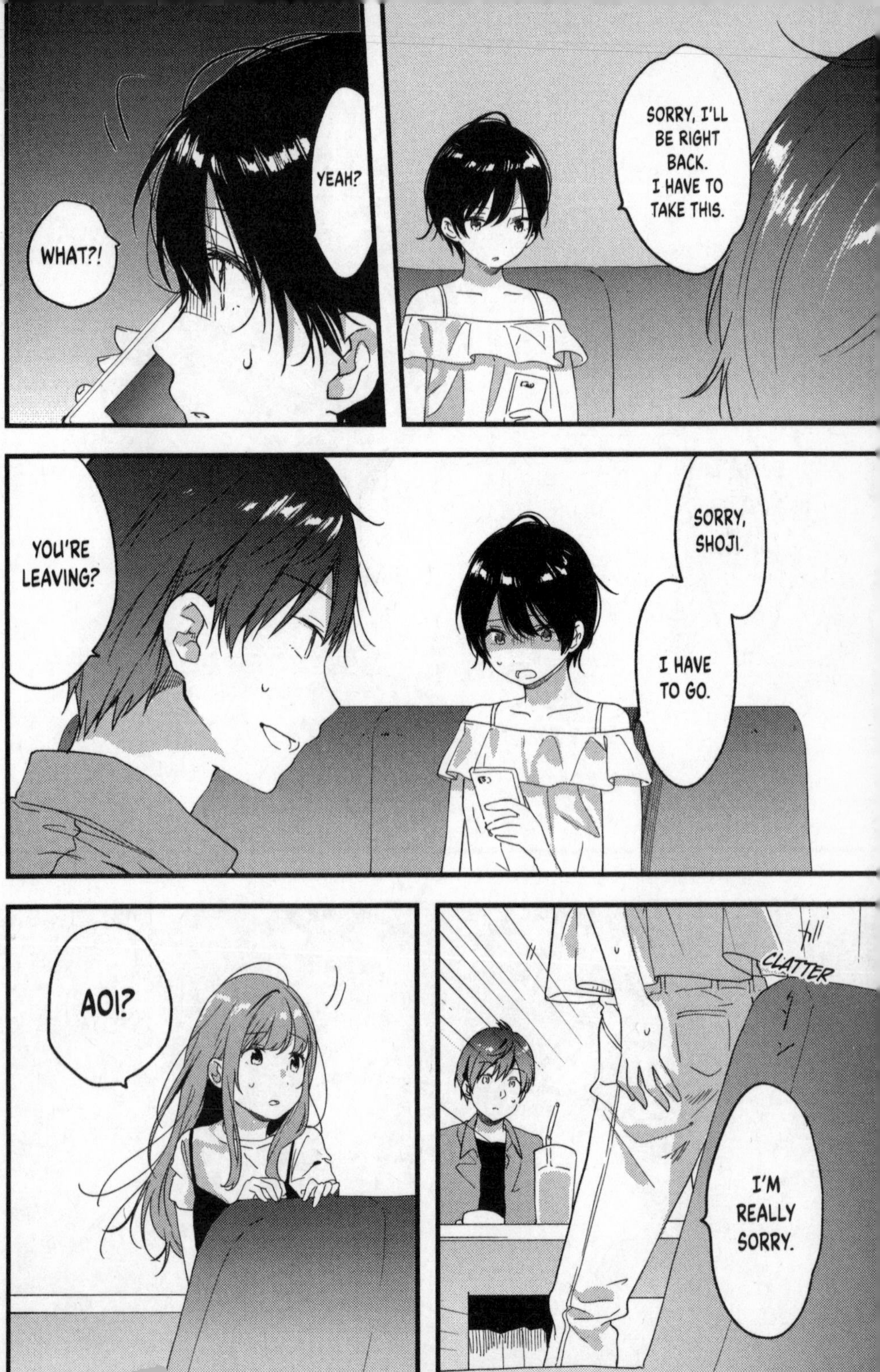
SORRY, I'LL BE RIGHT BACK. I HAVE TO TAKE THIS.
YEAH?
WHAT?!
SORRY, SHOJI.
I HAVE TO GO.
YOU'RE LEAVING?
CLATTER
I'M REALLY SORRY.
AOI?

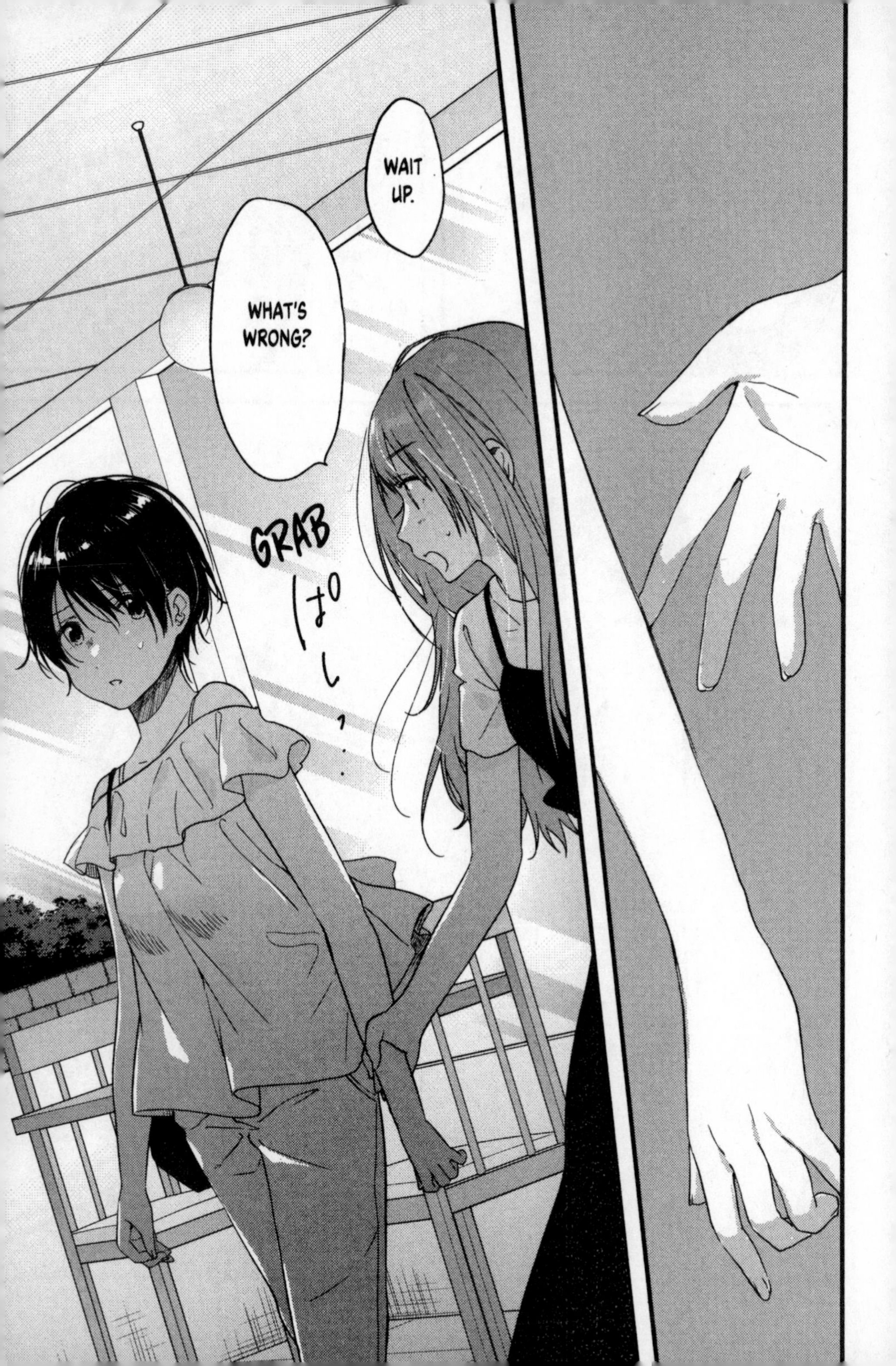
WAIT UP.
WHAT'S WRONG?
GRAB
ぱし

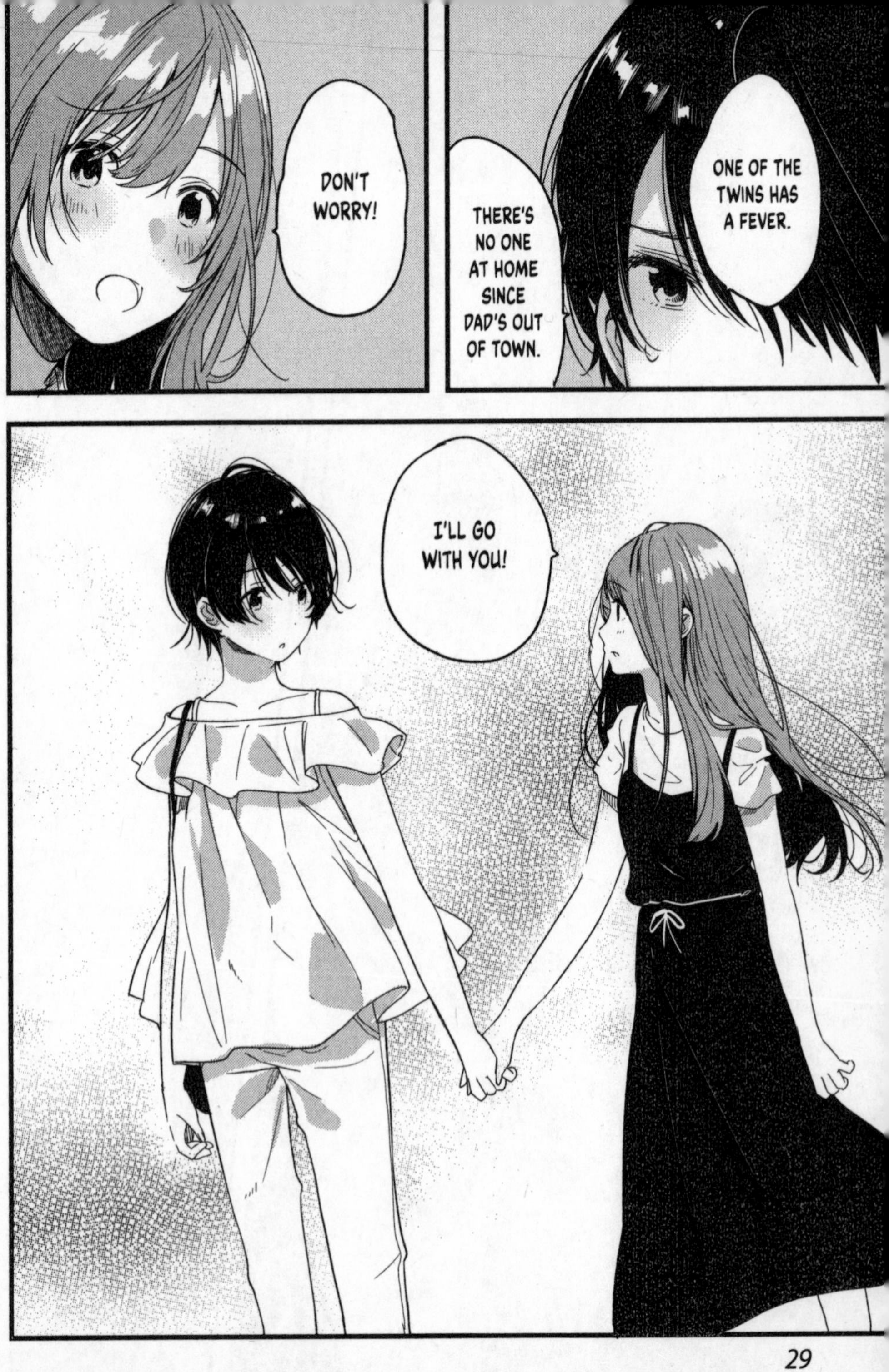
ONE OF THE TWINS HAS A FEVER.
THERE'S NO ONE AT HOME SINCE DAD'S OUT OF TOWN.
DON'T WORRY!
I'LL GO WITH YOU!

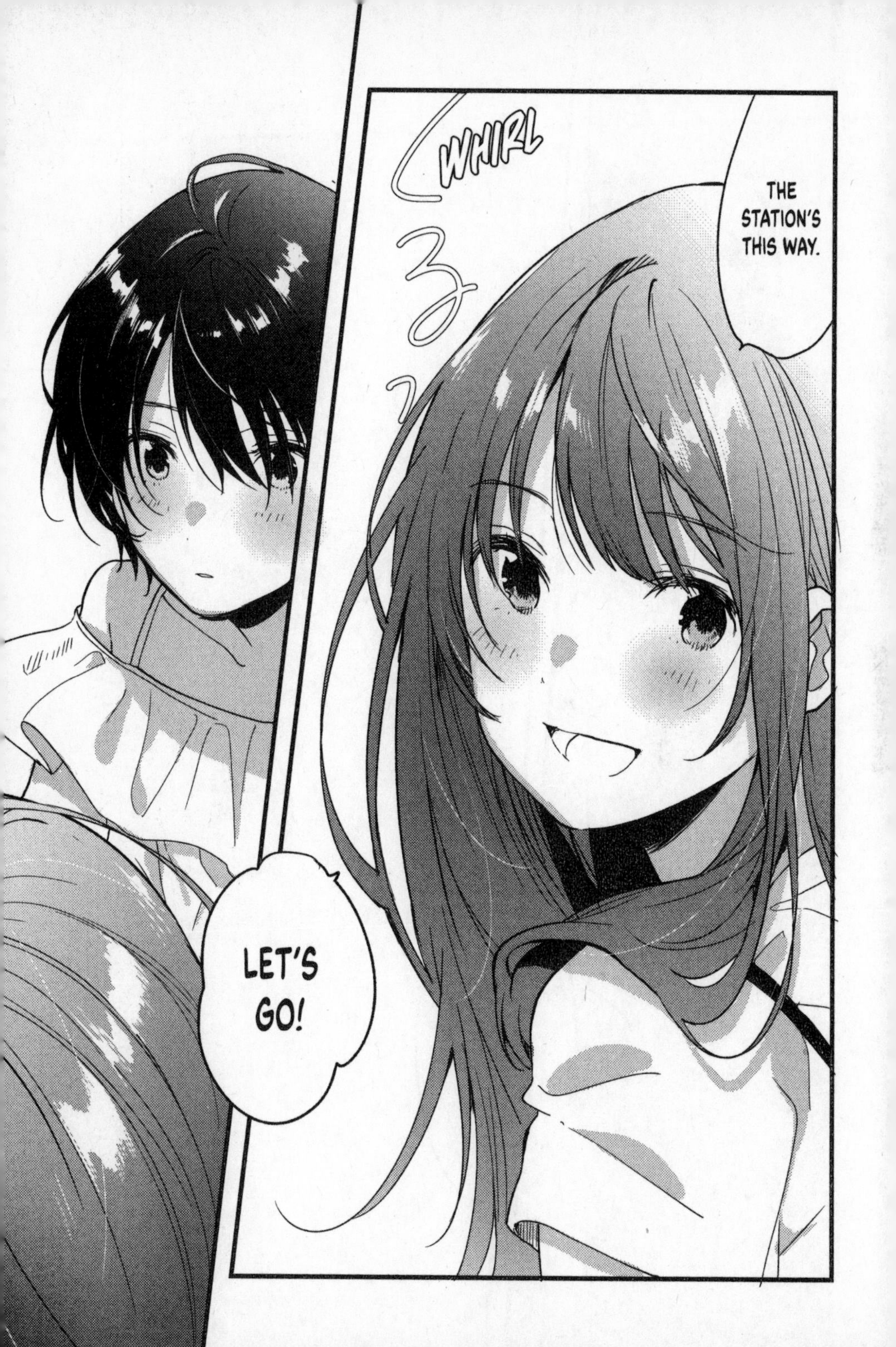
WHIRL
THE STATION'S THIS WAY.
LET'S GO!

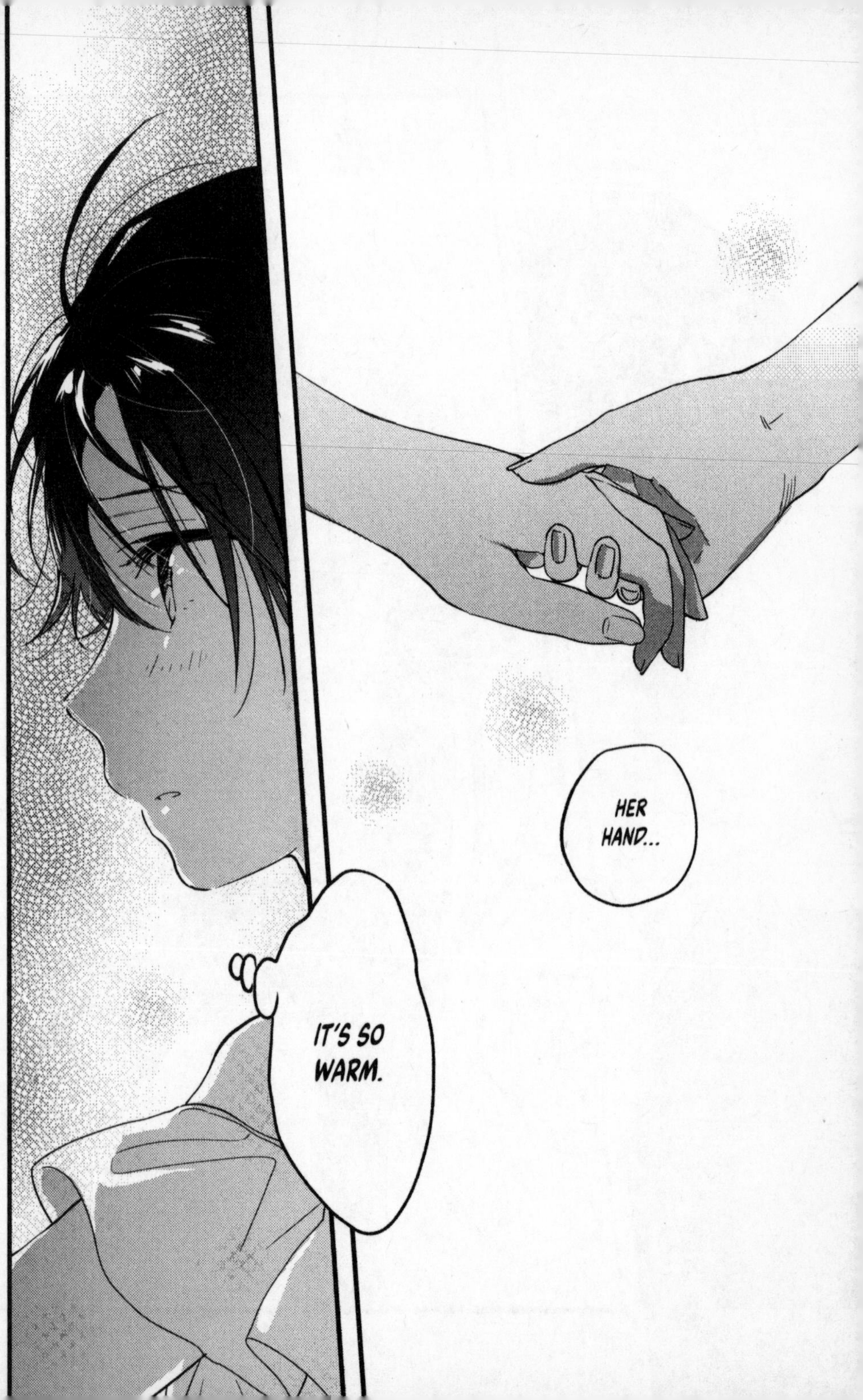
HER HAND...
IT'S SO WARM.

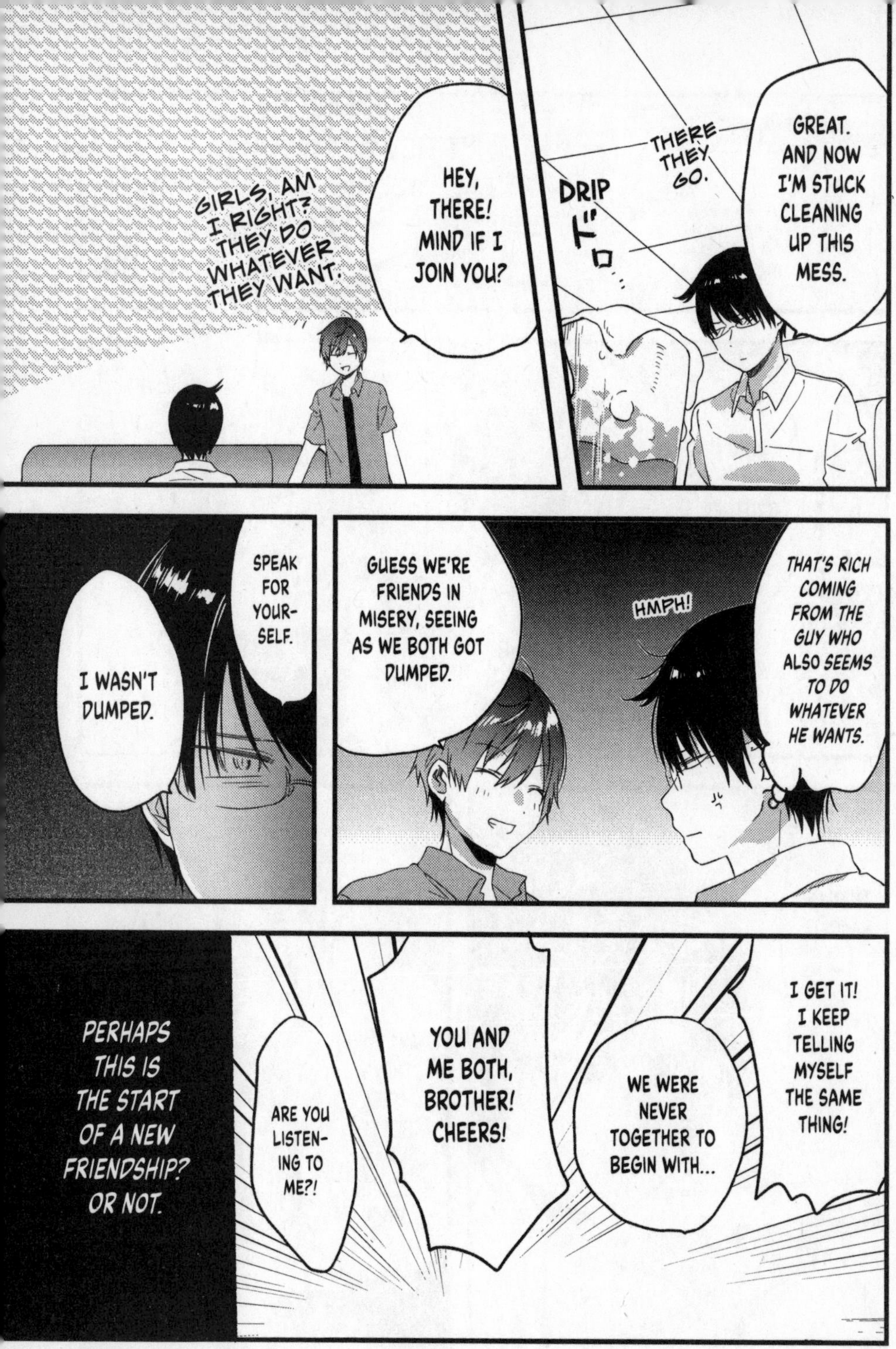
GREAT. AND NOW I'M STUCK CLEANING UP THIS MESS.
THERE THEY GO.
DRIP
ドロ…
HEY, THERE! MIND IF I JOIN YOU?
GIRLS, AM I RIGHT? THEY DO WHATEVER THEY WANT.
THAT'S RICH COMING FROM THE GUY WHO ALSO SEEMS TO DO WHATEVER HE WANTS.
HMPH!
GUESS WE'RE FRIENDS IN MISERY, SEEING AS WE BOTH GOT DUMPED.
SPEAK FOR YOUR-SELF.
I WASN'T DUMPED.
I GET IT! I KEEP TELLING MYSELF THE SAME THING!
WE WERE NEVER TOGETHER TO BEGIN WITH...
YOU AND ME BOTH, BROTHER! CHEERS!
ARE YOU LISTEN-ING TO ME?!
PERHAPS THIS IS THE START OF A NEW FRIENDSHIP? OR NOT.

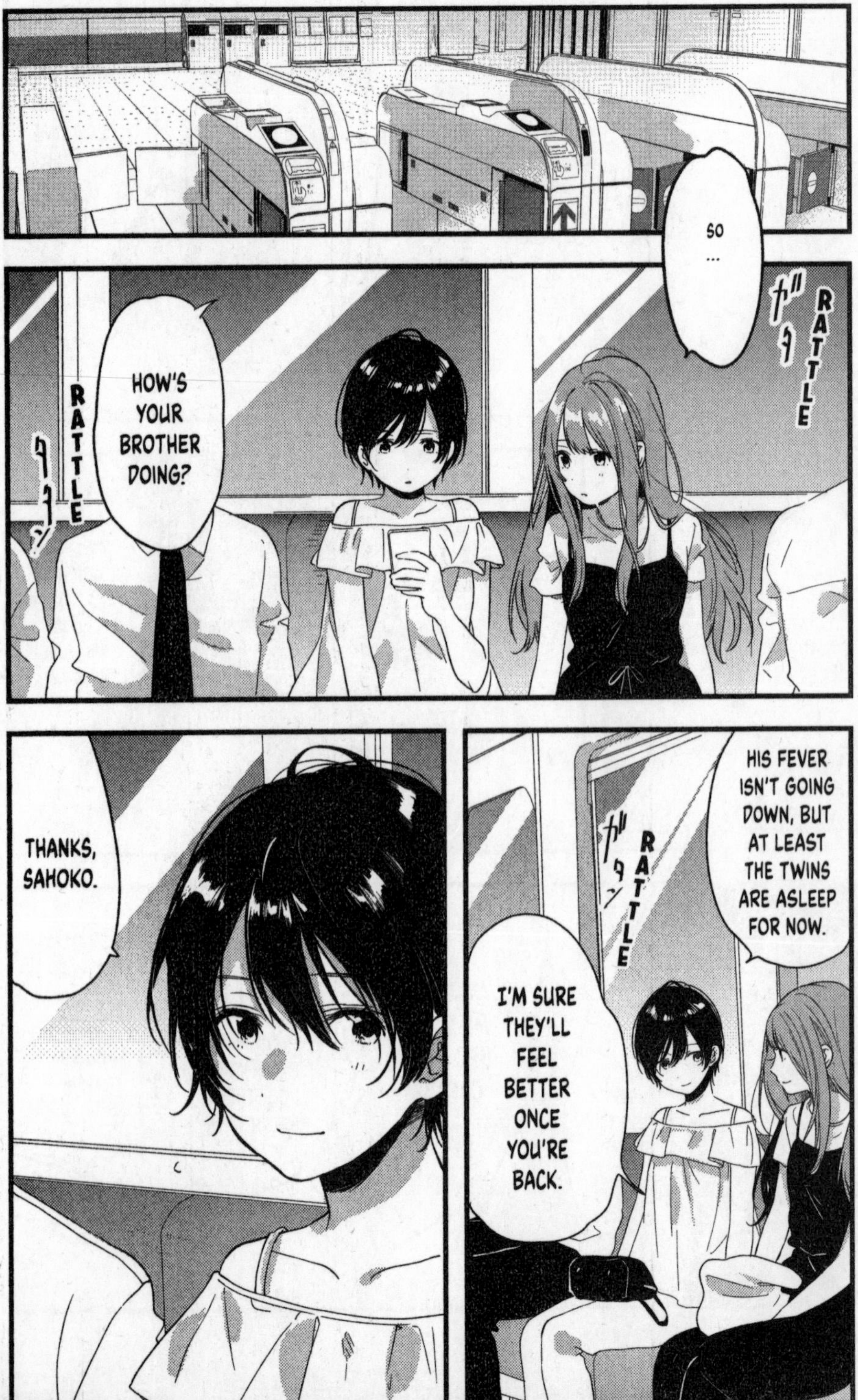
SO ...
RATTLE
HOW'S YOUR BROTHER DOING?
RATTLE
HIS FEVER ISN'T GOING DOWN, BUT AT LEAST THE TWINS ARE ASLEEP FOR NOW.
RATTLE
I'M SURE THEY'LL FEEL BETTER ONCE YOU'RE BACK.
THANKS, SAHOKO.

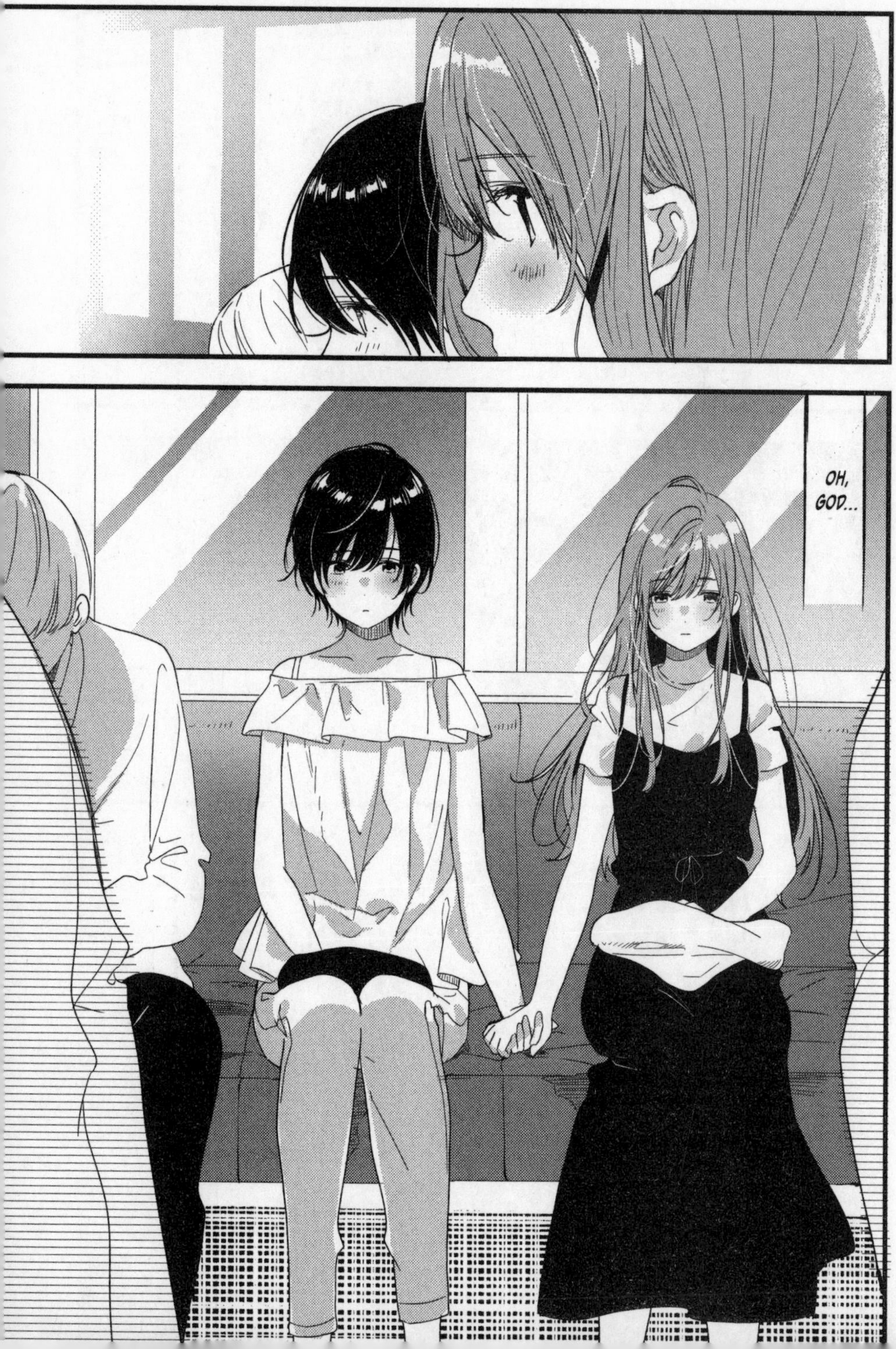
OH, GOD...

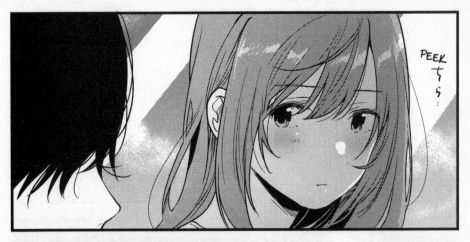

PEEK
ちら…
AM I ACTING RECKLESSLY, THINKING ONLY OF MYSELF?
I FEEL LIKE ALL I DO IS MAKE A MESS OF THINGS.

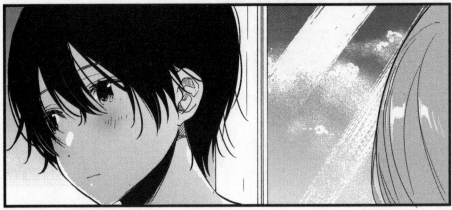

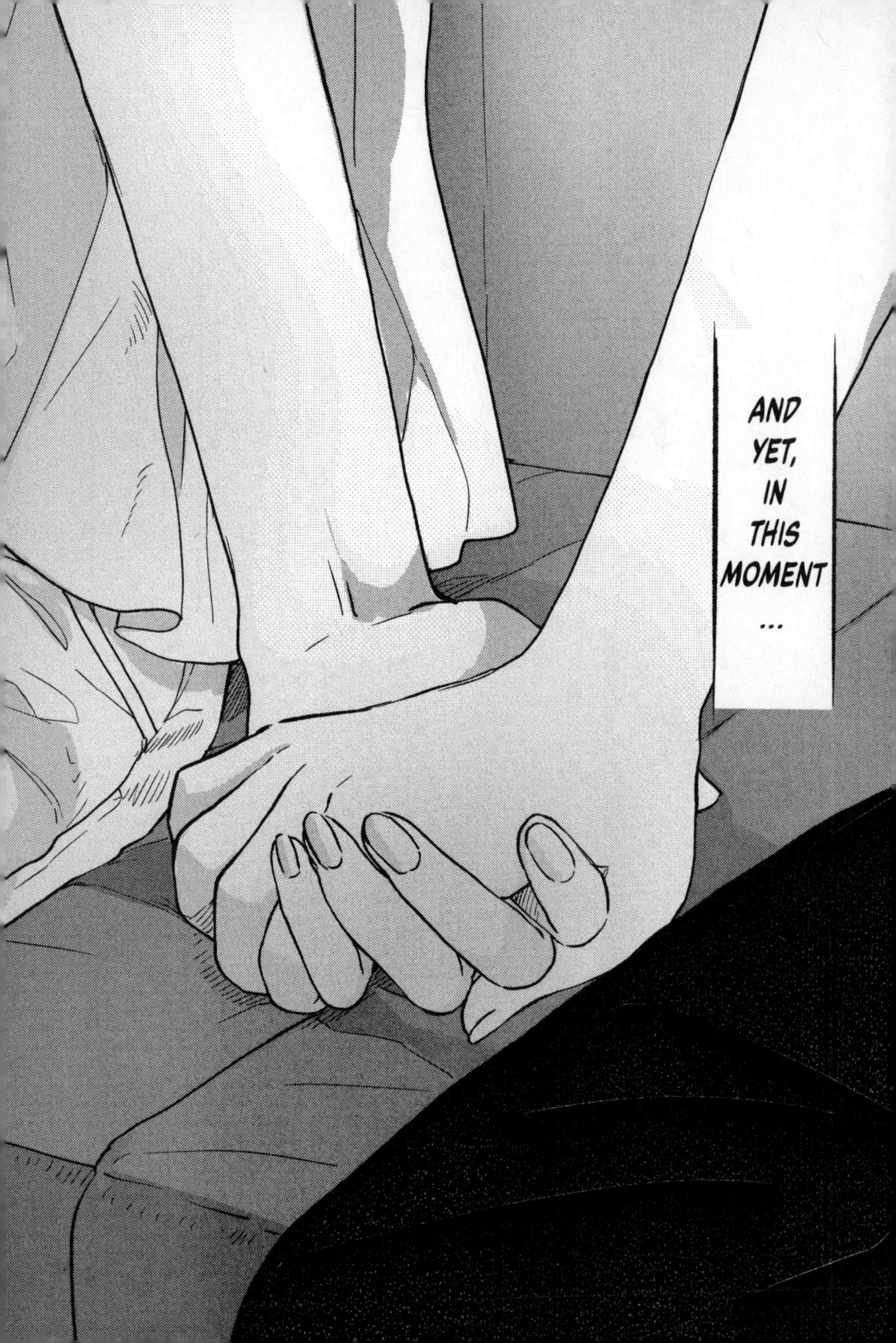
AND YET, IN THIS MOMENT ...

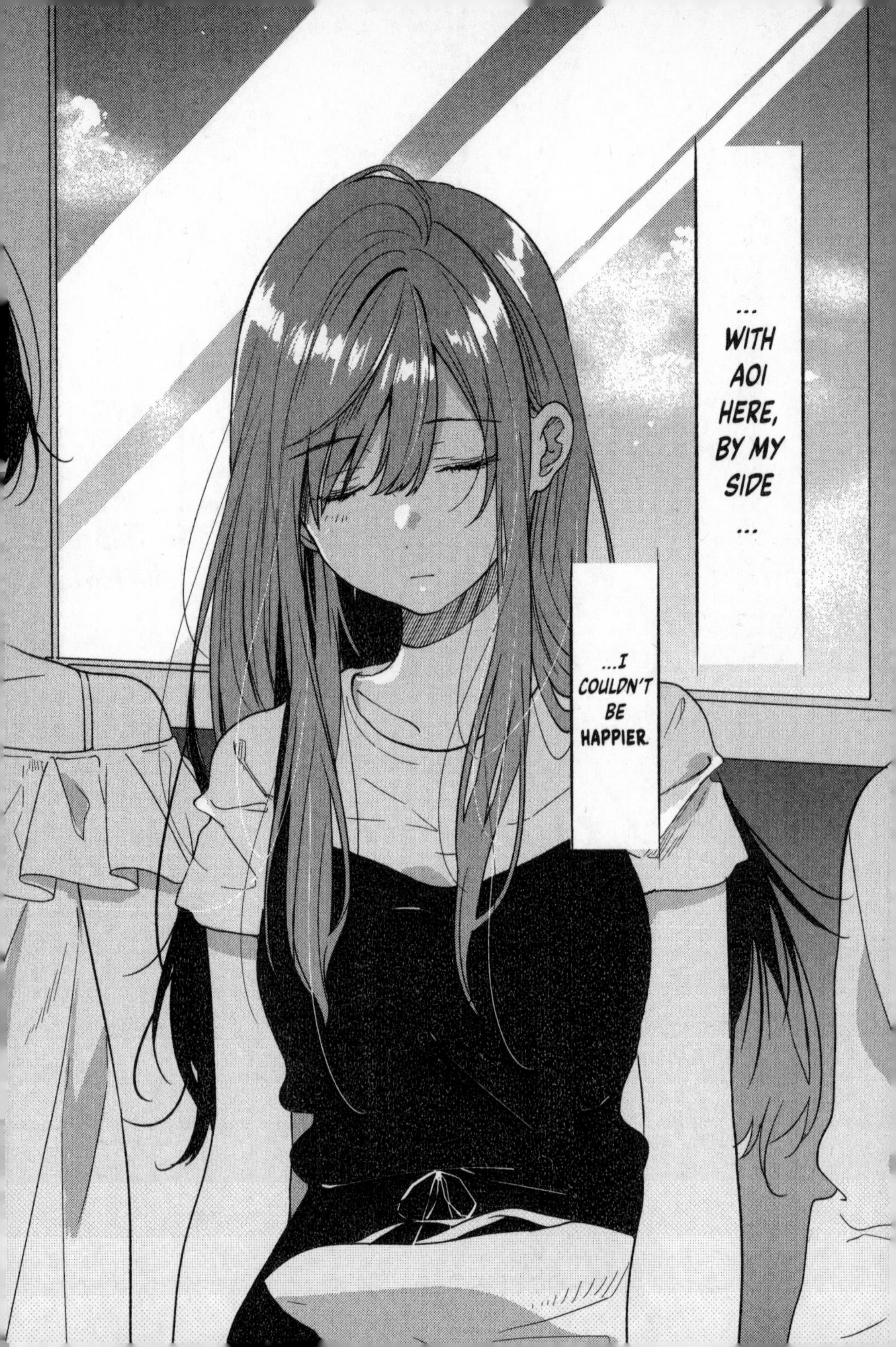
... WITH AOI HERE, BY MY SIDE ...
...I COULDN'T BE HAPPIER.

CHASING AFTER *Aoi Koshiba*

Summer | High School, Second Year

CHASING AFTER Aoi Koshiba

Winter | College, Third Year

Chapter 16: Crossroads 3

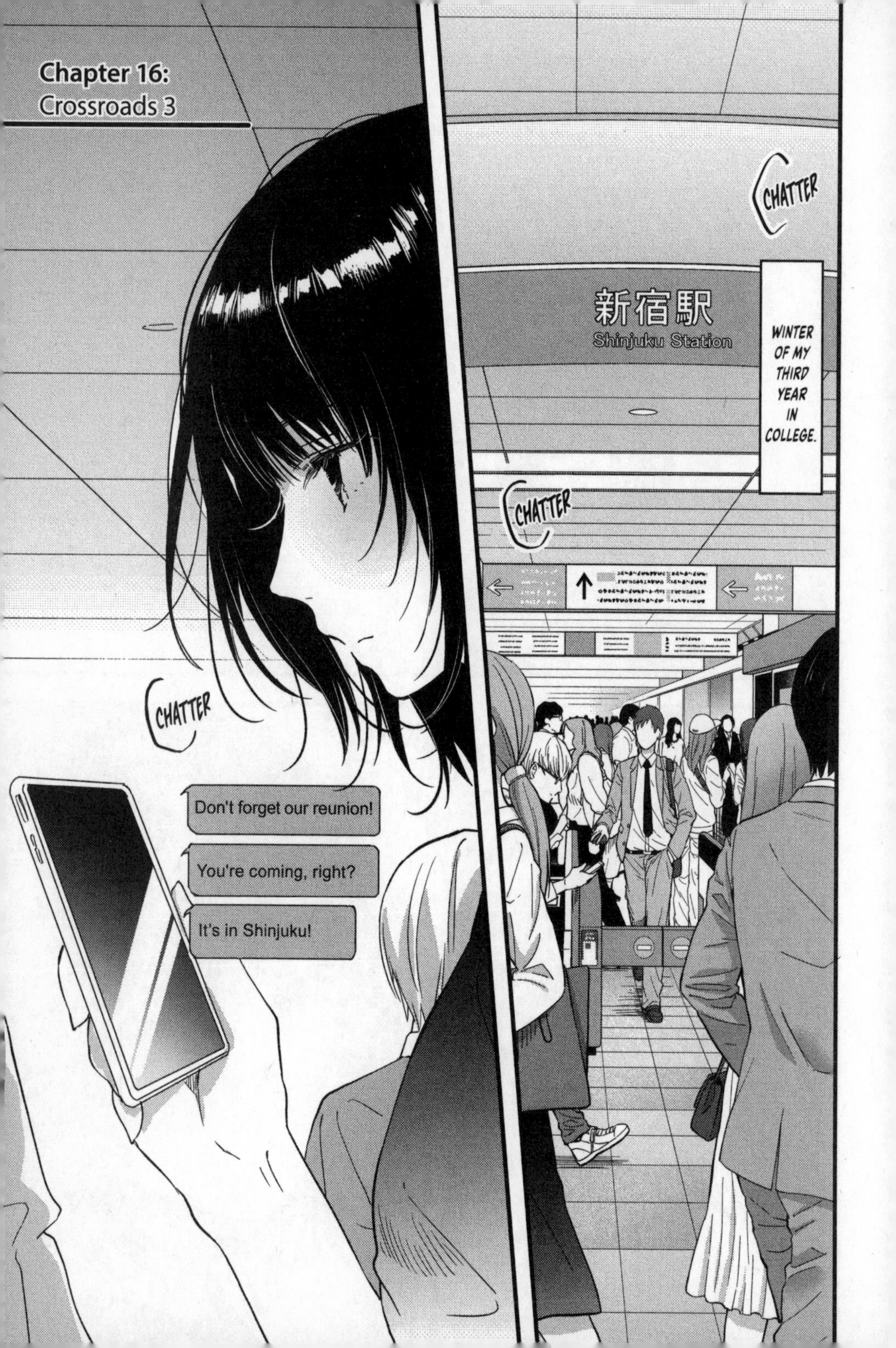
CHATTER
新宿駅
Shinjuku Station
WINTER OF MY THIRD YEAR IN COLLEGE.
CHATTER
CHATTER
Don't forget our reunion!
You're coming, right?
It's in Shinjuku!

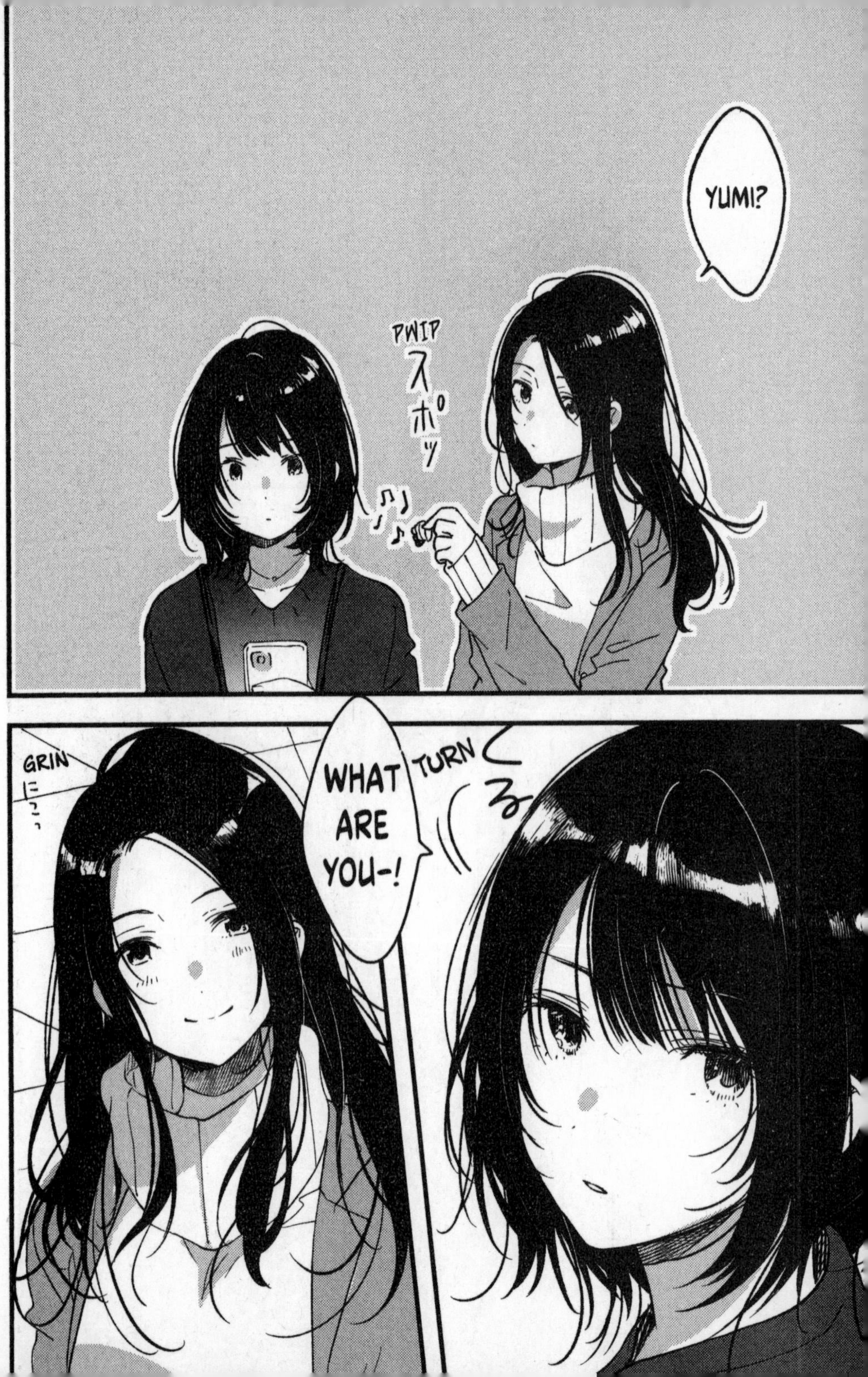
YUMI?
PWIP
スポッ
TURN
くる
WHAT ARE YOU-!
GRIN
にこっ

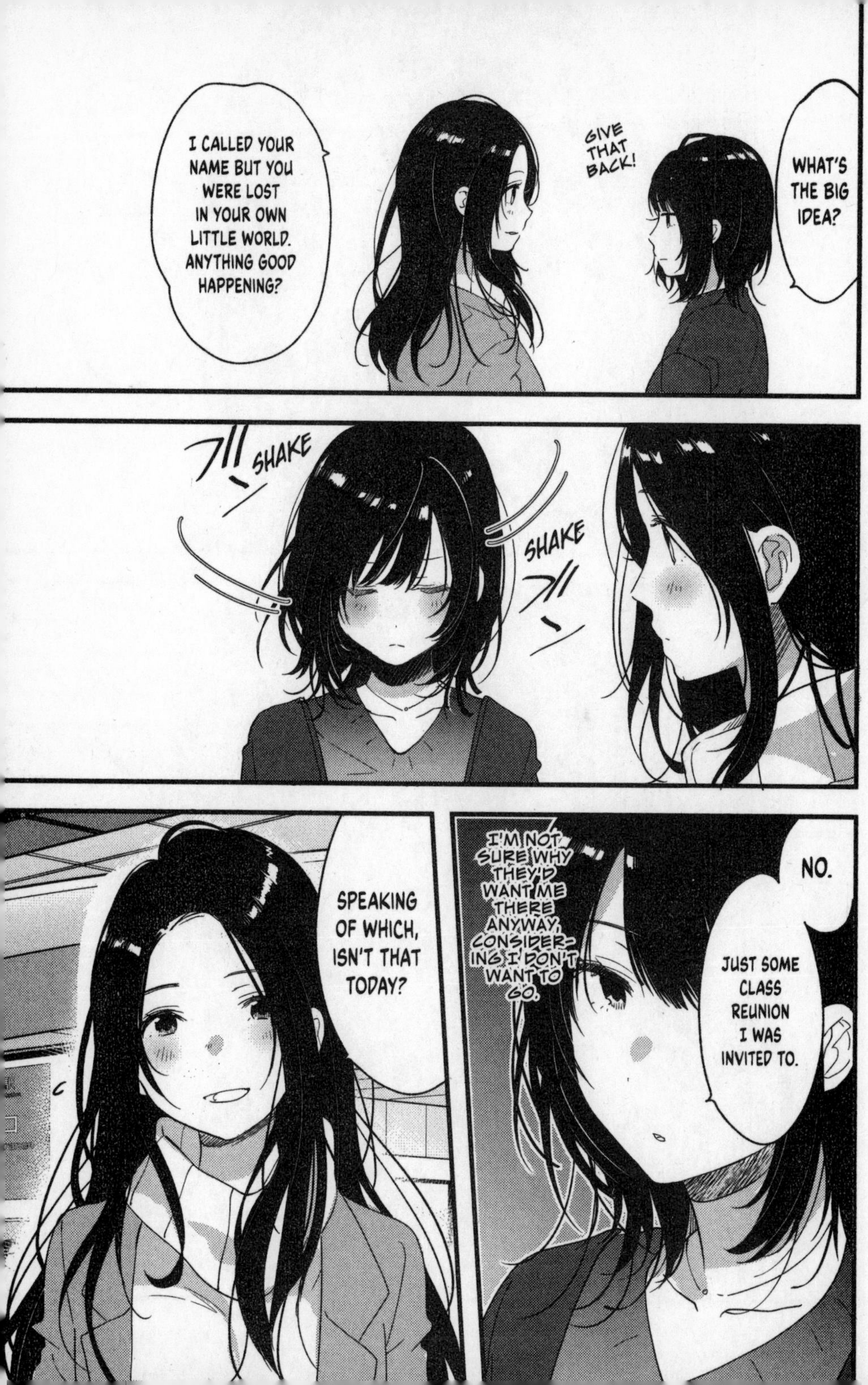
WHAT'S THE BIG IDEA?
GIVE THAT BACK!
I CALLED YOUR NAME BUT YOU WERE LOST IN YOUR OWN LITTLE WORLD. ANYTHING GOOD HAPPENING?
SHAKE
SHAKE
NO.
JUST SOME CLASS REUNION I WAS INVITED TO.
I'M NOT SURE WHY THEY'D WANT ME THERE ANYWAY, CONSIDERING I DON'T WANT TO GO.
SPEAKING OF WHICH, ISN'T THAT TODAY?

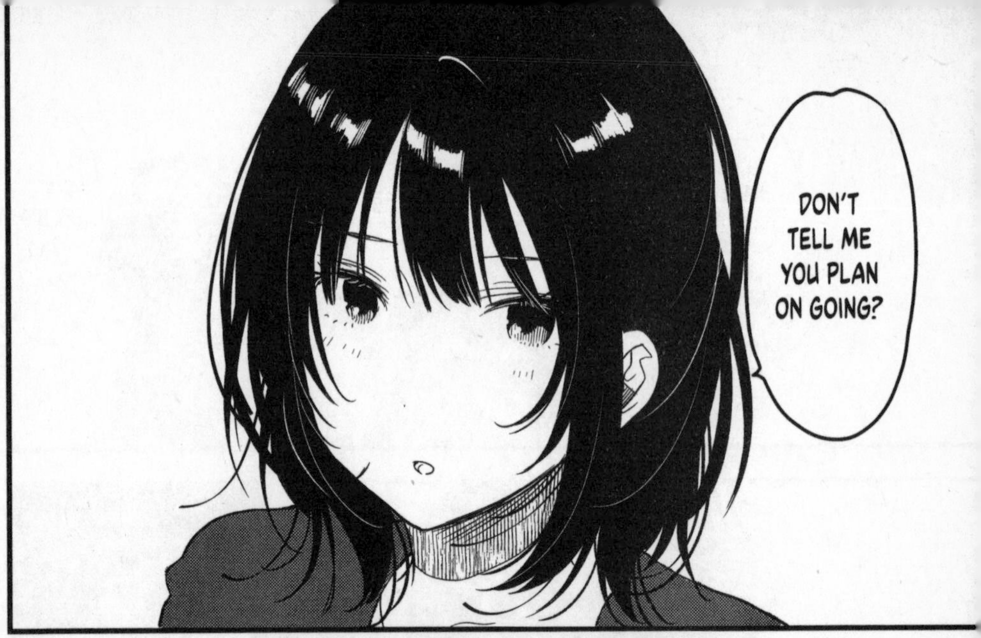
DON'T TELL ME YOU PLAN ON GOING?

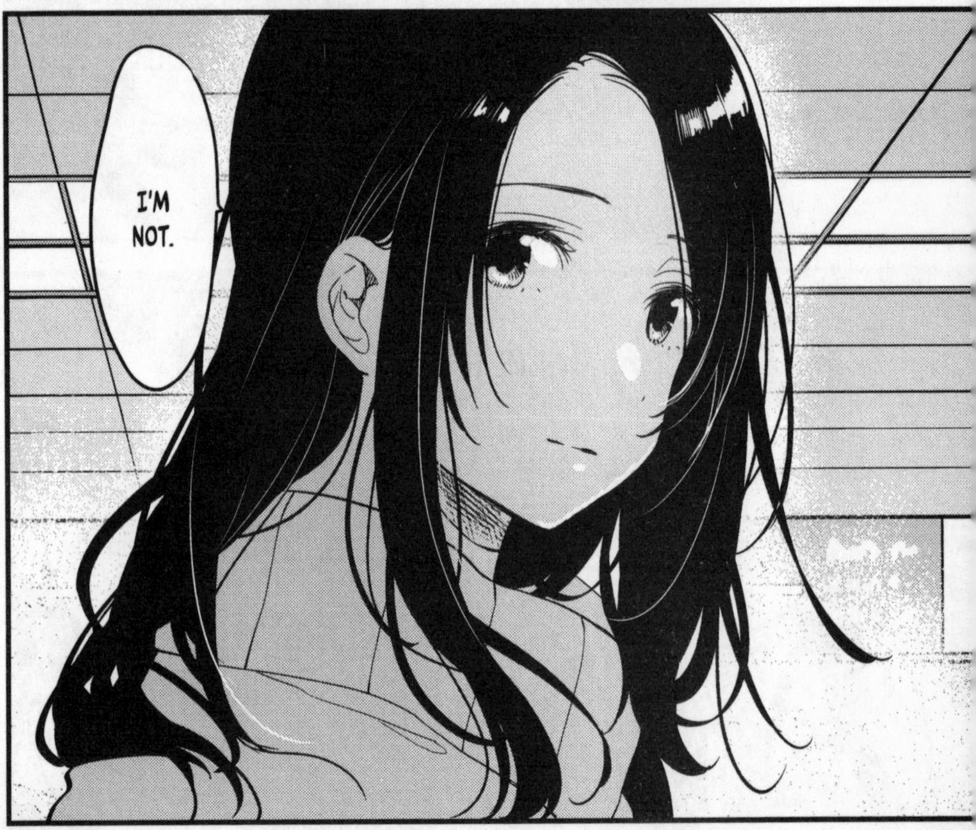
I'M NOT.

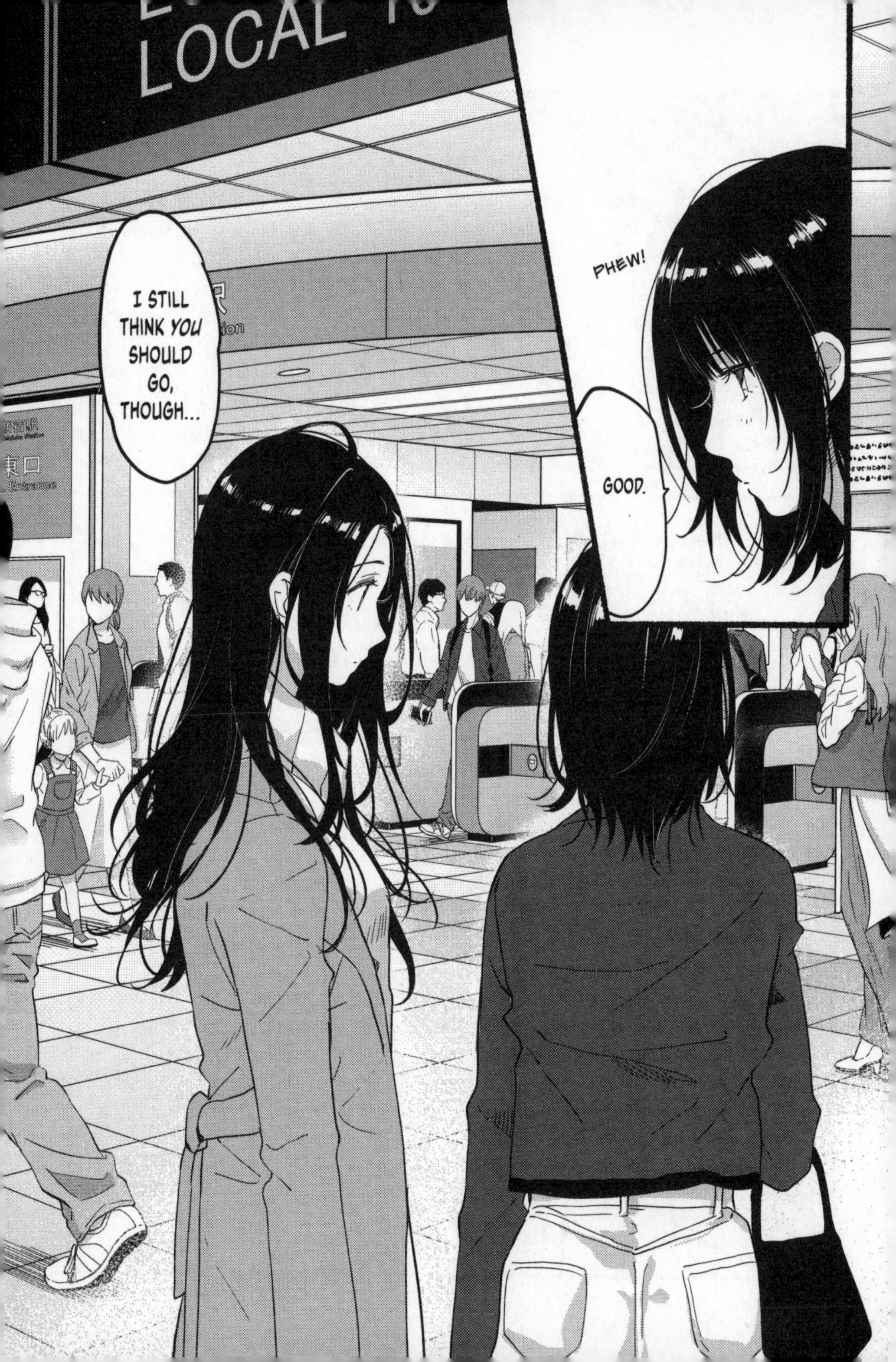
PHEW!
GOOD.
LOCAL
I STILL THINK *YOU* SHOULD GO, THOUGH...

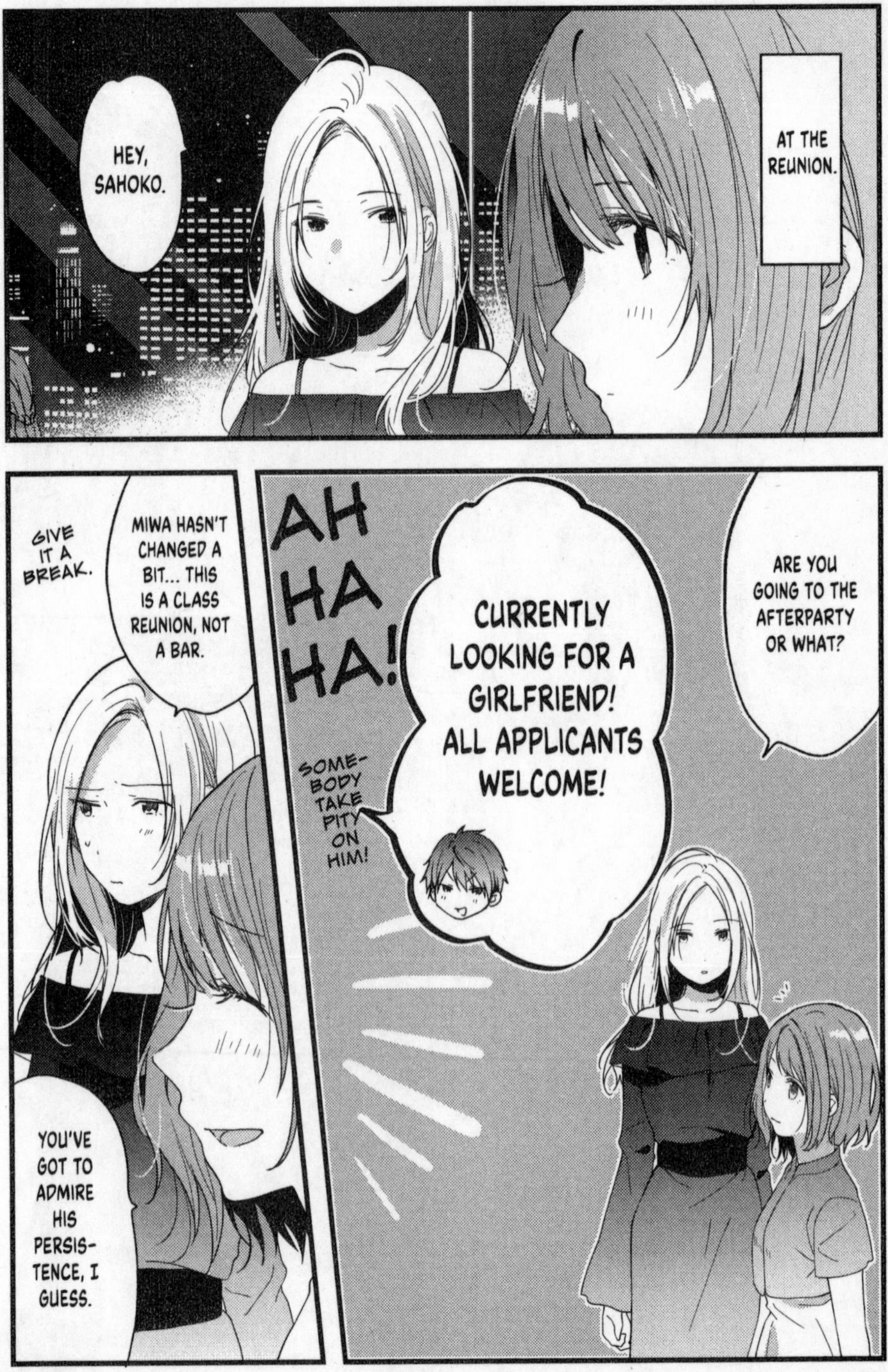
AT THE REUNION.
HEY, SAHOKO.
ARE YOU GOING TO THE AFTERPARTY OR WHAT?
AH HA HA!
CURRENTLY LOOKING FOR A GIRLFRIEND! ALL APPLICANTS WELCOME!
SOME-BODY TAKE PITY ON HIM!
MIWA HASN'T CHANGED A BIT... THIS IS A CLASS REUNION, NOT A BAR.
GIVE IT A BREAK.
YOU'VE GOT TO ADMIRE HIS PERSIS-TENCE, I GUESS.

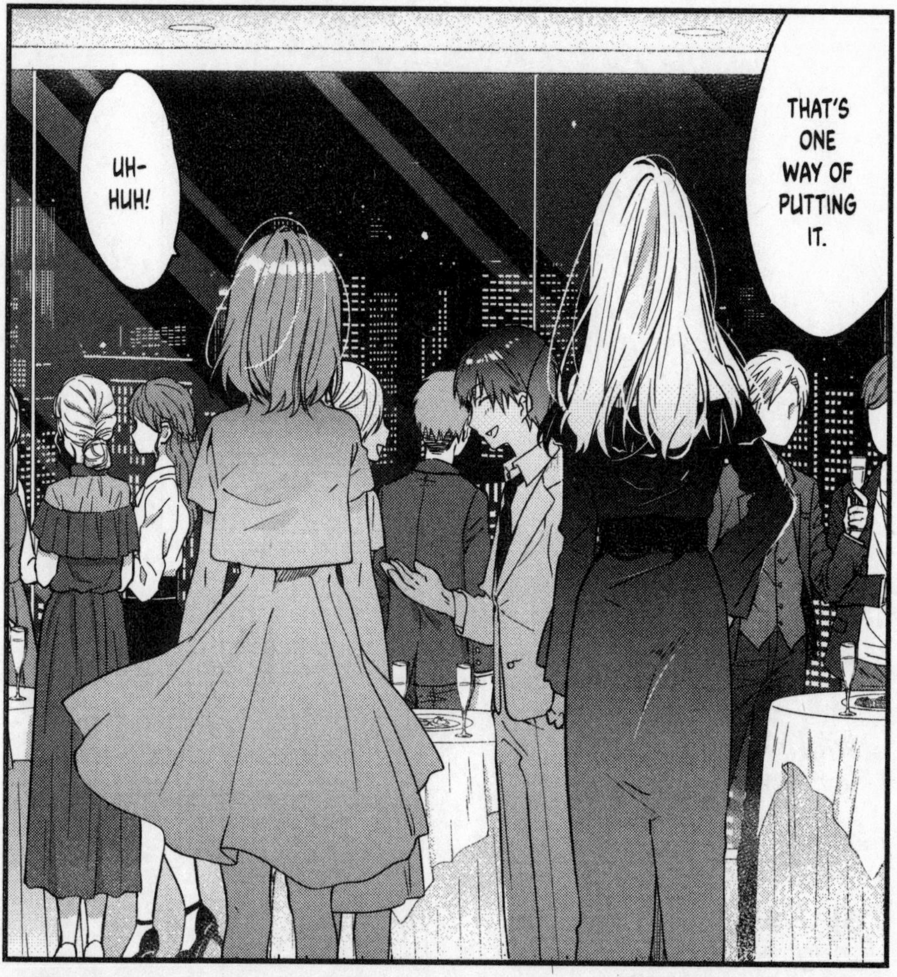
THAT'S ONE WAY OF PUTTING IT.
UH-HUH!

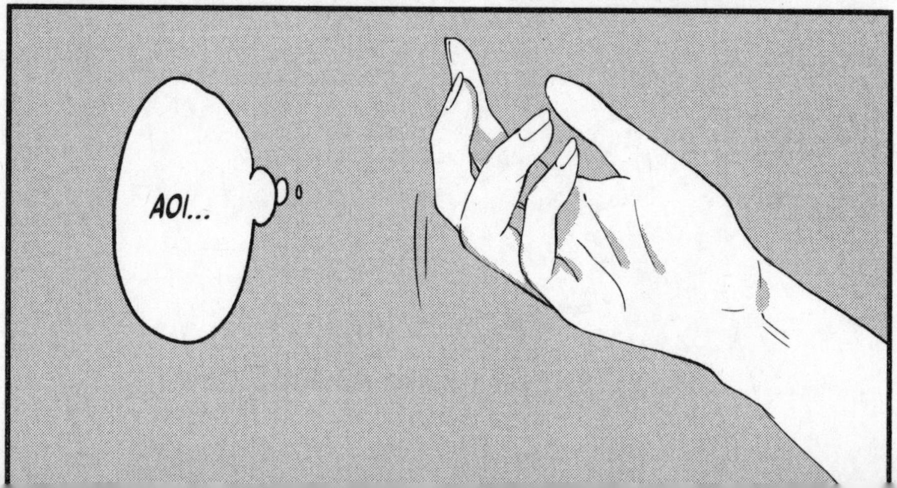
AOI...

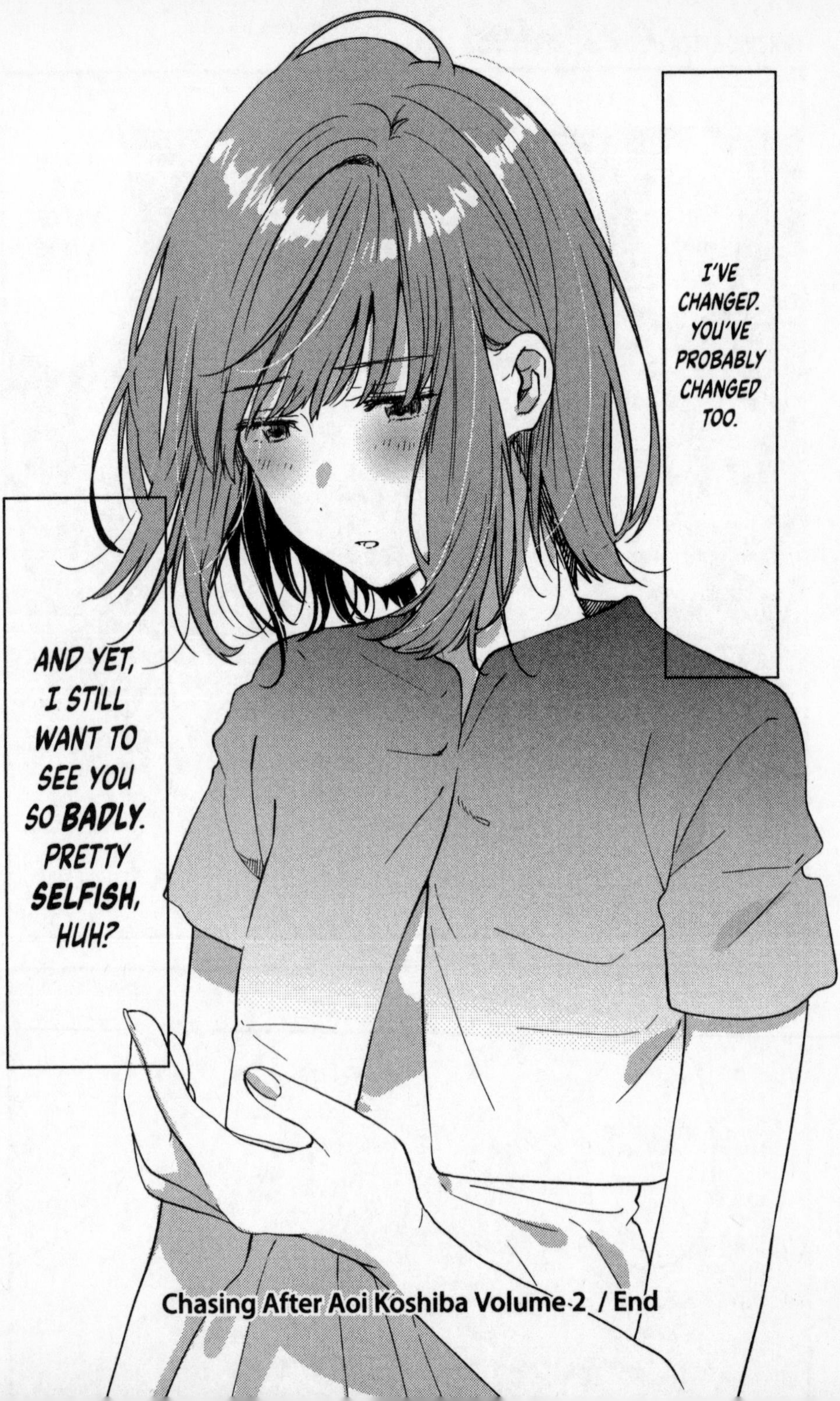
I'VE CHANGED. YOU'VE PROBABLY CHANGED TOO.
AND YET, I STILL WANT TO SEE YOU SO BADLY. PRETTY SELFISH, HUH?

Chasing After Aoi Koshiba Volume 2 / End

CHASING AFTER *Aoi Koshiba*

Winter | College, Third Year

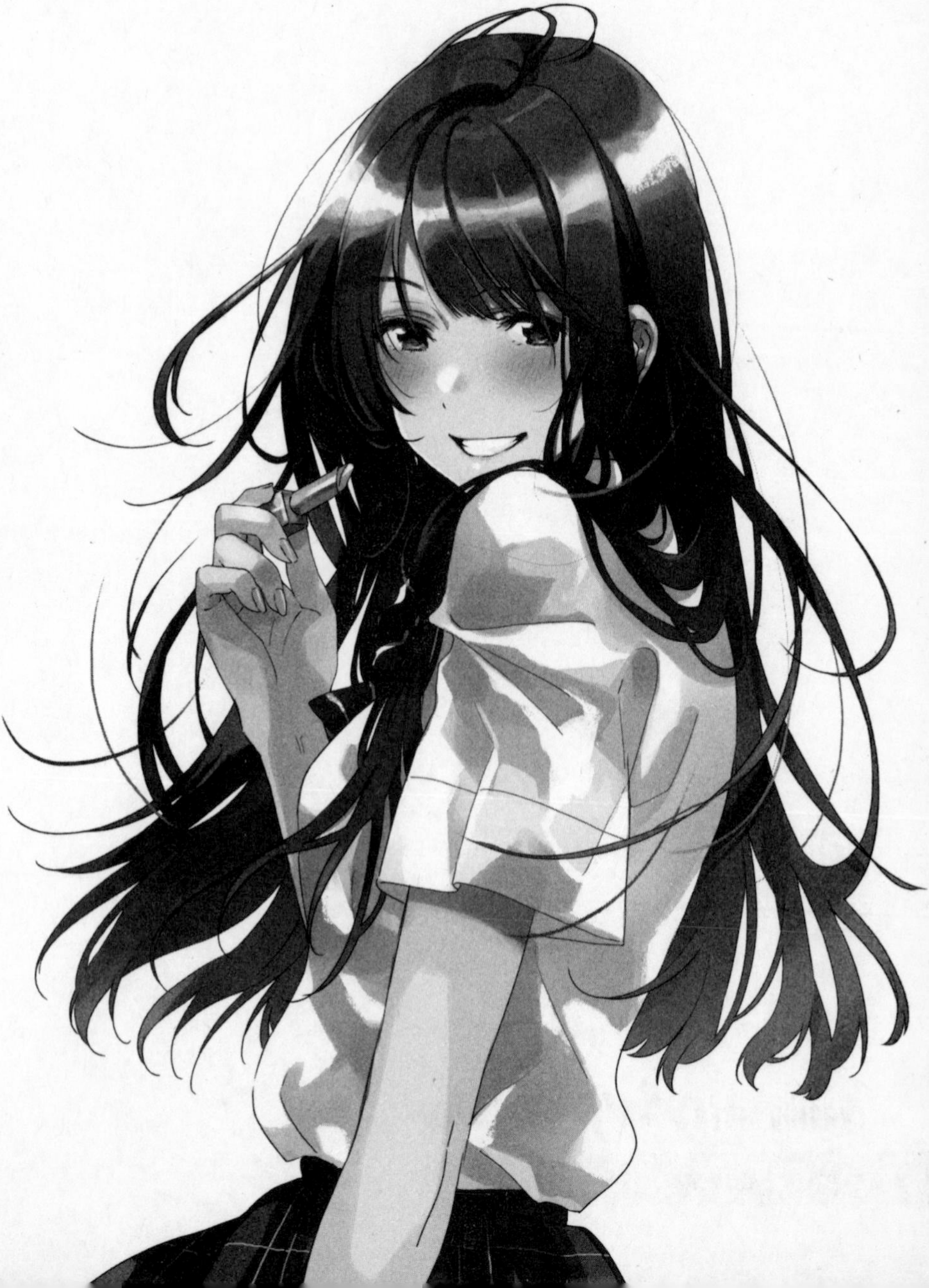

PERFECT WORLD

Rie Aruga

A TOUCHING NEW SERIES ABOUT LOVE AND COPING WITH DISABILITY

An office party reunites Tsugumi with her high school crush Itsuki. He's realized his dream of becoming an architect, but along the way, he experienced a spinal injury that put him in a wheelchair. Now Tsugumi's rekindled feelings will butt up against prejudices she never considered — and Itsuki will have to decide if he's ready to let someone into his heart...

"Depicts with great delicacy and courage the difficulties some with disabilities experience getting involved in romantic relationships... Rie Aruga refuses to romanticize, pushing her heroine to face the reality of disability. She invites her readers to the same tasks of empathy, knowledge and recognition."
—Slate.fr

"An important entry [in manga romance]... The emotional core of both plot and characters indicates thoughtfulness... [Aruga's] research is readily apparent in the text and artwork, making this feel like a real story."
—Anime News Network

KODANSHA COMICS

Perfect World © Rie Aruga/Kodansha Ltd.

CUTE ANIMALS AND LIFE LESSONS, PERFECT FOR ASPIRING PET VETS OF ALL AGES!

YUZU THE PET VET

1

BY MINGO ITO

In collaboration with NIPPON COLUMBIA CO., LTD.

Yuzu the Pet Vet © Mingo Ito / NIPPON COLUMBIA CO., LTD. / Kodansha Ltd.

For an 11-year-old, Yuzu has a lot on her plate. When her mom gets sick and has to be hospitalized, Yuzu goes to live with her uncle who runs the local veterinary clinic. Yuzu's always been scared of animals, but she tries to help out. Through all the tough moments in her life, Yuzu realizes that she can help make things all right with a little help from her animal pals, peers, and kind grown-ups.

Every new patient is a furry friend in the making!

The adorable new odd-couple cat comedy manga from the creator of the beloved *Chi's Sweet Home*, in full color!

Sue & Tai-chan

Konami Kanata

Sue is an aging housecat who's looking forward to living out her life in peace... but her plans change when the mischievous black tomcat Tai-chan enters the picture! Hey! Sue never signed up to be a catsitter! *Sue & Tai-chan* is the latest from the reigning meow-narch of cute kitty comics, Konami Kanata.

KC KODANSHA COMICS

A SMART, NEW ROMANTIC COMEDY FOR FANS OF *SHORTCAKE CAKE* AND *TERRACE HOUSE!*

LIVING ROOM

MATSUNAGA-SAN

Keiko Iwashita

Living-Room Matsunaga-san © Keiko Iwashita / Kodansha Ltd.

KC KODANSHA COMICS

A romance manga starring high school girl Meeko, who learns to live on her own in a boarding house whose living room is home to the odd (but handsome) Matsunaga-san. She begins to adjust to her new life away from her parents, but Meeko soon learns that no matter how far away from home she is, she's still a young girl at heart — especially when she finds herself falling for Matsunaga-san.

Young characters and steampunk setting, like *Howl's Moving Castle* and *Battle Angel Alita*

Beyond the Clouds © 2018 Nicke / Ki-oon

A boy with a talent for machines and a mysterious girl whose wings he's fixed will take you beyond the clouds! In the tradition of the high-flying, resonant adventure stories of Studio Ghibli comes a gorgeous tale about the longing of young hearts for adventure and friendship!

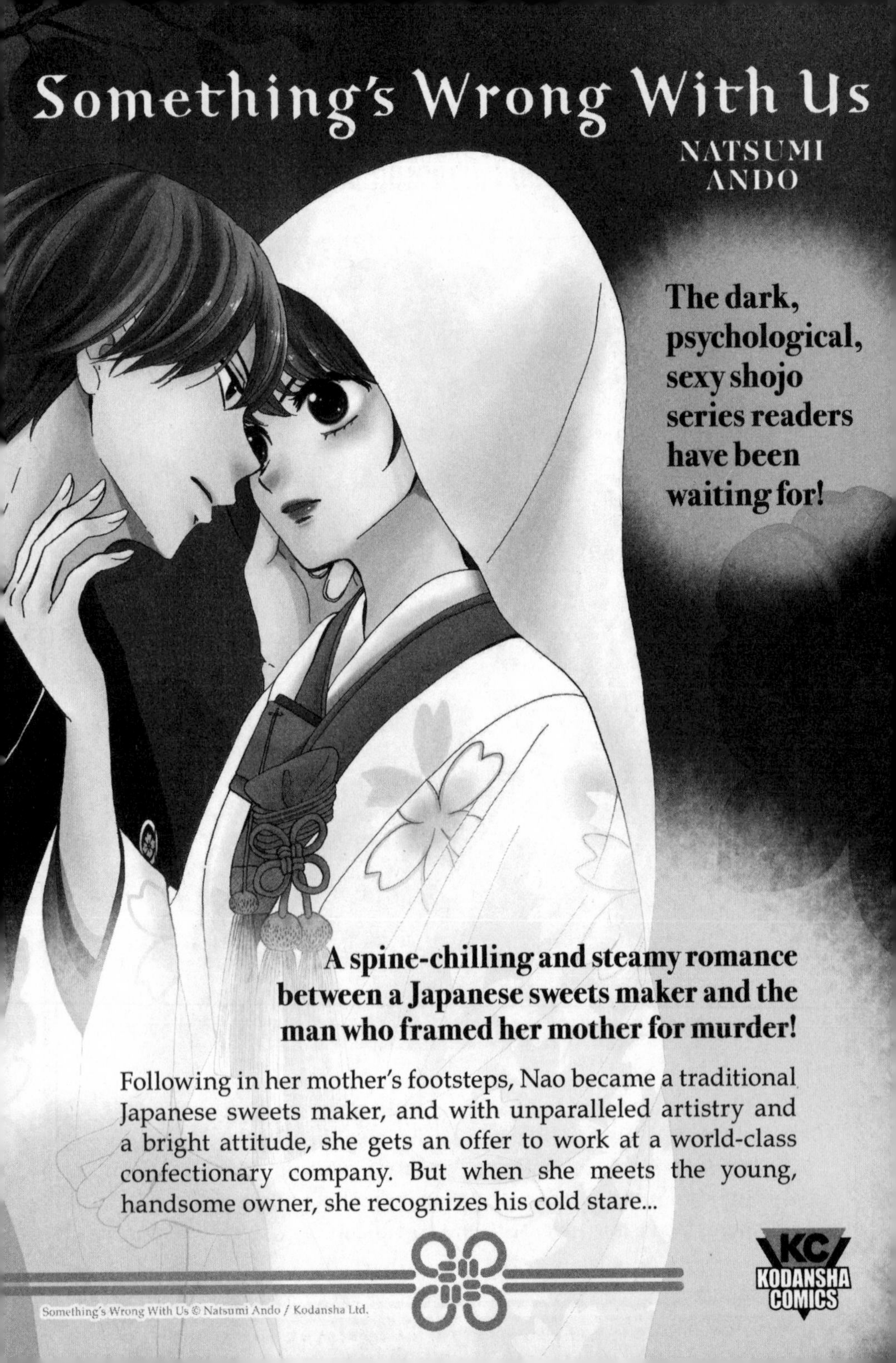
Something's Wrong With Us
NATSUMI ANDO
The dark, psychological, sexy shojo series readers have been waiting for!
A spine-chilling and steamy romance between a Japanese sweets maker and the man who framed her mother for murder!
Following in her mother's footsteps, Nao became a traditional Japanese sweets maker, and with unparalleled artistry and a bright attitude, she gets an offer to work at a world-class confectionary company. But when she meets the young, handsome owner, she recognizes his cold stare...
KC KODANSHA COMICS
Something's Wrong With Us © Natsumi Ando / Kodansha Ltd.

THE SWEET SCENT OF LOVE IS IN THE AIR! FOR FANS OF OFFBEAT ROMANCES LIKE WOTAOI

KINTETSU YAMADA

Sweat and Soap © Kintetsu Yamada / Kodansha Ltd.

In an office romance, there's a fine line between sexy and awkward... and that line is where Asako — a woman who sweats copiously — meets Koutarou — a perfume developer who can't get enough of Asako's, er, scent. Don't miss a romcom manga like no other!

Chasing After Aoi Koshiba 2 is a work of fiction. Names, characters, places, and incidents are the products of the author's imagination or are used fictitiously. Any resemblance to actual events, locales, or persons, living or dead, is entirely coincidental.

A Kodansha Comics Trade Paperback Original

Published in the United States by Kodansha Comics, an imprint of Kodansha USA Publishing, LLC, New York.

Publication rights for this English edition arranged through Kodansha Ltd., Tokyo.

First published in Japan in 2020 by Ichijinsha Inc., Tokyo.

ISBN 978-1-64651-188-4

Printed in the United States of America.

www.kodansha.us

9 8 7 6 5 4 3 2 1
Translation: Rose Padgett
Lettering: Paige Pumphrey
Editing: Michal Zuckerman
Kodansha Comics edition cover design by Adam Del Re

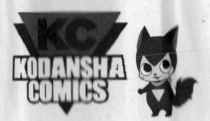

Publisher: Kiichiro Sugawara

Director of publishing services: Ben Applegate
Associate director of operations: Stephen Pakula
Publishing services managing editors: Alanna Ruse, Madison Salters
Production managers: Emi Lotto, Angela Zurlo